The Essays of Montaigne

A Critical Exploration

The Essays of Montaigne
A Critical Exploration

R. A. Sayce

*Reader in French Literature in the
University of Oxford and
Fellow of Worcester College*

Northwestern University Press

Library of Congress Catalog Card Number: 72-80212

ISBN 0-8101-0392-3

Printed in Great Britain

Contents

Preface

In writing this book I have incurred many debts, too numerous indeed to list, especially to all the librarians who have received me with so much kindness. However, I should like to express particular gratitude to M. and Mme Jean Mesnard and Mme Jeanne Veyrin-Forrer, whose generosity went far beyond the ordinary courtesies of the scholarly community. My wife has read and criticised every chapter and without her constant help and encouragement the book could never have been written. A debt of another kind will be obvious to anyone who reads these pages. It is to the memory of Pierre Villey, whose work on Montaigne looks ever more majestic as the years go by (which is not to say always right, of course). In particular, any statement about the date of composition or the sources of the *Essais* should be assumed to come from Villey unless otherwise specified: I have not thought it necessary to give a reference in every case.

Part of chapter 12 (pp. 301–8) is based on my contribution ('The style of Montaigne: word-pairs and word-groups') to *Literary style: a symposium*, edited by Seymour Chatman, London and New York, Oxford University Press, 1971.

R.A.S.

January 1972

Note on References

References are to the most conveniently accessible edition, the *Œuvres complètes*, ed. Thibaudet and Rat, Bibliothèque de la Pléiade, 1965 (TR): the letters (*a*), (*b*), and (*c*), inserted where the information is relevant, refer to the 1580 edition, the 1588 edition, and the Bordeaux Copy. Unfortunately the Pléiade text is not always reliable in details, and direct quotations are taken, apart from minor changes like the modernisation of i and j, u and v, and the addition of accents where necessary for intelligibility, from the Édition Municipale of the *Essais*, 5 vols, Bordeaux, 1906–33 (EM). Where reference to specific early editions was required, the following editions of the *Essais* have been cited: for 1580 Dezeimeris and Barckhausen, 2 vols, Bordeaux, 1870–3 (DB); for 1588 Motheau and Jouaust, 7 vols, Paris, 1886–9 (MJ); for 1595 Courbet and Royer, 5 vols, Paris, 1872–1900 (CR).

The following abbreviations are used:

BHR	*Bibliothèque d'Humanisme et Renaissance*
BSAM	*Bulletin de la Société des Amis de Montaigne*
CR	*Les essais*, ed. Courbet and Royer
DB	*Essais*, ed. Dezeimeris and Barckhausen
EM	*Les essais*, Édition Municipale
JV	*Journal du voyage*
MJ	*Les essais*, ed. Motheau and Jouaust
RHLF	*Revue d'histoire littéraire de la France*
TR	*Œuvres complètes*, ed. Thibaudet and Rat

Introduction

THERE are two sorts of books on Montaigne: those written from a particular viewpoint or with a particular object (for example to show that he is religious or irreligious, conservative or liberal) and those which make some attempt at a total picture of this most complex of all writers. The first may achieve a new illumination at the cost of distorting and falsifying; the second may run the risk of being duller and less original, but with some chance of showing him as he really is. The difficulties which beset any study of Montaigne, but especially any in the second category, are numerous. For a start, it is impossible (or at least not easy) to make any statement about him without immediately stating the contrary, to such an extent is his thought (though, as we shall see, thought is an inadequate word for the processes of his mind) made of antitheses, ambiguities, contradictions of every kind, to such an extent does it endeavour to grasp the full diversity of things. A sentence from Sextus Empiricus painted on the ceiling of the library at Montaigne gives the key: πάντι λόγῳ λόγος ἴσος ἀντίκειται (to any reason an equal reason can be opposed). It follows that quotations from the *Essais* taken in isolation can be highly misleading: as with the Bible, almost anything can be proved. Ideally every quotation should be related to the whole complex of attitudes, but this is hardly a practical possibility.

It follows too that, faced with such multiplicity, any critic tends to extract those elements which will make a Montaigne in his own image. For Gide as for Sainte-Beuve he is an agnostic or atheist; for Canon Müller a pious Catholic; for Camille Jullian an enlightened republican patriot of the late nineteenth century, an earlier incarnation of Renan; for Camille Aymonier a conservative and a royalist, a Machiavellian and almost a Maurrassian of the 1930s[1] (the list could be indefinitely extended). One of Montaigne's outstanding characteristics, remarked by a majority of perceptive readers, including some of the earliest,[2] is the way in which he seems to reveal to everyone that person's own thoughts and feelings. The temptation to project oneself into him is therefore understandable, though every effort must be made to resist it.

It seems then that the best way of proceeding is to accept as a starting-point and indeed as the central fact about Montaigne the contradictory nature of the truth he expresses, to try at least to give full and equal weight to the conflicting sides of his intellect and character. In this way we may hope to avoid the distortions of single-minded criticism. Even in this method, however, a danger lies concealed: that of forcing the *Essais* into a dualist pattern of straightforward clashes between simple opposites (like conservatism and liberalism). In fact, the contradictions are many-sided, and cover a whole range of intermediate positions as well as the extremes.

A further difficulty is that not only is it hard to say anything about Montaigne which does not need immediate correction, it is hard to say anything which he has not already said himself, and this includes the description and criticism of the *Essais*. As is well known, he portrays himself in all his moods and activities, physical and mental, but this naturally includes his principal activity, the writing of essays. We are therefore confronted not only with an observer (of the world and of himself) but also with an observer of this observer, and so, it sometimes appears, of what is almost an infinite regress. The relation between subject and object in such a case may well seem all but indefinable.

It follows from this (or at least is closely connected with it) that the Proustian distinction between man and writer, which has become something like an axiom of modern criticism, is very difficult to apply to Montaigne. The author and the book are, or seem to be, inseparable, are consubstantial as he himself says:

1 For all these see Bibliography.

2 e.g. the Dutch painter Pieter van Veen (1563–1629), who notes in the margin of his copy of the *Essais* (now in the British Museum): 'je trouue un infinite des parties en cest autheur qui quasiment ressemblent mon humeur' (Paris, 1602; B.M., C.28.g.7, 4K6ʳ). On this copy see Boase in *Mélanges Lefranc*, pp. 408–17; also Thorpe in *Rivista di letterature moderne* (1952).

Je n'ay pas plus faict mon livre que mon livre m'a faict, livre consubstantiel à son autheur, d'une occupation propre, membre de ma vie; non d'une occupation et fin tierce et estrangiere come tous autres livres.[1]

For other men, writing books may be a superficial activity which does not engage the whole being (how far the claim of absolute originality in this respect is justified we shall consider later); for him book and life continually interpenetrate at all points. Yet, difficult though it is, the separation must to some extent be made, and the intentional fallacy remains a fallacy even when Montaigne is its subject. What in the life, it may be argued, is relevant to the book has already found its place there (sometimes undergoing the transmutation which is characteristic of works of art). In particular, evidence drawn from the events of his life about Montaigne's religious and political views is by no means decisive, or even always admissible, when we examine the impact of his book. For these reasons biographical questions will not generally be dealt with here unless they have a specific bearing on particular points.[2]

If it is hard to separate the man and the book, it is even harder to separate thought and expression, content and form. This is true of almost any great writer, but in Montaigne the form of the essay is so closely moulded to the thought, what he has to say is so totally immanent in the language he uses (vocabulary, syntax, imagery), that his case may be regarded as quite exceptional, at any rate among prose writers. At the same time, if analysis is to make any progress at all, the distinction between thought and expression probably has to be made.

But almost the greatest difficulty, closely related to the last, is that of isolating 'aspects' of Montaigne, of removing for examination any part of the continuum presented by the *Essais*. Everything hangs together, all the themes are interwoven in unbroken sequence. If one piece is pulled out for inspection, all the rest are likely to come crashing down after it. As usual, he himself says it for us:

vostre fantasie n'en peut, par souhait et imagination, remuer un point, que tout l'ordre des choses ne renverse, et le passé et l'advenir.[3]

---

[1] II, xviii: EM ii, 453; TR 648.

[2] And also because the life has recently been treated in exhaustive and masterly fashion (D. M. Frame, *Montaigne: a biography*, 1965).

[3] III, ii: EM iii, 35; TR 793.

3

He is talking about the order of the universe and the chain of causation, but it is equally true of the *Essais* and the way they are organised. He cannot be subdivided and classified: his image of children playing with quicksilver and trying to arrange it in countable bits[1] applies all too well to the critic's efforts to impose some sort of rational order on the fluid argument. Yet, obviously, some kind of classification is essential, themes and attitudes must in some way be separated if we are to attain a serious understanding and avoid a mere reproduction of the original confusion (a confusion which, it is hardly necessary to add, has its own subtle laws and order). Similarly, whatever arrangement we adopt, some recurrent treatment of the same topics is inevitable, I hope at a progressively deeper level. Thus war, to take a simple example, has to be considered as part of Montaigne's picture of himself, as part of his experience of the world, as a mirror of his religious and political attitudes. To place together the whole discussion of his attitude to war would merely produce a different series of repetitions. This is still more true of such major themes as his diversity or mobility.

To these general difficulties, which really all spring from the form of the *Essais,* must be added others which are more particularly linked to the thought and to Montaigne's historical position. So much of his thought on so many subjects has passed into the common currency of European civilisation (and not only European) that we may easily overlook its extreme originality at the time of writing. This statement too requires contradiction. Montaigne is highly original but he is also highly derivative (he openly boasts of his thievings[2] and whole passages are taken verbatim from classical authors, especially Plutarch). It seems then that a close historical study is needed if we are to separate him from his sources and define his true originality. Nor is it only a matter of direct borrowings: his ideas (his scepticism in particular) take their place in the general development of Renaissance thought and it would seem to be impossible to appreciate him fully without relating him to this development. Yet this approach too has its dangers. History helps us to understand but also to misunderstand. Montaigne's originality (like that of a scientist) often springs not from the modification of what he has read in books but from a fresh and direct look at the world, the sort of

[1] III, xiii: TR 1043.
[2] 'mes larrecins' I, xxvi: EM i, 190; TR 146.

4

look which is possible at any time. To put him back into his temporal context may sometimes falsify his thought and this, I suspect, has happened, for example in discussions of his political outlook. History tends to suggest that nothing is original: the work of the source-hunters has decomposed even the most powerfully original thinkers (a Rousseau or a Marx, for instance) to the point where every major conception (and most of the minor ones) is seen as a borrowing from some precursor, or at least an unconscious echo. All this in a way is true, and the evidence such studies provide of the continuity of human intellectual activity is important and exciting, even if it diminishes the stature of individuals. None the less, new combinations of familiar or peripheral concepts produce essentially new totalities: originality is not entirely an illusion. Moreover, a work of literature, or a work of art, does not exist just at one point of time, that of its creation. It continues to exist, and that is why we study or read it. And in existing it changes its meaning. Montaigne himself offers an outstanding example: the *Essais,* which were passed with a few minor objections by the Roman censor in 1581, were placed on the Index in 1676. A different set of circumstances had made people see the book in a different way, or had drawn out meanings which were only latent in it. Though these changes of view are themselves explicable in historical terms, we see that a work has a post-history as well as a pre-history. At a deeper and more internal level Montaigne in his portrait of himself and in his depiction of what he calls *le passage* (the inner movement of the mind) is so far in advance of his time that it is impossible to achieve anything more than partial and fragmentary explanations by studying his models and sources. This applies in particular to the use of such terms as Renaissance, mannerism, or baroque (though they do illuminate some aspects and discussion of them is unavoidable). History comes in, even when we are considering these most original sides of Montaigne, but it is our history rather than his. Readers of Proust and Joyce can perceive in Montaigne things which were largely invisible to earlier readers or at any rate did not seem very important to them. In a word, a great original creator cannot be tied to a limited period: we must use the historical method without becoming its prisoners.

The emphasis in this study will therefore be on Montaigne's future (in relation to his own time) rather than on his past, on what he means to us rather than on how he came to be what he was.

There are indeed other dangers in laying too much stress on the ways in which he anticipates more recent thoughts, feelings, or attitudes, in particular the danger of distorting him by reading back our own preoccupations into his work. At the same time it is astonishing to see in how many ways he seems our contemporary, and no doubt each generation must interpret Montaigne (like any great writer) afresh. The danger of distortion is to be avoided as much by philological as by historical methods: by close attention to the exact meaning of what he says.

If these questions can be successfully resolved, a still larger problem awaits us. It may seem, in view of the diversity and contradictions we have observed, that Montaigne's thought and attitudes are made up of a mere formless eclecticism. This is by no means the case. Unity is there (very much so) in spite of the contradictions, as we can see from the difficulty we have already found in breaking down the fabric of the *Essais* into manageable component parts. The crucial point is well put by P. Mansell Jones: 'For their elucidation the search of some principle of unity is both a necessity and a peril.'[1] And the peril is confirmed, once again, by Montaigne himself:

> Ceux qui s'exercent à contreroller les actions humaines, ne se trouvent en aucune partie si empeschez, qu'à les r'appiesser et mettre à mesme lustre.[2]

It consists, clearly, in the risk of forcing and systematising, of omitting important elements, for the sake of a unity which may thus turn out to be spurious. Here more than anywhere it is necessary to divest ourselves as far as possible of all *a priori* assumptions (including the one already made about the unbroken continuity of the *Essais*), to proceed empirically, and to see whether unity does emerge naturally from what we find.

This recital of difficulties is not meant, or not meant primarily, as an excuse. In seeing what the difficulties are, and there is no doubt that they are formidable, we may at least have formed some impression of the general outline of Montaigne's literary position and character and of the central problems with which we shall have to contend, the questions which we must attempt to answer. There remains, it is true, one difficulty, not only arduous but insuperable, which has been stated by Jean Prévost:

1 *French introspectives*, p. 34.
2 II, i: EM ii, 1; TR 315.

pour retrouver le mouvement de la pensée d'un homme, il faut lui être supérieur sur tous les points, le *contenir* dans toute son étendue. Ce projet fait assez rire quand il s'agit de Montaigne.[1]

Indeed, and there is nothing much to be done about it. Criticism of any great writer demands some awareness of the critic's own limitations, and the total picture which we suggested earlier as the ideal is not in fact attainable. At the same time it would be wrong to stand in too much awe. If we cannot achieve a complete understanding, we can at least try to do justice to the many-sidedness of Montaigne, to be receptive to what he has to tell us, and to prefer what he says to our own preconceptions. He himself (though he often seems unfavourably disposed towards interpretations of the *Essais*) gives some encouragement:

Un suffisant lecteur descouvre souvant és escrits d'autruy des perfections autres que celles que l'autheur y a mises et apperceües, et y preste des sens et des visages plus riches.[2]

[1] *La vie de Montaigne*, pp. 10–11.
[2] I, xxiv: EM i, 163; TR 126.

※ 2 ※

The Text of the Essays

IN 1570 Montaigne sold his office of counsellor in the Bordeaux
Parlement (to his friend Florimond de Raemond) and retired
to his château of Montaigne, near Saint-Émilion, where an in-
scription in the library dated 28 February 1571, his thirty-eighth
birthday, records his intention of devoting the rest of his life to
peace and leisure in the bosom of the Muses, far from the burdens
of public affairs. The history of the *Essais* may be said to begin at
this point. A year later, in the essay *Que philosopher, c'est
apprendre à mourir,* he observes that he reached the age of thirty-
nine a fortnight ago,[1] so that by this time the book was well under
way. What led him to start it he explains in what may be a still
earlier essay, *De l'oisiveté.* In the idleness he had sought his mind
had behaved like a bolting horse, giving birth to so many fantastic
monsters that 'pour en contempler à mon aise l'ineptie et
l'estrangeté, j'ay commancé de les mettre en rolle, esperant avec
le temps luy en faire honte à luy mesmes.'[2] The very first essays,
usually considered dry and imitative, hardly seem to bear out this
highly coloured description, but this is perhaps because the usual
judgement is a relative one, comparing the early with the later
essays rather than appreciating them in themselves. From this
point on the pre-publication development of the *Essais,* although
much depends on conjecture, is fairly well mapped, thanks above
all to the great work of Pierre Villey:[3] it will be discussed later
when necessary.

1 I, xx: TR 82.
2 I, viii: EM i, 36; TR 34.
3 *Les sources et l'évolution des Essais de Montaigne.* Some doubt has recently
been cast on Villey's methods, but the main structure of his argument still
holds fairly firm.

8

The textual history of the published *Essais* is of quite exceptional importance, transcending its technical interest, because it reflects and clarifies the mobility of Montaigne's self-portrait. He is not displaying (like most portraits) a fixed and permanent character but the continuous change of a developing personality: the interpolations, corrections, and excisions of the different editions allow us to capture at least some of these changes. Textual variants throw interesting light on any author, but in Montaigne they touch the very substance of his being. In other cases it is usually possible to establish a definitive text, early or late, which can be regarded as *the* work; in Montaigne this scarcely makes sense because each stage has equal validity, each contributes something essential to the moving figure. The textual problem is therefore simply one aspect of the general problem of the nature of the book, but it has the advantage of furnishing accessible concrete evidence amidst the Protean fluidity.

The first edition of the *Essais* was published in 1580, in two small octavo volumes, by Simon Millanges, the leading printer and bookseller of Bordeaux at the time. Why Montaigne chose a local rather than a Parisian firm is not entirely clear: he had already had experience of dealing with Parisian booksellers in connection with the publication of his translation of Sabunde (Gourbin and Sonnius, 1569) and of the works of La Boétie which he had prepared for the press (Morel, 1571-2). The most likely explanation is modesty. He was not yet confident of the value of his work, as the deprecating tone of the preface *Au lecteur* illustrates: 'ce n'est pas raison que tu employes ton loisir en un subject si frivole et si vain.'[1] Later on, when the success of the essays was assured, he remarked that in Guyenne he paid printers, elsewhere they paid him;[2] it seems probable therefore that the edition was brought out at his own expense. It is perhaps worth noting that there are two issues with different title-pages. The earlier, of which only five copies are known to me,[3] runs simply *Essais de Michel de Montaigne*. The second adds his titles: *Seigneur de Montaigne, Chevalier de l'Ordre du Roy, & Gentil-homme ordinaire de sa Chambre* (in 1582 he is also *Maire et Gouverneur de Bourdeaus*). The most likely explanation for the change is Montaigne's own insistence, in striking contrast with his later

---

[1] EM i, 2; TR 9. [2] III, ii: TR 786(c).
[3] Bibliothèque Municipale, Bordeaux; London University Library; Bibliotheca Bodmeriana, Geneva; Yale; Princeton.

mockery of those who display their titles at the front of books.[1] In the 1588 edition he reverts to the simpler and in fact prouder form, keeping only the *Seigneur*. Apart from an innocent vanity which appears in him now and then, the 1580 change may be attributed to an inexperienced writer's need to seek support in extraneous and irrelevant qualifications.

Apart from *Au lecteur*, which is dated 1 March 1580 (thus no doubt enabling us to date the publication in the first half of the year) and which is of notable importance for the understanding of Montaigne's general conception of his work at this stage, the two volumes contain two books of essays (called chapters), fifty-seven in Book I and thirty-seven in Book II. Those at the beginning of Book I are very brief (often a page or two), but they expand in length as the work progresses and the centre-piece of Book II is the long *Apologie de Raimond Sebond*, which, even in this first state, could well make a book by itself. The subjects of the earliest chapters are minor problems of military action (*Si le chef d'une place assiegée doit sortir pour parlementer*) or practical morality (*Des menteurs*), but gradually they expand in depth as well as in length (*De la force de l'imagination, De la coustume, De l'institution des enfans* on education, *Des cannibales* on America, and so on). However, this expansive movement is by no means regular or unbroken, and the great essays, especially in Book I and to some extent in Book II, continue to be interspersed with more trivial reflections of the earlier type.

In 1582 Millanges published a second edition, 'revised and augmented'. It is generally regarded as a reprint of the first, with little independent value apart from a few corrections and additions. However, it is important for two reasons. Between the first and second edition Montaigne had accomplished his eighteen-month journey through Switzerland, Germany, Austria, and Italy, and these new and potent experiences are reflected in the changes of 1582: he introduces Italian proverbs, and quotations from Italian poets (Dante and Tasso particularly), allusions to Venetian customs and Roman antiquities, longer descriptions of watering places he had visited and incidents he had witnessed, like the execution of the brigand Catena in Rome[2] and the moving account of his meeting with the afflicted Tasso at Ferrara.[3] Secondly, we

[1] I, xl: TR 248. This passage was added in 1588.
[2] II, xi: TR 411.
[3] II, xii: TR 472.

see here for the first time, if only on a limited scale, the effect of interpolation and correction which we have already observed as a fundamental and not merely superficial characteristic of Montaigne's creative method. Changes are made for reasons of style, new images and illustrations introduced, word order modified to give greater force. There are signs too of a growing boldness (though this is by no means absent in the mature essays of 1580): to the remark that La Boétie would rather have been born at Venice than Sarlat (that is in a republic rather than a monarchy) he adds the typically laconic 'et avoit raison'[1] (he is not of course always laconic).

In 1587 another edition was published by the Paris bookseller Jean Richer (it was therefore the first Paris edition). However, it is a straight reprint of 1582 and fairly certainly Montaigne had no hand in it: there is no privilege and it may perhaps be regarded as pirated unless there was an agreement with Millanges; in either case it affords evidence of gathering popularity.

The edition published in Paris in the following year (1588) by Abel l'Angelier is very different. Montaigne went to Paris to supervise its publication (as well as to carry out a political mission for Henry of Navarre) and the date of the preface was changed to 12 June 1588, thus again fixing the approximate date of publication (confirmed by the privilege of 4 June 1588). Since it is described on the title page as the fifth edition and we have mentioned only three before it, it poses one of the minor enigmas of Montaigne scholarship: what has become of the missing edition? La Croix du Maine, a contemporary witness, speaks of editions printed at Rouen and elsewhere (not later than 1584),[2] but no copy has ever been found and it seems highly unlikely that whole editions of an unbanned book could disappear completely. Strowski mentions a possible Paris edition of 1584 'chez R. Estienne et L'Angelier',[3] but without evidence. More promising is the copy of the 1580 edition which belonged to Guillaume Guizot, with an extra III stamped on the date (therefore 1583),[4] but the most plausible, and technical, explanation is that of M. Jean Marchand: starting from the fact that several copies of the 1587

1 I, xxviii: EM i, 254; TR 193.
2 *Premier volume de la bibliotheque*, Paris, 1584, p. 328.
3 *Les essais, édition phototypique*, p. 7.
4 J. Le Petit, *Bibliographie des principales éditions originales d'écrivains français*, Paris, 1888, p. 100.

edition have the title-page removed, he supposes that Richer planned a new issue with a cancel title-page, a plan abandoned when Richer heard of the forthcoming l'Angelier edition.[1] To these hypotheses may be added a simpler one: apart from the possibility of mere oversight, the substitution of fifth for fourth edition may have been prompted by the desire to suggest that the book was selling better than it was, a trick not unknown even today.

This is a bypath of speculation. The importance of the 1588 edition lies in what follows 'Cinquiesme edition' on the title page: 'augmentée d'un troisiesme livre et de six cens additions aux deux premiers'. The third book was written by Montaigne from perhaps 1584 to the end of 1587 or the beginning of 1588.[2] It contains thirteen essays, all of substantial length, nearly all revealing an organic form and a depth of originality which surpasses his earlier work (though the difference from the latest essays of the 1580 edition must not be exaggerated). The six hundred additions (or thereabouts) to the first two books continue, but on a much larger scale, the method we have already observed in the 1582 edition: Montaigne rereads what he had written earlier and in reading is stimulated to new reflections which sometimes go far beyond their point of departure, enlarging, qualifying, setting off at a tangent, even contradicting.

No further essays were added, but almost as soon as the 1588 edition was published[3] Montaigne began to make new interpolations and corrections in the margins of his own copy of that edition (or perhaps, more accurately, on a set of the unbound sheets) and he seems to have continued this work almost up to his death in 1592. This, the famous Bordeaux Copy or *exemplaire de Bordeaux,* now in the Bibliothèque Municipale of the city, gives us Montaigne's final reflections and constitutes the principal piece of evidence for the establishment of his text. Unfortunately it was bound (or rebound?) in the eighteenth century, and the binder trimmed the edges of the leaves (as binders usually do), with the result that many ends of lines are missing. Other minor

[1] Jean Marchand, *Hypothèse sur la quatrième édition des Essais de Montaigne,* Bordeaux, Taffard, 1937.

[2] On this see Garapon in *Mélanges Frappier,* 1970, i, 321–7.

[3] Thus, if Florimond de Raemond is right, there is a reference to the Duc de Guise as still alive (murdered in December 1588); and there is one to Catherine de Médicis (died in January 1589). See Boase, *Revue du seizième siècle,* xv (1928), 263–4.

but not unimportant details are the restoration of the original date for the preface (1 March 1580), the insertion on the title page of the epigraph *Viresque acquirit eundo* (which epitomises Montaigne's growing confidence in the value of the book), and the inclusion on a blank leaf of a series of instructions, in his own hand, to the printer on questions of spelling and punctuation. These instructions, together with the alteration of 'Cinquiesme edition' to 'Sixieme', prove conclusively that Montaigne was preparing a new edition and not simply writing for his own amusement.

This is not quite the end of the history of the original text, for an edition based (directly or indirectly) on the Bordeaux Copy was published in Paris in 1595, shared between Abel l'Angelier and Michel Sonnius. The title-page claims that the new material increases the size of the book by one-third. How it was prepared for the press is a question of some complexity. It is preceded by a long preface by Marie de Gournay, Montaigne's *fille d'alliance* or adopted daughter, who explains that she was finishing the work of preparation in 1594 in Paris[1] (again confirmed by the privilege of 15 October 1594), that Mme de Montaigne had sent her 'these last writings' for her to publish[2] and that Mme de Montaigne had been assisted by Pierre de Brach (the Bordeaux poet),[3] that Mlle de Gournay had worked from a copy sent to her, and that another copy had remained at Montaigne.[4] This last must be the Bordeaux Copy itself, since its continuous presence in the area is attested (Mme de Montaigne gave it to the monastery of the Feuillants in Bordeaux, whence it passed to the Bibliothèque Municipale after the Revolution). The reasonable inference from all this is that Mme de Montaigne or Pierre de Brach (more probably the latter) had made a copy of the Bordeaux Copy, which they sent to Mlle de Gournay in Paris,[5] which was used for the printing, and which is now lost. However, it is just conceivable that Montaigne himself had made a second copy during his lifetime, though his motive for doing so would be obscure. The textual status of the 1595 edition is thus hard to define with precision. Where the binder has trimmed the edges of the Bordeaux Copy it is justifiable to turn

1 *Essais*, 1595, ĩ2ᵛ.
2 ã2ᵛ.
3 ĩ2ʳ.
4 ĩ2ʳ.
5 Eighteen months after Montaigne's death (i.e. about March 1594): see Gournay, *Les advis*, Paris, 1641, p. 994.

to the 1595 edition for the missing words; some additions in 1595 not in the Bordeaux Copy can be attributed to Montaigne's use of paste-on slips when there was no more room in the margins (there are often insertion marks or traces of paste at these points), and here again the 1595 edition can be taken as authoritative; some variants are clearly due to the editorial intervention of Mlle de Gournay or Pierre de Brach, and these can be ignored; finally there are some which do not fit any of these categories, which have the ring of Montaigne although there is no trace of them in the Bordeaux Copy, and these it is difficult to reject out of hand. Although, therefore, Montaigne's own hand in the Bordeaux Copy is bound to have supreme authority, the 1595 edition also has some independent status.

Some further peculiarities of the 1595 edition may be briefly noted. Some copies (especially those with the Sonnius imprint) lack the preface *Au lecteur*. The reason is explained by Mlle de Gournay in her short preface to the 1598 edition:[1] it had been mislaid at the moment of printing and had later reappeared. Those that have it are dated 12 June 1580, a contamination which confirms the temporary loss of the corrected 1588 preface and the need to botch something up in a hurry. One chapter (I, xiv) has been moved, to become I, xl, with consequent renumbering of all the chapters between: the new order is followed by all the editions based on 1595, that is nearly all until the end of the nineteenth century. The reason for the shift is a still unsolved mystery: if it was pure accident it seems surprising that Mlle de Gournay should have left it as it was in the later editions she published; on the other hand, its logical place (in so far as there is a logical order) is the original rather than the new one. At the end of the 1595 preface Mlle de Gournay says that she has corrected various errors in ink: 'Ie ne puis apporter trop de precaution ny de curiosité, sur une chose de tel merite'.[2] These corrections, in her own hand, are found in all the copies I have seen (and there are similar corrections in the 1635 edition). When we consider the labour of correcting every copy by hand in this way, the point has an obvious bearing on Mlle de Gournay's scrupulous care as editor and on the reliability of the 1595 edition, whose authority is thereby strengthened. Her care is further exemplified by the

---

[1] But already in manuscript in one of the copies of 1595 at the Plantin-Moretus Museum, Antwerp.
[2] ĩ2ᵛ.

cancels found in some copies. As in the case of 1580, there is a second issue of 1595, of which I have seen five copies.[1] The main differences are a cancel title-page, the omission of the privilege, and probably a new cancel (2L3-4). The most likely, though conjectural, explanation is that l'Angelier took over the remaining stock of Sonnius and reissued it with his own imprint.

Though Mlle de Gournay continued to publish editions of the *Essais* throughout her long life (those of 1598, 1608, 1617, 1625, and 1635 are of particular interest) and though in view of her connection with the original publication none can be entirely rejected, the 1595 edition marks the end of the main textual tradition. We thus have five stages of the work or five layers of text: 1580, 1582, 1588, the Bordeaux Copy, and 1595. Of these 1582 and 1595 can be regarded as secondary, though none the less important. The significance of this, and the justification for a fairly full treatment of the textual problem, lies in the fact that these stages set out the milestones in the movement of Montaigne's thought. In what is one of the most revealing as well as the most familiar statements about his work he says:

> Je ne peints pas l'estre. Je peints le passage: non un passage d'aage en autre, ou, comme dict le peuple, de sept en sept ans, mais de jour en jour, de minute en minute.[2]

To seize the movement from minute to minute it will be necessary to examine the verbal fabric of the *Essais* in detail, but textual criticism shows the cruder movement, almost exactly 'de sept en sept ans'. That is why the best modern editions designate at least the three principal phases by means of special symbols.

The *Essais* as we have them are not quite complete. Montaigne tells us that a servant stole several drafts, including a chapter on the comparison of modern weapons with those of the Romans.[3] Part of this missing essay has been worked in to the present II, ix (*Des armes des Parthes*). In any case the lost essays must be early (the two passages are in the 1580 edition and speak of the theft as in a fairly distant past), and their loss is not a matter of too deep regret.

[1] Bibliothèque de l'Institut, Paris; Plantin-Moretus Museum, Antwerp; King's College, Cambridge; Harvard; Sotheby's sale, 5 Oct., 1971. Another was sold at auction in Paris in 1961 (Jacques Mégret, 'Remarques sur le "Montaigne de 1595"', *Le bouquiniste français*, Jan. 1962, pp. 7-9).

[2] III, ii: EM iii, 20; TR 782.

[3] II, ix: DB i, 338; II, xxxvii: TR 737.

In the general presentation of the text in the early editions the most striking feature is the absence of paragraphing (the only major exception, for no apparent reason, is I, xlvii, *De l'incertitude de nostre jugement*). Among modern editors only Courbet and Royer follow Montaigne in this respect, and it would indeed be difficult to expect an editor to carry fidelity to the point of making the book almost unreadable for those accustomed to modern usage. At the same time, it is important to remember that Montaigne himself does not use paragraphs. Any analysis of structure based on paragraph units is obviously impossible; at a deeper level, the continuous flow of the original, within each essay, contributes something to the depiction of thought in uninterrupted movement. In speaking of the unfaithful servant, Montaigne remarks that he was employed in writing the essays ('qui me servoit à les escrire soubs moy'). Therefore at least part of the essays were presumably dictated (he also used a secretary for parts of the *Journal du voyage*), though the marginalia of the Bordeaux Copy are nearly all in his own hand; this again may have some bearing on the conversational character of his style (or, more accurately, of the conversational impression it gives).

Modern editors, if they do not modernise the spelling, generally at least regularise it (with the exception of the Édition Municipale). Something is no doubt lost thereby, since, though Montaigne claims to be indifferent to the pedantic details of spelling and punctuation,[1] we have seen that he includes in the Bordeaux Copy a list of instructions to the printer on just these points (a typical example of the separation of the man inside the *Essais* and the man outside them). However, the modernising of punctuation in recent editions (even the Édition Municipale) is a much more serious matter: not only is the rhythm subtly altered, but stylistic arguments based on sentence and clause divisions have to be advanced with great caution.

Montaigne's constant revision of the text at all stages is, as we have seen, not merely the concern of any careful writer for greater accuracy and more refined expression reflected in superficial if significant changes: it is a vital part of the work itself, going to the deepest roots of his purpose, the record of his thought in movement. More than this even, it presents an aspect of the infinite regress, the observer observing and observed: his judge-

[1] III, ix: TR 942.

ment is stimulated by all his experience, and this inevitably includes what he has already written, which leads him to ever new
comments and reflections, glancing off at all kinds of unexpected
angles. No treatment of his thought or style is therefore possible
without constant reference to the mobile state of the text. The
revisions can be classified as corrections or substitutions, suppressions, transpositions, and interpolations. He himself substantially
denies the existence of the first class:

(*a*) Au demeurant, je ne corrige point mes premieres imaginations
par les secondes; (*c*) ouy à l'avanture quelque mot, mais pour
diversifier, non pour oster.[1]

J'adjouste, mais je ne corrige pas.[2]

These statements, like much of what Montaigne says about himself, are true in a general way and convey very well the sense of
continuity, of addition piled on addition. But they are not true in
detail. There are in fact numerous corrections and substitutions,
both of thought and of form: how numerous can be seen from a
cursory glance at the Bordeaux Copy. A single example will show
the sort of wry and ironical honesty which can be revealed in a
minute verbal correction. In 1580, speaking of the spurious
advantages of kingship, he wrote that for an intelligent and well-
born man 'la royauté n'adjoute rien à son bon'heur'. In the
Bordeaux Copy this becomes 'la royauté adjoute peu à son
bon'heur'.[3] The qualification (Montaigne had clearly reflected
that the advantages of kingship were not as negligible as all that)
stands in subdued and humorous counterpoint with the original.
Suppressions have sometimes the effect of giving greater concentration and vigour (though Montaigne's vigour is not usually at-
tained by concentration); where they affect the thought, by the
excision of views which might be dangerous (not very frequent),
they will be discussed later. Transpositions, not common, are
interesting because they demonstrate at least some concern for
relevance, not on the face of it an outstanding characteristic of
Montaigne, and a feeling for the place where an idea will produce
its most powerful effect. More subtly, a subversive opinion may
pass more easily in one context than in another.[4]

[1] II, xxxvii: EM ii, 575; TR 736-7.
[2] III, ix: EM iii, 228; TR 941.
[3] I, xlii: EM i, 339; TR 255.
[4] For discussion of an interesting example see Frame, *Biography*, pp. 300-1.

However, the most important changes are naturally the interpolations. Some essays, especially but not exclusively the earliest, consist in their final version almost entirely of interpolations. Thus II, xx (*Nous ne goustons rien de pur*), a brief reflection of hardly a page in 1580, is expanded and given life by the additions of 1588 and the Bordeaux Copy. A more telling and less obvious example in a much more central essay is I, xiv (*Que le goust des biens et des maux depend en bonne partie de l'opinion que nous en avons*): in the first printing Montaigne promises to discuss the three evils of death, poverty, and pain, but in fact poverty is hardly mentioned and is only fully treated in the later interpolations. The full, rounded, solid plan is therefore only gradually achieved. More complex patterns in a smaller compass within the essays are formed by the interweaving of additions at different stages.[1] Frequently, he starts a new train of thought, or turns the argument against himself, or sharpens irony by the addition of a concrete detail as in the description of a foolish pedant:

(*a*) et si estoit homme de lettres et de reputation, (*b*) et qui avoit une belle robe.[2]

On the whole it is remarkable how ingeniously and unobtrusively Montaigne welds his interpolations into the fabric of the existing essay, maintaining the continuity which is so characteristic. A single example will illustrate his way of doing it. In 1588 he writes:

De se tenir chancelant et mestis, de tenir son affection immobile et sans inclination aus troubles de son pays et en une division publique, je ne le trouve ny beau ny honneste: il faut prendre party.[3]

In the Bordeaux Copy, after 'honneste', a long passage is added, which ends:

(*c*) Ce seroit une espece de trahison de le faire aus propres et domestiques affaires: aus quels necesseremant (*b*) il faut prendre party (*c*) par application de dessein.[4]

The joint is quite invisible. But there are a few exceptions where possessives are left hanging, referring to antecedents far back in

[1] A particularly good illustration is in I, ix: TR 35–6.
[2] I, xxv: EM i, 180; TR 138.
[3] III, i: MJ v, 170.
[4] EM iii, 5; TR 770.

the text. Thus 'Et les gens de village de ce païs'[1] seems to refer to the peasants of Libya, just described in a Bordeaux Copy addition, but ought to refer to those of Arcadia, as in 1580. These rare slips do not invalidate the general principle. A much graver problem is that of interpolations introduced *before* publication, particularly between 1571 and 1580, which of course leave no trace in the published editions but which must have been fairly numerous because of Montaigne's method of working. In particular their existence must cast doubts on Villey's dating of the composition of each essay: even when a date is certain, it really applies only to a single passage, not necessarily to the essay as a whole.[2] A possible example among many of pre-1580 interpolation is *Des menteurs* (itself largely built up of post-1580 additions): about halfway through the final version, the sentence '(*a*) Ce n'est pas sans raison qu'on dit, que qui ne se sent point assez ferme de memoire, ne se doit pas mesler d'estre menteur'[3] bears all the marks of a Montaigne introduction in the early essays; the actual introduction of 1580, beginning '(*a*) Il n'est homme à qui il siese si mal de se mesler de parler de memoire', with its personal note and verbal echo of the other passage, looks very much like a later reflection. Sometimes the probability seems greater: at one point in *De l'art de conferer* (III, viii) there is considerable confusion between Pompey and Tacitus, *il* serving for both. The chances are that the bit about Pompey has been interpolated and that the point of juncture comes at 'ainsi je ne l'en crois pas'.[4] At any rate the possibility of such interpolations must always be borne in mind. It may be remarked in passing that heavy concentrations of additions help to draw attention to the themes and problems which Montaigne has most at heart.

The title he chose for his book constitutes in itself one of his greatest claims to originality. He is in fact the first to use the word 'essay' in its modern sense: the word as well as the thing is his own. It is true that Sagon (Marot's enemy) had published in 1537 *Le coup d'essay de Françoys de Sagon*, but this is in verse and the meaning is only tangentially related to Montaigne's (who does say at one point 'Laisse, lecteur, courir encore ce coup d'essay',[5]

1 II, xxxvii: EM ii, 587; TR 746.
2 cf. Villey, *Sources et évolution*, i, 299. But he does not give full weight to the objection.
3 I, ix: EM i, 39; TR 36.
4 III, viii: EM iii, 201; TR 920.
5 III, ix: EM iii, 228; TR 941.

this first attempt). An interesting point made by Telle[1] is that the title up to 1588 is just *Essais* but from 1595 onwards *Les essais*: the original title is more modest, the later (not Montaigne's) assumes that the work is already well known. Frame's view that the title was found about 1578 may be accepted, though his suggestion that it was inspired by the Jeux Floraux of Toulouse (where it meant a final deciding test) seems less convincing.[2] How disturbingly new the title was can be seen in Naselli's Italian translation of 1590, where it appears as *Discorsi*, which has the effect of making the book sound much more ordinary, especially as it is followed by *morali, politici, et militari*, suggesting a familiar genre. When he writes in the dedication 'ma essendo questi Discorsi di cose gradi, di guerra, & di governi', Naselli shows that he does not understand the book as Florio does, but his reaction reveals what some contemporaries saw in it (the next Italian translation, Canini's of 1633, is called *Saggi*, the normal equivalent in modern Italian, with *Discorsi* as subtitle, a combination also adopted by Florio in *The essayes or morall, politike and millitarie discourses*).

When we come to determine the exact sense in which Montaigne used the word[3] we are struck by the number of possible meanings (a multivalence which is typical of him). Already in 1584 La Croix du Maine distinguishes two senses: (i) 'coup d'Essay, ou apprentissage' (a sense we have already met); (ii) 'experiences, c'est à dire discours pour se façonner sur autruy'.[4] Both interpretations are useful, but clearly only Montaigne himself can give us a precise answer. To take first a case where the book itself is not under consideration, he writes of La Boétie: 'Il l'escrivit par maniere d'essay, en sa premiere jeunesse'.[5] Here the sense is obviously that of *coup d'essai* or apprentice work, and Telle suggests that this is the origin of Montaigne's use of the term. Certainly this most modest of all the senses is very suitable as a starting-point, from which other more ambitious senses devel-

---

[1] E. V. Telle, 'A propos du mot «essai» chez Montaigne', *BHR*, xxx (1968).
[2] Frame, *Biography*, p. 184.
[3] This question has been much discussed: apart from Telle, see in particular A. Blinkenberg, 'Quel sens Montaigne a-t-il voulu donner au mot *Essais* dans le titre de son œuvre ?', *BSAM*, III, 29 (Jan.–March 1964), pp. 22–32.
[4] *Premier volume de la bibliotheque*, 1584, p. 328.
[5] I, xxviii: EM i, 238; TR 182(a).

oped. The most important of these occurs in a group of passages, all written before 1580 (but probably not before 1578):[1]

Quant aux facultez naturelles qui sont en moy, dequoy c'est icy l'*essay*. . . .[2]

C'est icy purement l'*essay* de mes facultez naturelles, et nullement des acquises. . . .[3]

Le jugement est un util à tous subjects, et se mesle par tout. A cette cause, aux *essais* que j'en fay ici . . . Si c'est un subject que je n'entende point, à cela mesme je l'*essaye*, sondant le gué de bien loing . . . Tantost, à un subject vain et de neant, j'*essaye* voir s'il trouvera dequoy luy donner corps. . . .[4]

. . . mon jugement ne se defferre poinct, duquel ce sont icy les *essais*.[5]

In all these cases Montaigne is trying out or testing his faculties or his judgement (the English word 'assay' presents a close parallel) to see how far they will take him. A later observation confirms this:

Si mon ame pouvoit prendre pied, je ne m'*essaierois* pas, je me resoudrois: elle est tousjours en apprentissage et en espreuve.[6]

He is testing himself and his opinions, never coming to a fixed conclusion. Another sense emerges in the final book:

En fin, toute cette fricassée que je barbouille icy n'est qu'un registre des *essais* de ma vie. . . .[7]

Here the sense, applied to life but reflected back on to the book, is rather that of 'experiences', which we have found in La Croix du Maine. It is sometimes said[8] that the word is never, or hardly ever, used of the individual essays, called simply chapters: in the passages considered, when the plural occurs, and in the general title, it refers to the whole series of soundings into the mind and its working, not to mere formal divisions. There is an important truth here, which should never be lost from view. However, two

---

1 For dates of composition see Villey, *Sources et évolution*, i, 356 ff.
2 I, xxvi: EM i, 188; TR 145(*a*).
3 II, x: EM ii, 100; TR 387(*a*).
4 I, l: EM i, 386; TR 289(*a*).
5 II, xvii: EM ii, 437; TR 637(*a*).
6 III, ii: EM iii, 21; TR 782(*b*).
7 III, xiii: EM iii, 379; TR 1056(*b*).
8 e.g. by Schon, *Vorformen des Essays in Antike und Humanismus*, p. 5.

passages (both late) may be taken as referring to individual essays in the modern sense:

> et, de mes premiers *essays*, aucuns puent un peu à l'estranger.[1]
>
> ... je redicterois ... autant d'*essais*. ...[2]

It seems that towards the end Montaigne is beginning to look at his book in a rather different way. In the same chapter he speaks of it as memoirs:

> Tant y a qu'en ces memoires ... on trouvera que j'ai tout dict, ou tout designé.[3]

Here the sense must be close to 'memoranda'.

Some general uses of the word, apart from the title, may help us to elucidate its nuances. One leads from 'experience' to 'experiment' (one of the senses given by Cotgrave for *essay*):

> J'imagine l'homme regardant au tour de luy le nombre infiny des choses, plantes, animaux, metaux. Je ne sçay par où luy faire commencer son *essay*. ...[4]

Man is looking at the whole world, and thus the word is closely linked with scientific inquiry. Of his family's habit of doing without doctors he says: 'il y a deux cens ans ... que cet *essay* nous dure',[5] and the word *experience* occurs in the same sense in the next sentence. The word 'essay' is thus intimately connected with the word 'experience', itself the title of Montaigne's last culminating chapter, and the twin senses of trial or testing and experience or experiment run through the whole fabric of the book.

Montaigne's minor works require some mention because they will be quoted for reference or comparison. Apart from the publication of the posthumous works of La Boétie (1571–2), with prefatory epistles of his own, they are the translation of the *Theologia naturalis* or *Liber creaturarum* of the fifteenth-century Spanish theologian Raymond Sabunde, or Sebon(d) as Montaigne spells it, and the *Journal du voyage en Italie par la Suisse et l'Allemagne en 1580 et 1581*. The translation of Sabunde (1569), made at the behest of Montaigne's father, is of importance because it inspired the *Apologie de Raimond Sebond* (an odd sort of

---

[1] III, v: EM iii, 114; TR 853(*b*).
[2] III, ix: EM iii, 230; TR 942(*b*).
[3] III, ix: EM iii, 254; TR 961(*b*).
[4] II, xxxvii: EM ii, 608; TR 762(*a*).
[5] II, xxxvii: EM ii, 583–4; TR 743(*a*).

apology in fact) and still more because it gave Montaigne a training in the handling of philosophical vocabulary and argument. Sabunde's scholasticism and dogmatic presentation of his ideas stand, however, at the opposite pole to Montaigne, and it is difficult to imagine that he would have been attracted to this author if it had not been for his father's insistence.

The *Journal du voyage* is a different matter. It was first published in 1774, from a manuscript found in the château of Montaigne, in three simultaneous editions edited by Meusnier de Querlon. Unfortunately the manuscript disappeared shortly afterwards and has never been recovered, which means that the editions, however imperfect, are the only authority. Although publication was simultaneous, the order of printing can be clearly established as: (i) two volumes, 12mo; (ii) one volume, 4to; (iii) three volumes, 12mo. The mysterious circumstances of the finding and loss of the manuscript, together with a certain disappointment at the relatively dry mode of narration and at the relatively conformist attitude to religion, have led to some doubts about its authenticity. Such doubts can hardly survive an unprejudiced reading, and the doubters tend to overlook the fact that the *Journal* was never intended for publication but merely as a private record. The first part was kept by a secretary, who is sometimes independent of his master; after the dismissal of the secretary Montaigne himself takes over, at first in French and then in Italian:

Assaggiamo di parlar un poco questa altra lingua, massime essendo in queste contrade dove mi pare sentire il più perfetto favellare della Toscana, particolarmente tra li paesani che non l'hanno mescolato et alterato con li vicini.[1]

This gay approach to the effort of learning a new language is typical of him; in spite of his modest disclaimers his Italian is in fact quite good, though rather slapdash.[2] The *Journal* constitutes a vivid account of life in Germany and Italy at the end of the sixteenth century; it provides invaluable evidence of Montaigne's keen intellectual and human curiosity, of his love of religious disputation, of his reactions to the works of art of ancient and

---

[1] *Journal*, ed. Lautrey, p. 328.
[2] See Aldo Rosellini, 'Quelques remarques sur l'italien du "Journal ed voyage" de Michel de Montaigne', *Zeitschrift für romanische Philologie*, lxxxiii (1967).

B

Renaissance Italy (though there are some blind spots here); and it is full of incidents and observations which are later worked into the *Essais* and comments which serve to illuminate them. He says in the *Essais* that he never wrote them away from home,[1] and the *Journal*, a temporary substitute for them, shows how strong his passion was for setting down his thoughts on paper, for watching himself as well as the world, and for crystallising in language what he had seen.

[1] II, xxxvii: TR 736.

Imitation and Originality:
Montaigne and Books

IF his own mind and the world refracted through it are
Montaigne's subjects, the instrument he uses to measure and
grasp them are primarily books. In spite of his dislike of
pedants and his frequent mockery of learning he was from his
earliest years a passionate reader: at the age of seven or eight
he was already reading Ovid's *Metamorphoses* (in the original,
of course) for pleasure,[1] and the earliest purchase of a book which
he is known to have made dates from 1549 when he was sixteen.[2]
The library, with its painted quotations from ancient authors, is
still the most interesting room in his famous tower, and the collection of books he assembled in it was a considerable one for the
time. In the 1588 edition he can claim a thousand volumes: 'ayant
mille volumes de livres autour de moy en ce lieu où j'escris. . . .'[3]
Coupled with the declaration that he never worked on the *Essais*
except at home, this shows that the composition of the work must
be seen against the background of the surrounding bookshelves.
His description is eloquent:

> La figure en est ronde et . . . vient m'offrant en se courbant,
> d'une veue, tous mes livres rengez à cinq degrez tout à l'environ.
> Elle a a trois veues de riche et libre prospet, et sese pas de vuide en
> diamettre.[4]

The views from the windows as well as the tiers of five shelves
must be taken into account.

About one hundred of the books from the library survive in

---

[1] I, xxvi: TR 175.
[2] Erasmus's edition of Terence (1538): see *BSAM* II, 8 (1940), p. 14.
[3] III, xii: EM iii, 348; TR 1033(*b*).
[4] III, iii: EM iii, 53: TR 806–7.

various collections,[1] and part of the rest has been reconstructed by Villey from the evidence of Montaigne's reading.[2] It is a typical Renaissance scholar's library, with the authors of antiquity occupying a prominent place (the Greeks often though by no means always in translation), not much theology, a number of modern commentators, but with particular emphasis on Montaigne's special interests and curiosity: history, including Turkey, China, and America (Lopez de Gomara's *Histoire générale des Indes occidentales*, Benzoni's *Histoire nouvelle du Nouveau Monde*, both translations); poetry, ancient and modern (neo-Latin; Italian – Petrarch, Ariosto, Tasso; French – Ronsard and du Bellay); miscellanies of Renaissance compilers like Crinitus, Egnatius, and Ravisius Textor; a few scientific or occult books like Martinus Poblacion on the use of the astrolabe or Cornelius Agrippa's *De occulta philosophia*; above all many philosophers and moralists.

Apart from his own, Montaigne seems to have seized every opportunity of visiting other libraries, as we see from the *Journal du voyage*. In particular he gives a long description of the Vatican Library, where he saw a Chinese book and a papyrus as well as a number of early manuscripts, the presentation copy of Henry VIII's attack on Luther, and Plantin's polyglot Bible.[3] He says in the *Essais* that he never travels without books in peace or war,[4] and this is confirmed by the *Journal* where he relates how his books were retained for examination by the Roman customs officers and were later damaged when his horse fell into a stream at San Chirico.[5] On the way he buys the works of Nicolas of Cusa in Venice and eleven comedies at the Giunta shop in Florence.[6] In Rome he makes a careful study of maps and guide books (no doubt including his copy of Mauro, *Le antichita della citta di Roma*, 1558, now in the Bordeaux Library) as a preparation for his sightseeing tours.[7]

Here then is a man who lives among books and is always accompanied by them. His references to his own learning (as to his

---

1 For a list see Bonnefon, 'La bibliothèque de Montaigne', *RHLF*, ii (1895), and additions in *BSAM*, especially 1938–40.
2 *Sources et évolution*, vol. i, especially pp. 273–83.
3 TR 1221–3.
4 III, iii: TR 806.
5 TR 1205, 1318.
6 TR 1185, 1296.
7 TR 1212.

memory) are nevertheless nearly always deprecatory: he is incapable of working for long, he cannot normally read for more than an hour at a time,[1] he confesses to having bought books, at least at first, just for show,[2] he skims through rather than studies them, remembering nothing in detail but keeping a residue which he forgets he has taken from someone else.[3] How far we can accept this at its face value is hard to say: there is an element of genuine modesty here but also a touch of the coquetry of a gentleman who does not wish to be confused with mere pedants and professional writers (the prejudice against learning and intellectual activity among the French nobility was at this time very strong).[4] At all events, his erudition is remarkable by modern standards.

However, when all these allowances are made, it remains true, as he explains in *Des livres*, that he relied a good deal on marginal notes and on a general judgement written at the end of a book which had specially interested him.[5] He quotes three examples (Guicciardini, Commines, the memoirs of the du Bellay brothers), and the habit is confirmed by some of his surviving books (for example his Caesar, now at Chantilly). An aside in the Guicciardini assessment tells us that 'quelque langue que parlent mes livres, je leur parle en la mienne' (that is, in French not Italian): the idea of an active conversation with books rather than a passive absorption is wholly characteristic of his method of reading. He stresses again and again that books are for him an exercise of judgement (a key concept in many other respects) and a spur to action rather than a means of instruction.[6] He also reads for entertainment, and expresses his attitude in terms of an evolution in time:

J'estudiay, jeune, pour l'ostentation; depuis, un peu, pour m'assagir; à cette heure, pour m'esbatre. . . .[7]

This conforms in some ways to the general development of his outlook, though, as with the general development itself, it should not be interpreted too rigidly.

He is also aware of the disadvantages and dangers of reading,

---

[1] TR 392–3, 919.
[2] III, iii: TR 807. But this perhaps refers figuratively to his studies rather than literally to books.
[3] II, xvii: TR 635.
[4] Montaigne himself comments on it (II, xvii: TR 642).
[5] II, x: TR 398–400.
[6] e.g. TR 241(*a*), 764(*a*), 797(*c*), 1016(*c*).
[7] III, iii: EM iii, 54; TR 807(*b*).

its laboriousness, its unhealthiness, the excessive pleasure it gives, its inferiority to conversation:

> L'estude des livres, c'est un mouvement languissant et foible qui n'eschauffe poinct; là où la conference apprend et exerce en un coup.[1]

He is particularly scathing about the rage for writing books in his own time, 'quelque simptome d'un siecle desbordé',[2] the sign of a decadent age; about the veneration inspired by the printed word; and in *De l'experience* about glosses, commentaries, and books on books, culminating in the heartfelt cry:

> Quand est-il convenu entre nous: ce livre en a assez, il n'y a meshuy plus que dire?[3]

a warning for writers about Montaigne, among others.

Yet few men have written better in praise of books. The apologia for reading in *De trois commerces* contains not only the well-known 'C'est la meilleure munition que j'aye trouvé à cet humain voyage'[4] but an enumeration of the services and comforts which books can offer. At a deeper level (here approaching criticism, to be considered later) he remarks that he is sometimes struck by the beauty of a passage but returning to it later, 'j'ay beau le plier et le manier, c'est une masse inconnue et informe pour moy,'[5] an experience which is not confined to him. In the same way, his perceptiveness and the fineness of his response appear (he is talking again about his bad memory) in 'les lieux et les livres que je revoy me rient tousjours d'une fresche nouvelleté'.[6] In short Montaigne presents an outstanding example of the real purpose of books: not as a substitute for experience but as an enhancement and enlargement of it (answering in advance the criticisms of a bookish education made by Rousseau in *Émile* and by Sartre in *Les mots*).

There can be no question here of repeating even in summary form Villey's great work on Montaigne's sources,[7] but some

---

1 III, viii: EM iii, 176; TR 900(*b*).
2 III, ix: EM iii, 205; TR 923.
3 III, xiii: EM iii, 364; TR 1044.
4 III, iii: EM iii, 52; TR 806.
5 II, xii: EM ii, 316; TR 549(*a*).
6 I, ix: EM i, 39; TR 36(*b*).
7 *Sources et évolution;* Édition Municipale, vol. iv. The former lists the identified sources alphabetically, the latter, most usefully, quotes the relevant passages from them in the order of the *Essais*.

notion of the extent and nature of his borrowings (or thefts) is required before we can approach the crucial questions: how did he incorporate them in his book and how does his reliance on them affect his originality?

After what has been said there is no need to emphasise that his principal sources are classical, and this immediately raises the problem of his knowledge of Greek. His own answer is that he has only 'une puerile et aprantisse intelligence'[1] of the language, insufficient for him to judge the accuracy of Amyot's translation of Plutarch,[2] but we have seen how much he was inclined to belittle his accomplishments of this sort. He was taught Greek as a boy,[3] there were a number of Greek books in his library (for example a Bible and Appian's history of the Roman civil wars), and there is a sprinkling of Greek quotations in the *Essais*. However, the possession of these books does not prove that he read them, and the quotations seem to come almost entirely from intermediate sources (thus Villey points out that all the quotations from Euripides are also found in the *Sententiae* of Stobaeus).[4] More seriously, it is certain that he read Plutarch and Herodotus in the French translations of Amyot and Saliat, as is proved (apart from his own statement in the former case) by numerous verbatim transcriptions. And he admits that he cannot appreciate the beauty of Plato's or Homer's language.[5] On the whole, though he may have been underrated in this respect by himself and others, it is difficult to deny Highet's conclusion that relative ignorance of Greek sets limits on his appreciation of classical antiquity.[6]

Yet when we have conceded that he read Greek authors mostly in translation (Latin or French), the range and depth of his acquaintance with the literature of antiquity remain formidable. He exaggerates when he speaks of 'mon livre massoné purement de leurs despouilles',[7] but it is the exaggeration of an indubitable truth. Among many statements of his love and admiration the

---

[1] II, x: EM ii, 103; TR 389. In editions to 1588 we find 'une moyenne intelligence' (MJ iii, 122). Is the correction due to greater honesty or greater modesty?
[2] II, iv: TR 344.
[3] I, xxvi: TR 173–4.
[4] *Sources et évolution*, i, 142.
[5] II, x: TR 394; II, xxxvi: TR 730.
[6] *The classical tradition*, Oxford, 1949, p. 188. See also Börje Knös, 'Les citations grecques de Montaigne', *Eranos*, xliv (1946).
[7] II, xxxii: EM ii, 526; TR 699(c).

most eloquent is perhaps a passage where he compares their greatness with his own gross clumsiness:

> Leurs escris ne me satisfont pas seulement et me remplissent;
> mais ils m'estonnent et transissent d'admiration. Je juge leur beauté;
> je la voy, si non jusques au bout, aumoins si avant qu'il m'est
> impossible d'y aspirer. Quoy que j'entreprenne, je doy un sacrifice
> aux graces, comme dict Plutarque de quelqu'un, pour pratiquer
> leur faveur,
> >   si quid enim placet,
> >   Si quid dulce hominum sensibus influit,
> >   Debentur lepidis omnia gratiis.
>
> Elles m'abandonnent par tout. Tout est grossier chez moy; il y a
> faute de jantillesse et de beauté.[1]

Here speaks the authentic voice of Renaissance humanism.

Apart from the Roman poets, who come in a special category
(and we might add Homer, who is placed among the three excellent men of II, xxxvi, though not on strictly poetic grounds),
his favourite writers are Plutarch and Seneca, 'ou je puyse comme
les Danaïdes, remplissant et versant sans cesse'[2] (as in the last
quotation the classical example springs naturally to corroborate the
classical thought). Apart from their influence in details these two
are of great importance for the form of the *Essais*, as we shall see.
Plutarch in particular, 'le plus judicieux autheur du monde',[3] is
often praised and still more often plagiarised. After them, frequently discussed and quoted, come (among the Greeks) Plato
and Aristotle, Herodotus (an inexhaustible mine of tall stories),
Xenophon, Sextus Empiricus (or rather Pyrrho through him);
among Latin authors Livy, Tacitus (greatly admired but with
some reservations), Pliny (the source of many unbelievable bits of
natural history), above all Caesar and Cicero (though Montaigne
has doubts about both as men and about Cicero as a writer).[4]

Indeed if he has strong preferences among authors on literary
grounds, he has equally strong feelings about the men of antiquity
as characters (and here we only partly leave the subject of books,
for he inevitably sees them through his reading, Plutarch's *Lives*
especially). Morally speaking (and it is essential not to forget this

---

[1] II, xvii: EM ii, 414–5; TR 620.
[2] I, xxvi: EM i, 188; TR 144(*c*).
[3] II, xxxii: EM ii, 528; TR 700. This essay is the *Defence de Seneque et de
Plutarque*.
[4] See Villey for a full list, including the *minores*.

when we come to consider charges of weakness or lack of heroism based on the self-portrait), the *Essais* are dominated by a series of noble figures, carefully, judiciously and justly weighed, the faults penetratingly observed but never allowed to obscure the greatness: Epaminondas (repeatedly eulogised), Alcibiades (the model of the *galant homme*), Alexander and Caesar (both with very deep shadows), and the most heroic, Cato the Younger, 'his dantem jura Catonem'.[1] But above them all, at any rate in the last stages of the *Essais*, towers Socrates, 'le maistre des maistres',[2] 'le plus sage homme qui fut onques',[3] 'ce personnage à tous patrons et formes de perfection'.[4] At the end of Montaigne's development he represents all or nearly all that Montaigne regarded as exemplary: sufficient but unostentatious courage (and really the greater for being unostentatious), indifference to death, keen intelligence but subordinate to wisdom. Appropriately Socrates makes his last (or, strictly, penultimate) appearance in the *Essais* to support the association of bodily and intellectual pleasures which concludes the final chapter. Montaigne was not indeed the first to praise Socrates highly (three earlier examples are Erasmus, Rabelais, and Guy de Bruès), but it may be doubted whether anyone had been so profoundly influenced. How far the position of Socrates as supreme model affects our view of Montaigne's religion will be considered later. For the moment nothing could establish more clearly the classical affiliation of the *Essais*.

What is most striking about his use of the classics is the way in which, seen through his eyes, antiquity is made alive.[5] Even when he is imitating most closely, he is always aware of ancient life as it was lived, never slipping into the arid lists or scholia characteristic of much classical scholarship in his time and since. He perhaps comes nearest to the methods of the classical scholars of his period in *Des coustumes anciennes* (I, xlix), with its disjointed notes on Roman customs (baths, lavatories, table manners, wine-drinking and so on). These notes are, however, assembled from different sources and given coherence by the theme of everyday behaviour and by the intuitive sympathy which brings it all to

---

[1] Virgil. Quoted in I, xxxvii: EM i, 304; TR 228.

[2] III, xiii: EM iii, 375; TR 1053(*c*).

[3] II, xii: EM ii, 224; TR 480-1(*a*).

[4] III, xiii: EM iii, 422; TR 1090. On the relationship see Frederick Kellermann, 'Montaigne's Socrates', *Romanic review*, xlv (1954).

[5] cf. Jean Prévost's remark that both La Boétie and Montaigne 'regardaient l'Antiquité comme chose vivante' (*La vie de Montaigne*, p. 68).

life. Both the technique, to some extent, and certainly the spirit of scholarship are remarkably present here. But if this essay is exceptional in its concentration on the sort of problem scholars deal with, the same easy familiarity runs through the *Essais* as a whole. It is true that (like Macaulay) he sometimes overdoes the assumption that his readers share this familiarity (children know the story of Croesus,[1] everyone knows the story of Scaevola,[2] and so on) but he was addressing an audience better informed in this respect than a modern one. Sometimes familiarity seems a little too easy, as when he speaks of 'ce maraut de Caligula'[3] or 'ce coquin de Neron';[4] obscure allusions (again more obscure to us) abound, like that to Xenophilus the Musician.[5] Sometimes his familiarity goes much deeper than these superficial indications of learning. His method can be seen at its most powerful in the spirited way he tells the hackneyed story of Androcles and the lion[6] (from Apion through Aulus Gellius) or the picture (from Plutarch) of Cato the Censor as governor of Sardinia, always on foot with a single official to carry his robe and a vase for sacrifices, 'et le plus souvent il pourtoit sa male luy mesme'[7] (this last touch is not in Amyot). He sees it and we see it: the secret lies once more in the union of learning and observation (which comes close to the imagination of the novelist), reading enriched by experience of life:

> ... j'allegue aussi volontiers un mien amy que Aulugele et que Macrobe, et ce que j'ay veu que ce qu'ils ont escrit.[8]

He sees everything on the same plane, books and life, and to some extent the present and the past. In fact he sometimes seems scarcely aware that the world of the ancients has ceased to exist (a point to which we shall return). So in speaking of a battle in which Pompey was defeated, he can speak (as often happens) of 'our ensigns, our legions',[9] identifying himself with the Romans. When he sets out to describe the cannibals of America (I, xxxi), he begins with Pyrrhus in Italy: the familiarity of ancient history serves as a stepping-stone to the unfamiliar

[1] I, xix: TR 77.
[2] I, xiv: TR 59.
[3] II, vi: EM ii, 50; TR 350.
[4] II, viii: EM ii, 92; TR 382.
[5] I, xx: TR 81.
[6] II, xii: TR 455–7.
[7] I, lii: EM i, 396; TR 296.
[8] III, xiii: EM iii, 382–3; TR 1059.
[9] II, xii: TR 454.

modernity of the New World. Conversely, antiquity is often seen
in modern terms, as when the effect of a siege engine (in Livy) is
compared to an arquebus shot.[1] More serious historical parallels
are constantly drawn. In particular the Roman civil wars recur
in explicit or implicit comparison with the French Wars of
Religion.[2] He returns again and again to the greatness of Athens,
Sparta (which he generally prefers), and above all Rome, the
state which contains in itself the sum of human history:

> Il comprend en soy toutes les formes et avantures qui touchent
> un estat; tout ce que l'ordre y peut et le trouble, et l'heur et le
> malheur.[3]

The title of *De la grandeur romaine* (II, xxiv) speaks for itself:
this is the touchstone by which the past and the present alike are
judged.

By the side of this massive inspiration (to talk of sources seems
in the end grossly inadequate) the use of modern (or medieval)
writers amounts to little and can be briefly summarised. Though
the library included many modern works, most of them were
continuations of, or commentaries on, the classics, and naturally
in Latin (an exception may be made for modern history). Of
medieval writers Montaigne quotes Dante (the *Divine Comedy*)
twice, but probably at second hand. He knew Boccaccio and
Petrarch well, and some historians, especially Froissart and
Commines; he refers in a playful way to the romances of chivalry,
especially *Amadis*. The *Theologia naturalis* of Sabunde, no doubt
the source of his most prolonged study of medieval thought, we
have already considered. Other Christian and theological sources
do not go much beyond the Bible and St Augustine (*De civitate
Dei*), and even in these cases the debt is limited: the great disproportion between classical and Christian sources has a clear
bearing on Montaigne's religious position.

Sixteenth-century sources are, as we should expect, much more
numerous, and again mostly in Latin. He makes use for example
of Erasmus, Cornelius Agrippa (a predecessor in scepticism), the
compilers already mentioned, Buchanan (his master at the Collège
de Guyenne), the poets (Johannes Secundus, Beza, Dorat,
Turnebus), and again numerous historians. He knows contempor-

[1] I, xlviii: TR 280.
[2] e.g. III, i: TR 781; III, viii: TR 920.
[3] III, ix: EM iii, 223; TR 937.

33

ary Italian literature very well, with references to or quotations from Machiavelli (who has considerable influence, negative or positive, on Montaigne's political thought), Castiglione, Aretino, the poets (especially Ariosto and Tasso, who are often quoted). The French sources reveal a similar pattern: Rabelais (with echoes of phrases like 'jusques au feu, mais exclusivement',[1] which suggests greater familiarity with the text than more systematic borrowings), the *Heptameron* of Margaret of Navarre, the poets once more (Marot, Ronsard, du Bellay, Guy du Faur de Pibrac), Jean Bodin (the *République* in particular), more historians, including many translations into French, especially the Spanish and Portuguese historians of voyages and colonisation.

What really matters, however, is what he does with these sources. As we have seen, almost every page carries direct quotations from the classics, and occasionally the moderns (these are the visible borrowings); even more numerous are nearly verbatim quotations or translations, unacknowledged (these are the invisible borrowings); and to them must be added the many allusions, references, or summaries. A single example of the second category will show how faithful (or in modern terms unscrupulous) Montaigne can be:

Montaigne	*Amyot*
Tesmoin le peuple Thebain: lequel ayant mis en justice d'accusation capitale ses capitaines . . . absolut à toutes peines Pelopidas, qui plioit sous le faix de telles objections, et n'employoit à se garantir que requestes et supplications: et au contraire Epaminondas, qui vint à raconter magnifiquement les choses par luy faites . . . il n'eut pas le cœur de prendre seulement les balotes en main; et se departit l'assemblée, louant grandement la hautesse du courage de ce personnage.[2]	Car les Thebains, estans leurs capitaines accusez . . . à peine absolurent Pelopidas, qui plioit à telles obiections, & les supplioit: Et au contraire, Epaminondas qui vint à raconter magnifiquement les braues choses qu'il auoit faittes . . . ils n'eurent pas le cœur de prendre seulement les ballotes en main . . . ains se departirent de l'assemblée, en louant grandement sa haultesse de courage, & s'esiouissant & riant d'auoir ainsi ouy parler ce personnage.[3]

[1] III, i: EM iii, 4–5; TR 770. Cf. (e.g.) *Pantagruel*, Prologue.
[2] I, i: EM i, 5; TR 12.
[3] Plutarch, *Les œuvres morales*, Paris, 1572, f.139.

The minor changes are no doubt significant, but the main point is the copying of whole phrases and sentences. Multiplied as they are, such transferences inevitably constitute a major feature of the *Essais*. It is hardly necessary to point out that this was the regular practice of the time, that there was little if any stigma attached to it, and that Montaigne was a great deal less derivative than most of his contemporaries. None the less a problem remains: it is not easy to treat a passage like the one just quoted as if it were authentic Montaigne (and in spite of Villey's truly remarkable success in tracking down the most obscure borrowings there are certain to be others that he missed).[1]

Montaigne himself, as usual, is keenly conscious of the problem, and the numerous explanations and defences he offers, which vary considerably over the years, show how important he thought it. In the 1580 edition his approach is a humble one, he sees an immense gulf between himself and the authors of antiquity[2] and he does not claim to make his borrowings his own.[3] However, even here a more confident note begins to appear, in one of the latest 1580 essays. He is speaking of his thoughts (*imaginations*):

> Je les produisis crues et simples, d'une production hardie et forte, mais un peu trouble et imparfaicte; depuis je les ay establies et fortifiées par l'authorité d'autruy, et par les sains discours des anciens, ausquels je me suis rencontré conforme en jugement: ceux-là m'en ont assuré la prinse, et m'en ont donné la jouyssance et possession plus entiere.[4]

This sums up very well his growing conviction that he has something important to say and that his ancient sources lend strength to his own judgement. In the later stages this confidence increases markedly. In 1588, although he admits, in a famous phrase, that he has only made 'un amas de fleurs estrangeres', he now maintains that he is not hidden by his borrowings and that he only wants to show what is his own.[5] If some of his early essays 'puent un peu à l'estranger', he is now convinced of the essential originality of his work, 'et sa fin principale et perfection, c'est d'estre exactement mien'.[6] The Bordeaux Copy takes him further

1 See for example, in the Bibliography, articles by Dessein and Pertile.
2 I, xxvi: TR 145(*a*).
3 II, x: DB i, 340.
4 II, xvii: EM ii, 444; TR 641–2(*a*).
5 III, xii: EM iii, 347; TR 1033(*b*).
6 III, v: EM iii, 114; TR 853(*b*).

still. In an interpolation following the passage from *De l'institution des enfans* already discussed, he is prepared (though aware of the audacity of it) to claim something like equality with the ancients:

Si sçai je bien combien audacieusement j'entreprans moi mesmes à tous coups de m'esgaler à mes larrecins, d'aller pair à pair quand et eus, non sans une temerere esperance que je puisse tromper les yeux des juges à les discerner.

The argument culminates in a pregnant antithesis:

Je ne dis les autres, sinon pour d'autant plus me dire.[1]

This is certainly true and gives the key to the question of originality. Everything he quotes or imitates is reflected through his own mind, adapted to his purposes, absorbed into the texture of the book, made his own, so that (as with the interpolations) it is usually impossible, as he hopes, to discern the joints between his 'larcenies' and the rest. The method is not dissimilar to that of T. S. Eliot, in whose work poetic concentration makes the amalgam even more complete. In what may be his last statements on the subject (if we assume that the interpolations of the Bordeaux Copy were made in the order of the book, though this is a large assumption) Montaigne comes out strongly in favour of originality (we must not therefore overemphasise sixteenth-century tolerance of plagiarism):

Nous autres naturalistes estimons qu'il y aie grande et incomparable præferance de l'honeur de l'invantion à l'honur de l'allegation.[2]

And he observes in passing that he adapts his sources (perhaps including the direct quotations) by means of 'quelque particuliere adresse de ma main', so that they will not be merely foreign.

When we turn to his practice we find that these claims are generally borne out. Thus the impressive conclusion of the *Apologie* on the nature of time and being[3] is in its main lines not just an imitation but a transcription of Amyot's Plutarch (*Que signifioit ce mot E"?* in the *Œuvres morales*), but it is so interspersed with borrowings from other sources that the extent of the debt is partly concealed. This is not really a fair example because it is not quite unacknowledged ('A cette conclusion si

---

[1] I, xxvi: EM i, 190–1; TR 146(*c*). Repeated in a slightly different and less affirmative form in II, x: TR 387(*c*).

[2] III, xii: EM iii, 350; TR 1034(*c*).

[3] II, xii: TR 586–8(*a*).

religieuse d'un homme payen'), though neither the identity of the pagan author nor the limits of the quotation are exactly specified. From the same source comes the story of Archias which gives its title to *A demain les affaires* (II, iv), but here again Montaigne relates it to different stories, ancient and modern, with the same bearing, and draws new conclusions from them. In *De l'amitié* (I, xxviii) he obviously owes much to Cicero's *De amicitia* but he maintains that 'les discours mesmes que l'antiquité nous a laissé sur ce subject me semblent láches au pris du sentiment que j'en ay'.[1] And the story of Blosius, probably from Cicero, confirms this (Blosius, under interrogation on his part in the schemes of his friend Tiberius Gracchus and asked whether at his friend's command he would have set fire to the temples, replied 'He would never have commanded it', 'But if he had?' 'Then I would have obeyed').[2] The story is most moving in itself, but Montaigne's long commentary goes far beyond it and offers an excellent example of how he treats classical sources: he brings out subtly and convincingly the reasons which lie behind Blosius's answer (the unity of will between the two friends) and then binds it all up organically with his own relation to La Boétie. Again the process becomes more marked in the final stages of the *Essais*: thus at the beginning of *Du repentir* Montaigne admits that he contradicts himself, with a classical parallel:

> Tant y a que je me contredits bien à l'adventure, mais la verité, comme disoit Demades, je ne la contredy point.[3]

This again is from Amyot:

> Demades . . . dit qu'il s'estoit bien contredit à soy-mesme assez de fois selon les occurrences des affaires, mais contre le bien de la chose publique, iamais.[4]

It will be seen that Demades had said something commonplace; Montaigne has turned it into something profound.[5]

There is a broader interpretation of sources than these detailed considerations: the question of the origin of the essay form itself.

---

1 I, xxviii: EM i, 252; TR 191–2.
2 TR 187–8 (*a,c*).
3 III, ii: EM iii, 21; TR 782(*b*).
4 Plutarch, *Les vies des hommes illustres*, Paris, 1565, f.586ᵛ.
5 For a full discussion of Montaigne's handling of quotations see Metschies, *Zitat und Zitierkunst in Montaignes Essais*, 1966. A point of particular importance, to which we shall return, is the use of quotations to slip in subversive thoughts.

We have seen that Montaigne coined the word in this sense and even that he invented the form, but he must have had precursors and sources of inspiration. A book has been devoted to the subject[1] and, though it is not exhaustive, a brief summary will suffice here. A grave difficulty, in this as in other respects, lies in Montaigne's multiplicity: a different result will appear if we seek origins of the discursive form, the self-portrait, the analysis of mental processes (the 'espineuse entreprinse'), the depiction of mobility, and so on (and of course his full originality can only be appreciated when we take them all together). Thus when Thibaudet says that Marcus Aurelius (whom Montaigne never quotes and mentions once in passing) is the only writer of antiquity to show something of the same design, he is speaking of the self-portrait.[2] Montaigne in any case disagrees: he likes reading the letters to Atticus not only for their historical interest but because he discovers in them Cicero's 'humeurs privées'[3] (he naturally seeks what is most like himself). Much more interesting is a reference to Plato, interpolated in a passage where Montaigne excuses the apparent disorder of his writing:

> J'ay passé les yeus sur tel dialogue de Platon mi parti d'une fantastique bigarrure, le davant à l'amour, tout le bas à la rhetorique. Ils [the dialogues, presumably] ne creignent point ces muances, et ont une merveilleuse grace à se laisser einsi rouler au vent, ou à le sembler.[4]

This (an unmistakable reference to the *Phaedrus*) clearly turns on multiplicity and mobility, and it constitutes (especially 'à le sembler') a most perceptive description of the *Essais* themselves, about which Montaigne makes similar statements here and elsewhere. It is also no doubt true of Plato, but he is at once more logical (the changes of subject are slower and more controlled) and more outward-looking – the element of self-analysis is lacking. And of course the dialogue form, with its dramatic concretisation of characters, is fundamentally different from the essay in spite of the similarity in looseness of development (these considerations apply *a fortiori* to the Renaissance dialogue as practised for example, apart from the Italians, by Jacques Tahureau or Guy

---

1 Schon, *Vorformen des Essays in Antike und Humanismus*, 1954; see also Friedrich, *Montaigne*, ch. VIII.

2 *Montaigne*, p. 69.

3 II, x: EM ii, 111; TR 394(*a*).

4 III, ix: EM iii, 270; TR 973(*c*).

de Bruès). Another interpolation affirming the originality of the book and the self-portrait contains a mysterious allusion:

> Nous n'avons nouvelles que de deus ou trois antiens qui aient battu ce chemin; et si ne pouvons dire si c'est du tout en pareille maniere à cettecy, n'en conoissant que les noms. Nul despuis ne s'est jetté sur leur trace.[1]

As their works are lost it is difficult to say who these two or three were: Coste, repeated by subsequent commentators, suggests Archilochus, Alcaeus, and Lucilius but does not say on what grounds.[2] At all events we see that at this point Montaigne was not conscious of any precursor among the extant works of antiquity. There is, however, a much more serious candidate and that is Plutarch (whom Montaigne discusses soon after Plato):

> Il est des ouvrages en Plutarque où il oblie son theme, où le propos de son argument ne se treuve que par incident, tout estouffé en matiere estrangiere: voïes ses alleures au dæmon de Socrates.[3]

The *Demon of Socrates* (in the *Moralia*) is in fact the story of a conspiracy at Thebes, in dialogue form with much narration and many anecdotes. It is true that the demon plays a very small part but in spite of the discrepancy between title and content it is not really at all like a Montaigne essay. However, when we look at the *Moralia* as a whole, which apart from the dialogues are composed of prose disquisitions on subjects of everyday morality or prudence, the resemblance is more convincing. The titles of the opuscules for instance (in Amyot) *De la curiosité, De l'amitié fraternelle* (cf. I, xxviii), *Du trop parler* (cf. I, x), *Que les bestes brutes usent de la raison, De l'amour et charité naturelle des peres envers les enfans* (cf. II, viii), *De la vertu morale* (cf. II, xxix), *Les vertueux faicts des femmes* (cf. II, xxxv), could easily find a place in Montaigne; the works themselves, in their mixture of argument, definition, illustration, tall stories, allusions, are not at all unlike the *Essais*, though they seem arid and even banal in comparison. The tone too is quite like one of Montaigne's: a running fire of expostulatory, argumentative attack on accepted ideas. Plutarch too sometimes speaks of himself, but neither in depth nor at length. The richness, the variety, the unexpectedness, and

---

[1] II, vi: EM ii, 59; TR 358(c).
[2] *Les essais*, Paris, 1725, ii, 55.
[3] III, ix: EM iii, 270; TR 973(c).

perhaps the humour are missing. Even so, it must be admitted that Plutarch, although without the convolutions of Montaigne, has to some extent realised the basic form of the essay. This is not to say that Plutarch necessarily supplied the direct inspiration: it seems more likely that the form grew spontaneously out of Montaigne's first attempts, with perhaps some influence of Plutarch on the mode of this development.

Beside these ancient models, and Plutarch in particular, modern ones are of relatively little importance, though the possibilities are numerous, and some we have already considered. Petrarch, Erasmus (the *Praise of Folly*, the *Colloquia*, the *Adagia*), the writers of dialogues and letters, all have something in common with Montaigne but not the essential. However, a special category, that of the *exempla* and *leçons*, deserves rather more serious consideration.[1] A typical, and perhaps the most popular, representative is Pedro Mexia, whose *Silva de varia leccion* (1540) was translated into French with the title *Les diverses leçons* (1552): disquisitions, factual or argumentative, on questions of morality and conduct, of history, of literature, of science, of intellectual curiosity generally. The parallel with Plutarch is clear, though the *leçons* are as a rule shorter, narrower in scope, more miscellaneous, more anecdotic and trivial, less original, and much less coherently argued. But of course these are exactly the characteristics we have observed in the earliest essays of Montaigne, and in this case too some of Mexia's titles (in the French translation) will help to show the likeness (not necessarily the influence): *De la grandeur de l'empire Romain, & comme & en quel temps il commença à decliner* (cf. II, xxiv), *Combien est detestable le vice de cruauté, avec plusieurs exemples à ce propos* (cf. II, xi), *Comme on peut dire mensonge sans mentir* (cf. I, ix). The titles are desultory like the contents, which are little more than strings of examples. Still, this is in a way Montaigne's starting-point and it is difficult to resist the conclusion that the *leçons* furnish the initial impetus and that the development of the form brings it nearer to Plutarch (later of course going far beyond him).

Two questions remain about Montaigne's use of and attitude to books. His favourite reading was history and poetry: 'L'Histoire, c'est plus mon gibier, ou la poësie, que j'ayme d'une particuliere inclination.'[2] Both are important for the interpretation of the

---

[1] For a fuller discussion see Villey, *Sources et évolution*, ii, 3–33.
[2] I, xxvi: EM i, 188; TR 144.

Essais, history because it involves Montaigne's sense of time, poetry for many reasons, not least its close connection with his literary criticism.

History for him is primarily ancient history: we have seen how the classics supply him with innumerable anecdotes, illustrations, examples. Antiquity is the yardstick by which all else is judged. This is no more than we should expect from a Renaissance writer, but what is striking in Montaigne (apart from his frequent credulity) is that he seems to make little distinction between past and present. Again and again his ancient sources (Herodotus, Aristotle, Plutarch and Pliny especially) are cited as evidence of what actually exists in the world. Thus we are told (after Plutarch) that the eels in the fountain of Arethusa respond (in the present) to human voices, and this is evidence of the affinity between men and animals.[1] But though antiquity is ever present, modern history, as we should expect from the contents of the library, is drawn on extensively, both the history which comes from books and the contemporary events and incidents derived from personal experience or hearsay. Usually ancient and modern are mingled, again with little distinction of chronology. Thus in *De ne communiquer sa gloire* (I, xli) sacrifice of fame is illustrated by alternating examples: Catulus Luctatius and the Cimbrians, Charles V in Provence, Thracian ambassadors, the Black Prince at Crécy. More vivid still (and not surprisingly from the last stage) is the juxtaposition of two anecdotes recounting virtually the same story (a rich man handing over his wealth to others), one from Xenophon about a courtier of Cyrus the Great, the other about an old prelate Montaigne knew (probably the archbishop of Bordeaux).[2] The exact balance of ancient and modern in these two examples, as well as the continuity of history which results from the juxtaposition, is typical. Of course he is not alone in this sort of mixture: Mexia, for example, does it occasionally, Bodin frequently, and in a celebrated catalogue of strange deaths, ancient and modern,[3] Montaigne is for the most part simply following Ravisius Textor (even here he adds a personal example, the death of his own brother from a blow by a tennis-ball). None the less

---

[1] II, xii: TR 446. This is not peculiar to Montaigne: Bodin in the *Methodus* offers some rather absurd examples.

[2] I, xiv: TR 66-7.

[3] I, xx: TR 83-4.

the *Essais* gain force from the way in which their author ranges over the whole of history and his own time.

What has been said so far about the details of Montaigne's treatment of history suggests a rather naïve attitude. His reflections on the subject, however, go much deeper than this. What he takes from history, especially in the later stages, is, again, *examples,* that is to say illustrations of general truths (even though the accumulation of facts, real or alleged, sometimes amuses him). A change in the Bordeaux Copy shows how his view of this general significance developed. The 1580 text runs:

> Les historiens sont le vray gibier de mon estude: car ils sont plaisans et aysés, et, quant et quant, la consideration des natures et conditions de divers hommes, les coutumes des nations differentes, c'est le vray suject de la science morale.[1]

Already the historical examples are there for the general considerations they suggest, but the emphasis is on the diversity and relativity of human behaviour, one of the central themes of the first two books (for instance the *Apologie* and *De la coustume*). In the Bordeaux Copy, where the whole passage is rewritten ('Les Historiens sont ma droite bale . . .'),[2] the image is changed from hunting to tennis or perhaps trade ('ball' or 'bale');[3] what historians have to teach is less the external differences between men and nations than 'l'home en general' and the varied composition of his inner character. Diversity and relativity are still present, reinforced indeed, but they are now subordinate to man in general, the human condition, which dominates the Third Book. There is of course a danger, from the historian's point of view, in this attitude: if examples are only illustrations of general principles, it doesn't greatly matter whether they are true or not, and this is what Montaigne says about Plutarch (precise accuracy is not a matter of life and death in ancient history as it would be in a medical prescription).[4] The parallel with Aristotle on historical and poetic truth scarcely needs remarking.[5]

---

[1] II, x: DB i, 351.
[2] Cf. p. 115 below.
[3] See Huguet and EM (Lexique).
[4] I, xxi: TR 105(c).
[5] Again Montaigne makes it for us: 'Il y a des autheurs desquels la fin c'est dire les evenemans. La mienne . . . seroit dire sur ce qui peut avenir' (I, xxi: EM i, 133; TR 104).

This is not to say that Montaigne is unaware of the necessity of exact observation. It is the historian's duty to record all important events, including popular opinions and rumours;[1] he should ideally have practical experience of the events he describes, or at least similar events, and as in a judicial process he has to compare witnesses and evidence.[2] Montaigne therefore distinguishes two kinds of historian, the simple compilers and those who judge and interpret: the latter course is difficult and those who fall between are very dangerous. Clearly all this owes something to Bodin's *Methodus*. It is more surprising, in view of his moderation and love of tranquillity, to see Montaigne's preference for the historians of violence:

> Et les bons historiens fuient come un' eau dormante et mer morte des narrations calmes, pour regaigner les seditions, les guerres, où ils sçavent que nous les apelons.[3]

This, from the last stage, has an important bearing on his personality and his relation to his time. He points out too (a fact often overlooked even by good historians) that what is known about history is only a minute proportion of what is unknown.[4] In one essay, *De la gloire* (II, xvi), this fairly obvious, if neglected, point leads to the most subtle (and poetic) considerations on the limitations of historical knowledge, the fortuitousness of fame, the oblivion to which nearly all men and actions are consigned. A plangent gravity (very like Sir Thomas Browne but also typical of Montaigne, though less often remarked in him), 'La memoire non des chefs seulement, mais des batailles et victoires, est ensevelie',[5] is united with the humorous common sense which is also typical (a hundred years from now people will just about know that there was a civil war in France). A reflection on the accidents of history is thus connected with the meaning of existence.[6]

If history bulks larger in the *Essais*, poetry is more deeply felt:

> Dès ma premiere enfance, la poesie a eu cela, de me transpercer et transporter.[7]

1 III, viii: TR 921.
2 II, x: TR 397–8.
3 III, xii: EM iii, 335; TR 1023(c).
4 III, vi: TR 886.
5 II, xvi: EM ii, 402; TR 611.
6 On history see Guy Desgranges, 'Montaigne et l'histoire', *French review*, xxiii (1950).
7 I, xxxvii: EM i, 303; TR 228.

Apart from the discussions of poetry and individual poets, the large number of allusions and quotations are enough to bear this out: according to Miss Gracey's tables there are altogether nearly nine hundred quotations from poets.[1] And although Montaigne himself wrote only some Latin verse in his youth,[2] none of which has survived, his work as a whole is impregnated with poetic feeling as well as actual reminiscences.[3] However, his concern with poetry is inseparable from his literary criticism in general.

At the heart of his conception of poetry is the Platonic notion of the poet's fury or madness, which was already familiar from its adoption by Ronsard and the Pléiade. Montaigne perhaps carries it further and certainly understands it better. The most powerful statement comes, unexpectedly as so often, in the short essay on Cato the Younger (*Du jeune Caton*, I,xxxvii). After saying that at a low level poetry can be judged according to rules, he goes on:

> Mais la bonne, l'excessive, la divine est audessus des regles et de la raison. Quiconque en discerne la beauté d'une veue ferme et rassise, il ne la voit pas, non plus que la splandur d'un esclair. Elle ne pratique point nostre jugement; elle le ravist et ravage.[4]

(There is much to be said for Thibaudet's view that the passage from which this comes is the finest piece of criticism in the French language;[5] we might place beside it Péguy on Racine's *Iphigénie*).[6] It follows from this conception that a poet is by no means the same thing as a mere versifier,[7] now a commonplace. More importantly, there is no absolute distinction between verse and prose, since the test of poetry is not the form but the degree of intensity achieved:

> Mille poëtes trainent et languissent à la prosaïque; mais la meilleure prose ancienne ... reluit par tout de la vigueur et hardiesse poetique, et represente l'air de sa fureur.[8]

---

[1] Phyllis Gracey, *Montaigne et la poésie*, 1935 (a sensible and useful account of the whole matter).

[2] III, v: TR 853.

[3] Gracey (pp. 35–6) speaks rightly of 'son imagination essentiellement poétique'.

[4] I, xxxvii: EM i, 303; TR 227–8(c).

[5] *Montaigne*, p. 473.

[6] *Victor-Marie comte Hugo*, Paris, Gallimard, 1947, pp. 157 ff.

[7] I, xxvi: TR 170.

[8] III, ix: EM iii, 271; TR 973(b).

We have here a key not only to Montaigne's critical theory but to the poetic character of the *Essais* themselves. It should be added that, translating Seneca, he takes as the principal attribute of poetry the force given by concentration, like air in a trumpet.[1] The constant emphasis on fury and intensity is enough to refute Thibaudet's assertion that La Fontaine would have been the true poet for Montaigne:[2] without disrespect to La Fontaine, it may be suggested that Montaigne's idea of poetry was far deeper and higher. And the question transcends his literary criticism, in fact opens up another dimension of his work. There is in him not only cautious moderation (with its hint of mediocrity) but passion and enthusiasm, reflected at many other points.[3]

The suggestion of pre-Romanticism in this general theory appears also in his interest in popular poetry, altogether exceptional in his period. He appreciates not only Gascon villanelles[4] but the songs of the Brazilian Indians, two of which (a war song and a love song) he quotes in translation.[5] The love song with its grass-snake motif he describes as anacreontic: he needs an ancient landmark to give him his bearings but this does not interfere with his receptiveness towards the unexpected and unfamiliar. The same interest emerges in his Italian travels, when he notes the presence of extemporary rhymers in nearly all the inns and gives a long account of an illiterate peasant poetess.[6] Nature, he concludes elsewhere, gives birth even in the least cultivated nations to works which can compete with the highest productions of art.[7] Again we see that in him, in spite of appearances, everything hangs together: there is a close connection between his literary taste and the primitivism which forms a vital strand in his whole system of thought. It is in keeping with this liking for simplicity and genuineness (though now perhaps antimannerist rather than pre-Romantic) that he objects strongly to the affectations of

---

[1] I, xxvi: TR 144.
[2] *Montaigne*, pp. 479–80.
[3] W. G. Moore points out an interesting parallel between Montaigne and Longinus on poetic ecstasy ('Montaigne and Lucretius', *Yale French studies*, 1967, p. 111). Longinus was at this time hardly known, and Montaigne's anticipation (so to speak) may be regarded as a not insignificant element in the origins of pre-Romanticism.
[4] I, liv: TR 300.
[5] I, xxxi: TR 211–2.
[6] *JV*: TR 1254, 1279.
[7] I, xxv: TR 136(c).

contemporary poetry, the abuse of neologisms, or the 'fantastic elevations' of Spanish or Petrarchan poets.[1]

At many points in the *Essais* but particularly in four chapters (*De l'institution des enfans*, I, xxvi; *Des livres*, II, x; *De trois commerces*, III, iii; *Sur des vers de Virgile*, III, v) Montaigne deals, however glancingly, with some of the major problems of critical method. It is easy, he says, for someone reading a page of Virgil to exclaim 'How beautiful!':

> Mais d'entreprendre à le suivre par espauletes et de jugement exprès et trié vouloir remarquer par où un bon autheur se surmonte, par où se rehausse, poisant les mots, les frases, les invantions une apres l'autre, ostez vous de là![2]

This is of course a recipe for what is now called close reading. It would be too much to say that Montaigne was the first to use this method: it is foreshadowed in ancient critics, Longinus especially, and the laborious efforts of innumerable commentators (Muret on Ronsard for example) cannot be overlooked. But, unlike the commentators, Montaigne weighs aesthetic values, not just grammatical points, factual allusions, parallels, or sources of ideas. And such reading is a discovery, a revelation: he had found in Livy a hundred things which someone else would have missed, Plutarch a hundred more, which the author had perhaps never thought of. Whether this is a sound critical principle is still under discussion: at any rate he goes on (of Livy, but is equally true of his criticism in general) to show its depth:

> A d'aucuns c'est un peur estude grammerien; à d'autres, l'anatomie de la philosofie, en la quelle les plus abstruses parties de nostre nature se penetrent.[3]

In sharp contrast with the theories of the Pléiade, he insists on originality if not of subject at least of form, disposition and language, as the supreme test of a book:[4] again, though this was not altogether new, he seems to anticipate the future.

It would take too long to show in detail how these principles are applied to individual works. There are scattered references to the drama, in which he took a keen interest from the time when he

---

[1] III, v: TR 851; II, x: TR 391.
[2] III, viii: EM iii, 195; TR 915(c).
[3] I, xxvi: EM i, 203; TR 156(c).
[4] III, viii: TR 919. cf. p. 36 above.

performed in school plays. However, the Latin poets (Catullus, Lucretius, Horace, Virgil) are his preferred subject, but the prose writers too are often discussed, for instance in an acute analysis of Cicero's style.[1] He makes frequent use of comparison, Seneca and Tacitus, Seneca and Plutarch (more than once), or Virgil and Ariosto, where criticism by metaphor (the movements of a bird) is brilliantly displayed.[2] Ronsard and du Bellay could hardly be more exactly and succinctly characterised than in 'les riches descriptions de l'un et les delicates inventions de l'autre'.[3]

But to convey Montaigne's full quality as a critic, one or two detailed illustrations are necessary. The essay *Du jeune Caton* is peculiar in two ways: criticism precedes the quotations, which makes for a feeling of suspense and even excitement, and the main weight of criticism comes in a long interpolation of the Bordeaux Copy which includes the general remarks already quoted and prolongs the suspense still further. The interpolation begins with a series of gradations, assigning each poet to his place in the scale of admiration (beginning thus at the end of the critical process):

> Or devra l'enfant bien nourry trouver, au pris des autres, les deus premiers [Martial and Manilius] treinans, le troisieme [Lucan] plus vert, mais qui s'est abatu par l'extravagance de sa force; estimer que là il y aroit place à un ou deus degrez d'invantion encores, pour arriver au quatriesme [Horace], sur le point du quel il jouindera ses mains par admiration. Au dernier [Virgil], premier de quelque espace, mais la quelle espace il jurera ne pouvoir estre remplie par nul esperit humain, il s'estonera, il se transira.[4]

Equally striking here are the depth of response which the highest poetry inspires in him, the awareness of the unbridgeable gap which separates the highest from the very good, and at the same time the sense of relative values which prevents him from doing injustice to those lower in the scale. He then (after the general observations) goes on, still reversing the normal order of critical procedure, to characterise, most penetratingly, three Latin poets (one of whom is not among those quoted):

[1] II, x: TR 393–4.
[2] II, x: TR 392.
[3] I, xxvi: EM i, 221; TR 170.
[4] I, xxxvii: EM i, 303; TR 227(*c*).

premierement une fluidité gaye et ingenieuse; depuis une subtilité aiguë et rellevée; enfin une force meure et constante. L'example le dira mieus: Ovide, Lucain, Vergile. Mais voyla nos gens sur la carriere.

We then return to the original text of 1580 and the quotations on which the rest is based:

> Sit Cato, dum vivit, sane vel Cæsare maior,

dict l'un [Martial].

> Et invictum, devicta morte, Catonem,

dict l'autre [Manilius]. Et l'autre [Lucan], parlant des guerres civiles d'entre Cæsar et Pompeius,

> Victrix causa diis placuit, sed victa Catoni.

Et le quatriesme [Horace], sur les loüanges de Cæsar:

> Et cuncta terrarum subacta,
> Præter atrocem animum Catonis.

Et le maistre du chœur [Virgil], apres avoir étalé les noms des plus grands Romains en sa peinture, finit en cette maniere:

> his dantem jura Catonem.[1]

The essay ends at this point. To have built so much on these single lines reveals considerable subtlety but above all intensity of poetic feeling. And suggestions of pre-Romanticism should not be allowed to obscure the essential classicism of Montaigne's taste, seen here in his sure differentiation between the strained grandeur of Lucan and the simple majesty of Virgil.

The contradiction can perhaps be resolved when we look at another example of close reading, this time of a single longer passage (eight lines of Lucretius on Mars and Venus). There is the same combination of intense reaction and precise detail, the same contrast between directness and artifice of language:

> Quand je rumine ce «rejicit, pascit, inhians, molli, fovet, medullas, labefacta, pendet, percurrit», et cette noble «circunfusa», mere du gentil «infusus», j'ay desdain de ces menues pointes et allusions verballes qui nasquirent depuis. A ces bonnes gens, il ne falloit pas d'aigue et subtile rencontre; leur langage est tout plein et gros d'une vigueur naturelle et constante; ... Il n'y a rien d'efforcé, rien de treinant, tout y marche d'une pareille teneur.

But it is not just a matter of simplicity or even of vigour. This direct language has the power to transport and to ravish, to give depth and life:

---

[1] EM i, 304; TR 228(c)(a).

Ce n'est pas une eloquence molle et seulement sans offence: elle est nerveuse et solide, qui ne plaict pas tant comme elle remplit et ravit, et ravit le plus les plus forts espris. Quand je voy ces braves formes de s'expliquer, si vifves, si profondes, je ne dicts pas que c'est bien dire, je dicts que c'est bien penser.

Form and content are thus united. And finally the language is lifted up by the imagination of the poet:

C'est la gaillardise de l'imagination qui esleve et enfle les parolles.[1]

Classicism here is no set of rules or even a principle of moderation but an insistence on the full strength of language to convey the most powerful experiences.

Some of Montaigne's critical opinions may not seem very surprising now (though still fresh), but it may be doubted whether anyone at this period or earlier, at least since antiquity, had talked about books in such a simple, natural and intelligent way, with such penetration and such profound feeling for the essence of poetry and style. In his criticism we find part of the answer to the problem of originality: he responds to his classical models with a keenness of aesthetic understanding which is far removed from the pedestrian routine of the merely learned, and this understanding is made explicit as it is not generally by the poets (like Ronsard) who no doubt experienced it equally. We find also a gravity and a sense of greatness in art much at variance with the picture usually given of Montaigne. He is here perhaps revealing the deepest level of himself.

---

[1] III, v: EM iii, 111; TR 850–1(*b*). On Montaigne's treatment of imagination see I. D. McFarlane, 'Montaigne and the concept of the imagination', in *The French Renaissance and its Heritage*, 1968.

4

The Study of the Self:
the Observer Observed

IT may be that in the past too much emphasis has been placed
on the self-portrait as the sole centre of the *Essais*. Montaigne,
it may be argued, stands a long way from the true introspective, the anxious introvert (like Amiel or even Rousseau). His
book, like himself, is open to the world, its concrete existence, its
sights, sounds and smells, to people, things, events, ideas. The
introspective is balanced, in a new contradiction, by a realist (in
the literary sense) and a philosopher capable of handling abstract
and impersonal thought. Even so, these diverse elements can in
their turn be subsumed in the unity of the self-portrait: everything he thinks or experiences, at whatever level of sense or
intellect, is reflected through himself and contributes something
to the total picture of himself. This is certainly his own view. He
declares more than once that he is not conveying knowledge of
things but of himself,[1] or, more subtly:

> Il y a plusieurs années que je n'ay que moy pour visee à mes pensees,
> que je ne contrerolle et estudie que moy; et, si j'estudie autre chose,
> c'est pour soudein le coucher sur moi, ou en moy, pour mieus dire.[2]

At all events there can be no doubt that for him, at least at
the time of the 1580 preface, the principal and indeed the only
object of the book is the depiction of himself. He has written it,
he says, for the benefit of his relations and friends, so that they
can remember him after his death (this modest explanation, no
doubt due once more to the nervousness of a writer making his
first independent public appearance, was to change considerably

---

[1] II, x: TR 387(*a*), 389(*a*).
[2] II, vi: EM ii, 59; TR 358(*c*).

later on, and in any case it does not explain the fact of publication, vital for a full understanding of his attitude and purpose). He will show himself simply, without artifice, 'car c'est moy que je peins' (the parallel with painting is already established); he will reveal his faults as much as decency will allow and if he had been among the nations which still live according to the original laws of nature (this prominent allusion to the New World is also significant) he would have painted himself in complete nakedness (here again the initial reticence is gradually cast aside as confidence increases). But though some of the qualifications and prudent hedgings of the preface are to be abandoned, the central statement, though modified in some important ways, remains essentially firm: 'Ainsi, lecteur, je suis moy-mesmes la matiere de mon livre.'[1] We may not accept it entirely, but we cannot ignore it.

Of course, the preface was written nearly halfway through the period of composition of the *Essais*, and the conception of the self-portrait did not emerge all at once. The very earliest essays, as we have seen, are strings of anecdotes and reflections couched in the impersonal mode of the *leçons*. Even in this first stage, however, progress is rapid. At the end of the very brief *De l'oisiveté* (written according to Villey in 1572) we find what is probably the first reference to the plan of the self-portrait and a humorous account of its genesis.[2] And the following essay (*Des menteurs*, also 1572) begins with the first complaint about the weakness of his memory. Unfortunately in both these cases we have to take into account the possibility of pre-1580 interpolations, particularly easy to introduce at the beginnings and ends of chapters. However, the end of *De l'oisiveté* with its 'Dernierement' cannot have been added very much later, and although the explanation (again with its touch of self-deprecation) is a little far-fetched, there is no reason to doubt that the immediate origin of the self-portrait (and of the *Essais*) springs from a sense of unsatisfied idleness.

From this point onwards the self-portrait continues to develop in theory and practice. Another essay of the same period, this time a major one, *Que philosopher, c'est apprendre à mourir*, is strongly marked with Montaigne's personality.[3] But still in the 1580 edition, two great essays, *De l'exercitation* (II, vi, perhaps

---

1 Au lecteur: EM i, 2; TR 9.
2 Cf. p. 8 above.
3 I, xx. See particularly TR 88–9(*a*) (bearing in mind once more the possibility of interpolation).

1573-4) and *De la præsumption* (II, xvii, perhaps 1578), carry the depiction of the self almost as far as it will ever go. The earlier one describes Montaigne's fall from a horse, the concussion he suffered, and the exact sequence of the sensations he experienced. It may be that there is something new here not only in the *Essais* but in the whole of literature. The later of the two, though less strikingly original and less deeply penetrating, is perhaps even more important for the extent of self-revelation and for the discussion of the mode of procedure. A remark deleted in the Bordeaux Copy shows that the idea still had the freshness of novelty: 'c'est une humeur nouvelle et fantastique qui me presse, il la faut laisser courir';[1] and also that a strong internal pressure was at work. Though the *Apologie* is notable for the paucity of references to the self (being untypical in this as in other respects), we can see that the self-portrait is fully developed, at least in its general lines, by 1580. That the Third Book enlarges it, enriches it, discards the restrictions imposed on it by prudery, and puts it in a somewhat different perspective – all this is sufficiently well known and will be illustrated later. But fundamentally nothing is changed. We must, however, bear in mind, as always, the effect on the first two books of the post-1580 additions. The very early impersonal essays are transformed by passages, often inserted at the end, which relate the preceding historical anecdotes or general reflections to the author's own experience (for example I, i, iii, v, vii). *De l'exercitation* offers a particularly good illustration: the analysis of sensations (the observer) is there in 1580, but the highly important remarks on how and why it is being performed (the observer observed) are added in the Bordeaux Copy. All this speaks both for and against Villey's evolutionary theory. Clearly the self-portrait is born at a point later than the beginning of the *Essais* and develops in acuity and wealth of detail, and to some extent in conception, right up to the end of the Third Book. On the other hand, the starting-point occurs very early, very soon after the earliest impersonal essays, and the development is complete in essentials by 1580, so that it is impossible to accord absolute pre-eminence to the Third Book.

Turning now from the question of evolution (though it will be impossible to avoid it altogether), we may inquire how Montaigne views the portrayal of the self in general, expanding

[1] II, xvii: MJ iv, 246.

and sometimes modifying the ideas of the preface. The parallel with painting, already adumbrated there, recurs in the frequent use of the word *peindre*. This is only a metaphor, but occasionally he carries the analogy further. Thus he speaks of a portrait of himself, bald and greying, to which the painter has given not a perfect face but Montaigne's own.[1] Still more convincing is a reference to a self-portrait by René, King of Sicily, which Montaigne says he had seen at Bar-le-Duc. He goes on:

> Pourquoy n'est-il loisible de mesme à un chacun de se peindre de la plume, comme il se peignoit d'un creon?[2]

The connection between his method and that of the painter is clearly understood by him, and this will be of importance when we come to consider his relations with the art of his time. He stresses the completeness of the self-portrait, giving it, again as in painting, a spatial dimension:

> Je me presente debout et couché, le devant et le derriere, à droite et à gauche, et en tous mes naturels plis.[3]

This is to be taken in part physically but above all psychologically; the latter stands alone when he speaks of finding in the study of himself infinite depth and variety.[4]

So far the tone of his reflections on the subject has been fairly cool, detached, and rational, in keeping with the Greek injunction 'know thyself' which he is fond of quoting. He is, or claims to be, looking at himself as an impartial judge. There are rare moments however, when a different mood appears, when he reveals, as might indeed be expected in view of the nature of his project, not just a coolly amused but a passionate interest in himself:

> moy, je regarde dedans moy: je n'ay affaire qu'à moy, je me considere sans cesse, je me contrerolle, je me gouste ... moy je me roulle en moy mesme.[5]

In passages like these there is more than a suggestion of self-love, indeed of narcissism, which might be held to justify the strictures of Pascal and Malebranche. It must be emphasised, however, that it is only one element in the infinite depth and variety, and a

---

[1] I, xxvi: TR 147(*a*).
[2] II, xvii: EM ii, 438; TR 637.
[3] III, viii: EM iii, 203; TR 922.
[4] III, xiii: TR 1052.
[5] II, xvii: EM ii, 444; TR 641(*a*).

subdued element at that. A full understanding of Montaigne is none the less hard to achieve without some awareness of this undercurrent. It may furnish the key to the problem of publication, already mentioned: if he was writing for himself and his friends alone, as he says in the preface, why did he bother to publish at all? He addresses himself to the question in *Du dementir*, repeating, in a famous and memorable image, that his work is destined for neighbour, kinsman, friend:

> Je ne dresse pas icy une statue à planter au carrefour d'une ville, ou dans une Eglise, ou place publique ... C'est pour le coin d'une librairie, et pour en amuser un voisin, un parent, un amy, qui aura plaisir à me racointer et repratiquer en cett' image.[1]

He goes on to say that his only contact with the public has been to use its speedier tools of writing (that is printing) and that he has had to resort to printing in order to save the trouble of making several manuscript copies.[2] The second part of this statement, even less convincing than the first, is suppressed in the Bordeaux Copy, no doubt for its lack of candour. The Third Book gives a different answer: 'Je suis affamé de me faire connoistre'; he adds, it is true: 'ou, pour dire mieux, je n'ay faim de rien ...'[3] but too late. He would even, if he could, give an account of his death to the public.[4] This passion for self-exposure (a necessary basis for any great autobiographer) takes us a long way from the apologetic tone of the preface or the involved excuses of *Du dementir*. It might be argued that we have here not so much evolution as the development of something already latent, but the distinction is more subtle than real. When, therefore, in one of the latest additions he says: 'J'ose non sulement parler de moi, mais parler sulemant de moi',[5] he is speaking the truth in a very broad sense (though, as always, it is only one side of the truth).

He is naturally aware that this self-obsession lays him open to criticism from the point of view both of Christian humility and of conventional good manners, and that it requires justification and defence. In the first edition, once more, he adopts an apologetic tone, speaking of 'cette sotte entreprise'[6] (thus admitting in

---

1 II, xviii: EM ii, 452; TR 646–7(a).
2 MJ iv, 266.
3 III, v: EM iii, 77; TR 824(b).
4 III, xii: TR 1034(b).
5 III, viii: EM iii, 202; TR 921(c).
6 II, viii: EM ii, 69; TR 364(a).

advance Pascal's 'Le sot projet qu'il a de se peindre') and in the preface of 'un subject si frivole et si vain'.[1] But he already brushes aside the objection of good manners:

> Je me trouve icy empestré és loix de la ceremonie, car elle ne permet ny qu'on parle bien de soy, ny qu'on en parle mal. Nous la lairrons là pour ce coup.[2]

And he goes on to argue, less powerfully, that great men are known by their actions but humbler persons can be excused if they make themselves known in the only way open to them (this is closely connected with the argument, written about the same time, of the statue for the library rather than the public square, where again the tone is deprecating: his subject is so sterile and meagre as to escape the charge of ostentation).[3] In the latest additions the mood is very different and he passes from defence to counter-attack: instead of the frivolity and vanity, the stupidity and sterility of his preoccupation with himself, he stresses its difficulty and its usefulness[4] (in what this usefulness consists must await later discussion) and he turns the tables by reproaching his critics with their failure to look into themselves:

> Si le monde se pleint de quoi je parle trop de moy, je me pleins de quoi il ne pense sulement pas à soi.[5]

Once again he has moved from self-doubt to self-confidence and has triumphantly anticipated the objections of seventeenth-century rationalism, puritanism or etiquette, with its dislike of the exuberant egoist. This applies particularly to Pascal: our last quotation might be aimed at him, so well does it match the criticisms in the *Pensées*, so clearly express the point in terms a Christian cannot help but acknowledge.

What we have been considering so far is Montaigne's programme, not its realisation, his own version of what he is doing, or wants to persuade the reader that he is doing, rather than what he actually does. This poses a very serious critical problem which will arise whenever his own statements about the *Essais* require discussion and which may eventually take one very close to the heart of the work. The problem lies of course in the status of

---

1 Au lecteur: EM i, 2; TR 9(*a*).
2 II, xvii: EM ii, 408; TR 615(*a*).
3 II, xviii: TR 647(*a*).
4 II, vi: TR 358(*c*).
5 III, ii: EM iii, 21; TR 782–3(*c*).

C

these 'critical' or programmatic statements. We have said that the intentional fallacy remains a fallacy even when we are dealing with Montaigne and we cannot necessarily assume that what he says he is going to do is what he does. On the other hand these statements of intention are not, as is usually the case, extraneous to the work, they are an integral component of it, part of what we have to examine. The resulting interaction of the work and statements about it (themselves part of the work), the play of reflections, constitute one of the major characteristics of the *Essais* and one which will demand fuller study. For the moment it may be said that though these statements are highly relevant evidence, they are not necessarily conclusive: the relation between the work and its reflection in the work is not necessarily a simple one of direct and exact correspondence (any more than the relation between the self-portrait and the self). Our next step therefore must be to look at both the method and the content of the self-portrait. It would indeed be tedious, after so many others, to extract all the details and reproduce in a more systematic way what Montaigne says about himself in order that we may show what sort of man he was (or represented himself to be). On the other hand, how he portrays himself cannot be entirely separated from the details of the portrait, and its quality, not just its extent, depends on the accumulation of a multitude of separate touches.

In defining the portrait it seems reasonable to start from externals and work gradually inwards, from the background of family, friends, social position, events of life, to the physical man, habits and personality, and finally to the central core of mind and character. Though reasonable, and no doubt the least unsatisfactory, this procedure immediately involves us in difficulties both of a general philosophical and a particular critical kind. Philosophically, since Descartes, it is not easy to accept the background or even the physical man as part of the self to be portrayed. Briefly (for the whole question will demand fuller consideration), it may be replied that Montaigne, in spite of his scepticism, is far removed from solipsism: his doubt, except in certain limited ways, does not extend, like Descartes's, to the existence of external reality. The other difficulty, which we have already encountered and which springs from the nature of his mind and writing, is closely related to the first and in a way helps to answer it: external and internal are so intermingled as to constitute a single view.

His family plays quite a large part in the *Essais*. He exaggerates its nobility, speaking of Montaigne as the birthplace of most of his ancestors, though in fact his father was the first to be born there,[1] and he conceals, or at least does not mention, its prosaic commercial origins. His father, greatly loved and admired, his brothers and daughter are frequently mentioned, his mother not at all. There are many references to his marriage, few, directly, to his wife: the exact nature of their relations is a biographical question into which we need not enter, but the marriage seems to have been a typical *mariage de convenance*, moderately satisfactory, with, on his side, some esteem and a good deal of irritation, all best summed up in, significantly, a later addition:

Qui pour me voir une mine tantost froide, tantost amoureuse envers ma femme, estime que l'une ou l'autre soit feinte, il est un sot.[2]

This, incidentally, is an excellent example of the fine balance of contradictory sentiments in Montaigne which makes him so hard to pin down. On the whole we can conclude that his feelings for his family, apart from his father, were dutiful rather than powerful and that women as persons did not count a great deal for him (but there arises here the much larger question of his attitude to women in general, which may lead us to modify this conclusion).

The case of his male friendships is very different and it was to them that he gave his affections without reserve. It is worth remarking, keeping to the evidence of the *Essais* and the *Journal*, that his friends included some of the most eminent men of his time: Henry IV, Amyot, Jacques Peletier du Mans, Monluc, Turnebus, Muret, and (by correspondence) Justus Lipsius. But clearly the great emotional event of his life was his friendship with Étienne de La Boétie (died 1563), celebrated in *De l'amitié* and often mentioned elsewhere. *De l'amitié* culminates in one of the best known and most moving of all definitions of love or friendship:

(*a*) Si on me presse de dire pourquoy je l'aymois, je sens que cela ne se peut exprimer, (*c*) qu'en respondant: Par ce que c'estoit luy; par ce que c'estoit moy.[3]

As often, the supreme statement comes in a late addition. It has been argued with some force that Montaigne's account of this friendship is more of a literary exercise, inspired by ancient

---

[1] III, ix: TR 948.
[2] I, xxxviii: EM i, 307; TR 230(*b*).
[3] I, xxviii: EM i, 245; TR 186–7.

models, than a genuine experience.[1] The genuineness of the experience cannot seriously be doubted, as is shown by the entry in the *Journal du voyage* (not intended for publication) where Montaigne is suddenly overcome by the memory of La Boétie, nearly twenty years after his death.[2] But certainly the expression of the experience, as we saw in the last chapter, is influenced and partly determined by literary tradition and convention. It has also been argued that the friendship exercised a decisive influence on the genesis and form of the *Essais*: left without the man who could share all his thoughts, Montaigne turned for compensation to the recording of his thoughts on paper and communication with his readers.[3] This again can be accepted, as an element in the formation of the book, and it is borne out by some passages in the text; but again it should not be overstressed, since Montaigne soon soars above La Boétie and anything his example could offer. The memory remains as a subdued elegiac strain, and not only in the First Book, but it would be a mistake to regard it as central. A mere footnote, on the other hand, is the later friendship with Marie de Gournay, the *fille d'alliance,* which only began in 1588 and is only mentioned once directly, in a 1595 addition of not wholly certain authenticity. We have seen how much the transmission of the *Essais* owes to Mlle de Gournay, but she cannot be said to have influenced their actual creation.

As far as social position is concerned, Montaigne generally speaks of himself as being of middle rank.[4] This must surely refer to the middle rank of the nobility (he was not of course a grandee) but the fact that he looks upon himself thus has wider implications, to which we shall return, for his political and social attitudes. On the other hand, the *Essais* reveal, though without ostentation, that he was a rich man (which we should know in any case from external sources): he remarks in passing that a hundred men had been working for him.[5] Unostentatious though such references are, they were enough to infuriate his seventeenth-century critics. Guez de Balzac demands to know why he should

1 Floyd Gray, 'Montaigne's friends', *French studies,* xv (1961).
2 TR 1270.
3 e.g. Anthony Wilden, 'Par divers moyens on arrive à pareille fin: a reading of Montaigne', *Modern language notes,* lxxxiii (1968). Cf. also Frame, *Biography,* pp. 63, 81–3.
4 e.g. III, ix: TR 931.
5 III, xii: TR 1025.

tell the reader that he employed a page.[1] But if he had a page there seems to be no reason why he should not have said so in a complete portrait of himself (of course it was to the very conception of the self-portrait that the seventeenth-century critics fundamentally objected). He certainly identifies himself on numerous occasions with the military nobility (*noblesse d'épée*), ignoring the bourgeois origins of his family and his own legal career. He sometimes speaks of himself as a courtier and if he frequently stresses his almost total lack of ambition (confirmed by the fact that his major public office, the mayoralty of Bordeaux, was virtually forced on him, like the part he played in political negotiations), it is due not only to modesty and ethical principles but also to his consciousness of the independence of a country gentleman.

This independence and the tranquillity of mind and conscience he associates with it are, it is true, seriously threatened by the civil wars which rage all round him, 'qui suis assis dans le moiau de tout le trouble des guerres civiles de France'.[2] This was perhaps written about 1574: some ten years later, in *De la vanité* (which contains the fullest treatment of his experience of the wars), things have got so much worse that he can speak of the near-collapse of ordered society in his neighbourhood.[3] Behind the *Essais* and indeed running through them there is thus a background of extreme violence, which should never be lost from view: the famous tower was never a tower of ivory. And the wars inflicted a hard test of abstract philosophical and moral theories, stoical, epicurean, or whatever name we decide to give to them: if there is tranquillity in the *Essais*, it is not easily won. His attitude, it must be admitted, falls short of the highest heroism. His house may be destroyed if necessary, but he will do his best to save it, as far as duty allows,[4] and there are many references to his success in achieving this aim. He sums it all up, in a striking link between outer and inner life, when he says:

> J'essaie de soubstrere ce coin à la tempeste publique, comme je fois un autre coin en mon ame.[5]

Once more, as so often and in spite of contradictions, all is of a piece. His independence is not merely an effect of social position but an essential part of himself.

[1] *Discours critiques*, XIX (*Œuvres*, Paris, 1665, ii, 660).
[2] II, vi: EM ii, 52; TR 352(*a*).   [3] III, ix: TR 933(*b*).
[4] III, i: TR 770.
[5] II, xv: EM ii, 387; TR 601(*c*).

The external events of his life are recorded from birth or even before (in one of the rare contributions to the self-portrait in the *Apologie* he quotes himself as an example of an eleven-month gestation)[1] almost to death, but in an entirely unsystematic and incomplete way: thus, as we have seen, his legal career, which lasted some fifteen years, is never directly mentioned and hardly ever alluded to. Although his work can be called autobiographical in some respects, it is not his purpose to write an autobiography (for a chronological record of his life we have to turn to the entries in his copy of Beuther's *Ephemeris historica* and, for a limited period, to the *Journal du voyage*).

The self-portrait proper may be said to start (for us not for him, since his remarks on the subject are scattered through the *Essais*) with his outward appearance, his physique, deportment, dress.[2] On the whole he stresses the less attractive aspects, especially his smallness and the embarrassment it causes him, his loud voice, his roughness with servants.[3] On the other hand (and there is contradiction here as in more serious matters) he cultivates certain elegances, like the carrying of a stick or cane, to the point of affectation,[4] and his open and easy manners win confidence, even at a first meeting.[5] His tastes and habits are revealed to us, throughout the *Essais* but particularly in the last chapter of Book III, perhaps more fully than had ever been attempted before.[6] He eats greedily, his table manners are bad, fish for him has a more exquisite taste than meat, he doesn't care for salads or fruit (except melons) but his appetite can put up with anything except beer, he could dine without a tablecloth but hardly without a white napkin, which he makes very dirty, he doesn't use a spoon and fork much, he cannot drink wine or water neat, he likes nice smells and hates bad ones, he scratches his ears and fidgets. These minute details are indeed trivial and have been much criticised, not only in the seventeenth century. But their concreteness, apart from its

---

[1] II, xii: TR 539.

[2] For a summary of passages dealing with these matters see Frame, *Biography*, pp. 63 ff. It should, however, be noted that the interesting statement about white teeth, chestnut beard and so on (TR 624) may not refer to Montaigne himself.

[3] III, xiii: TR 1065–6.

[4] II, xxv: TR 669.

[5] III, i: TR 769.

[6] When Plutarch tells us (in *Des propos de table*, *Œuvres morales*, 1572, f. 373E) that for a long time he abstained from eating eggs, we are struck by the exceptional character of the information.

picturesque attraction, serves to bring the writer before us so completely and so frankly, so shamelessly even, that we are less disposed to worry about omissions in the external record. When he goes further, to lament the smallness of his penis or to describe in detail the passing of stones or his behaviour at stool, we see once again the passion for revelation and communication, unrestrained by mere propriety or convention, which goes to the making of the great autobiographical writer; we find confirmation too that in the Third Book he has abandoned the reservations of the preface, to show himself 'tout entier et tout nud'. And although these disclosures present him as strongly individual, they also speak for humanity, since not these but similar peculiarities belong to everyone.

Two themes of larger significance need to be looked at separately and rather more fully. One is travel (here again we perceive the difficulty of distinguishing the picture of himself from the picture of the world around him: for the moment we are concerned as far as possible with the first). We have come upon many indications of a firm and stable local centre of the *Essais* (for instance descriptions of tower and library, the statement that he never works on his book away from home). This strongly fixed centre, whether we look at it from the point of view of his books and classical learning or, more literally, from that of geographical surroundings, family ties, Gascon dialect, country upbringing and acquaintance with people of all classes ('Je suis né et nourry aux champs et parmy le labourage')[1] is vitally important for the understanding of Montaigne. Yet it is even more important to seize the contrary principle of mobility, which seeks to break away from all these ties, physically, intellectually, and emotionally. It is again in *De la vanité* that the material amassed during the Italian journey (factually recorded in the *Journal*) and other travels is put to fullest use. Of the reasons he gives for leaving his settled home the most significant are escape from the monotony of domestic life, dislike of the present state of France, cosmopolitanism, and love of diversity.[2] He is aware that the keen pleasure he takes in travel is a sign of inner dissatisfaction and restlessness,[3] and when he says that he knows what he is fleeing from

[1] II, xvii: EM ii, 436; TR 636.
[2] III, ix: TR 925 ff.
[3] III, ix: TR 966.

The Essays of Montaigne

but not what he is looking for[1] he reveals a deep-lying disquiet in strong contrast with the image of prudent conformism which is sometimes attached to him. At any rate the picture of a man on horseback runs through the *Essais* and has to be set against Michelet's caricature: 'Quand je me trouve enfermé dans cette *librairie* calfeutrée, l'air me manque.'[2] Montaigne himself gives the answer: 'J'ayme les pluyes et les crotes, comme les canes.'[3] There is no lack of fresh air here.

The second great theme is that of illness, age, and death. Here the presence of an evolutionary element is undeniable. In the early essays he boasts of his good health and ignorance of pain.[4] After he has been afflicted by one of the most painful of diseases, the stone, the note changes and before 1580 he is writing:

Je suis aus prises avec la pire de toutes les maladies, la plus soudaine, la plus douloureuse, la plus mortelle et la plus irremediable.[5]

From this point onwards (though they never obscure the dominant mood of joy and acceptance in the Third Book) we find recorded the progress of the illness, accompanied by the signs of advancing age and premonitions of death. The physical symptoms, his mental reactions to them, and his struggles or acceptance are alike described with detached precision, though not without an undercurrent of emotion. What is most remarkable is the range of his reactions and the delicacy with which he notes them, from gay defiance (even in the latest stage):

je [ne] laisse de me mouvoir comme devant et piquer apres mes chiens, d'une juvenile ardeur, et insolente . . .[6]

through determined resistance or stoical resignation, emphasising the consolations (his conversation and bearing in company are not disturbed), to the excruciating descriptions of the worst moments:

On te voit suer d'ahan, pallir, rougir, trembler, vomir jusques au sang, . . . rendre les urines espesses, noires, et effroyables, ou les avoir arrestées par quelque pierre espineuse et herissée qui te pouinct et escorche cruellement le col de la verge. . . .[7]

---

[1] III, ix: TR 949.
[2] *Histoire de France*, Paris, 1856, x, 401.
[3] III, ix: EM iii, 242; TR 951.
[4] e.g. I, xiv: TR 56(a).
[5] II, xxxvii: EM ii, 577; TR 738(a).
[6] III, xiii: EM iii, 400–1; TR 1073–4(c).
[7] III, xiii: EM iii, 395; TR 1069(b).

Here, though the physical suffering is intense, stoical self-control is still uppermost. A more tragic note occasionally pierces the stoicism as when, a little later in the final essay, he describes (or rather, marvellously suggests) the relief of passing a stone, combined with the knowledge that his life is passing with it:

> C'est quelque grosse pierre qui foule et consome la substance de mes rouignons, et ma vie que je vuide peu à peu, non sans quelque naturelle douceur, comme un excrement hormais superflu et empechant.[1]

This comparison of life to an excrement is of some, not wholly obvious, significance. What seems contemptuous is in fact an acceptance of life, and illness, as a natural process from which no physiological operation need be excluded and which receives more explicit statement in the moving and beautiful retrospect of his life from the vantage-point of old age:

> J'en ay veu l'herbe et les fleurs et le fruit; et en vois la secheresse. Hureusemant, puis que c'est naturellemant.[2]

Death, which he had approached so closely at the moment of his accident, is of course part of the same gentle process:

> C'estoit une imagination . . . non seulement exempte de desplaisir, ains mesléc à cette douceur que sentent ceux qui se laissent glisser au sommeil.[3]

So far we have been considering the externals of the self-portrait, though as we have progressed the line between external and internal has become increasingly hard to draw. The inner representation of character is in a way the whole of the *Essais* (as we have seen, even when he looks at the world outside himself he is concerned above all with his own reactions to it), and it is made up of innumerable contradictory details. Here again any attempt at a full summary would merely repeat what Montaigne himself has written unsystematically and many of his critics systematically: only such salient features can be considered as assist us towards the understanding of method and the judgement, however tentative, of the result.

The first group of qualities, mental and moral, which he stresses

---

[1] III, xiii: EM iii, 401; TR 1074(*c*).
[2] III, ii: EM iii, 37; TR 794(*c*).
[3] II, vi: EM ii, 54; TR 354(*a*). The word *glisser*, which adds so much to the effect, is a correction of the Bordeaux Copy (the original was *emporter*).

in himself, all closely linked, is centred on slowness of mind (the dullest boy in the whole province, he says),[1] absence of memory, laziness, sleepiness, nonchalance, indifference, coldness. There is a progression here from amiable if not admirable characteristics to self-centredness (naturally) and egoism. A recurrent theme is his reluctance to concern himself with the affairs of others, to commit himself fully when he does so[2] (the case of La Boétie may be regarded as a single outstanding exception), to incur obligations, to explain, apologise or deny. The death of his children ('two or three') has left him almost unmoved.[3] Hatred is as foreign to him as strong affection.[4] And in general, a frequently repeated asseveration, his slowness and coldness make him free from all violent passions (with one important exception, love or rather sex):[5] he is particularly indifferent to avarice and ambition, liking neither to exercise nor endure command. Tranquillity, not glory, is his central object:

> Toute la gloire que je pretans de ma vie, c'est de l'avoir vescue tranquille: tranquille [non] selon Metrodorus, ou Arcesilas, ou Aristippus, mais selon moi.[6]

All this adds up to a fairly familiar picture, open to favourable or unfavourable interpretation: on the one hand, equity, equanimity, balance, detachment from the evil passions of his time; on the other, an indifference to the sufferings of humanity in general, an unremitting devotion to his own comfort, a triumph of egocentricity:

> Je vis du jour à la journée; et, parlant en reverence, ne vis que pour moy: mes desseins se terminent là.[7]

But, before we try to decide which of these two interpretations is nearer the truth, there is another group of qualities which seems to stand in marked contrast to the first. A few slight indications suggest some doubts about the familiar picture. When he says that he is 'extremement oisif, extremement libre',[8] the addition of the superlatives puts his idleness and freedom from constraint in

1 II, viii: TR 378.
2 e.g. III, x: TR 981.
3 I, xiv: TR 61(c).
4 'Aussi ne hay-je personne;' III, xii: EM iii, 359; TR 1040.
5 III, v: TR 871.
6 II, xvi: EM ii, 394; TR 605.
7 III, iii: EM iii, 54; TR 807.
8 II, xvii: EM ii, 423; TR 626(c).

a different light, giving them an intensity of experience which is not compatible with coldness. He does nothing without gaiety,[1] he is unsuspicious,[2] he is subject to sudden, though slight and brief, attacks of emotion,[3] all of which are at variance with a totally dispassionate and calculating character. So, perhaps, are his keen curiosity and delight in variety. But these are minor examples of shading which lend vividness and relief to the picture without altering it fundamentally. There are more far-reaching contradictions. He says that, though he cannot cry, he feels tender compassion for the afflictions of other people.[4] We are not bound to take his word for it, and this may be no more than the sentimentality which sometimes accompanies coldhearted egoism. Other passages make this view difficult to sustain. Cruelty horrifies him,[5] his sympathies go to the unhappy and the vanquished,[6] the suffering of others inspires in him an acute physical distress:

La veue des engoisses d'autruy m'engoisse materiellement, et a mon sentimant souvant usurpé le sentimant d'un tiers.[7]

In fact one of his characteristics is an extreme sensibility, which plays an important part in his thought as well as in his self-portrait. It may not be irreconcilable with egoism but it cannot be squared with crude egoism: our interpretation of him can never be simple. It is reflected too in his sympathy with animals, often expressed (again sensibility and thought go together). It appears in his aesthetic feeling, in his response not only, as we have seen, to poetry but to material objects like glass ('Tout metal [m']y desplait au pris [d']une matiere claire et transparante'),[8] to works of art (stronger than is usually supposed, though it is not an educated response like that he gives to poetry) and to nature:

quand je me promeine solitairement en un beau vergier, si mes pensées se sont entretenues des occurrences estrangieres quelque partie du temps, quelque autre partie je les rameine à la promenade, au vergier, à la douceur de cette solitude et à moy.[9]

---

1 II, x: TR 389.
2 III, xii: TR 1038.
3 III, v: TR 868.
4 II, xi: TR 409.
5 e.g. III, viii: TR 900.
6 III, xiii: TR 1079–80.
7 I, xxi: EM i, 121; TR 95(c).
8 III, xiii: EM iii, 386; TR 1062.
9 III, xiii: EM iii, 419; TR 1087–8.

It is impossible to understand Montaigne without taking into account this intense sensibility, moral and aesthetic. At the same time, here as elsewhere, all these strands are brought back to himself: 'tranquille non selon Metrodorus . . . mais selon moi', 'ne vis que pour moy', 'à la douceur de cette solitude et à moy'. Montaigne's sensibility in a way transcends egoism, but it is self-centred in a quite literal sense. And it is closely associated, especially in the later stages of the *Essais*, with his capacity for pleasure. The moral and philosophical implications of his hedonism need to be discussed in their own context: for the moment it is enough to say that hedonism is not an abstract doctrine but a vital ingredient of his temperament and of the self-portrait. Here again, though, a corrective is necessary: if he accepts himself with all his propensities, he also, for the sake of his tranquillity, pushes them (without actually resisting them) in the direction of moderation: 'J'esguise mon courage vers la patience, je l'affoiblis vers le desir.'[1]

Nor should we overlook the group of qualities centred on frankness, his hatred of lying, dissimulation and feigning, his indignant refusal to believe that he could ever be capable of ingratitude, treachery or malignity, his judgement uncorrupted by passion (especially enmity). All this again is perfectly compatible with egoism but not with moral laziness or cowardice. More importantly, we shall see how far these personal qualities (as in the case of hedonism) are projected into a general ethical system.

For the present it is clear that frankness, apart from its importance for the consideration of Montaigne's character, has a special bearing on the candour of the self-portrait (which again is not quite the same thing as its truth or truthfulness), and we have already seen how far it carries him. He reveals his most secret thoughts and actions and is unsparing towards his weaknesses:

plus je me hante et me connois, plus ma difformité m'estonne, moins je m'entens en moy.[2]

à peine oseroy-je dire la vanité et la foiblesse que je trouve chez moy.[3]

But it would be wrong to suppose that the tone is generally one of grave confession or self-abasement: what dominates is a

---

[1] III, vii: EM iii, 169; TR 895.
[2] III, xi: EM iii, 313; TR 1006.
[3] II, xii: EM ii, 315; TR 548(*a*).

humorous self-mockery. His life, he says, is exemplary, provided that you take it as the opposite of what is to be followed.[1] His account of how he obtained letters of Roman citizenship is wittily placed at the end of the essay on vanity. He makes fun of his physical smallness when, at the moment of the accident, a huge horse and rider charge down 'sur le petit homme et petit cheval'.[2] His humour has a distinctly modern ring when he calls the *Apologie* 'ce long et ennuyeux discours'[3] or renounces any posthumous praise which will be given him not because he is worthy of it but because he is dead.[4] The same spirit can be seen even in the *Journal du voyage*: thus when, out of respect for his wisdom and learning, he is consulted on a case by Italian doctors he laughs to himself ('Me ne rideva fra me stesso'),[5] a good summary of his general attitude to himself. Very frequently these wry digs at himself are interpolated: for instance, a 1580 attack on pedants who get all their knowledge from books is completely modified by an addition to the Bordeaux Copy where he admits that he himself is exactly the same.[6]

These then are the bare outlines of the self-portrait. We have seen some of the fundamental contradictions it embraces, but not perhaps the full extent to which it is constructed of small contradictory touches. Thus he has often been ill, he has rarely been ill (both these, of course, before the major illness developed); he follows his hounds, as we saw, with youthful ardour in spite of his illness, but a couple of pages later he has given up all violent exercises (only, to complicate matters further, the second passage was written before the first); in his house there reigns an absence of ceremony and he even forgets such simple courtesies as receiving guests, but immediately afterwards (admittedly in a later interpolation) he boasts that he could keep a school of etiquette (French style);[7] similarly, though at a much deeper level, he is happiest (sometimes only happy) in solitude, but he is outward-looking, born for society and friendship;[8] he is sensitive and insensitive; he has very strong sexual impulses ('Jamais homme n'eust ses

[1] III, xiii: TR 1056.
[2] II, vi: EM ii, 53; TR 353.
[3] II, xii: EM ii, 370; TR 588.
[4] III, iv: TR 816.
[5] *Journal*, ed. Lautrey, p. 363.
[6] I, xxv: TR 135.
[7] I, xiii: TR 48(*b*)–49(*c*).
[8] III, iii: TR 801.

approches plus impertinemment genitales'),[1] but he is (some-times) capable of chastity. Above all there is the contrast between mobility, diversity, inconstancy (and contradiction) on the one hand, on the other, less prominently but noticeably none the less, an insistence on a stubborn continuity of opinion and judgement.[2] These contradictions, and many like them, offer no great difficulty of interpretation: each statement is the truth of the moment; once again he may contradict himself but he does not contradict truth. Moreover they do not exceed the quantity of conflicting impulses, motives, thoughts, to be found in any fairly complex character. What makes Montaigne remarkable (and up to his own time unique) is the completeness and honesty with which he records these contradictions and the skill, or art, which builds them all into the picture of a single individual.

But though the contradictions can be resolved easily enough in this way, we still have to face the question of the 'truth' of the self-portrait as a whole, not just its internal coherence but its correspondence to external reality. This is much less easy, in fact extremely difficult. It might appear simple to compare the *Essais* with a straightforward biography and see what the differences are, but genuine external evidence is quite sparse and no biographer of Montaigne could afford to neglect the largest body of information at his disposal, the *Essais* themselves (with the *Journal du voyage*, which, not being intended for publication, is less open to doubt but still necessarily subjective). The result is inevitably in part a reproduction of what Montaigne himself has said: we cannot appeal from one to the other. The consubstantiality of man and book which he proclaims is indeed hard to break. Where it is possible to check with independent documents we find, not un-expectedly, sometimes confirmation and sometimes opposition. Thus in his account of his conduct as mayor of Bordeaux,[3] where all the details can be verified, he turns out to be exactly right. More generally, the disinterestedness to which he lays claim is borne out by a speech to the Bordeaux Parlement in 1565 in which he argued that it would be wrong for them to make any request tending to increase the profits they drew from their offices[4] (of course disinterestedness comes easily to the rich). On his hatred

---

[1] III, v: EM iii, 135; TR 868.
[2] e.g. II, xii: TR 553; III, ii: TR 790.
[3] III, x: TR 982–3.
[4] Frame, *Biography*, p. 55.

of falsehood and lying a contemporary witness brings striking corroboration: in the margin at the point where Montaigne speaks of himself as 'enemi juré de toute falsification'[1] Florimond de Raemond (a friend admittedly) noted: 'l'auteur se peint au vrai tel qu'il estoit'.[2] Of Montaigne's scrupulous exactitude in minor details an example is the deletion in 1582 of the statement that he would not be able to manage a horse and its equipment[3] (after his return from Italy he knew that he could).

On the other hand we have seen how he exaggerates the antiquity of his family and disguises his legal career, speaking of himself as a soldier (of which he had little real experience) rather than as a lawyer (which he was for about fifteen years). One of the most serious accusations against him is that made by Rousseau (after Malebranche):

> J'avois toujours ri de la fausse naïveté de Montaigne, qui, faisant semblant d'avouer ses défauts, a grand soin de ne s'en donner que d'aimables.[4]

There is no doubt much to support this. After saying that, from laziness and negligence, he has never bothered to look at his title deeds, he goes on:

> Que ne ferois je plus tost que de lire un contract, et plus tost que d'aller secouant ces paperasses poudreuses, serf de mes negoces ? ou encores pis de ceux d'autrui, comme font tant de gens, à pris d'argent ?[5]

He admits an amiable absent-mindedness but not that he himself had belonged to the profession he despises. It is difficult to deny a certain disingenuousness here and in several similar passages.[6] But the most far-reaching difference between the picture of the *Essais* and what is revealed by other sources does not lie in these minor examples of fairly innocent and superficial vanity but, on the contrary, in an exaggerated modesty. What he says about his ponderousness and dullness is belied (though not perhaps completely invalidated) by a contemporary account of another speech he made (in 1563), when he is said to have 'expressed himself with

---

1 I, xl: RM i, 327; TR 246.
2 Pierre Bonnet, 'Une nouvelle série d'annotations de Florimond de Raemond', *BSAM*, III, 10 (1959), 18–19.
3 II, xvii: DB ii, 231.
4 *Confessions*, ed. van Bever, Paris, 1927, ii, 390.
5 III, ix: EM iii, 215; TR 931(c).
6 Especially III, i: TR 774.

all the vivacity of his character'.[1] His lack of memory is refuted by the range of his quotations and references (whatever aids he may have used), his laziness by the translation of Sabunde if by nothing else: in both cases the faults he confesses without much justification are more attractive than the learning and industry he might more truthfully have claimed. Rousseau's charge does seem to stick, in some respects at least. It could of course be replied that his faults, real or feigned, *are* lovable, certainly more lovable than Rousseau's.

However, the point of all this is not to catch Montaigne out, to convict him of some sort of deception (what he is telling us is what he thought about himself, how he looked to himself, and this is hardly capable of objective refutation), but to show the complexity of the relations between the self of the *Essais* and the man who wrote them. It would be silly to follow fashion and talk about a *persona* in the work, a fictional character quite separate from the real man. The book and the man are indeed consubstantial. Still, consubstantiality in its original and best-known sense implies difference as well as unity, and so it is here. The self of the *Essais* is in some ways subtly different from the Montaigne who can to some extent be reconstructed from external evidence; it is vastly more complex and on the whole less admirable, with more weaknesses. This is partly the difference between an internal and an external view (which emerges well enough from the contrast we perceive in the *Essais* between his pride of bearing and inner self-mockery), a difference which constitutes a psychological universal. But it is also partly the transformation of reality which operates in any work of art. As he says himself in the sentence preceding the remark about consubstantiality: 'Me peignant pour autrui, je me suis peint en moy de colurs plus nettes que n'estoint les mienes premieres.'[2] The self of the book may be better or worse than the original – this matters only a little – but above all it acquires from the mode of presentation a depth of interest which the external man could never lead us to expect. Even here Proust's axiom of the separateness of the man and the artist remains partly true, however closely entangled they may be. As so often for Montaigne we are forced to an antithetical conclusion: they are the same, they are not the same.

We have spoken of the internal view, and Michelet calls the

1 Frame, *Biography*, p. 54.
2 II, xviii: EM ii, 453; TR 648(*c*).

The Study of the Self: the Observer Observed

Essais 'première description exacte, minutieuse, de l'intérieur de l'homme'.[1] This, self-evident though it may seem, has not found universal acceptance. P. Mansell Jones observes:

> We must agree, in any systematic sense Montaigne is not an introspective. His self-revelations are sporadic intuitions rather than conscious pieces of self-analysis.[2]

We must also agree, in so far as Montaigne does nothing systematically, is indeed the embodiment of anti-system, and Mansell Jones's argument (too complex to be summarised without injustice) has the merit of stressing the importance of judgement,[3] and of calling attention to much in Montaigne that is not self-portraiture. All the same, Michelet is right, and Montaigne's self-analysis is of a depth and quality which go far beyond sporadic intuitions. The minute account of his feelings after the accident has already been considered: though the objection may be made that this is a reaction to an external stimulus, it is soon transposed into an introspective key. A less famous example (one among many) is a description of the growth and decline of love, the more remarkable in that it already figures in the 1580 edition and in the generally impersonal *Apologie*. For its full complexity to be manifest it must be quoted at length:

> Je n'ay point grande experience de ces agitations vehementes (estant d'une complexion molle et poisante) desquelles la pluspart surprennent subitement nostre ame, sans luy donner loisir de se connoistre. Mais cette passion qu'on dict estre produite par l'oisiveté au cœur des jeunes hommes, quoy qu'elle s'achemine avec loisir et d'un progrés mesuré, elle represente bien evidemment, à ceux qui ont essayé de s'opposer à son effort, la force de cette conversion et alteration que nostre jugement souffre. J'ay autrefois entrepris de me tenir bandé pour la soustenir et rabatre (car il s'en faut tant que je sois de ceux qui convient les vices, que je ne les suis pas seulement, s'ils ne m'entrainent); je la sentois naistre, croistre, et s'augmenter en despit de ma resistance, et en fin, tout voyant et vivant, me saisir et posseder de façon que, comme d'une yvresse, l'image des choses me commençoit à paroistre autre que de coustume; je voyois evidemment grossir et croistre les avantages du subjet que j'allois désirant, et agrandir et enfler par le vent de mon imagination; les

1 *Histoire de France*, x, 399.
2 *French introspectives*, p. 30.
3 For a full study of this aspect see La Charité, *The concept of judgment in Montaigne*, 1968.

difficultez de mon entreprinse s'aiser et se planir, mon discours et ma conscience se tirer arriere; mais, ce feu estant evaporé, tout à un instant, comme de la clarté d'un esclair, mon ame reprendre une autre sorte de veuë, autre estat et autre jugement; les difficultez de la retraite me sembler grandes et invincibles, et les mesmes choses de bien autre goust et visage que la chaleur du desir ne me les avoit presentées.[1]

A long passage like this brings home forcibly the difficulty of compartmentalising Montaigne. Form and content (the self-revelation is practically indistinguishable from the style), introspection and general reflection go together. Even so, the dominant here is clearly the minute differentiation of successive states of mind, a 'conscious piece of self-analysis' without any doubt. Both the method and the central theme (that love is a creation of the lover and his passions) come very close to Proust. The analysis of the emotions of love is, it is true, characteristic of sixteenth-century and even more of seventeenth-century literature, but here there is practically nothing of the formal and stereotyped system of expression in which it is usually conveyed. Once again we can only wonder at the fresh look Montaigne gives to life and the way he breaks through any merely temporal classification.

The self-portrait then is a complete one, not in the sense that every conceivable detail is shown (which would hardly be possible and in any case would not be compatible with Montaigne's method of proceeding by separate and unsystematic approaches) but in the sense that every side of his life, physical and mental, external and internal, is at some point included. It emerges clearly from all that has been said that the inner, psychological portrait predominates. However, the relation between portrait and painter is still more complex than has been suggested so far. It is not only a matter of the internal and external portrait or of the correspondence between portrait and reality. The very notion of a self-portrait necessarily implies a doubling of personality or at any rate of functions within the self: someone is living and acting, someone is watching him live and act. As usual he is himself fully conscious of what is going on, even by 1580:

Et puis, me trovant entierement despourveu et vuide de toute autre matiere, je me suis presenté *moy-mesmes à moy*, pour argument et pour subject.[2]

1 II, xii: EM ii, 320–1; TR 552(a).
2 II, viii: EM ii, 69; TR 364(a).

Moy qui m'espie de plus prez, qui ay les yeux incessamment tendus sur moy. . . .[1]

The final stage, again as usual, brings a more unequivocal statement:

Je ne m'aime pas si indiscretemant et ne suis si ataché et meslé à moi que je ne me puisse distinguer et considerer à quartier: come un voisin, come un arbre.[2]

In all these cases it is clear that there is an observing self and an observed self,[3] in the last that the observer possesses an objectivity which the observed self lacks.

Thus far, though it may be doubted whether this duality had received such deliberate expression in modern literature, the phenomenon itself is not so very remarkable. It is implied in the Greek 'know thyself', it must be present in any painter working on a self-portrait, it is (perhaps partly under Montaigne's influence?) a commonplace in the French drama of the seventeenth century. What complicates matters is that in the case of Montaigne the principal activity he is engaged in is precisely that of writing essays. It follows that the observer himself is under observation, that duality is hardly a sufficient description of what is taking place. We have not just a painter painting a picture of himself but a painter painting a picture of himself painting a picture and so on, in fact something like an infinite regress. Montaigne in one of his most profound statements about his own work catches the process at the vanishing point where it may be said to reach infinity:

. . . d'autant qu'à point nomé j'escris de moy et de mes escris come de mes autres actions, que mon theme se renverse en soi . . .[4]

So, paradoxically but characteristically, the multiplicity of selves and points of view leads in the end to a new unity in which all are fused.

[1] II, xii: EM ii, 315; TR 548(*a*).
[2] III, viii: EM iii, 202; TR 921(*c*).
[3] 'C'est l'homme à la fois observateur et sujet de son observation' (Nisard, *Histoire de la littérature française*, Paris, 1889, i, 438).
[4] III, xiii: EM iii, 366; TR 1046(*c*).

✠ 5 ✠

The Self and the World

IN spite of his introspection Montaigne, like Gautier, was a man for whom the external world existed. As we have already suggested, the two sides are almost inseparable: the world outside him is refracted through himself, offering perpetual occasion for judgement and observation (and for observation of his own reactions to it); the study of the self is constantly enriched by the absorption of what he has observed. The mind cannot move in a void, it must have something to work on:

> ... il semble que l'ame esbranlée et esmeuë se perde en soy-mesme, si on ne luy donne prinse: il faut tousjours luy fournir d'object où elle s'abutte et agisse.[1]

This is not to deny what has been said about the existence of true introspection, but the principle stated here holds good for the book in general.

The basis of appreciation of the external world is of course the senses. Their reliability and mode of operation present serious problems to Montaigne, as to all philosophers, but for the moment what matters is his own sensory range, his sensibility, sensuousness, sensuality. The pure pleasures of the imagination, he says, are no doubt the highest, but he does not pretend to rise to them: for him they are always mixed, 'intellectuellement sensibles, sensiblement intellectuels'.[2] We have already seen something of his voluptuous interest in material objects, their shape, consistency, taste, smell. The effect on the mind of disagreeable sensations is a commonplace, but he conveys the sensation itself, 'ce

[1] I, iv: EM i, 23; TR 25(a).
[2] III, xiii: EM iii, 418; TR 1087.

74

bruit aigre et poignant que font les limes en raclant le fer',[1] not so well as Shakespeare:

> I had rather hear a brazen canstick turn'd,
> Or a dry wheel grate on the axle-tree,

but there is an imaginative kinship. Touch and taste are involved in:

> Ferons nous a croire à nostre peau que les coups d'estriviere la chatoüillent? Et à nostre gout que l'aloé soit du vin de Graves?[2]

or temperature, superbly, in the description of the retreat of the ten thousand:

> d'entre eus plusieurs morts, plusieurs aveugles du coup du gresil et lueur de la nege, plusieurs stropicz par les extremitez, plusieurs roides, transis et immobiles de froid . . .[3]

This comes from Xenophon (Castellio's Latin translation), but the source is much less vivid. A whole essay, though short, *Des senteurs* (I, lv), is devoted to the sense of smell, to the way, for example, in which scents cling to his moustaches, or actually affect his mood. This quite exceptional intensity of reaction to sense impressions, his sensual-aesthetic approach to life, are fundamentally poetic, or at least part of what may be called the poet's equipment, as the parallel with Shakespeare suggests.

With keen sense perception goes, naturally and almost inevitably, a keen response to beauty in all its manifestations. Miss Gracey speaks of his 'sensibilité extrême pour tout ce qui est beau',[4] a characteristic which is highly important and often overlooked. His feeling for natural beauty, scarcely equalled in his time, at least in prose writing (Shakespeare once more offers the obvious parallel), emerges mainly in the *Journal du voyage*. The reason for this seems clear enough: natural description is only incidentally relevant in the *Essais*, in the *Journal* it is the spontaneous outcome of each day's new experience. Wherever he goes, especially in the Alps and the Apennines, he is likely to give brief but unconventional and extraordinarily felt notations of the surrounding landscape.[5] One or two examples will suffice for illustra-

[1] II, xii: EM ii, 359; TR 580.
[2] I, xiv: EM i, 65; TR 55.
[3] I, xxxvi: EM i, 298; TR 224.
[4] *Montaigne et la poésie*, p. 33.
[5] See also Buffum, *L'influence du voyage de Montaigne*, 1946, pp. 10-12.

tion. Thus the Inntal (the secretary is writing, presumably to dictation):

> Ce vallon sambloit à M. de Montaigne representer le plus agreable païsage qu'il eust jamais veu; tantôt se resserrant, les montaignes venant à se presser, et puis s'eslargissant à cette heure, de nostre costé, qui estions à mein gauche de la riviere, et gaignant du païs à cultiver et à labourer dans la pente mesme des mons qui n'estoint pas si droits; ... et puis descouvrant des plaines à deux ou trois etages l'une sur l'autre, et tout plein de belles meisons de gentil'homes et des eglises; et tout cela enfermé et emmuré de tous costés de mons d'une hauteur infinie.[1]

Wild rocks, 'les uns massifs, les autres crevassés et interrompus par l'ecoulement des torrens',[2] made a strong impression in the South Tyrol, after Brixen. Even better (and now from Montaigne himself) is the description of the mountains round Foligno:

> Bien louin audessus de nos testes, nous voions un beau vilage, et sous nos pieds, comme aus Antipodes, un autre ... cela mesme n'y done pas mauvès lustre, que parmi ces montaignes si fertiles l'Apennin montre ses testes refrongnées et inaccessibles, d'où on voit rouller plusieurs torrans, qui aïant perdu ceste premiere furie se randent là tost après dans ces valons des ruisseaus très plesans et très dous. Parmi ces bosses, on descouvre et au haut et au bas plusieurs riches pleines, grandes parfois à perdre de veue par certain biais du prospect. Il ne me samble pas que nulle peinture puisse represanter un si riche païsage.[3]

It may seriously be asked whether anyone before Montaigne had succeeded in conveying the sensations of travel in high mountains as well as this: the villages above and below, the multiplicity of levels, the dizzy transformation of normal conceptions of dimension, are rendered with astonishing sharpness. And afterwards we must probably await Rousseau (and even he lacks this freedom of vocabulary) to find anything similar; even Goethe, who followed much the same route, is decidedly inferior in his imaginative response. The same spirit, which could be called pre-Romantic, is found in his admiration for sea-views, like that of the sea, the islands, Leghorn and Pisa, 'une des plus belles vues du monde'.[4] But the word 'pre-Romantic' is misleading in a way: we have

[1] TR 1164.
[2] TR 1171.
[3] TR 1245–6.
[4] TR 1305.

here an illustration of the inadequacy of historical yardsticks, of Montaigne's capacity for seeing the world with fresh eyes, unencumbered by literary conventions (though the reference to painting suggests that pictures may have helped him to this sort of vision).

This is the private world of the *Journal*. In public, in the *Essais*, such delicate and anachronistic sensibility is kept under control, reduced to brief allusions (some of which, like the view from the library windows or the beauty of an orchard and the sweetness of solitude, we have already observed). Thus he attributes much of the effect of watering-places to 'des promenades et exercices à quoy nous convie la beauté des lieux où sont communément assises ces eaux'.[1] The tone is more abstract but the feeling is the same. He even, and in an early essay, bases an aesthetic argument (apparently much in advance of its time) on the impressions produced by natural scenery:

... pour rendre une veuë plaisante, il ne faut pas qu'elle soit perduë et escartée dans le vague de l'air, ains qu'elle aye bute pour la soustenir à raisonnable distance.[2]

(That is to say, a beautiful view must have a focal point to guide the eye.) It is hard to see where, apart from direct observation, he could have got this from, unless again from a study of landscape painting (the quotation from Lucan which follows was added in 1588 and describes a different phenomenon). He is also, though this is less unusual or surprising, keenly aware of human beauty.[3]

The last examples show how close his feeling for beauty in nature is to feeling for beauty in art, and we have already come upon several examples of his interest in painting especially, which in a way may be said to furnish the central metaphor of the book. Such passages are in fact extremely numerous and refute the charge that he was blind to the visual arts (though, as we have seen, he was not trained to appreciate them as he was to appreciate literature). He is particularly attracted by the practice and technique of painting, more than once describing a painter at work (admittedly using what he sees as illustration of a philosophical or moral argument rather than for strictly aesthetic ends), for instance when he observes that for painters the lines of the face

[1] II, xxxvii: EM ii, 601; TR 756 (added in 1582).
[2] I, iv: EM i, 23; TR 25(a).
[3] e.g. II, xii: TR 464; II, xvii: TR 622–4; III, xii: TR 1035–6.

may indicate laughter or tears and that in the early stages of a portrait it is impossible to tell which is which.[1] Architecture is a frequent source of images, but direct description is mostly to be found in the *Journal*, though there are cases in the *Essais* like the admiring evocation of Roman amphitheatres (derived from Lipsius) in *Des coches*.[2] Ultimately, however, art for him means less than morals and nature.

J'ay veu, cependant qu'on s'entretenoit, au haut bout d'une table, de la beauté d'une tapisserie ou du goust de la malvoisie, se perdre beaucoup de beaux traicts à l'autre bout.[3]

The 'beaux traicts' at the lower end of the table are clearly concerned with human conduct and motive rather than with the mere beauty of a tapestry. On a grander scale (but perhaps less authentically Montaigne):

Ce n'est pas raison que l'art gaigne le point d'honneur sur nostre grande et puissante mere nature. Nous avons tant rechargé la beauté et richesse de ses ouvrages par nos inventions, que nous l'avons du tout estouffée.[4]

'Art' here is probably to be taken in a more extended sense than the modern one, all the products of human ingenuity. The message, anticipating Rousseau, is none the less clear: in spite of his aesthetic sensibility Montaigne is more concerned with nature than with art.

Nature, of course, means more than mountains, and in dealing with any philosophical or poetic writer (and Montaigne is both) we will probably have to take account of his cosmology, the idea he has of the universe. Here a familiar difficulty presents itself in a more acute form: Montaigne's cosmology is to a large extent a reflection of the extraordinarily varied speculations of Greek antiquity (with some admixture of modern science). What appear to be intuitions of astonishing boldness and prescience can often be traced to Greek sources, and where no source is known we may still suspect the same origin. Since what matters to us is his view of reality as a whole rather than where he got it from, it will be best, except incidentally, to leave aside the question of sources and try to see how the world appeared to him.

[1] II, xx: TR 656.
[2] III, vi: TR 883–4.
[3] I, xxvi: EM i, 201–2: TR 155.
[4] I, xxxi: EM i, 268; TR 203.

It must be admitted that his cosmology, mainly contained in the *Apologie,* is basically of the old-fashioned kind. The earth is literally at the bottom, 'au dernier estage du logis et le plus esloigné de la voute celeste',[1] with the moon above it and, higher still, serene spheres in which incorruptible celestial bodies move in stately measure.[2] He believes in the four elements[3] (an important component of Sabunde's argument), but of course no other coherent theory had yet been advanced.

On the other hand, his insatiable intellectual curiosity leads him to advance (if only sceptically, as evidence of the diversity and uncertainty of human science) many theories which do not accord with this simple Aristotelian scheme. Thus he admits the possibility that the earth moves round the sun, citing Cleanthes and Nicetas but also Copernicus, who 'de nostre temps . . . a si bien fondé cette doctrine qu'il s'en sert tres-regléement à toutes les consequences Astronomiques';[4] he adds, in his usual sceptical way, that a thousand years from now a third opinion may reverse the two earlier ones. Copernicus had already been discussed in greater detail (though without the important point about mathematical regularity) by Guy de Bruès:[5] still, Montaigne shows here his awareness of the greatest scientific discovery of the sixteenth century and an accurate appreciation of its significance as then understood. Elsewhere he suggests that ('as some say') the universe may be contracting: this is in direct opposition to more recent theories, but it certainly upsets the static world-picture and the use he makes of it to cast doubt on the possibility of precise measurement of time conveys a hint of relativity. He does not dispute the orthodox Christian view of the age of the world, but he quotes other estimates, going as far as the 400,000 years of the Chaldeans.[6]

Of particular interest, in view of the later history of the idea, are his references to the plurality of worlds. It is true that he makes fun of those who imagine mountains and valleys (and human colonies) on the moon, or think that the earth is a luminous

1 II, xii: EM ii, 158; TR 429(*a*).
2 I, xxvi: TR 160(*c*) (from Seneca); II, xii: TR 428(*a*).
3 I, xx: TR 94(*c*). Again from Seneca, but Montaigne accepts the notion without question.
4 II, xii: EM ii, 322; TR 553(*a*).
5 *Les dialogues,* 1557 (ed. Morphos, 1953, p. 149). See also Jean Plattard, 'Le système de Copernic dans la littérature française au XVIe siècle', *Revue du seizième siècle,* i (1913). He does not, however, mention Bruès.
6 II, xii: TR 556(*c*).

star.[1] For these fantasies about the moon he quotes Anaxagoras, Plato, and Plutarch, and in spite of his scepticism he thus marks a link with Wilkins, Cyrano de Bergerac, and other literary precursors of space travel. More seriously, he quotes Lucretius, Plato, Democritus, and Epicurus to show the probability of other worlds exactly similar to ours (or very different), since nothing in the universe is unique nor can God's power be limited.[2] Though he is in no way original here, he continues Cornelius Agrippa[3] and he anticipates Fontenelle and some of the speculations of modern cosmology.

All this is enough to cast some doubt on Thibaudet's remark that 'Le monde pour lui, sous son apparence multiple, est bien quelque chose de limité'.[4] Montaigne contrasts Ptolemy's clear and definite view of the world with the uncertainty of his own time: 'une grandeur infinie de terre ferme'[5] has been discovered and no one knows what lies beyond. He is now talking about the earth rather than the cosmos, but the principle holds good for both. His attitude is perhaps summed up in:

(b) Si nous voyons autant du monde comme nous n'en voyons pas, nous apercevrions, comme il est à croire, une perpetuele (c) multiplication et (b) vicissitude de formes.[6]

There is here not only the multiplicity acknowledged by Thibaudet but a perpetual multiplication. But this universe is not only infinite in variety, it is also unified (and here once more we may perceive a connection between the structure of Montaigne's world-picture and the structure of his work):

Il se trouve une merveilleuse relation et correspondance en cette universelle police des ouvrages de nature ...[7]
rien ne s'est ingeré en cet univers, qui n'y tienne place opportune.[8]

It is equally true of the *Essais* that 'comme en nature le contrere se

1 II, xii: TR 429(*a,c*).
2 II, xii: TR 505–6, 556.
3 *De incertitudine et vanitate scientiarum*, Paris, I. Petrus, 1531, f. 60.
4 *Montaigne*, p. 359.
5 II, xii: EM ii, 324; TR 555(*a*).
6 III, vi: EM iii, 157–8; TR 886. This looks like a translation from the preceding Cicero quotation (*De natura deorum*, I, xx), but in fact Montaigne has considerably altered the end of the quotation and the essential part, the multiplication and vicissitude of forms, seems to be his own.
7 II, xxiii: EM ii, 476; TR 662.
8 III, i: EM iii, 2; TR 767.

vivifie par son contrere'.[1] Contradictions give life to each other and so create harmony rather than disrupt it. In the same way, just as in economic affairs profit for one can only be achieved at the expense of others, so in the physical world one thing can only grow at the expense of another.[2] Everything is interdependent and coherent.

Having seen how Montaigne looks at the universe, we can now ask what he conceives to be man's place in it. It is in some ways a Pascalian vision (as Thibaudet has also observed), and of course Pascal was directly inspired by it. An individual, even a kingdom, is a minute speck in comparison with the vastness of nature:

> Mais qui se presente, comme dans un tableau, cette grande image de nostre mere nature en son entiere magesté; qui lit en son visage une si generale et constante varieté; qui se remarque la dedans, et non soy, mais tout un royaume, comme un traict d'une pointe tres-delicate: celuy-là seul estime les choses selon leur juste grandeur.[3]

Here, though the disproportion is humiliating, the picture remains serene. The *Apologie* is much crueller in its depiction of man's insignificance. He is at once the frailest and proudest of creatures, 'logée icy, parmy la bourbe et le fient du monde, attachée et clouée à la pire, plus morte et croupie partie de l'univers. . . .'[4] This is exactly Pascal's tone. But Montaigne does not perceive the strength of the *roseau pensant* argument (though crushed by the universe, man is still superior to it because he knows it). In fact, in one of his most eloquent passages, he considers the argument and rejects it:

> Qui luy a persuadé que ce branle admirable de la voute celeste, la lumiere eternelle de ces flambeaux roulans si fierement sur sa teste, les mouvemens espouvantables de cette mer infinie, soyent establis et se continuent tant de siecles pour sa commodité et pour son service ? Est-il possible de rien imaginer si ridicule que cette miserable et chetive creature, qui n'est pas seulement maistresse de soy, exposée aux offences de toutes choses, se die maistresse et emperiere de l'univers, duquel il n'est pas en sa puissance de cognoistre la moindre partie, tant s'en faut de la commander ? Et ce privilege qu'il s'attribue d'estre seul en ce grand bastimant, qui ayt la suffisance d'en recog-

---

[1] I, xx: EM i, 101; TR 80(c).
[2] I, xxii; TR 106.
[3] I, xxvi: EM i, 204; TR 157(a). Cf. Pascal, *Pensées*, ed. Lafuma, Paris, 1951, i, 134–5.
[4] II, xii: EM ii, 158; TR 429(a).

noistre la beauté et les pieces, seul qui en puisse rendre graces à l'architecte et tenir conte de la recepte et mise du monde, qui luy a seelé ce privilege? Qu'il nous montre lettres de cette belle et grande charge.[1]

It is a magnificent representation of the gratuitous spectacle of the universe and of the contrast between its infinity and man's nothingness (and the view of man implied will demand later consideration), entirely worthy of Pascal. But of course Montaigne lacks something which Pascal has, the secure grasp of modern scientific developments which raises the similar passages in the *Pensées* above the level of noble eloquence. Still, the central idea is unquestionably there. A final quotation, with another allusion to the plurality of worlds, will take us back to our central theme:

Ce grand monde, que les uns multiplient encore comme especes soubs un genre, c'est le miroüer où il nous faut regarder pour nous connoistre de bon biais.[2]

The spectacle of the universe is thus again related to man, but above all the mirror image reinforces the conclusion that, with this as with other aspects of reality, the study of the world and the study of the self are indissolubly linked.

So far we have considered mainly the world in the sense of cosmos, but Montaigne is naturally much more concerned with this earth, with what he sees around him, at home or on his journeys, and with the greater world which he knows from hearsay or more fully (if not always accurately) from the works of the sixteenth-century cosmographers and travellers[3] as well as the historians. Among European countries Italy is, as might be expected, the one which is most familiar to him and which appears most often in the *Essais*. Apart from anecdotes (like the execution of Catena), observations of detail are introduced in passing for illustration or analogy, like the Italian use of umbrellas or parasols[4] or the comparison of Indian untouchables giving warning of their approach to Venetian gondoliers shouting at corners[5] (a remarkably vivid example of Montaigne's capacity for precise notation and his use of it to explain the unknown in terms of the known).

[1] II, xii: EM ii, 156; TR 427(*a*).
[2] I, xxvi: EM i, 204; TR 157.
[3] On this aspect of his reading see (apart from Villey) Atkinson, *Les nouveaux horizons de la Renaissance française*, 1935.
[4] III, ix: TR 951.
[5] III, v: TR 828.

Some of these details (and many besides) are to be found in the *Journal du voyage*; perhaps more typical of the *Essais* are the general reflections they inspire. Thus *Sur des vers de Virgile* includes a sketch of Italian *mores* and character: there are a greater number of beautiful women than in France (contradicted by the *Journal*) but in supreme beauties the two countries are about equal; the same is true of mental characteristics—brutality (probably in the sense of stupidity) is incomparably rarer in Italy, but the number of truly elevated characters is not dissimilar; bravery is universal among the French but the highest examples are to be found in Italy; marriage for Italian women is constraint and servitude.[1] If we are prepared to admit the possibility of generalising about national characters at all, we must be struck by the shrewdness of these judgements, still partly valid. His journey had left him with a very good impression of the Germans and the Swiss, notable for their honesty and truthfulness. As always, he looks for the tell-tale differences of customs which confirm his relativism, as when he compares German stoves with French fires and remarks that it makes a German ill to sleep on a mattress, an Italian on a feather bed, or a Frenchman without fire and curtains.[2] More remote European countries are mentioned: the Irish, 'our neighbours', wear scarcely any clothes in spite of the cold[3] and (in the 1595 edition only):

C'est par l'entremise de la coustume que chascun est contant du lieu où nature l'a planté: & les sauvages d'Escosse n'ont que faire de la Touraine, ny les Scythes de la Thessalie.[4]

It must be admitted that this, though powerfully expressed, is something of a commonplace rather than an original observation: Erasmus had said that an Irishman would not change places with an Italian[5] and Pascal later repeated the idea in words very similar to Montaigne's.[6]

However, the main weight of his observation naturally bears on France, of which he had most direct experience, and here the breadth of the picture, the handling of narrative in anecdote, and the vivacity of detail reveals gifts akin to those of the novelist, if

1 III, v: TR 861.
2 III, xiii: TR 1058.
3 II, xii: TR 434.
4 I, xxiii: CR i, 133–4.
5 *Moriae encomium*, Strasburg, 1511, C1ʳ.
6 *Pensées*, ed. Lafuma, i, 133.

less sustained (this is not, of course, peculiar to him, since before the development of the modern realistic novel a number of writers naturally anticipate its methods even though using other forms). Such glimpses of everyday life, being scattered through the *Essais*, cannot easily be systematised, but they may be illustrated. So we find numerous references to dress and manners (usually disapproving), like the new fashion of farthingales[1] or the older one of codpieces,[2] the false teeth and padded thighs of women (used as an analogy for the pretences of science),[3] the characteristically French custom of kissing as the normal greeting between the sexes,[4] or 'nos baisemains et nos inclinations serpentées' (unknown to simple savages).[5] Often such rapid perceptions are built up into scenes or pictures: there are those who use their wills like apples to reward and punish the heirs who please or displease them (a typical scene from a comedy, or novel)[6] or, still more vivid, and worth quoting in full to show how Montaigne seizes reality, the picture of the soldier and the scholar:

> Celuy que tu vois grimpant contremont les ruines de ce mur, furieux et hors de soy, en bute de tant de harquebuzades; et cet autre, tout cicatricé, transi et pasle de faim, deliberé de crever plutost que de luy ouvrir la porte, pense tu qu'ils y soyent pour eux? ... Cettuy-ci, tout pituiteux, chassieux et crasseux, que tu vois sortir apres minuit d'un estude, penses tu qu'il cherche parmy les livres comme il se rendra plus homme de bien, plus content et plus sage? Nulles nouvelles. Il y mourra, ou il apprendra à la posterité la mesure des vers de Plaute et la vraye orthographe d'un mot latin [Browning's grammarian in fact].[7]

The apostrophe to the reader ('tu vois'), the soldiers' arquebus-shots and scars, the scholar's catarrh and bleary eyes, the range and diversity of the vocabulary from the learned *pituiteux* to the vigorous, though not yet popular, *crever*, all this produces an impression of outstanding visual power. But, as usual in these cases, the picture is not offered for its own sake, it illustrates an argument (here the folly of doing things for glory or for posterity rather than for the good of one's own soul). And, again as usual,

[1] II, xv: TR 598.
[2] I, xliii: TR 261.
[3] II, xii: TR 518.
[4] III, v: TR 859–60.
[5] II, xii: EM ii, 179; TR 445.
[6] II, viii: TR 378.
[7] I, xxxix: EM i, 314; TR 235–6(*a*).

the tone is humorous. All sorts of incongruity come into play: not only the obvious ones of disproportion between the effort and the result or the contrasts of vocabulary, but the subtle unexpectedness of the identity shown to exist between the soldier's violent fury and the scholar's peaceful and secluded labours (both prepared to sacrifice their lives for their absurd projects).[1] It is to be noted that this remarkably finished example of Montaigne's descriptive technique is already in the 1580 edition. The same is true of the well-known deathbed scene at the end of *Que philosopher, c'est apprendre à mourir:*[2] the weeping women and the pallid servants, the darkened room and the candles, the doctors and preachers crowding at the bedside, combine to create an atmosphere of solemnity and horror as well as a vivid pictorial (and auditory) representation of the way death came to a sixteenth-century nobleman. It will be seen that, though the tone is normally humorous, Montaigne is equally successful with serious and tragic subjects. The parallel with the novel is, however, closest when Montaigne goes beyond the picture to introduce a narrative element, that is in his sustained anecdotes. We need not take too seriously the story of Marie-Germain, the girl who took a great leap and found that she was a boy (reproduced almost verbatim from the *Journal du voyage*)[3] or that of the gentleman whose only interest in life was the movement of his bowels.[4] But when we come to the dean of Saint-Hilaire at Poitiers, who stayed in his room, never emerging, for twenty-two years,[5] or the exceptionally brilliant story (especially in the Bordeaux Copy additions) of the old man (identified with Montaigne's friend the Marquis de Trans) gulled by his family and servants so as to be in complete ignorance of the affairs he thought he was managing,[6] we have a premonition of the world of Balzac. To exact observation of manners and skill in handling narrative Montaigne joins the keenest sense for oddity of character.

What has been said is sufficient to show something of the social range of his observation. From kings and courtiers (of whom he disapproves, though he sometimes speaks as if he were one of

---

1 On Montaigne's humour generally see Keith C. Cameron, *Montaigne et l'humour*, 1966.

2 I, xx: TR 94.

3 I, xxi: TR 96(*b*); cf. TR 1118-9.

4 III, ix: TR 922-3.

5 II, viii: TR 372.

6 II, viii: TR 373-4.

them), through the humanists, soldiers, lawyers and physicians who appear frequently, to the peasants of Périgord or the beggar at his door, he furnishes a fairly complete view of contemporary French society (there is, however, little reference to the commercial classes). Apart from the familiar hymn of praise to Paris (he is French only through it, he says, perhaps with some exaggeration),[1] the city is often mentioned: thus he regrets that he will not live to see the completion of the Pont-Neuf.[2] But country life is, as we should expect, much more extensively treated. Montaigne appears, for example, as a landowner, an ignorant and incompetent one, it is true (his incompetence, like his amateurishness in writing, is no doubt exaggerated). Thus he complains that his agent is never satisfied with the weather (if it is good for the vines, it is bad for the meadows)[3] and he professes ignorance of the simplest matters, the names of tools or how his wines are made.[4] Yet he also reveals a deep feeling for the natural processes involved: 'Le vin s'altere aus caves, selon aucunes mutations des saisons de sa vigne',[5] a marvellously apt conclusion to an essay which deals with the way in which men's deeds live after them.

We have already considered the impact of civil wars on Montaigne's self-portrait and we shall have to consider them again later from the point of view of his attitude towards them, but war and politics cannot be ignored here since they are so much a part of his apprehension of French reality (and this inevitable recurrence of the same subject offers one more illustration of the difficulty of subdividing him, of breaking him down into watertight compartments). For the moment we are viewing war simply as material of experience, without reference to its moral implications, and in this respect his response to it is as keen and indeed sometimes as appreciative as to any other facet of the diversity of the world. There is no occupation as pleasant as military life, he says, and goes on to praise its masculine comradeship, the freedom of conversation, and the stirring effect of martial music.[6] But, as usual, he does not confine himself to generalities, and the *Essais* (especially *De la vanité*) are full of particularised impressions of

[1] III, ix: TR 950.
[2] III, vi: TR 880.
[3] III, ix: TR 925.
[4] II, xvii: TR 636; III, ix: TR 929.
[5] I, iii: EM i, 22; TR 24(*c*).
[6] III, xiii: TR 1075(*b*).

the hazards of war. We have already seen the soldier in the breach, but:

> On n'est pas tousjours sur le haut d'une bresche . . . On est surpris entre la haye et le fossé; il faut tenter fortune contre un poullaillier; il faut dénicher quatre chetifs harquebousiers d'une grange.[1]

This is war as seen by Stendhal or Tolstoy with all its muddle and pettiness. Here, though glory is demolished, there is still a note of excitement, but generally it is horror that predominates, as in the descriptions of torture:

> Je sçay qu'il s'est trouvé des simples paysans s'estre laissez griller la plante des pieds, ecrazer le bout des doits à tout le chien d'une pistole, pousser les yeux sanglants hors de la teste à force d'avoir le front serré d'une grosse corde . . .[2]

This is the France depicted at almost the same time in the first book of d'Aubigné's *Tragiques*. Or sometimes there is a grim humour as in the story (which relieves the catalogue of suicides of *Coustume de l'isle de Cea*) of the woman of Toulouse raped by several soldiers: 'Dieu soit loüé, disoit-elle, qu'au moins une fois en ma vie je m'en suis soulée sans peché!'[3] (though one suspects that this may be a traditional joke). It is indeed true, as M. Lebègue remarks, that Montaigne and his contemporaries writing about the Wars of Religion strike a chord that still reverberates for the twentieth-century reader.[4]

Such reactions to war are those of an observer of outstanding acuteness but the observations themselves were available to anybody. It must not be forgotten, however, that Montaigne occupied a privileged situation as a political observer, and his comments on contemporary affairs are made from a national (and international) standpoint. Thus he alludes to the abdication of Charles v,[5] the execution of Horn and Egmont,[6] or the assassinations of William of Orange and the Duc de Guise.[7] But clearly he is more interesting when he draws directly on personal experience, as in the recital of the death of Moneins, the royal lieutenant in Guyenne, killed

[1] II, xvi: EM ii, 395; TR 606(*a*).
[2] II, xxxii: EM ii, 530; TR 702.
[3] II, iii: EM ii, 33; TR 338.
[4] 'La littérature française et les Guerres de Religion', *French review*, xxiii (1950), 213.
[5] II, viii: TR 370-1.
[6] I, vii: TR 32.
[7] II, xxix: TR 689-90(*b*).

D

by a crowd of rioters in Bordeaux in 1548, or his own decisive and successful intervention as mayor in rather similar circumstances, which is contrasted with the Moneins affair.[1] On a more exalted level are the character sketches of great political figures, like that of Henry IV (not named, but there can be little doubt about the identity of the subject).[2] Montaigne tells us that he had been urged to write an account of the events of his time because of his impartiality and the access which fortune had given him to the leaders of the different parties.[3] This familiarity is certainly reflected in the *Essais*.

It will be readily seen that what we have been discussing is in fact the part played by experience in the book. We have here, needless to say, one of the central strands in Montaigne's thought, emerging in the final essay (*De l'experience*) as perhaps the most important strand of all. So far we have considered it in relation to the observing self, as the raw material of judgement and self-exploration, and as the sheer enjoyment of the multiplicity of the world. It has other implications which will require further study. For the moment we must notice that as his horizon widens beyond the confines of Europe, although some of these connections persist, the element of personal experience naturally gives way to the purely bookish. Yet this would not quite be a true conclusion either. Although for his remarks on exotic countries, which are very numerous, he must inevitably rely on the reports of others (and sometimes very fanciful reports), his interpretation of them is illuminated and controlled by his observation of the familiar: his experience of the remote remains in a way a lived experience.

The passages dealing with America (especially in *Des cannibales* and *Des coches*) are the most famous, the most original, and the most important for an understanding of Montaigne, but references to eastern countries are much more frequent (though individually less extensive).[4] The main reason for this is no doubt the larger quantity of information available. Among eastern countries it was predictably Turkey that interested him, and his contemporaries, most.[5] The Ottoman empire was then at the zenith of its power and was felt in Europe as an ever-present threat (thus the *Journal*

---

[1] I, xxiv: TR 129–30(*b*).
[2] III, x: TR 986.
[3] I, xxi: TR 104–5(*c*).
[4] On this see Atkinson, *Les nouveaux horizons*, p. 325.
[5] Atkinson (p. 250) observes that there were twice as many books and ten times as many pamphlets devoted to Turkey as to America.

du voyage makes a number of references to the incursions of corsairs, as far north as Pisa, to defensive towers and systems of warning cannon, or to former slaves who had escaped from Turkish captivity).[1] In the *Essais* there is praise for Turkish valour 'la race Hottomane, la premiere race du monde en fortune guerriere',[2] military discipline, and warlike frugality (Turkish soldiers live on water, rice, powdered meat, and, if necessary, the blood of their horses);[3] many illustrations come from Turkish history, especially the atrocious murders of the seraglio, or religious practices, for example the sect whose members fast, keep silence, and slash themselves with knives.[4] As he goes further east Montaigne's details become on the whole less precise: he tells the story of the Assassins (a familiar theme),[5] and is much impressed by the legendary figure of Tamburlaine, whom he imagines with 'des sourcils eslevez, des naseaus ouvers, un visage affreus et une taille desmesurée'.[6] Apart from elephants and the juggernaut,[7] he displays considerable familiarity with two Indian institutions, the caste system, which we have already encountered (he got this from Simon Goulart's translation of Osorius's history of Portugal), and suttee, of which he gives a long and detailed description, beginning 'Un homme escrit encore de noz jours':[8] in fact, many earlier writers, ancient (including Cicero and Plutarch) and modern, had spoken of it. The East Indies, not as a rule sharply marked off from India, afford a good example of the attraction which the exotic held for Montaigne, in the sumptuous description of the suicide of a nobleman in Malacca:

Il fit dresser un eschafaut plus long que large, appuié sur des colonnes, royallement tapissé et orné de fleurs et de parfuns en abondance. Et puis, s'estant vestu d'une robe de drap d'or chargee de quantite de pierreries de haut prix, sortit en rue, et par des degrez monta sur l'eschafaut, en un coing du quel il y avoit un buchier de bois aromatiques allumé.[9]

1 e.g. TR 1225, 1252, 1268, 1303.
2 II, xxi: EM ii, 470; TR 659.
3 I, xlviii: TR 282.
4 III, v: TR 857. This is from Postel: see EM iv.
5 II, xxix: TR 690.
6 III, ii: EM iii, 28; TR 787.
7 II, iii: TR 342. But Montaigne ('En certain Royaume de ces nouvelles terres') does not seem to be fully aware that this is in India. His source Mendoza (see EM iv) places it in southern India (Tuticorin).
8 II, xxix: EM ii, 507; TR 685-6; Cf. also I, xiv: TR 51-2.
9 II, iii: EM ii, 34; TR 339(c).

This again, with some modifications including the word 'aromatiques', is from Goulart, but it shows Montaigne's almost naïve admiration for magnificence and his far from naïve capacity for matching the language to the subject, a necessary, and neglected, counterbalance to the wry and sceptical humour which characterises so much of his writing. Even more interesting for the modern reader are the occasional references to China, still a country that was scarcely known to Europeans. He observes that we boast of the invention of artillery and printing, but these inventions had been made a thousand years before in China, at the other end of the world[1] (a fact which only recently has received full attention). Again, following Mendoza's history of China, he praises Chinese arts and political institutions, in many ways superior to ours,[2] thus anticipating the great vogue of *chinoiserie* which only begins to develop seriously in the second half of the seventeenth century. Inevitably he is indebted to authors like Mendoza for his information: where he is superior to them is in his perception of the consequences for our whole conception of civilisation.

But if references to Asia (especially Turkey) are more numerous, those to the New World have a much greater impact on the reader and much deeper consequences for Montaigne's thought. We have seen (on p. 51 above) that the 1580 preface includes a prominent reference to 'those nations who are said still to live under the sweet liberty of the first laws of nature', and are thus accorded a place among the leading themes of the book as they appeared to the author at the moment of first publication. A number of passages in the *Essais* themselves bear witness to the effect the discovery of a new continent had on him, as when he speaks of 'ce monde nouveau, qui a esté descouvert du temps de nos peres par les Espaignols'[3] or 'ce nouveau monde des Indes occidentales'[4] or 'Nostre monde vient d'en trouver un autre.'[5] Of course the expression 'New World' was perfectly familiar by the time Montaigne wrote (thus it occurs in a Latin poem by La Boétie addressed to Montaigne and published in 1571),[6] but he

1 III, vi: TR 886. Also derived from Mendoza.
2 III, xiii: TR 1049(c).
3 II, xii: EM ii, 219; TR 477(a).
4 II, xii: EM ii, 326; TR 556(b).
5 III, vi: EM iii, 158; TR 886.
6 *Œuvres complètes*, ed. Bonnefon, 1892 (reprinted 1967), p. 208. Cf. Frame, *Biography*, p. 75.

brings out its full significance, marvelling always at the transformation of accepted attitudes which it has achieved. His astonishment is summed up by the Senecan quotation in *Des cannibales*, 'viri a diis recentes':[1] the men of these new regions have just issued from the hands of the gods. In an effort to place the new in relation to what is known and to foresee the consequences for the future, he evokes Plato's Atlantis and ideal republic[2] and predicts that the discovery of other similar worlds may follow.[3] But it is still the present reality that interests him most.

For his information about America he relied mainly, as we have seen, on the works of Lopez de Gomara, and Benzoni translated by Chauveton. To these should perhaps be added the works of Las Casas, the Spanish defender of the Indians, and the eyewitness accounts of Villegagnon's expedition to Brazil (especially important for *Des cannibales*) by the Franciscan cosmographer André Thevet[4] and the Protestant pastor Jean de Léry.[5] Even here, however, there is an element of personal observation, though Montaigne may have exaggerated it. Indian captives were brought to France from the beginning of the sixteenth century (Chinard records an example at Rouen in 1509)[6] and sometimes took part in pageants: thus at Henry II's entry into Rouen in 1550 a Brazilian scene was set up in a wood, when three hundred naked Indians disported themselves, fifty of them real Brazilians, the rest Frenchmen who had been there and spoke the language.[7] A similar display, though with less concern for verisimilitude, was put on for Charles IX's entry into Bordeaux in April 1565, and Montaigne could therefore easily have seen it.[8] However, Rouen was the great centre of French trade with America, and not surprisingly it was there, in 1562, that he met and conversed with three Brazilians

1 I, xxxi: EM i, 270; TR 204(c).
2 I, xxxi: TR 200, 204.
3 II, xii: TR 555; III, vi: TR 886.
4 *Les singularitez de la France antarctique*, Paris, 1557.
5 *Histoire d'un voyage fait en la terre du Bresil, autrement dite Amerique*, La Rochelle, 1578. On all these writers and their relation to Montaigne, see also Chinard, *L'exotisme américain dans la littérature française au XVIe siècle*, 1911.
6 *L'exotisme américain*, p. 6.
7 *C'est la deduction du sumpteux ordre plaisantz spectacles et magnifiques theatres dresses, et exhibes par les citoiens de Rouen ...* , Rouen, 1551, K3ᵛ. On this entry cf. Armstrong, *Ronsard and the Age of Gold*, p. 137; McGowan, 'Form and themes in Henri II's entry into Rouen'.
8 Frame, *Biography*, p. 56; Chartrou, 'Les entrées solennelles à Bordeaux au XVIe siècle', *Revue historique de Bordeaux*, xxiii (1930), 99–102.

through an interpreter.[1] Moreover, he had with him for a long time as a servant a man who had spent ten or twelve years in Brazil and who apart from his own recollections introduced sailors and merchants with American experience to his master;[2] he had himself tried the Brazilian equivalent of bread;[3] and it seems that he assembled at Montaigne a collection of objects which had been brought back from America:

Il se void en plusieurs lieux, et entre autres chez moy, la forme de leurs lits, de leurs cordons, de leurs espées et brasselets de bois dequoy ils couvrent leurs poignets aux combats, et des grandes cannes, ouvertes par un bout, par le son desquelles ils soustiennent la cadance en leur dancer.[4]

Cabinets of exotic curiosities like these were a common feature of the houses of princes and great noblemen during the Renaissance and afterwards, but we see in Montaigne's collection an expression of a genuine interest, not a mere ornament. Chinard is no doubt right in suggesting that he has exaggerated the importance of personal contacts like these and diminished the part played by books, which in fact supplied the bulk of his material.[5] It is, however, more revealing to consider that we have here another example of Montaigne's view of books not as a substitute for experience but as an adjunct to it,[6] of his passionate eagerness to enlarge and control his reading by whatever direct evidence he finds at hand. Even when dealing with distant America, he does his best to grasp the concrete reality through books but also through eye witnesses and artefacts.

The consequences of the preoccupation with America are pervasive and far-reaching: for the moment we are concerned with it simply as evidence of this grasp of external reality. Passing allusions are found in many essays, but detailed discussion is concentrated in three: the *Apologie* (to some extent), *Des cannibales,* and *Des coches.* The description of the life, customs and beliefs of the Brazilians in *Des cannibales* is precise, so far as one can judge accurate, and at the same time most lively. It matters little that Montaigne still believes that America touches

[1] I, xxxi: TR 212–3.
[2] I, xxxi: TR 200–3.
[3] I, xxxi: TR 205.
[4] I, xxxi: EM i, 272; TR 206.
[5] *L'exotisme américain*, pp. 195–6.
[6] Cf. p. 28 above.

the East Indies or is separated from them only by a narrow strait.[1] What does matter is the vividness of his picture, both physical and moral, and the way it is arranged so as to place the indigenous inhabitants in the most favourable light, which is what distinguishes him from most of his printed sources like Thevet and Léry. Thevet's style, for example, is very flat and dull in comparison, but the real point is his lack of sympathy and understanding, the qualities which create the beauty and poetry of Montaigne. *Des cannibales* is concerned with primitive Brazil and its happy tribes living in a state of unspoiled nature; *Des coches* treats of the civilised states of Mexico and Peru:

> L'espouventable magnificence des villes de Cusco et de Mexico, et . . . le jardin de ce Roy où tous les arbres, les fruicts et toutes les herbes . . . estoyent excellemment formez en or; comme, en son cabinet, tous les animaux qui naissoient en son estat et en ses mers; et la beauté de leurs ouvrages en pierrerie, en plume, en cotton, en la peinture, montrent qu'ils ne nous cedoint non plus en l'Industrie.

and the sombre and touching theme of their extinction. The next sentence goes on:

> Mais, quant à la devotion, observance des loix, bonté, liberalité, loyauté, franchise, il nous a bien servy de n'en avoir pas tant qu'eux: ils se sont perdus par cet advantage, et vendus, et trahis eux mesme.[2]

But this takes us away from the concrete reality of America to the use Montaigne makes of it, a much larger subject to which we shall return. None the less, the first part of the passage offers another illustration of his powerful attachment to the physically graspable, even at a distance and through the intermediary of literary sources. Many other examples could be given, like the description of the road from Quito to Cuzco[3] or of the postal system of the Incas[4] (both from Gomara).

However, this outline of Montaigne's view of America would hardly be adequate if we did not at least hint, anticipating later developments, at the persistent argument which underlies it, the equality of mankind, even the superiority of unspoiled natural man as found in America to the Christian and 'civilised' nations of Europe.

[1] I, xxxi: TR 201.
[2] III, vi: EM iii, 159; TR 887.
[3] III, vi: TR 893-4.
[4] II, xxii: TR 662(*b*).

Ils sont sauvages, de mesmes que nous appellons sauvages les fruicts que nature, de soy et de son progrez ordinaire, a produicts: là où, à la verité, ce sont ceux que nous avons alterez par nostre artifice et detournez de l'ordre commun, que nous devrions appeller plutost sauvages.[1]

No theme could be more central to his purpose.

Looking back now on his view of the world as a whole, familiar or exotic, we can see that the *Essais* constitute not only a self-portrait but a kind of general anthropology. The *Apologie* and *De la coustume* in particular (but only to a greater degree than the other essays) are full of observations of the most diverse human customs, traditions, and institutions, not, in spite of appearances, assembled at random but chosen for their pertinence to the same pervasive theme. As usual these observations are based partly on personal experience, partly on the reports of others. Thus to the description of the simple and untarnished existence of the American Indians can be joined that of the isolated community of Lahontan in the foothills of the Pyrenees, whose idyllic happiness was undisturbed by lawyers and doctors; but, as with the Indians, ruin followed when these agents of civilisation gained admittance.[2] Direct observation on his home ground (he was patron of the living of Lahontan) produces the same results as the indirect accounts of America. It might almost be said, allowing for the difference of time and scientific temper, that there is something of Frazer in the way he pieces his various reports together. But of course these reservations are capital. Together with the exact observation of local *mores* or the careful way in which he collects and checks the evidence of travellers to America goes a readiness to accept any story which serves his turn, ancient or modern (and as we have seen in the case of history he does not always seem aware of the distinction), countries which have a dog as king,[3] where men have eyes and a mouth in their chest or change into wolves and mares and back again.[4] *De la coustume* especially is an extraordinary mixture of the true and the fantastic: a long list puts side by side, all treated alike, genuine customs such as exogamy or female circumcision and fables such as the country of the Amazons.[5] In spite of so many excursions

[1] I, xxxi: EM i, 268: TR 203.
[2] II, xxxvii: TR 758-9.
[3] II, xii: TR 430.
[4] II, xii: TR 506.
[5] I, xxiii: TR 110-3.

into fantasy, he undoubtedly has an anthropologist's eye. A couple of examples (from the *Essais,* without considering the many in the *Journal du voyage*) will suffice to illustrate it: at home the behaviour of gipsy women after childbirth[1] and abroad the king of Mexico, changing his clothes four times a day and never using anything more than once.[2]

Still, he would not be himself if he did not feel the need to explain his attitude to truth and falsehood in these matters, and he does so in several important statements. One argument is that nothing can be imagined so fantastic that it will not correspond to some real practice somewhere:

> J'estime qu'il ne tombe en l'imagination humaine aucune fantasie si forcenée, qui ne rencontre l'exemple de quelque usage public, et par consequent que nostre discours n'estaie et ne fonde.[3]

The examples which follow are pretty incredible, but it is difficult to deny the force of the point in general. In a famous passage he takes a slightly different (though not contradictory) line, admitting that some of the tales he recounts may not be strictly in accordance with fact but maintaining that even so they reveal something of what human beings are capable of:

> Aussi en l'estude que je traicte de nos meurs et mouvemens, les tesmouignages fabuleus, pourveu qu'ils soient possibles, y servent comme les vrais. Advenu ou non advenu, a Paris ou a Rome, a Jan ou a Pierre, c'est tousjours un tour de l'humeine capacité, duquel je suis utilement advisé par ce recit. Je le vois et en fois mon profit esgalement en ombre que en corps.[4]

Though this is not the attitude of a scientific anthropologist, it is hard to gainsay him. We are here, once again, very close to Aristotle's view of poetic as opposed to historical truth,[5] and also to the *vraisemblance* of seventeenth-century classical theory, though Montaigne, as we should expect, puts it in a less abstract and simpler way.

Beyond the fairly detached concern with anthropology, whether scientific or poetic, lies something else, where a still stronger moral sense comes into play. This is his cosmopolitanism, most sharply

---

1 I, xiv: TR 58.
2 I, xxxvi: TR 224(*b*); from Gomara.
3 I, xxiii: EM i, 141; TR 109.
4 I, xxi: EM i, 133; TR 104(*c*).
5 Cf. p. 42 above.

reflected in the *Journal du voyage* and the parts of the *Essais* inspired by his travels. One reason for his grand tour was the wish to escape from warring and fanatical France, but deeper propensities are involved. 'Il n'a pas nos préjugés', as Maurice Barrès said, rejecting him from the fold of French nationalism. When he travels it is not to find Gascons in Sicily, he has left enough of them at home: he would rather meet Greeks or Persians.[1] In general he avoids the society of Frenchmen abroad: if three of them were alone in the Libyan desert they would immediately start to fight.[2] He makes the classic tourist's complaint that everybody in the streets of Rome addresses him in French.[3] He conforms as far as he can to the customs of the country he is in, as his secretary says, 'car en tant qu'en lui est il se conforme et range aus modes du lieu où il se treuve', and so in Augsburg wears a German fur bonnet.[4] He praises Rome because all foreigners are at home in it and there is no xenophobia.[5] As always he presents another side, and some of his reactions to Italy are indeed those of an insular Frenchman. However, as Guy Desgranges has pointed out,[6] his outlook is strongly contrasted with the nationalism of du Bellay and the Pléiade. As an example of the self-satisfied French attitude he so much detests we might quote Jacques Tahureau (or at least Le Cosmophile, a participant in the *Dialogues*):

... l'instruction d'vn seul homme de bon iugement edifie plus en vne heure, que ne font tous les barragouins & diuers langages de mille nations étrangeres en dix ans.[7]

The dislike of meeting his fellow-countrymen and his willingness to adapt himself to local ways are no doubt fairly superficial (though none the less significant) expressions of his temperament. At a rather deeper level is the love of travel for its own sake, which we have already come upon.[8] In a most revealing passage of the *Journal du voyage* the secretary says of his master (perhaps from dictation):

Je croy à la vérité que, s'il eut été sul avec les siens, il fut allé

[1] III, ix: TR 964.
[2] II, xxvii: TR 675.
[3] *JV*: TR 1204.
[4] *JV*: TR 1157.
[5] *JV*: TR 1236.
[6] 'Montaigne et l'histoire', *French review*, xxiii (1950), 376 n. 22.
[7] *Les dialogues* (1565), ed. Conscience, Paris, 1870, p. 107.
[8] Cf. p. 61 above.

plustost à Cracovie ou vers la Grèce par terre, que de prendre le tour vers l'Italie. . . .

And a little later:

Il disoit aussi: qu'il lui sembloit estre à mesmes ceus qui lisent quelque plaisant conte, d'où il leur prent creinte qu'il vieigne bientost à finir, ou un beau livre; lui de mesme prenoit si grand plesir à voïager à son aise. . . .[1]

The comparison of a journey to a story or a book is particularly striking. This feeling of liberty in travel, real or imaginary, is echoed in still stronger terms in the *Essais*:

Je suis si affady apres la liberté, que qui me deffenderoit l'accez de quelque coin des Indes, j'en vivroys aucunement plus mal à mon aise.[2]

He does not say whether he means the East or the West Indies: in either case what matters is the way in which his imagination is constantly occupied with these distant prospects. Even the most banal reflection can be poetically expanded by this vision of the whole world. Life, he says, is insecure, and risks have to be taken: Caesar incurred debts of a million in gold in order to become Caesar. He then goes straight on, typically, from the highest to the humblest:

Et combien de marchans commencent leur trafique par la vente de leur metairie, qu'ils envoient aux Indes
Tot per impotentia freta ?[3]

Even better, the same illustration for a rather different theme (how reprehensible passions can inspire virtuous actions), is:

puis que l'avarice peut planter au courage d'un garçon de boutique, nourri à l'ombre et à l'oysiveté, l'assurance de se jetter si loing du foyer domestique, à la mercy des vagues et de Neptune courroucé, dans un fraile bateau. . . .[4]

In the last resort, however, Montaigne's cosmopolitanism means, even more than this poetic grasp of the world, a total acceptance of the diversity of human life, a refusal to be bound by prejudices of time and place. Not only every country, he says,

[1] TR 1176–7.
[2] III, xiii: EM iii, 370: TR 1049.
[3] I, xiv: EM i, 76; TR 63–4.
[4] II, i: EM ii, 9; TR 321.

but every city and every profession has its own manners.[1] This diversity is indeed part of the pleasure of travelling: 'La diversité des façons d'une nation à autre ne me touche que par le plaisir de la varieté. Chaque usage a sa raison'[2] (the enclosure of the sentence between the two near-synonyms *diversité* and *varieté* is itself noteworthy). But pleasure points to a deeper lesson, the absurdity of judging by parochial standards, which finds its positive expression in the declaration:

Non parce que Socrates l'a dict, mais parce qu'en verité c'est mon humeur, et à l'avanture non sans quelque excez, j'estime tous les hommes mes compatriotes, et embrasse un Polonois comme un François, postposant cette lyaison nationale à l'universelle et commune.[3]

We have here not only a noble profession of faith in humanity but an anticipation of one of the dominant lines of thought in the seventeenth and eighteenth centuries.

Once again we see the difficulty of compartmentalising Montaigne. However much we try to concentrate on a single aspect of his complex literary personality (here his rendering of external reality), we find that it has necessary implications for the whole of his thought (here leading to the diversity of life, to relativism, and ultimately to liberalism). However, we are now in a position to appreciate better the delicate balance between introspection and awareness of the external world, though it is perhaps not strictly correct to speak of balance. The two sides in fact form an indissoluble unity but not, as we shall see, a static one.

---

[1] I, xiii: TR 49.
[2] III, ix: EM iii, 258; TR 964.
[3] III, ix: EM iii, 240; TR 950.

℀ 6 ℀

Movement and Change

AT the beginning of *Du repentir*, after characterising the
continuous change which is active in all things, even the
most apparently solid, Montaigne makes one of his best-
known and most important statements about himself, his self-
portrait, and his method of delineating it (part of which I have
already quoted:[1]

> Je ne puis asseurer mon object. Il va trouble et chancelant, d'une
> yvresse naturelle. Je le prens en ce point, comme il est, en l'instant
> que je m'amuse à luy. Je ne peints pas l'estre. Je peints le passage:
> non un passage d'aage en autre, ou, comme dict le peuple, de sept
> en sept ans, mais de jour en jour, de minute en minute. Il faut
> accommoder mon histoire à l'heure. Je pourray tantost changer,
> non de fortune seulement, mais aussi d'intention. C'est un contrerolle
> de divers et muables accidens et d'imaginations irresoluës et, quand
> il y eschet, contraires: soit que je sois autre moymesme, soit que je
> saisisse les subjects par autres circonstances et considerations.[2]

In the last three chapters we have considered the *Essais* for the
most part as a single object existing all at once at the same point
of time. Though this is partly true and is in any case necessary
for the purpose of initial understanding, it is also to miss what
constitutes the most profound originality of the work. The self-
portrait is a mobile one, the world described is a world in motion.
The more we examine these lines, the greater their complexity
appears. Not only is the universe in motion but the man who
observes it and the observer of the observer. Nothing, in the inner
or the outer worlds with which, as we have seen, Montaigne is

[1] p. 15 above.
[2] III, ii: EM iii, 20–1; TR 782(*b*).

concerned stays still long enough to be recorded with precision. Contradictions are inevitable, consistency is impossible. So it is that instead of attempting to depict a permanent essence, of things or of himself, which he admits he is unable to seize or comprehend ('nous n'avons aucune communication à l'estre'),[1] he undertakes to represent the *passage,* the movement itself. We must not be misled by the apparent modesty of some of these reflections. He is in fact making what is perhaps as ambitious a claim as any writer has ever made: to register the movement of thought not in crude blocks ('de sept en sept ans'), like a nineteenth-century *Bildungs- roman,* but microscopically, at the moment these changes take place ('de jour en jour, de minute en minute'). The self-portrait and the picture of the world thus receive an extra dimension, that of time. We have already seen that a self-portrait in this detail and depth is something new in literature. The addition of the element of mobility makes the claim quite astonishing, and it is probable that nothing similar was to be attempted until Proust, whom Montaigne in many ways foreshadows. Of course, a claim is not the same as its realisation, and it remains to be seen whether he does it or merely says that he does.[2]

In anticipatory parentheses, another sentence demands atten- tion here: 'Je le prens en ce point, comme il est, en l'instant que je m'amuse à luy'. The dominant tense of the *Essais* (unlike, for example, that of an autobiography) is the present: what he sees, thinks or feels now. This may at first seem in contradiction with the whole idea of movement, since the present tense is normally self-contained, the expression of a state of experience detached from past and future, from origins and consequences. But reflec- tion shows that the present is essentially unstable, a vanishing point in time, which belongs to the past as soon as attention is concentrated on it, is in fact essentially mobile. Montaigne's picture of movement is thus composed of a series of present moments and is implicit in them.[3]

This is indeed a simplification, both of the general character of the present tense and of Montaigne's handling of time. A mere

---

[1] II, xii: EM ii, 366; TR 586.

[2] For a fuller study of the devices by which movement is recorded, see my article, 'Montaigne et la peinture du passage', *Saggi e ricerche di letteratura francese,* iv (1963); also Jean Starobinski, 'Montaigne en mouvement', *Nouvelle revue française* (1960).

[3] On this, and Montaigne's treatment of time in general, see Georges Poulet, *Études sur le temps humain,* 1950, pp. 1–15.

succession of discrete instants, though it would convey a sense of movement, would do it in a very mechanical way. The element of flexibility is introduced largely by the operation of memory (and we have seen that his protestations about his bad memory do not correspond to the facts). Obviously he does not limit himself to the immediate present, nor follow a strictly chronological order; instead he moves backwards and forwards along the skein of his memories:

> Que l'enfance regarde devant elle, la vieillesse derriere: estoit-ce pas ce que signifioit le double visage de Janus? Les ans m'entrainent s'ils veulent, mais à reculons![1]

Or again:

> mon entendement ne va pas tousjours avant, il va à reculons aussi.[2]

This Janus-view, which embraces the present and the past, enables him to survey life and himself with a liberty which is far removed from any mechanical progression. And the variations in the time-scale which ensue are naturally expressed in variations of tense. 'Je suis venu jusques icy bien à mon aise.'[3] Such reflections, marked by the use of the perfect, occur frequently: the second observer pauses to look back and contemplate the path travelled so far. This was an elementary example. A more complex one, which also has an important bearing on the general theme of mobility, is:

> Je veux representer le progrez de mes humeurs, et qu'on voye chaque piece en sa naissance. Je prenderois plaisir d'avoir commencé plustost et à reconnoistre le trein de mes mutations.[4]

The conditional and the perfect infinitive express what might have been: a continuous record of change from the beginning of his intellectual life. But a more detailed study of style will come later. For the moment it is enough to stress that the conception of moving thought is already present in 1580 and does not wait for the Third Book.

With these warnings in mind (the flexibility of the time-scale and the presence of mobility from a quite early stage), we may now return to the central claim, 'de jour en jour, de minute en minute.

---

1 III, v: EM iii, 70; TR 819.
2 III, ix: EM iii, 228; TR 941.
3 II, xi: EM ii, 122; TR 402.
4 II, xxxvii: EM ii, 575; TR 737(a).

Il faut accommoder mon histoire à l'heure.' We have seen that he says he lives from day to day: in fact he says it twice.[1] He had judged something to be so with the whole force of his mind, but every day he discovers that he has changed his mind and that the original judgements were false.[2] This is in the *Apologie* and contributes to the main argument on the unreliability of reason: once again we can perceive the connection between his literary temperament, the inner form of his writing, and the philosophical ideas he puts forward. On the other hand he sometimes for amusement maintains an opinion contrary to his own and then finds that he is convinced by it.[3] The self-portrait and the day-to-day movement are still more firmly linked when he says (again in a relatively early essay):

> Je ne vise icy qu'à découvrir moy mesmes, qui seray par adventure autre demain, si nouveau apprentissage me change.[4]

Here is someone for whom every day begins a new life.

The movement from day to day is on a much finer scale than that which can be measured in seven-year periods (like the intervals between the editions), but it is still broad enough to be perceptible (it is in fact the characteristic procedure of the diarist). Changes from hour to hour and minute to minute are a different matter, and their representation may seem all but impossible. Here it is necessary to introduce another famous passage which, with the beginning of *Du repentir*, constitutes Montaigne's most profound statement about the nature of his work:

> C'est un' espineuse entreprinse, et plus qu'il ne semble, de suivre un' allure si vagabonde que celle de nostre esprit; de penetrer les profondeurs opaques de ses replis internes; de choisir et arreter tant de menus airs de ses agitations.[5]

Once more, the understatement of 'et plus qu'il ne semble' must not lead us to misjudge the truly extraordinary character of the project, at that time or at any time. The implications of the sentence are inexhaustible, the metaphors and the adjectives particularly. At this point it is the first aim that is most relevant, the attempt to follow the wandering motions of the mind. Clearly

1 I, xiv: TR 66(*b*); III, iii: TR 807(*b*). Cf. p. 64 above.
2 II, xii: TR 546(*a*).
3 II, xii: TR 549(*b*).
4 I, xxvi: EM i, 191; TR 147(*a*).
5 II, vi: EM ii, 59; TR 358(*c*).

this *allure* is a movement (literally 'gait'), and to follow it means concerning oneself with intervals of at most a minute: in fact the process is continuous. Here we have the key to Montaigne's depiction of himself and his thought (again the word is chosen for want of a better) in unbroken development. It points to one of his supreme originalities: 'dans la plupart des auteurs, je vois l'homme qui écrit; dans Montaigne, l'homme qui pense', says Montesquieu.[1] In most writers other than poets and novelists, creators of imaginative literature, thought is arranged and frozen by long reflection in neat compartments; in Montaigne it is captured as it rises from its almost unfathomable source.

We have observed a number of references to the broader scales, and there are similar references to the finer scale of hours and minutes.

Ainsi je ne pleuvy aucune certitude, si ce n'est de faire connoistre jusques à quel poinct monte, pour cette heure, la connoissance que j'en ay.[2]

Once again, all the stress is on the moving present; or, with still more far-reaching consequences for the nature of the self-portrait:

Moi asture et moi tantost somes bien deus.[3]

The change from minute to minute finds expression in a cry of alarm which is the more remarkable since it appears in a very early essay, though it may have been interpolated before 1580:

A chaque minute il me semble que je m'eschape.[4]

Montaigne's acute sense of time in its smallest subdivisions comes through very strongly in remarks like these. Of course they, and many like them, are still generalisations, they show his consciousness of his method rather than the method itself. The ways in which he makes visible the progress of his thought as he thinks it and follows the wandering movements of the mind are essentially linguistic and formal, and only a detailed analysis at the verbal level[5] could demonstrate them fully.

---

[1] *Œuvres complètes*, ed. Masson, ii (1950), 200.
[2] II, x: EM ii, 100–1; TR 387.
[3] III, ix: EM iii, 229; TR 941(c).
[4] I, xx: EM i, 108; TR 86(a).
[5] For which see my article 'Montaigne et la peinture du passage'; also F. Gray, *Le style de Montaigne*, 1958.

The principal means he employs is association of ideas. In formal composition ideas are given a logical structure in which points are ordered and treated one by one. In spontaneous thought, whether silent or as in familiar conversation, one thing leads to another without any apparent logical connection and a subsequent attempt at reconstruction suggests that the links are formed by tangential switches of theme. So it is for Montaigne. With his uncanny insight into the workings of his own mind and writing he defines the mechanism quite precisely:

> C'est l'indiligent lectur qui pert mon subjet, non pas moi; il s'en trouvera tousjours en un coin quelque mot qui ne laisse pas d'estre bastant [sufficient], quoi qu'il soit serré. . . . Mon stile et mon esprit vont vagabondant de mesmes.[1]

Style and mind follow the same irregular movement. But it is the 'word in a corner' which gives the key. A typical essay (we must except the *Apologie* and a few others) seems at first to have no order at all, any number of ideas are thrown out, and the link that binds them is hard to see. Yet in fact the result is anything but disjointed: sharp breaks are rare and for most of the time continuity is maintained by words, phrases and allusions which give rise to a new train of thought or take us back to the central subject of the essay. Examples of the latter can be found in two of the most apparently rambling essays, *De la præsumption* and *De la vanité*, where the keywords of the titles recur at strategic points, just when the thread seems irrevocably lost. A single example may suffice to illustrate the former, though every mature essay is full of them. *Des boyteux* starts with the Gregorian calendar, introduced into France in 1581, which opens up a train of reflection on the uncertainty of chronology and the difficulty of keeping a register of things of the past; things are then linked to causes by word-play (*choses* and *causes*, the word in a corner); then we are told that people spend a great deal of time in the search for causes of things that do not exist (anticipating though not mentioning the strange 'fact' about lame people which only comes at the end of the essay); and this leads naturally to a discussion of miracles.[2] So far we have only the overture of the essay. It goes on to opinions and how they are maintained in

[1] III, ix: EM iii, 270; TR 973(c).
[2] III, xi: TR 1002–4. For a fuller analysis of *Des coches* from this point of view, see my article 'Baroque elements in Montaigne', *French studies*, 1954, and pp. 272–4 below.

argument to the detriment of truth, the difficulty of opposing generally held opinions, the need for prudence in judging anything especially in legal decisions (all this mingled with further reflections on causes and miracles), witchcraft trials (the main point of the essay in spite of the title), the unimportance of his own opinions: then a sharp apparent break, the lame and their prowess in love, which is yet linked to the opening argument on causes, and finally the variety of human opinions, the ignorance of things and their causes (*chose* and *causa* together again). This is a very rough summary which fails to convey all the twists and turns of the argument, but at least we can see the glancing fashion in which a Montaigne essay develops, how it is held together by recurrent keywords (in this case *opinion, chose, cause*).

Association operates mainly through vocabulary; it is, viewed linguistically, a semantic phenomenon. But the immediate movement of thought is also expressed by syntactic means, open-ended constructions which look backwards as well as forwards (the Janus-view again), irregularity, inconsequentiality, entangled clauses, ambiguity. A long sentence in Montaigne may occasionally look like a period in Cicero or Bossuet, but close analysis reveals something very different. A single, though difficult, example presents most of these features (we shall have to return to these questions of sentence-structure in a later chapter):

> Il ne nous faut pas aller chercher ce qu'on dict des voisins des cataractes du Nile, et ce que les philosophes estiment de la musique celeste, que les corps de ces cercles, estant solides et venans à se lecher et froter l'un à l'autre en roulant, ne peuvent faillir de produire une merveilleuse harmonie, aux coupures et muances de la quelle se manient les contours et changemens des caroles des astres; mais qu'universelement les ouïes des creatures, endormies come celles des Ægiptiens par la continuation de ce son, ne le peuvent apercevoir, pour grand qu'il soit.[1]

We are at once struck by the complexity of the subordinate clauses, not the ordered complexity of a logical period but each springing, almost gushing, from the one that precedes. This is the general effect but it is not all. Montaigne offers two analogies, one local and one universal, for the way in which custom dulls the senses: the Egyptians do not hear the cataracts of the Nile (from Cicero), people in general do not hear the music of the spheres. But the

---

[1] I, xxiii: EM i, 138; TR 107(*c*).

first analogy ('ce qu'on dit des voisins des cataractes') is left in the air and is gradually merged with the second: only at the end and then obliquely by another subsidiary analogy ('endormies comme celles des Ægiptiens'), is its sense made plain. Each clause serves to explore one of the 'replis internes'. The pattern of the sentence reveals in miniature the pattern of an essay like *Des boyteux*: one thing leads to another and it is only by the closest inspection that we can see how they join. This example is indeed almost too good. The impression given is that of spontaneous thought, but the beauty and intricacy of the imagery and the final unification of the two analogies belong to a different order, that of the work of art, a difficulty to which we shall have to return.

None the less, these examples, few though they are, may help us to understand what Montaigne means by the passage from minute to minute. The very texture of words, sentences, essays, shows us thought in the process of creation, how it moves at a deeper level than logic, without regard for superficial consistency, from one idea or conception to the next. We know that he changes and contradicts himself (though not truth). Here, and on virtually every page, we can watch him changing.

And this brings us back to the general nature of the self-portrait in movement. The opening sentence of *Du repentir* puts it in another way: 'Les autres forment l'homme; je le recite et en represente un particulier bien mal formé....'[1] The others, the didactic systematisers, put forward ideal models for man; he is content to show in some sort of chronological order what one man is like. *Être* and *passage* are already contrasted. But the predominant emphasis is on the instability of the self, the flux which underlies what we are accustomed to think of as a single character or personality:

Non seulement le vent des accidens me remue selon son inclination, mais en outre je me remue et trouble moy mesme par l'instabilité de ma posture....[2]

Je m'entraine quasi où je penche, comment que ce soit, et m'emporte de mon pois.[3]

Et quand seray-je à bout de representer une continuelle agitation et mutation de mes pensées ...?[4]

[1] III, ii: EM iii, 20; TR 782.
[2] II, i: EM ii, 6; TR 318–9(*b*).
[3] II, xii: EM ii, 316; TR 549(*b*).
[4] III, ix: EM iii, 204; TR 923.

These statements are a few among many, a persistent leitmotiv. Once again the parallel with Proust is irresistible. In order to grasp the phenomenon we have stressed the divisions, *de minute en minute,* but what confronts us is a personality in continuous change.

So far we have been considering movement in the self-portrait, but some examples have already suggested generalisation and extension from the self to man. It is indeed clear enough that mobility is not confined to the writer of the *Essais,* it is a universal characteristic of humanity: 'Nostre vie n'est que mouvement.'[1] This is from the final essay, but we find it plainly stated long before in a well-known sentence in the first essay of all: 'Certes c'est un subject merveilleusement vain, divers, et ondoyant, que l'homme.'[2] Without necessarily accepting Villey's date of 1578 for the whole essay (one among several hypotheses),[3] we cannot doubt that this sentence must have been written at a much later date than the position of the essay might lead us to believe: still, it is present in 1580 and we can conclude that a mature view is firmly established by the time of the publication of the first edition. The theme, like that of movement in the self, runs through the *Essais,* but one essay in particular is centred on it, *De l'inconstance de nos actions* (II, i). It has been plausibly suggested by Villey[4] that *De l'inconstance,* at the beginning of Book II, echoes *Par divers moyens on arrive à pareille fin* at the beginning of Book I, which contains the 'vain divers et ondoyant' passage: this heavy emphasis on the theme affords evidence of its primordial importance for Montaigne, at least at the moment of the first edition. In spite of its brevity, *De l'inconstance de nos actions* offers the most complete account Montaigne gives of the dissolution of the personality into an assemblage of multiple facets, with the consequent impossibility of pinning any single personality down. It is here, probably, that he comes closest to Proust. Against the universal flux he sets an ideal of constancy and singleness of purpose, but it is presented as largely unrealisable. The contrast has unexpected implications for history and criticism. Even good writers, he remarks most penetratingly, try to reduce a man to an image of consistency, forcing his actions into the same mould; when he

---

[1] III, xiii: EM iii, 402; TR 1074(*b*).
[2] I, i: EM i, 6; TR 13(*a*).
[3] *Sources et évolution,* i, 348–9.
[4] ibid.

does something which will not fit they attribute it to dissimulation.[1] He is talking about history, but what he says applies also to literature as interpretations of Molière's *Misanthrope* testify. There are other consequences of human inconstancy, spread through the *Essais*. Movement and continuous change belong to the body as well as to the mind, and the two, as always in Montaigne, are closely associated:

> Il est certain que nostre apprehension, nostre jugement et les facultez de nostre ame en general souffrent selon les mouvemens et alterations du corps, lesquelles alterations sont continuelles.[2]

This is from the *Apologie,* and the conclusion drawn shortly afterwards is that, since the body with its continual changes exerts a powerful influence on the mind and judgement there is scarcely a single hour in a human life when the judgement achieves an unperturbed efficacity.[3] Once again the central thread of the *Apologie* joins the central thread of the whole work. Of these alterations in the body the broadest and most universal is the process of aging:

> Mais conduicts par sa main, d'une douce pente et comme insensible, peu à peu, de degré en degré, elle [nature] nous roule dans ce miserable estat, et nous y apprivoise.[4]

This is the movement of life itself, gradual and imperceptible like the movement of thought in the *Essais*. On the other hand, beliefs and opinions possess a life and movement of their own, apart from the body and, indeed, apart from the individuals who hold them: 'elles ont leur revolution, leur saison, leur naissance, leur mort, comme les chous.'[5] The jokingly trivial comparison gives added point to an observation which has something of Vico about it and points towards the history of ideas.

It must be admitted, however, that apart from occasional insights like this one the notion of the human mind as essentially mobile and unstable is less profoundly original than the working out of the same notion in the self-portrait. In *De l'inconstance de nos actions* much comes from Seneca on the same theme.[6] Even

---

[1] II, i: TR 315.
[2] II, xii: EM ii, 313; TR 547.
[3] II, xii: TR 548.
[4] I, xx: EM i, 112; TR 89(*b*).
[5] II, xii: EM ii, 329; TR 559.
[6] The *Epistles*; cf. EM iv.

more telling is the close of the *Apologie,* where we find not only 'Nous n'avons aucune communication à l'estre' but also:

> Finalement, il n'y a aucune constante existence, ny de nostre estre, ny de celuy des objects. Et nous, et nostre jugement, et toutes choses mortelles, vont coulant et roulant sans cesse.[1]

This sums up on the most universal plane the conception of movement which we have studied in the details of its working. It is central to an understanding of Montaigne. Yet it is derived in essentials from Amyot's Plutarch, quoted verbatim a little later:

> Car c'est chose mobile que le temps, et qui apparoit comme en ombre, avec la matiere coulante et fluante tousjours, sans jamais demeurer stable ny permanente.[2]

In the first passage Montaigne (if he has not taken it from some other classical source) has endowed the idea with a greater sense of urgency, almost of panic, which contrasts with the calm majesty of Plutarch, but the idea itself is the same. The notion of universal human mutability is in fact a commonplace of both ancient (or Renaissance) and Christian thought.[3] But it is pointless to assess the originality of a writer, especially in the sixteenth century, by marking off borrowings and plagiarisms like these. What Montaigne has done is to extend and deepen the concept of mutability, using it as an organising principle which pervades his whole work, dominating its thought and giving life to its form.

These last quotations remind us that not only the individual self, not only humanity, but the whole world is in a state of flux. We may now return to the opening of *Du repentir* and consider the passage which precedes that quoted at the beginning of this chapter:

> Le monde n'est qu'une branloire perenne. Toutes choses y branlent sans cesse: la terre, les rochers du Caucase, les pyramides d'Ægypte, et du branle public et du leur. La constance mesme n'est autre chose qu'un branle plus languissant.[4]

The words *branle, branloire, branler,* all denoting movement, especially a dancing or oscillatory movement, are among

---

[1] II, xii: EM ii, 366; TR 586.
[2] II, xii: EM ii, 369; TR 588. Cf. *Les œuvres morales,* Paris, 1572, f. 357ʳ; and p. 36 above.
[3] For the idea in its commonplace form cf.: 'As tu perdu la memoire de l'instabilité et incertitude des choses ?' (Bruès, *Dialogues,* ed. Morphos, p. 108).
[4] III, ii: EM iii, 20; TR 782.

Montaigne's favourites. Here we see further evidence of his complexity and perhaps a sort of scientific intuition. The phrase 'et du branle public et du leur' is not easy to explain. Clearly everything has not a single but a double movement, its own and that of the world in general. In what exactly this movement consists he does not say, but the conjunction with the reference to the moving earth suggests that he took the theories of Copernicus more seriously than the brief account in the *Apologie* might lead one to suppose. The sense is perfectly plain in terms of modern science; in terms of sixteenth-century cosmology it is less easy to understand.[1] It is tempting to conclude that we are confronted here with an instinctive grasp of recent discoveries which hardly became public and general before Galileo. Again we might compare Pascal on the two infinities: of course, as we saw earlier, Montaigne lacks Pascal's technical command of scientific questions but both share a gift for perceiving the human consequences of theories which appear to have only technical interest. There is indeed a simpler explanation, that Montaigne was imbued with the philosophers of antiquity and their views on the flux of all things, but this explanation is by no means incompatible with the first. Finally, the last sentence of the passage quoted suggests that constancy, or stability, is itself only a slower motion. This represents an advance on *De l'inconstance de nos actions*, where constancy was recognised as possible if unlikely. The notion of mobility has now dissolved all that is apparently most resistant to change.

Movement and change then are everywhere present, in the continents themselves (another curious anticipation of recent discoveries):

(*b*) Il semble qu'il y aye des mouvemens, (*c*) naturels les uns, les autres (*b*) fievreux, en ces grands corps, comme aux nostres.[2]

in seas and rivers and sand.[3] This applies too, as we should expect, to human institutions, to war,[4] to the French language,[5] to political states especially:

Les maladies et conditions de nos corps se voyent aussi aux estats

[1] Rat's explanation (TR 1620), 'le mouvement de lente désagrégation qui se produit dans chacune des choses créées', does not seem wholly convincing, though this may be taken as one of the complex processes involved.
[2] I, xxxi: EM i, 266; TR 201.
[3] I, xxxi: TR 201–2.
[4] II, xv: TR 601.
[5] III, ix: TR 961.

et polices: les royaumes, les republiques naissent, fleurissent et fanissent de vieillesse, comme nous.[1]

The idea of the rise and decline of empires is, it is true, as much of a commonplace as that of mutability itself; what is slightly less so is the relating of political change to physiological, and very much less so the consistent working out of the theme in all the aspects of thought and feeling. But a much more far-reaching and personal rendering of the same phenomenon can be found in:

Le pis que je trouve en nostre estat, c'est l'instabilité, et que nos loix, non plus que nos vestemens, ne peuvent prendre aucune forme arrestée.[2]

Here the movement of institutions and laws is likened to the movement of fashion in clothes. The full implications of this will require further consideration: for the moment it may be noted that instability, though inherent in the nature of things, is not necessarily or always a subject of approval. Still larger, and probably more original, ideas are adumbrated when to historical change is added the difference between historical periods:

si nous voyons tantost fleurir un art, une opinion, tantost une autre, par quelque influance celeste; tel siecle produire telles natures et incliner l'humain genre à tel ou tel ply; les espris des hommes tantost gaillars, tantost maigres, comme nos chams. . . .[3]

We have seen that Montaigne often seems to ignore this difference when he is talking about the details of history; at any rate he shows here that he is well aware of the principle. He is now trembling on the verge of the idea of progress, later to play such a capital part in the intellectual history of Europe. He actually states it, at least in outline, in one of the late additions to the last essay:

Nos opinions s'antent les unes sur les autres. La premiere sert de tige à la seconde, la seconde à la tierce. Nous eschelons ainsi de degré en degré. Et avient de là que le plus haut monté ha souvant plus d'honneur que de merite; car il n'est monté que d'un grain sur les espaules du penultime.[4]

Anticipated by Bruès, Bodin and others, he here anticipates Bacon, Descartes, Pascal, and Fontenelle, all those who in the following

---

1 II, xxiii: EM ii, 476; TR 662–3.
2 II, xvii: EM ii, 441; TR 639.
3 II, xii: EM ii, 330; TR 559–60(*b*).
4 III, xiii: EM iii, 366; TR 1046(*c*).

century helped to give shape to the idea of progress.[1] The argument of the first of these two quotations, though offering a different solution, touches on the central problem of Fontenelle's *Digression sur les anciens et les modernes*. It must be admitted that Montaigne's statement of it is a grudging admission rather than a splendid vision (flux and progress are not at all the same thing), but it is one possible variation on the principle of ubiquitous movement and so finds a necessary if unobtrusive place. In particular, the analogy of the man climbing on the shoulders of his predecessor has a long history, going back at least to Bernard of Chartres in the twelfth century.[2] It is later taken up by, among others, Mersenne and, in a modified form, Pascal.[3] Montaigne is thus himself a link in a long chain.

This, though important for later history, occupies only an incidental place in the *Essais*. Much more characteristic of Montaigne is the rejection of scientific pretensions to knowledge of the world:

> Et de cette mesme image du monde qui coule pendant que nous y sommes, combien chetive et racourcie est la cognoissance des plus curieux![4]

Something so fluid can hardly be seized, at least by purely intellectual means. But it can be felt:

> Tout ne branle-il pas vostre branle? Y a-il chose qui ne vieillisse quant et vous? Mille hommes, mille animaux et mille autres creatures meurent en ce mesme instant que vous mourez.[5]

This is partly inspired by Seneca, but it conveys something more, Montaigne's sense of the union of the individual and the cosmos.

---

[1] For its general development see J. B. Bury, *The idea of progress*, 1920; Hubert Gillot, *La querelle des anciens et des modernes en France*, 1914. Neither, however, mentions these crucial statements in Montaigne, to which should be added a third, the passage in the *Apologie* where he remarks that what is unknown to one century is revealed to the next and that sciences and arts are not created all at once but are gradually brought to perfection (II, xii: TR 543).

[2] See Pierre Kohler, *Lettres de France*, 1943, p. 40; H. Gouhier, 'Les philosophes du XVIIe siècle devant l'histoire de la philosophie', *XVIIe siècle*, 54–5 (1962), pp. 6–7; D. dalla Valle, 'L'italianisme dans les poétiques baroques françaises', *XVIIe siècle*, 79 (1968), pp. 4, 11; and for a full discussion G. Sarton and others in *Isis*, xxiv–xxvi (1935–6).

[3] Pascal, *Œuvres*, ed. Brunschvicg, ii (1908), 137.

[4] III, vi: EM iii, 157; TR 886.

[5] I, xx: EM i, 118; TR 93.

✠ 7 ✠

The Human Condition

BUT, by another reversal, mobility is not all. Again at the beginning of *Du repentir* comes another fundamental statement:

> Je propose une vie basse et sans lustre, c'est tout un. On attache aussi bien toute la philosophie morale à une vie populaire et privée que à une vie de plus riche estoffe: chaque homme porte la forme entiere de l'humaine condition.[1]

The sense of the celebrated final phrase is perhaps more precise than a cursory reading might suggest. *Condition,* clearly enough, means the general disposition of human nature. *Forme* seems to be used in the technical sense of scholastic philosophy: the essential shape which marks humanity and to which individual differences can be accommodated[2] (Florio's translation 'stamp' gets very close to it). Thus this sentence is not contradicted by the numerous details we have observed of highly personal habits and idiosyncrasies. Still, it has moved a considerable way (another example of *passage*) from the opening sentence of the same essay ('je le recite et en represente un particulier bien mal formé'). He is now claiming to represent not just a single individual but the whole of moral philosophy and the whole of humanity, a big step from the total preoccupation with the self which we examined in chapter 4.

---

1 III, ii: EM iii, 21; TR 782(*b*).
2 See the helpful note in *Trois essais,* ed. Gougenheim and Schuhl, 1951, p. 67. Cf. also Bruès:
> Ronsard. Mais je considere universellement sa forme [i.e. man's] . . .
> Baïf. O grande et admirable excellence de l'homme! ô divine condition
>   d'iceluy!
> (*Dialogues,* ed. Morphos, p. 177.)

As in all aspects of Montaigne, the central theme itself has its antithetical term, without which it cannot be fully understood. Yet it would be a mistake to assume, as is sometimes done, that the extension of the self to embrace humanity is an innovation of 1588 and the Third Book. We have already seen how the feeling of mobility is carried on from the self-portrait to man generally. And there are plenty of indications of this generalising tendency from quite an early stage in the development of the *Essais*. At the very beginning, in an essay dated 1572 by Villey, Montaigne writes (we must add the usual warning that the passage may have been interpolated later):

> comme il nous advient à la chaude alarme d'une bien mauvaise nouvelle, de nous sentir saisis, transis, et comme perclus de tous mouvemens, de façon que l'ame se relaschant apres aux larmes et aux plaintes, semble se desprendre, se demesler et se mettre plus au large, et à son aise.[1]

The *nous* form here is indeed fairly banal in itself but we can feel the pressure of personal experience pushing through, inseparably from human experience in general. More to the point is:

> ... en l'estude que je fay, duquel le subject c'est l'homme. ...[2]

This stands, apparently at least, in stark contradiction with the frequent statements we have quoted to the effect that his subject is himself alone. It is from a later essay (?1578-9), but once again we see that a fundamental position is firmly stated before 1580. Nevertheless, and again as usual, it only finds its complete and mature expression in the Third Book and later. The process of development can be clarified by the textual history of a sentence in *Des livres*, which we have already discussed in part.[3] In the 1580 edition, as we saw, the reasons he gives for his liking for history are principally the consideration of the characters of different men and the customs of different nations, which form the true subject of moral science. This already bears a close resemblance to the key statement of *Du repentir*, but it remains an observation about historians, it is not related to what Montaigne himself is doing. It is allowed to stand in 1588, but in the Bordeaux Copy it becomes:

[1] I, ii: EM i, 10-11; TR 16(*a*).
[2] II, xvii: EM ii, 411; TR 617(*a*).
[3] p. 42 above.

Les Historiens sont ma droite bale: ils sont plaisans et aysez; et quant et quant l'home en general, de qui je cherche la conoissance, y paret plus vif et plus entier qu'en nul autre lieu, la diversité et verité de ses conditions internes en gros et en destail, la varieté des moïens de son assemblage et des accidans qui le menacent.[1]

Now history is seen as something which serves his own purpose, the search for knowledge of man in general, not essentially different from the formulation quoted earlier ('duquel le subject c'est l'homme') but thought out and elaborated in a subtly discriminating series of facets. We have here the approximate equivalent for the human condition of the 'espineuse entreprinse' passage for the self-portrait, the statement of a programme (though the word is hardly appropriate to Montaigne's glancing approach to things).

However, in recording the growing emphasis on universal significance we must not forget the simultaneously developing self-portrait; we must not abandon one idea to concentrate on another (a fatal error in dealing with Montaigne). The self-portrait too is affected by the stress on universality. Still in the astonishingly rich opening of *Du repentir*:

Les autheurs se communiquent au peuple par quelque marque particuliere et estrangiere; moi le premier par mon estre universel, comme Michel de Montaigne, non comme grammerien ou poete ou jurisconsulte.[2]

This is a variant on the contrast we have noticed between writing and thinking: writers in general appear as specialists, offering to the reader some sort of professional competence; Montaigne (the first, he says, in another bold but justified claim) presents the whole of himself, the man and not just the writer. So far this is a deepening, a stronger affirmation, of what he has already often said about his aim of painting himself; certainly there is no contradiction, though the emphasis is different. But later in the same essay he puts it in another way:

il n'est personne, s'il s'escoute, qui ne descouvre en soy une forme sienne, une forme maistresse, qui luicte contre l'institution, et contre la tempeste des passions qui luy sont contraires.[3]

[1] II, x: EM ii, 113; TR 396.
[2] III, ii: EM iii, 21; TR 782(c).
[3] III, ii: EM iii, 29–30; TR 789.

This is more serious. It seems that, in spite of what he has said so often before, there is a central part of the character which remains the same, which does not move, which is separate from the passions and impervious to education, good or bad. And, of course, he speaks of characters as if they could all be reduced to a single law, no longer maintaining the uniqueness of himself as an individual. The contradiction exists, certainly, but it can be resolved. Once more the key lies in the word *forme*: it is not a part of the character but an outline or general shape, within which diversity and mobility continue to operate; and it is not impervious to passions and education but struggles against them, a struggle which in itself is enough to create the agitation and flux we are now so familiar with. Nor, in a wider sense, is there an insoluble contradiction between the self-portrait and the effort to generalise from the self to man. The play of internal and external observation was bound sooner or later (but in fact from the beginning) to include the observation of humanity: it may be doubted whether complete self-absorption is possible even for the most dedicated introspective. But, as in other respects, the conscious realisation of the unity of self-portrait and general anthropology was a gradual one, though always present potentially. And to the end he maintains the movement between the two poles of individuality and universality, as in a late interpolation:

> Nous empeschons nos pensees du general et des causes et conduites universelles, qui se conduisent tres bien sans nous, et laissons en arriere nostre faict et Michel qui nous touche encore de plus pres que l'home.[1]

There is no contradiction, but to understand Montaigne it is necessary always to hold two ideas in the mind at once, never to forget the antithetical organisation of his thought.

A minor contradiction, closely tied to the last and less easy to reduce to unity, arises between the denial of didactic intention ('Je n'enseigne poinct, je raconte')[2] and its affirmation. As long as he is only talking about himself, his moods and passing fancies, he can claim that they have no wider meaning; but once he has posited a necessary resemblance between himself and the rest of mankind he is bound to regard what he says as a lesson, if only negatively:

[1] III, ix: EM iii, 213; TR 929(*c*).
[2] III, ii: EM iii, 23; TR 784.

Ce qui me sert, peut aussi par accident servir à un autre.[1]

Publiant et accusant mes imperfections, quelqu'un apprendra de les craindre.[2]

We need not try too hard to resolve this contradiction: it is part of the picture of changing attitudes, and even here ('par accident', 'mes imperfections') a place is reserved for the inalienably individual.

Montaigne, then, paints himself but he also paints humanity in himself. There is no contradiction, the two are inextricably mingled. One or two more examples may be adduced to make this vital point unmistakably plain. At the end of the description of himself in love which we have considered as an example of introspection he continues:

Nous ne sommes jamais sans maladie. Les fièvres ont leur chaud et leur froid; des effects d'une passion ardente nous retombons aux effects d'une passion frilleuse.[3]

With the passage from 'I' to 'we' introspection has turned to generality. Similarly, after the still deeper introspection of *De l'exercitation* and the account of his brush with death he goes on to draw conclusions, in a page of remarkable analysis, about the feelings of those who are really dying. Both examples are from 1580, further evidence of the early development of a link between the self and humanity in general.

Given that one of his main subjects is the description of the human condition, we are bound to discuss, at any rate in outline, what his view of it is. This is an arduous undertaking, partly because his view is itself in motion (though with some permanent underlying features), partly because no idea he expresses – and he expresses ideas on most topics of general human concern – is entirely irrelevant to it. It must include his conception of man and his life, of psychology and morality, and also, in the same duality as we have already noticed, of man's place in the world and his relation to nature. To speak of Montaigne as a philosopher is a little dangerous. He receives scant attention in professional histories of philosophy and even an admirer like Thibaudet denies

[1] II, vi: EM ii, 59; TR 357(c).
[2] III, viii: EM iii, 174; TR 899(b). It will be noticed that these and similar statements all seem to be late.
[3] II, xii: EM ii, 321; TR 552(a). Cf. p. 71 above.

him the title precisely because he is immersed in the *fieri*, becoming, rather than concerned with the essence of things.[1] The reason for the disqualification is not self-evident, but it has to be admitted that Montaigne's depiction of thought in its spontaneous stage, which we have seen to constitute his greatest originality, also separates him from nearly all philosophers (except Plato?), since philosophers furnish particularly apposite examples of thought frozen into logical forms. At the same time, Montaigne has much to say about philosophy, in its most restricted as well as in its broader senses, and some consideration of his position with regard to philosophical schools and problems is unavoidable.

We may begin with a fairly general question, his estimate of man in terms of optimism and pessimism. Both attitudes have been attributed to him, and with some show of reason: on the one hand the sceptic and Pyrrhonian who demolishes human reason and human dignity with it (taken by Pascal in the *Entretien avec M. de Saci sur Épictète et Montaigne* as the embodiment of man's misery without God), on the other the champion of the dignity and beauty of life against all bigotry or asceticism. Perhaps, as Villey argues, a chronological solution may explain the discrepancy, there may simply be an evolution from one position to the other; but this should not be assumed without careful examination of the evidence.

Certainly the *Apologie* presents a long and terrible picture of man's presumption, irrationality, and unrelieved worthlessness, both intrinsically and in comparison with the rest of the animal kingdom (it is no wonder that Pascal took so much from this essay).

La presomption est nostre maladie naturelle et originelle. La plus calamiteuse et fraile de toutes les creatures, c'est l'homme, et quant et quant la plus orgueilleuse.[2]

This strikes the keynote and is confirmed and substantiated in various ways throughout the essay. Calvin himself seems less deeply hostile to human nature. Montaigne's attitude is the more remarkable since Sabunde, whose apologia he is supposed to be writing, puts forward a highly optimistic view of man, excessively so, we may think, from the point of view of strict Christian orthodoxy. The *Theologia naturalis* is a paean of praise to the creation

---

[1] *Montaigne*, p. 418.
[2] II, xii: EM ii, 158; TR 429(*a*).

and man's noble place in it, quite at variance with both Montaigne and the Augustinian tradition:

> Aussi est-il assis au plus eslevé et plus digne lieu de l'univers [Montaigne, as we have seen, says 'la pire, plus morte et croupie partie de l'univers'] comme estant à la verité l'Empereur, le Roy, l'honneur de la nature.[1]

Everything in nature is made only for the service of man:

> Toute la gloire qui seroit au soleil, pour sa lumineuse grandeur est demeuree à l'homme, l'homme seul en joüist: par quoy c'est pour nostre seul contentement que toutes les choses ont ce qu'elles ont.[2]

Again Montaigne says the exact opposite.[3] It is true that Sabunde cannot entirely overlook the Fall, and when he comes to it he speaks in terms not too far removed from those of Montaigne.[4] However, it is the glory of man that predominates, even here where he is being denounced for his betrayal of it.

Though the *Apologie* is a special case, a similar contempt for mankind is frequent in the first two books.

> Tant sage qu'il voudra, mais en fin c'est un homme: qu'est il plus caduque, plus miserable et plus de neant?[5]

This note of disdainful misanthropy seems to be confined to the early stages of the *Essais*, and we may suspect a certain amount of bookish influence as in the close imitation of Seneca where life itself becomes an object of scorn (a nameless Stoic is speaking): 'Ce n'est pas grand' chose que vivre, tes valets et les bestes vivent.'[6] This is a fairly typical piece of Stoical detachment, frequent in the essays of 1580 dealing with death, like this one (*De juger de la mort d'autruy*) or *Que philosopher, c'est apprendre à mourir*. But it foreshadows a more famous version of the same thought, Villiers de l'Isle-Adam's 'Vivre? les serviteurs feront cela pour nous!'[7] Without suggesting that Villiers derived the idea from Montaigne, we may perceive an unexpected link between Stoicism and aestheticism, through the figure of the dandy and his cultivation of a sort of ataraxia.

---

[1] Montaigne's translation. *Œuvres complètes*, ed. Armaingaud, ix, 172.
[2] ibid., ix, 160.
[3] II, xii: TR 427.
[4] *Œuvres complètes*, ed. Armaingaud, x, 104.
[5] II, ii: EM ii, 19; TR 328(*a*).
[6] II, xiii: EM ii, 377; TR 594(*a*).
[7] *Axël*, Paris, 1890, p. 283.

E

This was something of a digression. Though much less common, similar expressions of disdain for man and life are to be found in the final stage, for example:

Nostre propre et peculiere condition est autant ridicule que risible.[1]

Nulle particuliere qualité n'enorgueillira celluy qui mettera quand et quand en conte tant de imparfaictes et foibles qualitez autres qui sont en luy, et, au bout, la nihilité de l'humaine condition.[2]

Il nous faut abestir pour nous assagir, et nous esblouir pour nous guider.[3]

The last anticipates, and no doubt inspired, a well-known and controversial passage in Pascal.[4] It must be admitted that all these are additions to 1580 essays and therefore likely to have been a continuation of their argument rather than completely new thoughts. Moreover, there is, in the first and last at any rate, a subtly different emphasis: in the first man is laughable rather than utterly miserable; in the last wisdom lies through ignorance (or stupidity), as earlier, but it is attainable and the passage is by no means wholly pessimistic. The same goes for an essay like *De la vanité* (III, ix) which certainly illustrates human folly but does it on the whole in a more indulgent and tolerant way than the *Apologie* and the other early essays quoted.

It is hardly necessary at this point to give examples of the acceptance of life found in the Third Book: it will require fuller treatment later on. For the moment we can say that it is already present, if not fully developed, in 1580, for instance in *De l'institution des enfans*, where the celebrated addition of the Bordeaux Copy on the pleasantness and easiness of virtue is preceded by the representation of philosophy as gay and festive rather than frowning and terrible, a passage already present in 1580.[5]

Villey's chronological evolution is thus largely justified in its broad lines as far as this aspect of Montaigne is concerned. Yet it needs to be flexibly argued. Once again we are confronted with two poles of thought. Man is a frail creature but if he recognises his limitations he is capable of a kind of greatness. The two

[1] I, 1: EM i, 390; TR 292(c).
[2] II, vi: EM ii, 62; TR 360(c).
[3] II, xii: EM ii, 213; TR 472(c).
[4] *Pensées*, ed. Lafuma, 1951, i, 240.
[5] I, xxvi: TR 160.

poles are harmonically connected, there is no fundamental contradiction; the first tends to dominate in the earlier essays, the second in the later, but they exercise their influence throughout. Man has an infinite capacity for good and evil, as a sentence from the 1580 edition shows: 'L'homme est capable de toutes choses, comme d'aucunes.'[1] Montaigne, capable of misanthropy and of faith in humanity, by giving vigorous, even exaggerated expression to both achieves a realistic balance between them.

Bearing this general view in mind and turning now to more limited aspects of the human condition, it seems reasonable to begin with one where the capacities of man are most completely engaged, education. Any model of education inevitably depends on a view of what human beings should ideally be; conversely, any view of man is partly conditioned by our view of his beginnings. Montaigne's theory of education has been much discussed, both in itself and in relation to educational history generally, so that here only a brief summary is required.[2] It is contained for the most part in *De l'institution des enfans* and, to some extent, in the preceding essay, *Du pedantisme*. The latter is mainly about schoolmasters, the former about methods of education from the point of view of the child. Together they form an admirable diptych. The *Institution*, though there are some references to schools, is primarily concerned, as in the case of Rousseau's *Émile*, with a single boy and the programme for his education by a tutor. This in a sense, and the same objection has been levelled against Rousseau, reduces the value of the model since it can only be practised with the children of the rich. For Montaigne the objection has some force: he was brought up in this way himself before he went to school (his autobiographical account of his own education is not the least valuable part of the essay), he was advising a great lady, the Comtesse de Gurson, on the education of her unborn son, and this no doubt seemed to him the natural path for a young nobleman to follow. But for both him and Rousseau there is perhaps a more important reason. By concentrating on a single child it was possible to bring out the requisites of an ideal education, which consideration of classes, discipline, and application to a variety of individuals would have made difficult: at least a loss of clarity would have resulted. In this respect also

[1] II, xii: EM ii, 308–9; TR 543(*a*).
[2] See particularly Paul Porteau, *Montaigne et la vie pédagogique de son temps*, 1935; Jean Chateau, *Montaigne psychologue et pédagogue*, 1964.

one man may be held to represent the human condition. Montaigne's child is a boy and though there are incidental remarks in other essays on female education he does not seem to have taken the subject very seriously. He is here at least the product of his time and more particularly, no doubt, of his class.

His own education at home was, as he describes it, a notable example of the application of the new principles of the Renaissance. He was woken by music, to avoid too brutal a shock, and he was taught Latin by a German tutor before he could speak Périgourdin or French, no one being allowed to use the vernacular in his presence.[1] This early use of the direct method was by no means confined to Montaigne's father. We find it suggested by Sir Thomas Elyot, before Montaigne was born:

> And if a childe do begyn therin at seven yeres of age, he may continually lerne greke autours thre yeres, and in the meane tyme use the latin tonge as a familiar langage: whiche in a noble manne's sonne may well come to passe, havynge none other persons to serue him or kepyng hym company, but such as can speake latine elegantly.[2]

Agrippa d'Aubigné claims to have learned Latin, Greek and Hebrew by the same method from his tutor Jean Cottin and to have known them all at the age of six.[3] We have here further evidence of the aristocratic background of Montaigne's educational ideas. He dislikes schools, both his own (the Collège de Guyenne) and in general, giving a ferocious picture of a typical scene of flogging and cries of terror.[4] Porteau argues that this picture is false, quoting a number of books to show that most writers of the time were on the side of leniency.[5] But the books were written by schoolmasters and the fact that they spend so much time in denying the need for savage punishment suggests that there was a great deal of it about. Montaigne undoubtedly writes from personal experience and describes an important part, though not the whole, of sixteenth-century school life. However, we are not so much concerned here with the historical or autobiographical truth of what he writes as with the conclusion he draws from his description, the contrast between what is and what ought to be:

---

[1] I, xxvi: TR 172-4.
[2] *The boke named The gouernour* (1531), ed. Croft, London, 1880, i, 54.
[3] *Memoires*, ed. Lalanne, Paris, 1889, p. 4.
[4] I, xxvi: TR 165.
[5] *Montaigne et la vie pédagogique*, pp. 82-99.

Combien leurs classes seroint plus decemment jonchees de fleurs
et de feuillee que de tronçons d'osier sanglans. J'y fairois portraire
la joye, l'alegresse, et Flora, et les graces, come fit en son escole le
philosophe Speusippus.[1]

This is a late addition, and the emphasis on joy in education is
stronger than in the original text of the essay. None the less this
humanity and the classical aura which surrounds it are wholly
typical.

The remarks on schools and colleges are incidental and the
single pupil, as we have seen, occupies the centre of interest. It
would be possible to examine in detail Montaigne's very interesting prescriptions for various departments of education: it seems
better to sum up the general spirit. Two principles are emphasised above all (in the end they are perhaps the same principle):
education as a preparation for life rather than for the transmission of learning; education as the training of judgement rather
than memory. Under the first we can include the place given to
physical education, with its Stoical implications, to the world and
society in educational formation, and to liberty in education: the
pupil must be taught to avoid evil not through lack of strength
or knowledge but through an effort of will, a doctrine which has
an important bearing on Montaigne's moral values generally.
Under the second comes in particular the insistence on critical
examination by the pupil of everything he is told; he must digest
and not merely ingurgitate. This is important not only because
it differentiates Montaigne from Rabelais and the early Renaissance, when the principle of magisterial authority was still powerful, nor because it anticipates the subsequent history of educational
theory, especially Rousseau, but because it prepares the way for
the development of the critical rationalism of the seventeenth
century. Books are not rejected (how could they be by
Montaigne?), but he condemns those who keep boys at them for
fourteen or fifteen hours a day, again a sign of disillusionment with
Rabelais, the early Renaissance, and the 'abîme de science'. From
this point of view, history is particularly valuable provided that
it is made an exercise of judgement not of facts, the opposite of
what Rousseau later says.[2] What emerges is that, as might be
expected, Montaigne's view of education is a fairly exact reflection

[1] I, xxvi: EM i, 215; TR 165(c).
[2] On all this see I, xxvi, *passim*.

of his general view of man and life: in particular we see that even in this relatively early essay the attitude towards them is fundamentally one of joyful acceptance. It is not surprising that he should regard education as the most important branch of human knowledge:[1] the context may have had some influence on the expression of this opinion at this moment, but it fits in with one side at least of his general purpose, the continuous exercise and training of judgement.

With education goes learning, principally discussed in *Du pedantisme*. Here we can be still briefer, since Montaigne's aristocratic prejudices are more in evidence and, as the title suggests, he gives us little more than a caricature of the contemporary scholar. Still, deeper considerations are involved, and some of the themes of the essay on education are already apparent, especially the view that learning must serve life rather than remain apart from it, that men of learning often err through lack of judgement, that parrot-learning is worse than useless, that moral considerations are uppermost: 'Toute autre science est dommageable à celuy qui n'a la science de la bonté.'[2] Here at least he is not far from Rabelais. But there is more than this. The critique of the learned leads naturally to praise of the unlearned, the critique of learning, balanced though it is, to the praise of ignorance. In this way, once more, a tangential theme, the mockery of men of learning, turns out to be intimately connected with a major one, scepticism and the uncertainty of all knowledge. It would be wrong, however, to leave the question without noticing that there is, as usual, another side. Learning is criticised, it is not rejected or despised, except in the persons of some of its more absurd practitioners. He denies that learning necessarily suffocates the mind: 'Mais il en va autrement: car nostre ame s'eslargit d'autant plus qu'elle se remplit.'[3] Here is a declaration of faith which again recalls Rabelais and shows that the spirit of the Renaissance is still living in Montaigne.

After education comes the life of the mature man, and among its particular aspects which he discusses the most important, and in some ways neglected, is that of marriage and sex. We have seen that he does not take female education very seriously. He makes fun of *femmes savantes* and the men who teach them, with more

[1] I, xxvi: TR 147.
[2] I, xxv: EM i, 182; TR 140.
[3] I, xxv: EM i, 172; TR 133.

than a hint of the spirit of Molière. Rhetoric, astrology, logic, all these make women sound ridiculous.[1] But, and here a more serious note enters, there are branches of knowledge which suit a woman's faculties and situation—poetry, history, some parts of philosophy: 'Voila, pour le plus, la part que je leur assignerois aux sciences.'[2] This seems pretty contemptuous. However, it should not be overlooked that these are just the subjects which Montaigne himself prefers and which he recommends in the ideal education of *De l'institution des enfans*. The difference between the sexes is not so wide as it appears.

When we pass to the treatment of women in general, we find a not dissimilar opposition. Montaigne's social attitudes are conservative, he is in this respect not much inclined to question received wisdom nor to adopt the liberalising tendencies of the new humanism (or, more accurately, of some humanists). So the most honourable occupation for women is housekeeping:[3] apart from maternal authority, itself capricious and unreliable, the power to command belongs by nature to men[4] ('Du côté de la barbe est la toute-puissance', as Molière's Arnolphe puts it), and this arises from superior endowment in reason and prudence.[5] More seriously, in view of the importance Montaigne attaches to it, women are not capable of friendship in the full sense, a point which is first advanced in 1580 in *De l'amitié*[6] and confirmed at greater length in 1588 in *De trois commerces*. In the conversation of women physical pleasure partly compensates for their intellectual deficiencies, but it is still not equal to the conversation of men.[7] All this, though more delicately put than usual, conforms well enough to the traditional anti-feminist line. Even so, most of these remarks are made in passing and are surrounded by qualifications which give a different impression from our bald summary (a summary of Montaigne is always inadequate). And when he addresses himself more directly to the question, in *Sur des vers de Virgile*, he reaches quite opposite conclusions. Women, he now says, are not wrong to reject the rules which

---

[1] III, iii: TR 800.
[2] III, iii: EM iii, 46; TR 801.
[3] III, ix: TR 952(*b*).
[4] II, viii: TR 379(*a*).
[5] III, iii: TR 805(*b*).
[6] I, xxviii: TR 185(*a,c*).
[7] III, iii: TR 802–3.

men have made without consulting them.[1] At the very end of the essay he goes further, affirming that there is really no essential difference:

> je dis que les masles et femelles sont jettez en mesme moule: sauf l'institution et l'usage, la difference n'y est pas grande.[2]

This was in 1588; the Bordeaux Copy adds the remark that Plato admitted women to all offices in his republic and that Antisthenes made no distinction between masculine and feminine virtue. Once again we find that Montaigne shows both sides of the coin and that a conservative position is in the end deeply modified. Here there can be little doubt about the presence of an evolutionary element: the less conventional position is reached only in a late essay.

Marriage is treated in a correspondingly cool tone, and here Montaigne again reflects the prevailing ethos of his society. He accepts the *mariage de convenance*, regards it as a family rather than an individual matter, prefers arrangement by a third party, and thinks nothing so likely to fail as marriages based on beauty or love.[3] The result is a relationship which is, and should be, restrained rather than ecstatic. We have already seen how Montaigne looked at it from the point of view of his self-portrait,[4] and the picture does not change much when generalised. Affection for wives is legitimate if kept within reasonable bounds;[5] this affection must not be confused with love, which is something quite different. But in the end marriage is not only a useful social institution but 'une douce societé de vie, pleine de constance, de fiance et d'ung nombre infiny d'utiles et solides offices et obligations mutuelles.'[6] A few sentences later it is a cage: the birds outside want to get in, those inside want to get out. The humorously balanced view is characteristic. On the whole Montaigne's view of marriage is partly that of the nobleman or rich bourgeois of his time, partly that of the detached philosopher impatient of human ties. It cannot be said that he makes any notably original contribution to a subject on which originality is difficult, though many of his asides are marked by great acuteness.

---

1 III, v: TR 832.
2 III, v: EM iii, 144; TR 875(b).
3 III, v: TR 827.
4 Cf. p. 57 above.
5 I, xxx: TR 196(a).
6 III, v: EM iii, 83; TR 829.

This is not at all true of his approach to sex in general. How audacious and how modern he is in this respect has perhaps hardly been stated. For a couple of centuries what he has to say on the subject belonged for his critics (as it did in life) to a realm of secret knowledge and veiled references.[1] Of course candour in these matters is the norm of sixteenth-century writing as of writing in most periods: it was only towards the middle of the following century in France that one of the recurrent waves of repression set in. We have only to think of Rabelais or Bonaventure des Périers, or above all Montaigne's contemporary Brantôme, to see that he is far from standing alone. He differs from Brantôme in that he is more intelligent, less concerned with mere anecdotes, always sure of the central place sexual behaviour must occupy in a study of the human condition. Without it Montaigne's man, like any man, would be incomplete. As usual, the topic recurs tangentially or parenthetically in a large number of essays but, as often, one essay, *Sur des vers de Virgile*, concentrates almost exclusively on it. The innocuous title is also typical of the essays in which he has something particularly bold and original to communicate.

As evidence of his greater depth when compared to Brantôme and the rest we might quote one justification for the importance he attaches to the subject:

> Tout le mouvement du monde se resoult et rend à cet accouplage: c'est une matiere infuse par tout, c'est un centre où toutes choses regardent.[2]

The notion of the sex act as a vital principle infused in everything and the centre of everything is interesting enough in itself, though perhaps not unparalleled. More than this, we can see here an instance of Montaigne's characteristic process of thought: the 'centre où toutes choses regardent' could also be applied to the relation between the self and the world in the *Essais*; the word *mouvement* is particularly notable and the whole conception of movement takes on a new potential from its context here. The details, sometimes hair-raising, sometimes hilarious, must be understood in their connection with this deeper purpose.

---

[1] Notable recent exceptions are Frame, Recksiek, and Hallie (see Bibliography).
[2] III, v: EM iii, 91; TR 835.

Nostre vie est partie en folie, partie en prudence. Qui n'en escrit que reveremment et regulierement, il en laisse en arriere plus de la moitié.[1]

This tells us that the picture of the human condition would be incomplete without the chapter on sex, but again it has much wider implications: life is serious, of course, but it is even more comic and it cannot be properly appraised without a strong dose of irreverence and folly (part of the lesson of Erasmus but Montaigne takes it further). At this point in the Bordeaux Copy there comes an addition which Montaigne subsequently erased. It is therefore not very legible, but he refers to *Au lecteur* ('ma preface liminere') and says that he has been emboldened to break the ice by the example of wise and sound authors and by the reception his work had encountered. At any rate there is no doubt that he is now prepared, as he was not at the time of the preface, to display himself 'tout entier et tout nud'.[2] I have said 'display himself' and though it might be possible in this as in other respects to separate the self-portrait from the description of the human condition it would be particularly arbitrary here. The whole point, of course, here as elsewhere, is that the two mingle and fuse.

It would be difficult, perhaps even a little tedious, to itemise the whole range of erotic experience reflected in Montaigne, since not much escapes him, whether he is discussing the practices of distant lands or his own, the external mechanics or the inner feelings aroused. As he goes on we see a marked development not only in frankness but also in tolerance or rather sympathy, since tolerance is always present. The act itself is first described rather timidly, in very abstract terms:

> . . . le plaisir nous transporte si fort hors de nous que nostre discours ne sçauroit lors faire son office, tout perclus et ravi en la volupté.[3]

(The object is to prove the contrary, the Stoic argument that even at these moments the reason can operate in a detached way.) The advance in precision can be seen in an addition of 1588 to *Nous ne goustons rien de pur*:

[1] III, v: EM iii, 132; TR 866-7.
[2] Cf. p. 51 above.
[3] II, xi: EM ii, 131; TR 409(*a*).

Nostre extreme volupté a quelque air de gemissement et de plainte.
Diriez vous pas qu'elle se meurt d'angoisse ?[1]

This, though very beautiful, is still restrained in comparison with
the wonderfully vivid account in *Sur des vers de Virgile*:

> Et, considerant maintesfois la ridicule titillation de ce plaisir, les
> absurdes mouvemens escervelez et estourdis dequoy il agite Zenon
> et Cratippus [i.e. severe and idealistic philosophers], cette rage
> indiscrette, ce visage enflammé de fureur et de cruauté au plus doux
> effect de l'amour, et puis cette morgue grave, severe et ecstatique
> en une action si fole, ... et que la supreme volupté aye du transy
> et du plaintif comme la douleur, je crois ... que l'homme est le jouet
> des Dieus.[2]

Here the emphasis is on the absurdity of the performance, but a
Bordeaux Copy addition brings a corrective touch:

> Somes nous pas bien brutes de nomer brutale l'operation qui
> nous faict ?[3]

Again the evolution towards greater acceptance is strongly marked
in these late passages.

To judge the range of experience we might begin with the
enumeration of strange customs in *De la coustume*: countries
where virgins do not conceal the pudenda, where unmarried girls
are not restricted in intercourse or abortion, where the *droit du
seigneur* is practised, where there are male brothels and marriages
between males.[4] This is a dry list, derived mainly from Gomara
and intended once more to bring out the relativity of traditions
and taboos. But many similar references are based on personal
experience or independent and reflective reading rather than on
convenient compilers. Thus in *Des boyteux* we have the superior
qualities of lame girls, with ingenious explanations, partly from
the ancients, partly Montaigne's own, and ladies in coaches and
female weavers, with an example from his own experience.[5] Or
there are the cases of phallic worship, found in most of the world,
he maintains, giving some very odd examples and adding from
his own experience the codpiece and the peculiarly shaped head-
dress worn by married women, but not widows, in his area.[6] Here

[1] II, xx: EM ii, 464–5; TR 655(*b*).
[2] III, v: EM iii, 117; TR 855.
[3] III, v: EM iii, 118; TR 856(*c*).
[4] I, xxiii: TR 110(*b*).
[5] III, xi: TR 1011–2.
[6] III, v: TR 836.

again we can observe the anthropologist's eye and the intelligence with which familiar things are related to what seems very remote from them. Similarly there is the humorous and rhetorical defence of the male member in *De la force de l'imagination* against charges of insubordination and rebellion[1] (one of the few cases in the *Essais* where he draws directly and extensively on his legal training). This, incidentally, may be another reaction against Sabunde, who says that human generation is produced by the involuntary action of a rebellious member.[2] Montaigne is making fun of the whole idea. But the idea in itself was fairly commonplace. Apart from codpieces he has a great deal to say about clothing. Total nudity is less exciting than the clothed body, the erotic is more powerful when half-hidden (with examples from Ovid and Martial).[3] This is of course an aesthetic, not a moral consideration. And elsewhere he asks a pertinent question:

Pourquoy a l'on voylé jusques au dessoubs des talons ces beautez que chacune desire montrer, que chacun desire voir ?[4]

The answer, naturally, is in order to stimulate desire still further. In the same way he is sceptical of verbal taboos. Forbidden words, he says, are the best known at all ages,[5] and he even expresses himself with indignation on the subject:

En fin qui desniaiseroit l'home d'une si scrupuleuse superstition verbale n'aporteroit pas grande perte au monde.[6]

It may be noted in passing that, though the matter seems trivial, this is not a characteristic conservative position. Taking advantage of this liberty of speech, he mentions necrophilia,[7] impotence and the cures for it,[8] or sadism, though without much stress on the last:

La volupté mesme cerche à s'irriter par la douleur. Elle est bien plus sucrée quand elle cuit et quand elle escorche. La Courtisane Flora disoit n'avoir jamais couché avecques Pompeius, qu'elle ne luy eut faict porter les merques de ses morsures.[9]

---

[1] I, xxi: TR 100–1(c).
[2] *Œuvres complètes*, ed. Armaingaud, x, 122.
[3] III, v: TR 858; cf. II, xii: TR 464.
[4] II, xv: EM ii, 384; TR 598.
[5] III, v: TR 825.
[6] III, v: EM iii, 132; TR 866(c).
[7] III, v: TR 860.
[8] e.g. I, xxi: TR 97–8.
[9] II, xv: EM ii, 382: TR 596–7(a), and the quotation from Lucretius which follows. Cf. also III, viii: TR 902.

There are scattered references to homosexuality and one fuller discussion, appropriately in *De l'amitié*. In 1580 there is only a discreet and damning allusion: 'Et cet' autre licence Grecque est justement abhorrée par nos meurs.'[1] In the Bordeaux Copy, however, he inserts a long and not at all unsympathetic account of the Greek attitude to the question.

This list could be considerably extended (it hardly seems necessary for instance to deal with his treatment of such standard topics as prostitution or cuckoldry except to say that, expectedly and like Molière later, he reacts against the general identification of a husband's honour with his wife's fidelity), but even as it is it will show how broad a picture of human sexuality can be discovered in Montaigne. The impression given may have been a little ponderous: in fact, as I suggested earlier, the whole treatment of the subject is irradiated with humour and vivacity, as in:

La bru de Pythagoras disoit que la fame qui se couche aveq un home, doit aveq la cote laisser aussi la honte, et la reprandre aveq le cotillon.[2]

Or, better known:

Nous imaginons bien plus sortablemant un artisan sur sa garderobe ou sur sa fame qu'un grand presidant, venerable par son maintien et suffisance.[3]

The contrast between the dignified trappings and the physiological reality is highly entertaining, but the implied comment on human credulity still more so. An example of sustained and most lively narration is the story of Jupiter and Juno:

... Juppiter fit à sa fame une si chalureuse charge un jour que, ne pouvant avoir patience qu'ell' eut gaigné son lict, il la versa sur le planchier et, par la vehemance du plaisir, oblia les resolutions grandes et importantes qu'il venoit de prandre aveq les autres dieus en sa court celeste: se vantant qu'il l'avoit trouvé aussi bon ce coup là, que lors que premieremant il la depucela à cachettes de leurs parans.[4]

This, from Plato and ultimately from Homer, provides further evidence of the way Montaigne brings the classics to life. There is a touch of the burlesque about it which distinguishes it from

---

[1] I, xxviii: EM i, 243; TR 185(*a*).
[2] I, xxi: EM i, 127; TR 99(*c*).
[3] III, ii: EM iii, 28; TR 788(*c*).
[4] I, xxx: EM i, 260; TR 197(*c*).

the episode in the *Iliad*, but its freshness, vigour and simplicity deserve the highest praise.

Still, such gaiety must not blind us to the seriousness of the subject or of Montaigne's attitude towards it. It hardly belongs to a discussion of his moral position, except indirectly: he is not far from Diderot and the 'inconvénient d'attacher des idées morales à certaines actions physiques qui n'en comportent pas' of the *Supplément au Voyage de Bougainville*. Even so, it could be maintained that this is itself a moral argument in the sense that it is immoral to confuse moral issues in this way. At any rate Montaigne is aware of some quasi-moral implications. Thus, though his attitude to women is for the most part the traditional one, as some of the examples quoted reveal, he argues in *Sur des vers de Virgile* not only, as we have seen, for the general equality of the sexes but also for equality in love, a view perhaps even more contrary to the spirit of his time; he attacks the double standard for men and women, or at least finds it surprising, something to be questioned.[1] More important still, however, is his profound undermining of conventional taboos.

(c) Pour le destruire [man] on cherche un champ spatieus en pleine lumiere; pour le construire, on se musse dans un creus tenebreus et contreint. (b) C'est le devoir de se cacher et rougir pour le faire; et c'est gloire, et naissent plusieurs vertus de le sçavoir deffaire.[2]

The paradox that killing a man is glorious, making one is shameful, is given its maximum force; and, as so often, the addition of the Bordeaux Copy gives poetic consistency to the abstract idea. Man is a miserable animal, unable to enjoy any pleasure without trying to create obstacles for himself above those which nature already offers, absurdly preferring local conventions ('les regles de ta parroisse') to universal laws.[3] These pages of *Sur des vers de Virgile*, interspersed with frequent comments in the margins of the Bordeaux Copy, are among the most human and humane parts of Montaigne's final message. In the last analysis he goes rather further and suggests, though cautiously through the mouths of ancient philosophers, that enjoyment is the only test.[4] Yet in a personal declaration on his conduct in his love affairs he shows

---

[1] III, v: TR 833.
[2] III, v: EM iii, 119; TR 856-7.
[3] III, v: EM iii, 121; TR 857-8. Cf. I, xxx: TR 198.
[4] II, xii: TR 567(*b,c*); III, ix: TR 968(*c*).

where he draws the line between what is permissible and what is not:

Ma conscience s'y engageoit aussi, jusques à la desbauche et dissolution; mais jusques à l'ingratitude, trahison, malignité et cruauté, non.[1]

After youth and maturity comes the last of the particular problems of the human condition, that is to say death. Montaigne's views on it have been discussed as much as anything in the *Essais* and it need not occupy us so long. Once again, though the subject appears in most, perhaps all, the essays, some are centred on it: of these the most important are *Que le goust des biens et des maux depend en bonne partie de l'opinion que nous en avons* (on the three major evils of death, poverty and pain), *Coustume de l'isle de Cea* (on suicide), and particularly *Que philosopher, c'est apprendre à mourir*. It will be noticed that all these are in the 1580 edition and that there is no essay directly on death in the Third Book, which is more concerned with life. In fact, evolution is easier to prove here than anywhere, and in this respect Villey's position commands assent. Nevertheless, though death has a subordinate place in the last essays, it is not really absent, and a constant preoccupation with it must rank as a characteristic of Montaigne. In an early essay he writes:

... comme est-il possible qu'on se puisse deffaire du pensement de la mort, et qu'à chaque instant il ne nous semble qu'elle nous tient au collet?[2]

And in one of the latest he says much the same thing, though personal experience has now replaced rhetoric:

Je sens la mort qui me pince continuellement la gorge ou les reins.[3]

... j'advoue qu'en voyageant je n'arrive gueres en logis où il ne me passe par la fantasie si j'y pourray estre et malade et mourant à mon aise.[4]

Death then is everywhere and at all times present. The argument drawn from this ubiquity in *Que philosopher, c'est apprendre à mourir* (it will be recalled that at least part of it was written as early as 1572) and related essays of 1580 is that coming

---

[1] III, v: EM iii, 136; TR 869.
[2] I, xx: EM i, 105; TR 84(a).
[3] III, ix: EM iii, 247; TR 956(b).
[4] III, ix: EM iii, 255; TR 961(b).

to terms with death is the principal aim of philosophy and therefore, paradoxically, of life. It is impossible to avoid death and the
vulgar solution of not thinking about it leads to a wretched failure
to face it when it comes. The only way then is to brace oneself
by continual effort and reflection, to think of it always. Clearly this
is the lesson of ancient Stoicism and quotations and imitations of
Plutarch and Seneca abound. This bald outline fails, as always with
Montaigne, to do justice to the twists and turns of the argument,
the bizarre illustrations, the notes of personal emotion, found even
in an early essay, but the central strand is the establishment of
death as the touchstone by which life is to be judged. In the later
essays of 1580 a shift of emphasis is already visible. Thus the
pupil of *De l'institution des enfans* is to receive lessons of philosophy which show him not just how to die but 'à sçavoir bien
mourir et bien vivre':[1] In *De l'exercitation* (which may not be
later than 1574) we see the turning-point. There is still the effort
to conquer fear of death by force of reflection, but a near approach
to death has gradually allowed a new thought to filter through,
that it may in fact not be so terrible, that stern preparation may
not after all be required: 'Pour s'aprivoiser à la mort, je trouve
qu'il n'y a que de s'en avoisiner.'[2] It is in this essay that, as we
have already seen, the reality of death, what actually happens, is
studied more closely and fully than in any other. The result of a
violent accident is rather like sleep, and death may well appear
in this guise. We have here one of the finest examples of the
modification of Montaigne's theoretical positions by the impact of
lived experience. In the Third Book the evolution, not to say *volte-
face*, is complete: 'C'est le vivre hureusement, non ... le mourir
hureusemant qui faict l'humaine felicité.'[3] He now wants to side-
step death, he is no longer concerned to put up a front of defiance;[4]
he finds that peasants and simple people die with as much
constancy as philosophers,[5] that preparation for death has caused
more suffering than death itself, and that in any case it is unnecessary because nature tells us how to behave when the moment
comes.[6] At the same point he quotes the sentence from Cicero
which had furnished the title and theme of *Que philosopher, c'est*

---

[1] I, xxvi: EM i, 206; TR 158(*a*). Cf. II, x: TR 388(*a*).
[2] II, vi: EM ii, 58; TR 357(*a*). Cf. Villey, *Sources et évolution*, ii, 405–6.
[3] III, ii: EM iii, 37; TR 794(*c*).
[4] III, ix: TR 956–7.
[5] e.g. III, xii: TR 1016(*b*).
[6] III, xii: TR 1028(*b*).

apprendre à mourir: 'Tota philosophorum vita commentatio mortis est', but now it is subjected to sharp criticism. He even goes so far as to say, in the Bordeaux Copy: 'Un quart d'heure de passion sans consequence, sans nuisance, ne merite pas des preceptes particuliers.'[1] The reader who has been given so many 'particular precepts' on the question in earlier essays is bound to think this a little offhand.

Yet although the evolution from one position (importance of preparation for death) to its opposite (unimportance of preparation for death) is thus established beyond doubt, at a deeper level there may be an element of continuity and a feeling which possesses greater human significance. A late addition to *Contre la faineantise* seems to represent the final stage very well:

> L'extreme degré de traiter corageusement la mort, et le plus naturel, c'est la voir non sulement sans estonement, mais sans soin, continuant libre le trein de la vie jusques dans elle.[2]

But this is only a restatement in more abstract terms of the familiar, early, and beautiful:

> ... que la mort me treuve plantant mes choux, mais nonchalant d'elle, et encore plus de mon jardin imparfait.[3]

Whether to be achieved through stern effort or evasive action, the object remains the same: the treatment of death as no more than an incident which hardly ruffles the surface of a serene life. Evolution, here as elsewhere, is largely the drawing out of latent potentialities. In the end death is accepted as a wholly natural part of life:

> Mais tu ne meurs pas de ce que tu es malade; tu meurs de ce que tu es vivant.[4]

With this penetrating observation (adapted from Seneca) the final stage has been reached, but it has been implicitly present all along.

So far we have been dealing with particular aspects of the human condition. All of them, of course, afford evidence of Montaigne's psychological insight, which is apparent in practically everything he writes, but, at the risk of some repetition, the ques-

1 TR 1028(*c*).
2 II, xxi: EM ii, 473; TR 661(*c*).
3 I, xx: EM i, 110; TR 87(*a*).
4 III, xiii: EM iii, 396; TR 1070(*c*).

tion does require to be considered in itself. Already Mlle de Gournay singles out his penetration in this respect:

> ... et l'anatomie parfaicte de leurs passions et mouvements internes: sur lesquelles actions et passions des hommes, ie ne sçay si iamais autre Autheur dict ny considera ce qu'il a dit et consideré.[1]

The claim of originality is expressed tentatively, but once again it is probably justified. Mlle de Gournay, in speaking of the 'mouvements internes', echoes Montaigne's own words. We have discussed the 'espineuse entreprinse' and some of its implications, but that was an interpolation of the Bordeaux Copy. It is interesting to observe that the same idea is already present, if not in quite so striking and profound a form, in the essays of 1580. One thing that the pupil of *De l'institution des enfans* must be taught is 'quels ressors nous meuvent, et le moyen de tant divers branles en nous'.[2] In similar words but with greater precision, *De l'inconstance de nos actions* ends:

> ce n'est pas tour de rassis entendement de nous juger simplement par nos actions de dehors; il faut sonder jusqu'au dedans, et voir par quels ressors se donne le bransle; mais, d'autant que c'est une hazardeuse et haute entreprinse, je voudrois que moins de gens s'en meslassent.[3]

Once again we see exactly how high he is aiming, in spite of his professions of modesty.

His most important contribution to psychological thought is no doubt the notion of the dissolving personality, the multitude of characteristics, motives, impulses, which we habitually reduce to an illusory unity. However, I have examined this at some length, both in relation to the self-portrait and to humanity in general. It is only necessary to add one or two points which have a more particular bearing on his psychological attitudes. One consequence of the total inconsistency of human beings, of the instability of all minds, is not only that the self and the world are difficult to grasp but that it is impossible to know other people: 'les autres ne vous voyent poinct, ils vous devinent par conjectures incertaines.'[4] Elsewhere he speaks of the misrepresentation of the

[1] *Les essais*, 1617, Preface, ẽ3ʳ. Her 1595 preface makes the same point, rather less well.
[2] I, xxvi: EM i, 206; TR 158(a).
[3] II, i; EM ii, 9; TR 321(a).
[4] III, ii: EM iii, 25; TR 785.

dead; but the living too are always judged to be other than they really are.[1] It is often said, and we have suggested some examples, that Montaigne anticipates the seventeenth century, but here he represents the antithesis of the confident psychology of a La Rochefoucauld, a Molière, or even a Racine. For all these writers the springs of human thought and action lie deep, but they are ultimately susceptible of quite simple explanations. Once more it is with Proust that the obvious parallel holds: Proust's novel is indeed built on just this universal misunderstanding. The philosophical problem of the possibility of knowing other minds lurks behind it, but for Montaigne it is a psychological rather than a philosophical problem.

On the other hand there is one point in which he does very much anticipate the following century and one of the major elements in Pascal's psychology of fallen man. The essay *De la diversion* is psychologically one of the most penetrating and shows Montaigne at his subtlest. Estienne Pasquier, not a particularly stupid man, said that he could never understand what was meant by 'diversion' in the *Essais*,[2] no doubt another sign of how far in advance of his time Montaigne was. The essay has two main themes. The first is a study of oblique ways of consoling, persuading and so on: this is what he means in the first place by diversion and it approximates to Pascal's *esprit de finesse*. The second, intimately linked to the first and more properly Pascalian, is summed up in the phrase 'nous pensons tousjours ailleurs'.[3] He goes on to explain: we escape from the present by thoughts of a better life, of the future of our children or our name, of vengeance on our enemies. In an addition to another essay it is put with still greater vigour:

Nous ne sommes jamais chez nous, nous sommes tousjours au delà. La crainte, le desir, l'esperance nous eslancent vers l'advenir, et nous desrobent le sentiment et la consideration de ce qui est, pour nous amuser à ce qui sera, voire quand nous ne serons plus.[4]

This is the second and much deeper sense of diversion. It is easy to recognise here the germ of one of the most famous arguments of the *Pensées*, the ills which arise from man's incapacity to sit

[1] III, ix: TR 961.
[2] *Lettres sur la littérature*, ed. Thickett, p. 44.
[3] III, iv: EM iii, 61; TR 812.
[4] I, iii: EM i, 14; TR 18(*b*).

still, to be content with his present lot. Elsewhere Montaigne uses two of the words which dominate Pascal's treatment of the theme:

> Cette opinion et usance commune de regarder ailleurs qu'à nous a bien pourveu à nostre affaire. C'est un objet plein de mescontentement; nous n'y voyons que *misere* et *vanité*. . . . Nous allons en avant à vau l'eau, mais de rebrousser vers nous nostre course c'est un mouvement penible.[1]

Such passages help us to understand why, in spite of his hostility to Montaigne, Pascal thought that a Christian had much to learn from him. Incidentally, there may seem to be a contradiction between this emphasis on man's preoccupation with the future and what we have said about the dominance of the present in Montaigne's conception of time. But of course he is rejecting the concern with the future, deliberately resisting the allurements of diversion, pulling himself and us back to present reality.

He anticipates the seventeenth century also, though in a less original way, in his insistence on the positive value of passions: anger, avarice, even fear, may lead to noble or useful actions.[2] Descartes is only the most eminent among the writers of the following period who prosecute these lines of inquiry.

Yet such reflections, interesting though they are, hardly do justice to the boldness of Montaigne's psychological thought. E. V. Telle, maintaining that Montaigne opens the way to psychoanalysis and modern psychiatry, hardly overstates the case when he says:

> On peut dire que Montaigne, en 1580, du point de vue de la méthode scientifique avait près de trois siècles d'avance sur son temps, et que seuls certains médecins, parmi ses contemporains, pouvaient pressentir son mérite.[3]

The workings of an unconscious mind are suggested in:

> car il y a plusieurs mouvemens en nous qui ne partent pas de nostre ordonance.[4]

or better (for this is perhaps a matter of reflex actions) in:

> Ma volonté et mon discours se remue tantost d'un air, tantost d'un

---

[1] III, ix: EM iii, 277; TR 979. Italics mine.
[2] II, xii: TR 550. On this question see Levi, *French moralists*, 1964, *passim*.
[3] 'A propos du mot "essai" chez Montaigne', *BHR*, xxx (1968), 228.
[4] II, vi: EM ii, 56: TR 355.

autre, et y a plusieurs de ces mouvemens qui se gouvernent sans moy.[1]

He treats dreams (he forgets the details of his own)[2] not in any mystical or prophetic way, but chiefly as evidence of character.[3] Even more clearly premonitory of Freud is the remark that:

Je treuve que nos plus grands vices prenent leur pli de nostre plus tendre enfance, et que nostre principal gouvernement est entre les mains des nourrisses.[4]

Similarly, children's games are not games but their most serious actions.[5] Behaviourism is foreshadowed in a remarkable study of the effect of emotion on thought: preachers are moved towards belief simply by the emotional force of their eloquence; the same is true of advocates and even martyrs (under the pressure of interrogations a man will go to the stake for a belief which among friends he would hardly have bothered to defend).[6] On the psychology of memory he observes that forgetting is not within our power: in fact, trying to forget something is the best way of imprinting it on the memory.[7] This has a vaguely Proustian ring, though the observation is not very remarkable in itself. At a much deeper level he conveys at least the first stage of Proust's involuntary memory when he points out the difficulty of remembering anything deliberately (memory is of course the subject of the sentence):

Or, plus je m'en defie, plus elle se trouble; elle me sert mieux par rencontre, il faut que je la solicite nonchalamment: car, si je la presse, elle s'estonne; et, depuis qu'ell' a commencé à chanceler, plus je la sonde, plus elle s'empestre et embarrasse: elle me sert à son heure, non pas à la mienne.[8]

Memory throws up its treasures at the least expected moments, efforts to make it do so are vain. Just so does Proust's narrator strive desperately to recover past sensations which can only return when the will is uninvolved.

On the whole, however, Montaigne's psychology is not notable

---

[1] III, viii: EM iii, 191; TR 912-3(*b*).
[2] III, v: TR 854-5.
[3] III, xiii: TR 1077-8.
[4] I, xxiii: EM i, 139; TR 107(*c*).
[5] I, xxiii: TR 108(*c*).
[6] II, xii: TR 549-50(*b*).
[7] II, xii: TR 474(*a*).
[8] II, xvii: EM ii, 433; TR 633(*a*).

so much for these brilliant anticipations as for the quality of his direct observation of human character, though here too in a way he anticipates. He is a *moraliste* in the French sense of the term, one who observes conduct and motive without didacticism, without necessarily committing himself on the rights and wrongs of what he observes. The form chosen by the *moraliste* is generally the aphorism or maxim, the general statement about behaviour (as in La Rochefoucauld, Vauvenargues, or Chamfort), or perhaps the anecdote or apologue (La Fontaine and La Bruyère strikingly combine the two). This literary genre may be called a French speciality, so much so that attempts to do the same thing in other languages never seem quite to come off: we may think of Lichtenberg's failure to achieve total concentration or Wilde's simple but none the less highly artificial reversals of accepted clichés. To say that Montaigne is the first representative of this great French tradition would be rash (we can perceive embryonic stirrings in many writers including Margaret of Navarre or even Marie de France), but he is its first great representative. As in the case of Proust, maxims have been extracted from the *Essais*,[1] but this does violence to both writers since their reflections are so deeply embedded in the context. Here we can hardly do more than give a few illustrations. Concise maxims of the La Rochefoucauld type do occur:

La vaillance a ses limites, comme les autres vertus. . . .[2]

Il est certaine façon d'humilité subtile qui naist de la presomption. . . .[3]

But both these lead to further discussion, and in general, as I have suggested, the keenest observations are not isolated but form an integral part of a larger argument; they cannot be reduced to a mere formula. Our being is cemented with evil qualities, ambition, jealousy, envy, cruelty:

car, au milieu de la compassion, nous sentons au dedans je ne sçay quelle aigre-douce poincte de volupté maligne à voir souffrir autruy; et les enfans le sentent.

This is supremely well observed, though he is not the first to

---

[1] Lablénie, *Montaigne auteur de maximes*, 1968. But Lablénie has many precursors, the first perhaps being Pasquier.
[2] I, xv: EM i, 84; TR 68(*a*).
[3] II, xxxvii: EM ii, 581; TR 741(*a*).

observe it. It is in fact the *suave mari magno* of Lucretius, which he goes on to quote, though much more subtly and truthfully worked out. But he does not stop at this point, and the continuation is even more striking:

> Desquelles qualitez qui osteroit les semences en l'homme, des-truiroit les fondamentalles conditions de nostre vie.[1]

The implications of this are far-reaching and perhaps terrifying.

> Ceux qu'on voit aux supplices courir à leur fin, et haster l'execution et la presser, ils ne le font pas de resolution: ils se veulent oster le temps de la considerer.[2]

This bears a close resemblance to La Rochefoucauld in the way apparent constancy is shown to be inspired by less creditable motives, but again it is part of a wider argument. The same is true of a syntactically similar formulation, one of many reflections on the theme of 'uneasy lies the head that wears a crown':

> Ceus qui sont en pressante creinte de perdre leur bien, d'estre exilez, d'estre subjuguez, vivent en continuelle angoisse, en perdant le boire, le manger et le repos: là où les povres, les banis, les serfs vivent souvant aussi joyeusement que les autres.[3]

It would be possible to give innumerable examples of this sort of direct and accurate notation of 'les fondamentalles conditions de nostre vie'. What distinguishes Montaigne from most of the later *moralistes,* who also observe accurately, is, as in so many aspects of his writing, the poetic feeling which illuminates and transfigures what might be pessimistic or cynical. How well he describes the haze of sensations experienced by a man falling asleep (Proust again)[4] or enters into the minds of American Indians seeing Europeans for the first time, the horses ('des grands monstres incogneuz'), armour ('une peau luysante et dure'), the thunder and lightning of firearms[5] (this wonderful passage is partly inspired by Gomara). But it is in more familiar, even banal, observations that the extreme delicacy of Montaigne's psychological notations is most evident:

[1] III, i: EM iii, 2; TR 768.
[2] II, xiii: EM ii, 375; TR 592(*a*).
[3] I, xviii: EM i, 94; TR 76(*c*).
[4] II, vi: TR 355(*a*).
[5] III, vi: EM iii, 159–60; TR 887–8.

Comme ceux que la tristesse accable et possede se laissent pourtant par intervalles tastonner à quelque plaisir et leur eschappe un soubsrire. . . .[1]

What could be more ordinary or more just? Or what we remember about dead friends:

Le souvenir d'un adieu, d'une action, d'une grace particuliere, d'une recommandation derniere, nous afflige.[2]

Or simplest and most poignant of all perhaps:

C'est chose tendre que la vie et aisée à troubler.[3]

It will be noted that these three last examples of the deep sensibility which emerges every so often from the usually humorous or mocking tone are all from the Third Book. Nowhere is it clearer that a purely historical explanation of Montaigne must be inadequate. Such observations are timeless and speak to all ages alike.

But if Montaigne is a *moraliste* in the French sense, a most penetrating observer of human conduct and motive, he is even more a moralist in the English sense, a man who is fundamentally concerned with ethical questions, with 'ought' rather than 'is'. The two are, it is true, not easy to keep separate when we are dealing with such a concrete writer. Even in his moral judgements his denial of didacticism remains partly valid and they tend to emerge, obliquely like everything else, from the fluid amalgam of anecdote, observation and comment. They are mobile, like all his judgements, and we must not expect mechanical consistency: none the less something like a coherent position develops in the end, the more coherent since, in their mature stage at least, they never depart from the foundation of psychological realism which we have just discussed. Villey's evolutionary theory works fairly well for Montaigne's moral attitudes, and it is possible, though we must not apply it too rigidly, to trace a development from Stoicism (virtue considered as a process of bracing oneself to bear all kinds of misfortunes) through Pyrrhonian scepticism (relativity of all moral values and, in the absence of any rational principles, the need to follow general custom, essentially Descartes's *morale provisoire*) to the final position, which is much more complex and requires fuller discussion. Here this evolutionary pattern will

[1] III, xii: EM iii, 336; TR 1024.
[2] III, iv: EM iii, 64; TR 814.
[3] III, ix: EM iii, 210; TR 927.

be considered only where necessary and in broad outline: the main emphasis will be on the enduring value of Montaigne's thought.

In the 1580 *Essais* the most important discussion of virtue comes not so much in the brief *De la vertu* (II, xxix), which argues that virtue is not true virtue without constancy, as in *De la cruauté*. Here Montaigne distinguishes between virtue and goodness. God is good, powerful, liberal and just, but not virtuous because virtue requires effort and difficulty:

> ... cette aisée, douce et panchante voie, par où se conduisent les pas reglez d'une bonne inclination de nature, n'est pas celle de la vraye vertu. Elle demande un chemin aspre et espineux.[1]

This is all of a piece with the earlier Stoical essays like *Que philosopher, c'est apprendre à mourir* which we have already considered and which stress the necessity of unremitting effort. It is the diametrical opposite of the conception expressed in the Third Book and the interpolations of the Bordeaux Copy, where the same image of the path or avenue is used to convey the gentleness and easiness of true virtue: 'La vertu est qualité plaisante et gaye',[2] or, in a well-known passage:

> Ceus qui l'ont aprochee, la tienent, au rebours, logee dans une belle pleine fertile et fleurissente, d'où elle voit bien sous soi toutes choses; mais si peut on y arriver, qui en sçait l'adresse, par des routes ombrageuses, gasonnees et dousfleurantes, plesammant et d'une pente facile et polie, come est celle des voutes celestes.[3]

Once more the *volte-face* is complete. But returning now to *De la cruauté* we can see how the change takes place. After saying that virtue is difficult and thorny, Montaigne begins to wonder whether Socrates or Cato the Younger could be called virtuous by this standard since everything comes so easily to them.[4] The tightly drawn argument proceeds by thesis, antithesis and synthesis: first comes an easy-going goodness, then rigid virtue, and finally supreme virtue from which all appearance of effort has vanished. This may well be the actual turning-point in the development from early Stoicism to the more flexible conceptions of the

---

[1] II, xi: EM ii, 122; TR 402(*a*).
[2] III, v: EM iii, 74; TR 822. The 1588 edition reads 'plaisante et voluptueuse'.
[3] I, xxvi: EM i, 209; TR 160-1(*c*). Cf. also I, xx: TR 80-1(*c*).
[4] II, xi: TR 402-3(*a*).

last stages. We catch Montaigne at the moment when he is changing his mind and it offers a striking example of the painting of *passage*, of thought in motion.

A more important question than whether virtue is easy or difficult is what it actually consists of: to this no simple answer can be given except in terms of the whole complex of moral attitudes. For the moment we can say that, apart from the initial association with constancy, a necessary counterpoise to ever-present flux, his idea of virtue is closely connected with that of conscience. Two essays, *De la conscience* and *De la liberté de conscience*, are much concerned with it, but it is by no means limited to them; even more important is the discussion in *Du repentir*. The only reward of virtuous actions is the satisfaction of one's own conscience, and this faith runs through the *Essais* without distinction of evolutionary stages: 'C'est le contentement qu'une conscience bien reglée recoit en soy de bien faire.'[1] Everything must be referred to an inner touchstone:

> Nous autres principalement, qui vivons une vie privée qui n'est en montre qu'à nous, devons avoir estably un patron au dedans, auquel toucher nos actions, et, selon iceluy, nous caresser tantost, tantost nous chastier. J'ay mes loix et ma court pour juger de moy, et m'y adresse plus qu'ailleurs.[2]

This stress on conscience has an almost Protestant ring, or would have if it were not for the fact that we can detect its origins in both Catholic thought and in the moral writers of antiquity (thus the last passage is followed by a quotation from Cicero which includes the word *conscientia*). However, it is significant that in mentioning with approval the kings of Egypt in Plutarch who made judges swear never to depart from conscience even if the kings themselves commanded it, he uses the word *conscience* where Amyot has only 'iniustement'.[3] There is perhaps some tendency to Christianise in what he says about conscience. Considered, however, in relation to his thought in general the matter appears in a somewhat different light.

> De fonder la recompence des actions vertueuses sur l'approbation d'autruy, c'est prendre un trop incertain et trouble fondement.[4]

[1] II, xvi: EM ii, 396; TR 607(*a*).
[2] III, ii: EM iii, 25; TR 785(*b*).
[3] III, i: TR 775; Plutarch, *Œuvres morales*, 1572, f. 189ʳ.
[4] III, ii: EM iii, 24; TR 785.

If moral rules are relative and uncertain like everything else, then, just as self-knowledge is the only certain knowledge, so the individual conscience is the only certain moral guide. Once more, in spite of the contradictions, everything hangs together. Rather than a Christian position we may see here an anticipation of the benevolence of the philosophers of the Enlightenment:

> Il y a certes je ne sçay quelle congratulation de bien faire qui nous resjouit en nous mesmes, et une fierté genereuse qui accompaigne la bonne conscience.[1]

It is difficult in this area to disentangle the strands of Christian and pagan or humanistic thought. What is essential is that inner reality is always preferred to outward show. He sums it up, still in *Du repentir*, in a declaration which is personal but may stand for his view of conscience in general:

> Qui me verroit jusques dans l'ame, encore ne me trouveroit-il coulpable, ny de l'affliction et ruyne de personne, ny de vengence ou d'envie, ny d'offence publique des loix, ny de nouvelleté et de trouble, ny de faute à ma parole; et quoy que la licence du temps permit et aprint à chacun, si n'ay-je mis la main ny és biens ny en la bourse d'homme François, et n'ay vescu que sur la mienne, non plus en guerre qu'en paix; ny ne me suis servy du travail de personne, sans loyer. Ces tesmoignages de la conscience plaisent; et nous est grand benefice que cette esjouyssance naturelle, et le seul payement qui jamais ne nous manque.[2]

This is his ideal of the man of honour and we cannot help being reminded of the fifteenth psalm, though again it has nothing of any specific religion. At any rate, in considering the diversity of his moral explorations we should not forget the presence of this firm centre.

If his profession of moral faith is firm and noble, it could also be called cautious: he speaks here of what he has not done rather than of what he has. Moderation, avoidance of extremes, even mediocrity in the Horatian sense, are generally thought to be characteristic of Montaigne, and though this is far from being the whole of him it clearly cannot be dismissed. Again one essay, *De la moderation,* is centred on the theme, but again it makes frequent reappearances, especially in *Du repentir* and the final essays of the Third Book. *De la moderation* is in striking contrast with the

---

1 III, ii: EM iii, 23; TR 784.
2 III, ii: EM iii, 23-4; TR 784-5.

exalted tone of the neighbouring *De l'amitié*. Excess of virtue is itself vicious:

> Nous pouvons saisir la vertu de façon qu'elle en deviendra vicieuse, si nous l'embrassons d'un desir trop aspre et violant.[1]

It may be remarked in passing that this is hardly consistent with Christian morals and leaves little room for the notion of sanctity. Similarly courage, if pressed too far, becomes temerity, obstinacy and folly;[2] even wisdom itself needs moderating, just as much as folly.[3] Put in positive terms, these principles lead to the well-known statements of the Third Book:

> (*b*) Le pris de l'ame ne consiste pas à aller haut, mais ordonnéement. (*c*) Sa grandur ne s'exerce pas en la grandur, c'est en la mediocrité.[4]

La grandur de l'ame n'est pas tant tirer à mont et tirer avant comme sçavoir se ranger et circonscrire.[5]

These remarks are absolutely central to our understanding of Montaigne's attitude to life, and must be set against his more revolutionary utterances. With moderation in the exercise of virtue goes a continual insistence on the importance of private as opposed to public actions. Heroic deeds are necessarily rare; the real test comes with the performance of the ordinary tasks of everyday life:

> Qui a de la valeur, si le face parestre en ses meurs, en ses propos ordineres, à traiter l'amour ou des querelles, au jeu, au lict, à la table, à la conduite de ses affaires, et œconomie de sa maison.[6]

This links up with the theme of constancy which cannot be established in sudden spurts, which can only be detected in the slow and unremarkable processes of familiar life. And this in turn reflects the whole method of the *Essais*, the gradual unfolding of thought and observation. The emphasis on private life and moderate virtue leads naturally – and here we are approaching something less often noticed – to an attack on fame and glory, on the fundamental values of the military nobility to which Montaigne ostensibly belonged. He constantly rejects the noble concept of

[1] I, xxx: EM i, 257; TR 195(*a*).
[2] I, xv: TR 68(*a*).
[3] III, v: TR 818(*b*).
[4] III, ii: EM iii, 28; TR 787.
[5] III, xiii: EM iii, 422; TR 1090(*c*).
[6] II, xxxvii: EM ii, 610; TR 764(*c*).

gloire and even the honour with which it was inseparably linked. To them he opposes the personal and individual standards of conscience: 'Toute persone d'honeur choisit de perdre plus tost son honeur, que de perdre sa consciance.'[1]

The emphasis on moderation and mediocrity may suggest a mediocre view of morality. This is not, however, true, although it has been often assumed. Especially in the Third Book, he brings out the extreme difficulty of moderation, of striking an exact balance between opposite excesses. Private virtue is more difficult than public, it is easier to speak like Aristotle and live like Caesar than to live and speak like Socrates.[2]

> Le peuple se trompe: on va bien plus facilement par les bouts, où l'extremité sert de borne d'arrest et de guide, que par la voye du milieu, large et ouverte. . . .[3]

The force of the argument and the originality of expression are alike undeniable. And, beyond this, moderation is not to be confused with pusillanimity:

> Rien de noble ne se faict sans hazard. . . . La prudence si tendre et circonspecte, est mortelle ennemye de hautes executions.[4]

We have here, in a late addition, an important note in Montaigne's morality and one which is too frequently overlooked.

With moderation and the virtues of private life goes something else, which is not exactly morality but which is not in the end separable from it, and that is the practical conduct of life. It would no doubt be generally agreed that it is a duty to organise one's own affairs as effectively as possible but when it comes to the details of how it should be done there is a feeling that they are merely selfish and not to be treated as moral problems at all. It may even be suggested that the terrible divorce in European history between high moral pretensions and monstrous actions (the treatment of the American Indians, to take an example close to Montaigne's heart) is partly due to a tradition of an impossible selflessness. Whatever we may think about this, such a divorce is far removed from Montaigne's way of thinking. Throughout the *Essais* the duty owed to one's neighbour and the duty owed to

---

[1] II, xvi; EM ii, 406; TR 614(*c*). Cf. also III, x: TR 996(*c*), where honour is opposed to order and reason.
[2] III, xii: TR 1032.
[3] III, xiii: EM iii, 422; TR 1090.
[4] I, xxiv: EM i, 165; TR 128(*b*).

oneself are intermingled and at the same time kept in balance by a sure sense of connections and distinctions. So a great deal of what he has to say takes the form of advice or discussion of how to act in practical situations. Most of the military essays like *Si le chef d'une place assiegée doit sortir pour parlementer* or *L'heure des parlemens dangereuse* come into this category, as do a number of minor essays on such subjects as *D'un defaut de nos polices* (on the desirability of a sort of information office in each town) or *De ne contrefaire le malade*. A good example is the very short *A demain les affaires*: starting from an anecdote in Plutarch it deals with the question of whether or not to open letters as soon as they are received; dignity suggests that they should be put aside but prudence often that they should be read at once, whatever the company. The question seems a trivial one but its interest lies in the way practical and moral considerations are interwoven. Of course essays like these present obvious and relatively simple examples. It is in the running commentary of major essays that the more penetrating observations occur. To give one instance, in *De mesnager sa volonté* Montaigne points out that in the conduct of affairs detachment is much more successful than passionate engagement:

> Nous ne conduisons jamais bien la chose de laquelle nous sommes possedez et conduicts.[1]

This again is closely linked to the doctrine of moderation, which is superior to ostentatious virtue in that it is better adapted to attaining the practical object of whatever we are doing. It throws a great deal of light (as does the whole essay) on Montaigne's view of the relation between the two duties, to self and others. It also anticipates the argument of Diderot's *Paradoxe sur le comédien* (the actor who lives the part is inferior to the one who remains detached). Diderot is speaking from an aesthetic standpoint, Montaigne from one somewhere between morality, practical efficiency and self-interest, but the distinction is not perhaps fundamental.

Yet when all has been said about moderation and practical good sense, there remains in Montaigne's morality something which seems to have little to do with these categories, something which is indeed profoundly subversive. This is the line of

---

[1] III, x: EM iii, 285; TR 985(*b*).

hedonism, of immoralism, of attack on rigid moral codes which subsequently leads through Diderot and Stendhal to Pater, Nietzsche, and Gide, the aspect of his ethics most pregnant with consequences for European thought and life. We have seen the precision with which he discriminates between the duty one owes to others and the duty one owes to oneself. But what is the duty one owes to oneself? A number of answers might be given and they might vary at different stages of the *Essais*. The primary answer, however, and the answer most typical of the final stages, is the duty of self-realisation, of self-perfecting, not in the sense of conformity to someone else's ideal but of the complete attainment of the inner logic of one's own being. How familiar, almost commonplace, these ideas have become! But this does not detract from Montaigne's originality when he propounded them.

It might seem at first sight that self-realisation could lead to other solutions besides hedonism, in an ascetic temperament to Stoicism for example. And so in theory it may. In practice, however, asceticism inevitably involves the repression of natural inclinations which for perfect self-realisation must be released. At any rate one might conclude, almost in agreement with Villey, that the Stoical strand in Montaigne's thought is an imperfect stage in the development of his potential self. I say 'almost in agreement' because we are confronted with a continuous process of self-discovery and self-revelation rather than an evolution neatly divided into three phases.

The presence of an epicurean element in Montaigne is familiar enough, but a brief outline is necessary if we are to grasp what is central to his thought on moral questions. Even by 1580 the notion of pleasure as duty is quite firmly stated, especially in *De la solitude*:

> Il faut retenir a tout nos dens et nos griffes l'usage des plaisirs de la vie que nos ans nous arrachent des poingz les uns après les autres, et les alonger de toute nostre puissance.[1]

'Il faut' is particularly noteworthy. Or again, at the end of the last essay of 1580 (*De la ressemblance des enfans aux peres*):

> Certes, je n'ay point le cœur si enflé, ne si venteux, qu'un plaisir solide, charnu et moëleus comme la santé, je l'alasse eschanger pour un plaisir imaginaire, spirituel et aërée [that is, glory].[2]

[1] I, xxxiv: DB i, 207–8.
[2] II, xxxvii: EM ii, 612; TR 766(a).

These examples, chosen among several, show that the leitmotiv of the Third Book is already clearly present in the first two, though it does not occupy the same dominant position. And it is true that in the early books the qualifications are more noticeable. Thus, at one extreme, there is the pessimistic note about the human condition which we have observed in the *Apologie*:

> mais la misere de nostre condition porte que nous n'avons pas tant à jouir qu'à fuir, et que l'extreme volupté ne nous touche pas comme une legiere douleur . . . Nous ne sentons point l'entiere santé comme la moindre des maladies . . . Nostre bien estre, ce n'est que la privation d'estre mal.[1]

And pleasure brings satiety (in *De l'inequalité qui est entre nous*): those who have too much of a good thing no longer enjoy it. Kings, choirboys, actors, the sultan in his harem:[2] the disparateness of the examples illustrates Montaigne's leaping and dancing intelligence, passing rapidly from one thing to another and perceiving the most unexpected affinities.

Such qualifications are also present in the Third Book and the interpolations of the Bordeaux Copy, though on the whole considerably muted. Thus, in an addition to *De l'institution des enfans*, virtue encourages pleasure even to the point of satiety if not quite of weariness ('jusques à la satieté . . . sinon jusques à la lasseté',[3] a step beyond the last reference), but still stops the drinker before drunkenness and so on. In other words, the only limit to pleasure is when it ceases to be pleasurable. Similarly in *De l'experience* temperance is associated with pleasure, not its scourge but its seasoning.[4] Hedonism is tempered by reason. But this, it is hardly necessary to say, is the standard epicurean argument and by no means confined to Montaigne. Again, consideration of pleasure cannot be divorced from that of pain, but pain is no argument against hedonism, since it serves to enhance pleasure by contrast: 'nature nous a presté la douleur pour l'honneur et service de la volupté et indolence',[5] followed by the remarks of Socrates, as his chains are removed, on the narrow alliance of pleasure and pain. Montaigne has travelled a long way from the con-

---

[1] II, xii: EM ii, 213; TR 472.
[2] I, xlii: TR 254–6.
[3] I, xxvi: EM i, 210; TR 161(*c*).
[4] III, xiii: TR 1091(*c*).
[5] III, xiii: EM iii, 398; TR 1072.

strained efforts to conquer pain by will-power of *Que le goust des biens et des maux.*

However, these reservations, if that is what they are, do not loom very large in the Third Book beside what is almost the hymn to pleasure of *Sur des vers de Virgile* or the end of *De l'experience.* Nor is it merely (and here we are approaching what is original in Montaigne) a matter of passive enjoyment of whatever life has to offer. On the contrary he stresses again and again the intelligent, conscious and active determination to seize and magnify each moment before it passes: 'à en poiser et estimer le bon heur et amplifier',[1] or 'Jusques aux moindres occasions de plaisir que je puis rencontrer, je les empoigne'.[2] Passages like these help to show that we are dealing with moral judgements and attitudes, with something like a recipe for life. And they are, as must be obvious, intimately connected with his conception of time. We have seen that Montaigne's tense is the present and that he records *le passage* by describing his feelings of the moment. And similarly here:

> Principallement à cette heure que j'apperçoy la mienne [life] si briefve en temps, je la veux estendre en pois; je veus arrester la promptitude de sa fuite par la promptitude de ma sesie, et par la vigueur de l'usage compenser la hastiveté de son escoulement: à mesure que la possession du vivre est plus courte, il me la faut rendre plus profonde et plus pleine.[3]

The key-words hardly need stressing: *heure, temps, promptitude, pois, sesie, hastiveté, escoulement, possession, courte.* The passage of time is no longer merely a matter of observation and record but of positive action. Once again everything hangs together. The dominance of the present tense is not only a matter of style, of the self-portrait, of the depiction of movement, of the metaphysics of time, but also of the general moral attitude. It may be objected that all this is nothing more than a restatement of the commonplace Horatian—and Ronsardian—*carpe diem.* True enough, but what marks Montaigne out is precisely the intense concentration not just on the day but on the instant, not only 'de jour en jour' but 'de minute en minute', and the vigour of his *sesie* which goes well beyond the gently anacreontic note of

---

[1] III, xiii: EM iii, 425; TR 1092.
[2] III, v; EM iii, 71; TR 819.
[3] III, xiii: EM iii, 424; TR 1092. On this question see also Poulet, *Études sur le temps humain*, pp. 11-15.

F

'Cueillez dès aujourd'hui les roses de la vie'. From this point of view the closest parallel among French moralists is one to whom he has been less often compared than to some others, and that is Stendhal. In both we find the *chasse au bonheur,* the exquisitely keen sense of overwhelming contentment, often arising from trivial things, and this as something not just to be experienced but to be achieved, as in a sentence already quoted: 'je les rameine [thoughts] à la promenade, au vergier, à la douceur de cette solitude et à moy.'[1]

Montaigne is not much given to prohibitions and condemnations. Still, any moral system must be partly defined by what is disapproved or rejected as well as by what is approved. The vices he dislikes are cruelty, lying and dissimulation, and perhaps even more strongly envy and malice. Jealousy and envy its sister are the worst vices for him (he has felt the first but not the second). Once again we are bound to admire the precision with which he makes the distinction. In *Du jeune Caton* he offers three explanations of the motives of detractors:

ils le font ou par malice, ou par ce vice de ramener leur creance à leur porteé, dequoy je viens de parler, ou, comme je pense plustost, pour n'avoir pas la veuë assez forte et assez nette pour concevoir la splendeur de la vertu en sa pureté naifve, ny dressée à cela.[2]

Montaigne does not usually waste time on his inferiors, but this is devastating. In one of the most significant corrections of the Bordeaux Copy (for, as he claims, he rarely makes corrections, at any rate of substance as opposed to style), in place of 'usures, veniances et paillardises' he puts 'la haine, l'avarice, l'injustice';[3] his idea of the gravest faults has clearly changed. This whole line of thought culminates in the attack in an interpolation towards the end of *De l'experience* on 'nostre esprit maladif, rabatjoye, qui nous desgoute d'elles [les voluptez naturelles] come de soi mesme'.[4] Finally, to return from the negative to the positive, and to the theme of detraction:

Pour juger des choses grandes et haultes, il faut un' ame de mesme, autrement nous leur attribuons le vice, qui est le nostre.[5]

---

[1] III, xiii: EM iii, 419; TR 1088.
[2] I, xxxvii: EM i, 302; TR 227.
[3] I, lvi: EM i, 410; MJ ii, 293; TR 304.
[4] III, xiii: EM iii, 417; TR 1086(c).
[5] I, xiv: EM i, 82; TR 68.

Once more it is necessary to stress his essential elevation of mind, a facet of his character as a writer which is often overlooked.

So far what we have been considering is the hedonism which is fundamentally a development of the epicureanism of antiquity and on which, certainly, Montaigne has imposed his own stamp. We can now approach the area in which he is more profoundly original, in which he anticipates rather than echoes, looks forward rather than back. This is of course the assault on, perhaps rather the undermining of, all rules and codes.

> Un jeune homme doit troubler ses regles pour esveiller sa vigueur, la garder de moisir et s'apoltronir. Et n'est train de vie si sot et si debile que celuy qui se conduict par ordonnance et discipline.[1]

We are already well on the way to Pater's 'our failure is to form habits', and indeed the whole concluding passage of *The Renaissance* is very close to Montaigne. He thinks little of timid and routine worthiness: 'certeine image de preud'homie scholastique, serve des præceptes, contreinte sous l'esperance et la creinte.'[2] True virtue, on the other hand, must be able to support itself without external aid, relying only on the seed of universal reason implanted in every man. Nor does it shrink from excess. Thus drunkenness, though, as we have noted, discouraged in a general way on hedonistic grounds, ought sometimes to be practised, not only in Germany as a concession to local custom but as an exercise in vigour.[3] And this is in *De l'institution des enfans* and written before 1580. In the Third Book the doctrine of excess is summed up in the brief and pregnant sentence: 'Estendons nostre possession jusque aux derniers moyens.'[4] We are here confronted by a real difficulty, which is of course that of reconciling excess with moderation. Perhaps we must simply admit this as typical of his contradictory approach to truth. It might however be suggested, paradoxically but seriously, that moderation itself must be treated with moderation, that it must be relaxed from time to time. At a deeper level, moderation for Montaigne is not mediocrity but a point of balance between conflicting forces of great intensity.

The rejection of rules leads naturally to its positive complement, a way of life marked by suppleness and flexibility. On a mainly

1 III, xiii: EM iii, 385; TR 1061.
2 III, xii: EM iii, 354; TR 1037(*c*).
3 I, xxvi: TR 166–7(*a*).
4 III, xiii: EM iii, 387; TR 1063(*b*).

physical plane we find it in 'un homme de guerre ... se doit accoustumer à toute diversité et inegalité de vie',[1] and in similar injunctions in *De l'institution des enfans.* Extended to moral life it appears in 'C'est estre, mais ce n'est pas vivre, que se tenir attaché et obligé par necessité à un seul train. Les plus belles ames sont celles qui ont plus de varieté et de soupplesse',[2] and in the whole of this opening of *De trois commerces,* not to speak of many other examples. Now *soupplesse* is clearly very close to Gide's *disponibilité,* the freedom to face each new situation untrammelled by habit, custom, precedent or law. What both reject is the reduction of morality to any merely routine system.

These principles emerge perhaps even more powerfully when they are applied in the sphere of moral judgements on individuals:

Ny les homes, ny leurs vies ne se mesurent à l'aune.[3]

or:

Quand on juge d'une action particuliere, il faut considerer plusieurs circonstances et l'homme tout entier qui l'a produicte, avant la baptizer.[4]

or again (on Alexander):

mais il est impossible de conduire si grands mouvemens avec les reigles de la justice: telles gens veulent estre jugez en gros par la maistresse fin de leurs actions.[5]

We see here a multiplicity of moral judgements: there are no rigid rules, each case is unique. In all this, yet again, everything hangs together: with relativism, of course, and 'l'homme ondoyant et divers', but more specifically with 'tout exemple cloche' and the extremely penetrating critique of language, definitions, and laws at the beginning of *De l'experience.* This is not to say that judgement is impossible (the examples quoted show the contrary) but certainly that it is very difficult and only to be achieved by complete understanding of all the circumstances. An almost inevitable consequence of the demolition of rules is that the wise man ('le sage') can do what he likes. Montaigne does not put

---

[1] III, xiii: EM iii, 385; TR 1061.
[2] III, iii: EM iii, 40; TR 796.
[3] I, xx: EM i, 118; TR 93(*c*).
[4] II, xi: EM ii, 127; TR 406(*a*).
[5] II, xxxvi: EM ii, 570; TR 733(*b*).

it as frankly as Rabelais but rather, as so often, by cunningly chosen quotations from ancient authors and then, as so often, by a physiological image. After quoting Diogenes on the opposition between nature and laws, he goes on:

> Pour les estomacs tendres, il faut des ordonances contraintes et artificielles. Les bons estomacs suivent simplement les prescriptions de leur naturel appetit.[1]

Here perhaps we think of Nietzsche rather than of Gide, of *Herrenmoral* and *Sklavenmoral*. The notion of an elite, a happy few with special privileges, is not strongly marked in Montaigne but it is certainly present in passages like these. Similarly, a little further on in *De la vanité*, a just man might do ten things in his life for which he could be hanged, another might never offend against the laws and yet not deserve the title of virtuous. Again we see the stress on positive as against negative morality.

To trace the history of these ideas from Montaigne to the present would go far beyond the limits of this study. In particular it would be necessary to examine the eighteenth and early nineteenth centuries in considerable detail, the Abbé Galiani or Diderot (the *Neveu de Rameau* and the *Supplément au Voyage de Bougainville*) or Balzac, or Stendhal perhaps more than anyone. However, since they have had such an immense influence not only on the thought but on the life of Europe and the world, we might consider briefly the three principal figures through whom (as well as through his own impetus) Montaigne has entered the mainstream of twentieth-century moral conceptions, that is to say Pater, Nietzsche and Gide (I am not putting them on the same level of intrinsic greatness). In all three cases, of course, the influence was direct and acknowledged. Each of them helps us to see how Montaigne avoids a too complete acceptance of the doctrines of immoralism. What distinguishes Pater, apart from an aestheticism which, though not foreign to Montaigne, certainly does not constitute a principal preoccupation in the *Essais* and apart from a far greater reliance on elusive implication, on speaking through the mouths of others, is his lack of direct contact with reality and his grave, even gloomy style. As always, style here is a matter of substance: Montaigne's humour and playfulness set his moral ideas in a fuller and more balanced proportion with life. We cannot imagine him burning with a hard gem-like

---

[1] III, ix: EM iii, 264; TR 968(*b,c*).

flame and though he might have approved of 'to maintain this ecstasy' he was too much of a realist to believe it possible.

Of the three the closest to Montaigne is no doubt Gide, who was so deeply permeated by the *Essais*. Here it is the polarisation of puritanism and liberty, and the resulting sense of tension and conflict (not an inferiority in itself) which marks the difference: Gide lacks Montaigne's serenity and tends to push both sides of his dichotomy to an extreme point. The *acte gratuit*, Lafcadio and Fleurissoire, are in a way contained in Montaigne's insistence that rules must be broken not for any specific advantage but simply to affirm one's superiority to them. Yet we can easily see what short work he would have made of a case like this, how soon it would have been caught in his net of checks and balances.

With Nietzsche, the most influential of the heirs of this side of Montaigne, the opposition becomes clearer still. The writer of 'L'homme ne peut estre que ce qu'il est, ny imaginer que selon sa portée',[1] would have had little sympathy with the notion of the superman. That was from 1580. The famous conclusion of the last essay: 'C'est une absolue perfection, et comme divine, de sçavoir jouyr loiallement de son estre', may seem to suggest the possibility of achieving a superior sort of humanity by the unfettered development of the personality without regard for codes and rules. But we must not forget the equally famous continuation:

(c) Et au plus eslevé throne du monde, si ne somes assis que sur nostre cul. (b) Les plus belles vies sont, à mon gré, celles qui se rangent au modelle commun (c) et humain, aveq ordre, mais sans miracle et (b) sans extravagance.[2]

The liberation Montaigne desires is not divorced from the potentialities of ordinary human beings. More seriously still, liberation for Nietzsche is inseparable from power, is in fact identified with the enjoyment of it. Power for Montaigne, whether political or personal, is not something which enters into the moral scheme. He sees it indeed as the enemy of the happiness he seeks, as a nuisance, and only to be assumed with the greatest reluctance. And we can, with caution, draw a wider conclusion. The French proponents of moral liberty lay all the stress on the *libido sentiendi* and make their case with so much freshness, gaiety and beauty

[1] II, xii: EM ii, 252; TR 501(a).
[2] III, xiii: EM iii, 430–1; TR 1096.

that they are difficult to resist. In the German tradition of which Nietzsche is the supreme representative (but even Goethe is not unmarked by it) the intrusion of the *libido dominandi* changes the scale of values.

However, we are left with the major difficulty. If morals are about relations with others and duties towards them, how can we consider in moral terms a system, or complex of attitudes rather, which seems to be entirely self-centred, to be constructed without reference to other people at all ('Il faut . . . n'espouser rien que soy')?[1] It will be seen that in a way we have turned in a full circle and that this is a re-statement in moral terms of the relation between the self-portrait and the picture of the human condition. In order to answer the question we have to view it in the general context of the *Essais*. When we do so, it becomes immediately clear that self-centredness is by no means incompatible with a sense of duty to others. In 'Il faut . . . n'espouser rien que soy' the stress is on *espouser*. Montaigne refuses to commit himself emotionally and totally to other people's interests and affairs, but this leaves him in a better position to judge in a detached way what he ought to do for them. A late addition to *Du dementir* shows the balance as he sees it : 'nous nous devons en partie à la societé, mais en la meillure partie à nous.'[2] His social obligations are exactly performed, but this leaves a vast area of life which is not covered by such duties and obligations, and it is one of Montaigne's greatest merits as a moralist that he concentrates on what should be done with this area. He is in fact a philosopher of leisure, which links him again with Nietzsche and Gide but marks him off from the long line of puritan moralists (of whom La Bruyère is no doubt the most eminent French representative). He does, it is true, share one thing with them, and that is a sense of the moral importance of time, but needless to say what he thinks should be done with time is very different. But to speak of duties and obligations to others is not quite sufficient. We must not overlook his extreme sensibility, his hatred of cruelty and injustice, his compassion for the poor and the unfortunate. Of course this could be explained in La Rochefoucauld's terms (unselfishness is disguised selfishness) and he himself almost admits it. What he dislikes in cruelty is the disturbance it causes to his own delicate nervous system, the projection of himself into the sufferer. How-

[1] I, xxxix: EM i, 315; TR 236(*a*).
[2] II, xviii: EM ii, 454; TR 648(*c*).

ever, this psychological explanation does not really affect the moral issue: first of all, we can see how rare a quality it is by comparing him with almost any of his contemporaries; secondly, his temperamental reaction is intellectually generalised, not without risk to himself.

We are still left with the distance we have noticed between him and his later emulators, and to account for this we are driven back to moderation. An article by Frederick Kellermann suggests that 'selon qu'on peut' and 'mentre si può' are more significant than 'Que sais-je?' for the understanding of Montaigne.[1] Certainly his keen sense of human limitations prevents him not only from attempting heroic and extraordinary virtues but also from carrying immoralism to its extreme logical conclusions.

Still, it would be a pity to end on this sedate and rather negative note. What is perhaps ultimately most striking in Montaigne's morality is its strong aesthetic orientation. So we have the story of Alexander drinking the potion offered by his physician while reading the letter which accused the physician of poisoning him:

je ne sçay s'il y a traict en sa vie, qui ayt plus de fermeté que cestuy-cy, ny une beauté illustre par tant de visages.[2]

Even more explicit is the interpretation of Cato's suicide. After speaking of 'une emotion de plaisir extraordinaire et d'une volupté virile', he goes on:

non pas esguisée par quelque esperance de gloire ... car cette consideration est trop basse pour toucher un cœur si genereux, si hautain et si roide; mais pour la beauté de la chose mesme en soy.[3]

The beauty of the thing in itself: this is exactly the language of post-Kantian aestheticism, and we are back with Pater, Nietzsche and the *acte gratuit*, though Montaigne's view of what constitutes moral beauty is no doubt very different. But this aesthetic attitude goes beyond admiration for the great men of antiquity to embrace the whole of life as when, in a well-known addition to *De l'institution des enfans*, he says of virtue: 'Elle aime la vie, elle aime la beauté et la gloire et la santé.'[4] And not only human life but animals, trees and plants also:

[1] 'The *Essais* and Socrates', *Symposium*, x (1956).
[2] I, xxiv: EM i, 165; TR 128(*b*).
[3] II, xi: EM ii, 124; TR 403(*a*). Cf. Conche, *Montaigne ou la conscience heureuse*, p. 77.
[4] I, xxvi: EM i, 210; TR 162(*c*).

... si y a-il un certain respect qui nous attache, et un general devoir d'humanité, non aux bestes seulement qui ont vie et sentiment, mais aux arbres mesmes et aux plantes. Nous devons la justice aux hommes, et la grace et la benignité aux autres creatures qui en peuvent estre capables.[1]

It is in this wide acceptance of life, far exceeding mere prudence or moderation, that Montaigne's liberation finds its fullest expression and all the apparent contradictions find their resolution.

[1] II, xi: EM ii, 139; TR 414(*a*).

☙ 8 ☙

The Mind of Montaigne:
Scepticism and Diversity

SO far we have looked at the human condition largely from
the point of view of the course of man's life, physical
and moral. This has naturally involved some insistence on
Montaigne's intellectual and even philosophical positions, his
Epicureanism in particular. These were not, however, the dominant considerations. Our next step must be to widen the field of
vision, to examine his attitude to more specifically philosophical
problems and to matters which transcend the life of the individual, even when that individual stands for man. This will constitute no real break with the last chapter (and we are coming to see
more and more that there are no real breaks anywhere in the
fabric of Montaigne's thought), but we shall now be concerned
less with man's life in itself than with his intellectual relation to
the world, still an essential ingredient of the human condition as
he views it.

Whether or not Montaigne is a philosopher in the technical
sense (that is to say whether he belongs to the category which
includes Descartes, Kant and Hegel) is hardly a question which
merits serious discussion: 'La question est de parolles, et se paye
de mesme.'[1] We have seen that he does not figure largely in
histories of philosophy written by philosophers. Two things are,
however, certain. One is that through Descartes he has exercised
a far-reaching influence on the development of modern philosophy
in its strictest sense. The other, more important for our immediate
purpose, is that he devotes a great deal of attention to the traditional problems of philosophy. This is particularly, though not

[1] III, xiii: EM iii, 366; TR 1046.

exclusively, visible in the *Apologie* with its vast survey of the philosophical systems of antiquity and their attitudes to various central questions such as the immortality of the soul or the supreme good. Of course it would be wrong to suppose that all this was based on reading of the original authors, though some of it was. Summaries of the views of different philosophers were available in writers like Cicero and Diogenes Laertius.[1] It remains true, as Jean Prévost has pointed out, that Montaigne developed an increasing capacity to grasp and dominate whole philosophical systems without adhering to them himself.[2] In general his attitude to philosophy is very much like his attitude to virtue. So far from being dull and solemn it is something to be approached in a mood of gaiety and playfulness:

> On a grand tort de la peindre inaccessible aux enfans, et d'un visage renfroigné, sourcilleux et terrible. Qui me l'a masquée de ce faux visage, pasle et hideux? Il n'est rien plus gay, plus gaillard, plus enjoué, et à peu que je ne die follastre.[3]

He is above all suspicious of sophistries, verbal tricks, logic-chopping, and deliberate obscurity. To these he opposes the objections of common sense which in some ways anticipate recent philosophical movements in their impatience with insoluble problems. Thus he remarks that when philosophers are called on to judge the rights and wrongs of a lawsuit or the actions of a man they are still trying to decide whether life and movement exist or what law and justice mean in the abstract.[4] In the last resort the aim of philosophy is living, not the mere acquisition of technical knowledge.[5] It is perhaps this practical orientation as well as his unsystematic form which has excluded him from the ranks of officially recognised philosophers.

We have already considered his Epicureanism as a general moral attitude rather than as a philosophy. His Stoicism has only been mentioned in passing, and because of the controversies it has aroused as well as for its intrinsic importance it demands separate attention; it must also involve a further look at Epicureanism, if only to see how far the two can be distinguished. In Stoicism

---

[1] On this see Hensel, 'Montaigne und die Antike', *Vorträge der Bibliothek Warburg 1925–1926*, Leipzig and Berlin, 1928, p. 70.
[2] *Vie de Montaigne*, pp. 175–6.
[3] I, xxvi: EM i, 208; TR 160(*a*). Cf. p. 143 above.
[4] I, xxv: TR 133(*c*).
[5] I, xxvi: TR 167.

we are dealing not just with Montaigne but with a widespread movement which occupied a preponderant position in the intellectual life of Europe in the second half of the sixteenth century and even in the first half of the seventeenth. Its influence can be detected in Jodelle and Garnier as well as in Shakespeare and the English Elizabethan dramatists, in La Boétie, and above all in the principal exponents of a Christianised Stoicism, Montaigne's contemporaries or near-contemporaries Justus Lipsius and du Vair. It is indeed about 1580, the date of first publication of the *Essais*, that the movement reaches its peak. Though the physical and metaphysical theories of the ancient Stoics are not wholly neglected, it is their moral philosophy which is at the centre of interest. To summarise, and perhaps to caricature, the sage or wise man of the Stoics tries by intense and deliberate effort to attain a mastery over himself and his passions, to maintain a rigid virtue which separates him from the common herd, to achieve a state of indifference to external things which makes him impervious to every possible misfortune, to poverty, pain, imprisonment, torture, death. Of all the philosophical systems of antiquity it is no doubt the simplest, the most consistent, and the narrowest. It is easily assimilated to Christianity because of the emphasis on perfection and the salvation of the individual; it is fundamentally incompatible with Christianity, as Pascal profoundly observed, because for the Stoics the individual can achieve this perfection unaided, Stoicism is rooted in pride. The vogue of Stoicism at this period is not hard to explain. The Wars of Religion in France and the Low Countries produced conditions in which the most innocent, and the most privileged too, were exposed to all the misfortunes just enumerated. As Montaigne himself says, ordered society had virtually collapsed, and it was natural to seek refuge in a doctrine which enabled the individual to stand firm, fortified by his internal resources alone. At a deeper level, and this accounts for the wider diffusion of the movement, even in countries which had been spared the horrors of civil war, there was the disappointment which followed the extravagant and unattainable hopes of the early humanists, a disillusionment which is reflected in the opening of the *Apologie*. Humanism was still strong, but the variety and openness of ancient thought tended to be abandoned for a doctrine which offered a bedrock of narrow certainty.

The presence of a Stoic element in Montaigne, especially in the early essays, is undeniable (though it was denied by Armaingaud).

For Villey, as we have seen, Stoicism was the first stage, the main theme of the early essays written before about 1574, but it was never deeply felt, a mere preliminary to the elaboration of the personal philosophy. Stoicism was succeeded by scepticism and scepticism by naturalism. It is worth noting that Montaigne's immediate contemporaries regarded him as a Stoic. Claude Expilly in the sonnet to Montaigne first published in the 1595 Lyons edition addresses him as 'Magnanime Stoïque', and Florimond de Raemond speaks of his 'philosophie courageuse et presque stoique'.[1] Among the early essays two, already mentioned more than once, present something like a standard model of Stoic opinions. These are *Que philosopher, c'est apprendre à mourir* and *Que le goust des biens et des maux depend en bonne partie de l'opinion que nous en avons*, the burden of which is that we can learn to conquer death, poverty and pain (though the essay is transformed and humanised by the later additions). All the emphasis is on preparation for these calamities by bracing the will to meet them: 'roidissons nous, et efforçons nous'.[2] Mastery of the passions will give us 'la vraye et souveraine liberté, qui nous donne dequoy faire la figue à la force et à l'injustice, et nous moquer des prisons et des fers'.[3]

> Stone walls do not a prison make,
> Nor iron bars a cage.

It is no wonder that the same doctrines attract two men caught up in the disasters of civil war. Montaigne himself is well aware of the connection between this Stoicism and contemporary events. In *De l'institution des enfans* his pupil must be inured to hardship

> pour le dresser à la peine et aspreté de la desloueure [dislocation of members], de la cholique, du cautere, et de la geole, et de la torture. Car de ces dernieres icy encore peut il estre en prinse, qui regardent les bons selon le temps, come les meschans. Nous en somes à l'espreuve.[4]

The same connection is clearly indicated by du Vair in *De la constance* (1594). It is unnecessary to go into all the details of Montaigne's Stoicism, but a few characteristic positions may

---

[1] *Erreur populaire de la papesse Iane*, Bordeaux, 1594, p. 159.
[2] I, xx: EM i, 107; TR 85(a).
[3] I, xx: EM i, 113; TR 90(a).
[4] I, xxvi: EM i, 199; TR 153(c).

serve to show that it is not limited to the schematic outline we have so far sketched. Men's wants are nearly all superfluous and artificial: the Stoics maintained that a man could live on an olive a day.[1] We have here, especially when taken in conjunction with the cannibals, a foreshadowing of Rousseau's central arguments. The Stoic contempt for death leads to the legitimacy of suicide as the supreme act of liberty in certain circumstances: this point is stated quite often and forms the main theme, though cautiously wrapped up, of *Coustume de l'isle de Cea*. Similarly, his coolness towards family ties and affections may be attributed to Stoicism as well as to temperament:

> Il faut avoir femmes, enfans, biens, et sur tout de la santé, qui peut; mais non pas s'y attacher en maniere que nostre heur en despende.[2]

This is one of the points at which Stoicism touches Christianity closely, but the difference of emphasis emerges here with some force: earthly affections and possessions are sacrificed not to the service of a higher power but to one's own peace of mind. Still more deeply part of his own essential attitude is the Stoic theory, on which the triumph over external misfortune rests, that men do not suffer from real evils but only from their own opinions of them (Epictetus is quoted in support).[3] The sage can thus dominate the world of experience, and we perceive a link between Stoicism and scepticism, no longer diametrically opposed.

However, the *Apologie* and the essays written about the same time mark a strong reaction against Stoicism which in the *Apologie* is subjected to the same kind of sceptical mockery as all the other philosophical systems of antiquity, except Pyrrhonism. The story of Possidonius is typical: suffering from a most painful illness which made him twist his arms and grind his teeth he refused to admit that this was real pain. Montaigne comments that he felt the same passions as a lackey but merely conformed to the verbal conventions of his sect.[4] It is noteworthy that du Vair tells the same story but with full approval.[5] In the Third Book the anti-Stoic feeling is more strongly expressed and we find a positive

---

[1] II, xii: TR 450(*a*).
[2] I, xxxix: EM i, 313; TR 235(*a*).
[3] I, xiv: TR 49–50(*a*).
[4] II, xii: TR 469(*a*).
[5] *La philosophie morale des stoiques* in *Traictez philosophiques*, Paris, 1606, p. 48.

alternative rather than just mockery. What is the point, he asks, of preparing oneself for misfortunes only some of which are likely to occur? In one of his finest and most telling images he says that it is like putting on your fur coat in midsummer because you will need it at Christmas.[1] The voluptuous nature of the image in itself suggests a turning away from Stoicism. For noble impassivity he now wants to substitute his own trust in nature, which he modestly calls stupidity:

> Qui ne peut atteindre à cette noble impassibilité Stoicque, qu'il se sauve au giron de cette mienne stupidité populaire.[2]

The development of his attitude towards death, which we have already discussed, offers a special though crucial example of this general change.[3]

So far, apart from the link we have observed between Stoicism and scepticism, Villey's position seems fully confirmed. In fact, however, this is not the whole story, and the Third Book and the Bordeaux Copy still exhibit numerous traces of Stoicism, for example:

> Qui ne couve point ses enfans ou ses honneurs d'une propension esclave, ne laisse pas de vivre commodéement apres leur perte. Qui fait bien principalement pour sa propre satisfaction ne s'altere guere pour voir les hommes juger de ses actions contre son merite. Un quart d'once de patience pourvoit à tels inconvenients.[4]

The first two sentences express standard Stoic principles couched in typically sententious form. We are again close to du Vair, though the tone is milder and the last sentence plays down the effort required in a way which is not quite that of the Stoics themselves. In *De la phisionomie* Montaigne recounts how he behaved when the testing time came and he was threatened with total ruin. Again, and still more powerfully, he makes the connection between a Stoic position and the circumstances of the time:

> En un temps ordinaire et tranquille, on se prepare à des accidens moderez et communs; mais en cette confusion où nous sommes depuis trente ans, tout homme françois, soit en particulier soit en general, se voit à chaque heure sur le point de l'entier renversement

---

[1] III, xii: TR 1027(*b,c*).
[2] III, x: EM iii, 301; TR 997.
[3] See p. 134 above.
[4] III, x: EM iii, 297; TR 994.

de sa fortune. D'autant faut-il tenir son courage fourny de provisions plus fortes et vigoureuses.[1]

The background of sixteenth-century Stoicism could hardly be better conveyed. He profits from these misfortunes to prepare himself for worse with the Stoic *sententia*: 'La vraye liberté, c'est pouvoir toute chose sur soy',[2] an echo of an even stronger statement at the beginning of *Sur des vers de Virgile*: 'Or je veus estre maistre de moy, à tout sens',[3] anticipating the line of *Cinna* which perhaps best expresses Corneille's Stoicism ('Je suis maître de moi comme de l'univers'). In Montaigne, however, as always, we must look at the context: here he must be master of himself to the extent of defending himself as much against temperance and wisdom as against pleasure and folly. In fact, the lessons of his early Stoicism have now borne fruit; they have been absorbed into a larger whole in which they constitute an essential but no longer preponderant element. There is an evolution of a kind but it cannot be divided into three clearly demarcated stages: not only are the later attitudes, as we have seen, potentially there from the beginning, but the early ones persist to the end.[4] We have a gradual enlargement of sensibility and sympathies rather than a linear progression. More important still is the place we must assign to courage and firmness in Montaigne's scheme of things: these qualities are in the Third Book less ostentatiously present than in the early essays but they are present none the less.

As a footnote to this discussion we may add that Stoicism and Epicureanism, like Stoicism and scepticism, are by no means as sharply differentiated as might appear at first sight. Thus when Seneca advises Lucilius to choose death (suicide) rather than continue a life of pomp and self-indulgence, Montaigne comments that it sounds like Stoicism but is in fact derived from Epicurus.[5] In *De la cruauté* he contradicts the common opinion which makes the Stoics more rigorous. At this point he treats the opinions of the two schools together as if they were the same, and speaks (in the first edition, it should be noted) of

[1] III, xii: EM iii, 334; TR 1022–3.
[2] III, xii: EM iii, 334; TR 1022.
[3] III, v: EM iii, 70; TR 818.
[4] For an interesting critique of Villey's views on stoicism and evolution see Boon, 'Émendations des emprunts dans le texte des essais dits "stoïciens" de Montaigne', *Studies in philology*, lxv (1968).
[5] I, xxxiii: TR 216(*a*).

cette brave et genereuse volupté Epicurienne qui fait estat de nourrir mollement en son giron et y faire follatrer la vertu, luy donnant pour ses jouets la honte, les fievres, la pauvreté, la mort et les geénes [tortures].[1]

This is no doubt a fair picture and it suggests that, though the mood (*follatrer, jouets*) is very different, the ultimate aim, indifference to the blows of fortune, is the same. On the other hand, he maintains in the Bordeaux Copy that according to the precepts of Cato's sect (the Stoics presumably) the wise man must be experienced in all natural pleasures.[2] And it is in the 1580 edition, in *De la gloire*, that he includes the text of Epicurus's letter to Hermachus and quotes with warm approval the Epicurean maxim 'hide your life', which he interprets as a recommendation to prefer private life to public.[3] All this further confuses the notion of evolution.

When we examine his views on more restricted subjects we can see how his general philosophical positions are worked out in detail. As we might expect he is scornful of scholastic logic and indeed of formal logic in general. The mockery of *barroco* and *baralipton* (medieval mnemonic formulae for types of syllogism) in *De l'institution des enfans* is well known.[4] A more far-reaching attack occurs in *De l'art de conferer* where reason and scholastic logic are contrasted:

Ce dernier [an opponent in argument] ne voit rien en la raison, mais il vous tient assiegé sur la closture dialectique de ses clauses et sur les formules de son art.

And logic itself is called in question:

Qui a pris de l'entendement en la logique? où sont ses belles promesses?[5]

But he does not confine himself to rhetorical questions and satirical digs. The remarkable critique of definitions begun in *Des livres* and carried further in *De l'experience* brings out the reasons for his distrust of formal logic. In the former he says that he understands plain words and wants to go on to the real point rather than waste time in having them defined (as by Cicero):

1 II, xi: EM ii, 123; TR 402(*a*).
2 III, xiii: TR 1089(*c*).
3 II, xvi: TR 602–3(*a*).
4 I, xxvi: TR 160.
5 III, viii: EM iii, 181; TR 904–5.

Pour moy, qui ne demande qu'à devenir plus sage, non plus sçavant ou eloquant, ces ordonnances logiciennes et Aristoteliques ne sont pas à propos: je veux qu'on comance par le dernier point; j'entens assez que c'est que mort et volupté; qu'on ne s'amuse pas à les anatomizer: je cherche des raisons bonnes et fermes d'arrivée. . . .[1]

In *De l'experience* he shows that definitions are not only a waste of time but strictly impossible since one word is replaced by another which itself requires definition and so on *ad infinitum*:

Une pierre c'est un corps. Mais qui presseroit: Et corps qu'est-ce? – Substance, – Et substance quoy? ainsi de suitte, acculeroit en fin le respondant au bout de son calepin. On eschange un mot pour un autre mot, et souvent plus incogneu. Je sçay mieux que c'est qu'homme que je ne sçay que c'est animal, ou mortel, ou raisonnable.[2]

The conclusion is plain common sense but we must look at the path which has led him to it and the concentrated intelligence with which the argument is conducted. Again he here anticipates Pascal, the discussion of definitions in *De l'esprit géométrique*. Pascal, as usual, is less universally sceptical and narrows the argument down to a distinction between what is definable and what is not. Still, there can be little doubt that the inspiration of his mathematically more solidly based argument came from Montaigne.

So far we have seen how Montaigne undermines the apparatus of traditional logic. We must now ask what he proposes to substitute for it. A first answer is given in 1580 in *De l'institution des enfans* where he lists a series of precepts for the conduct of argument. His pupil must only fight with his equals, he must practise relevance and brevity, he must always admit the truth whether advanced by his adversary or revealed to him by fresh consideration, he must always preserve his liberty of judgement. But these ideas are much more fully and subtly worked out in the Third Book, in *De l'art de conferer*. Incidentally we have here, as with the treatment of definitions, a good illustration of the relation between the Third Book and the first two, not so much a reversal of attitude as an extension and deepening of positions already adumbrated. Pascal called Montaigne 'l'incomparable auteur de l'*Art de conferer*',[3] a judgement often quoted but rather less often

---

[1] II, x: EM ii, 110; TR 393.
[2] III, xiii: EM iii, 366; TR 1046(b).
[3] In *De l'esprit géométrique* (*Œuvres*, ed. Brunschvicg, ix, 284).

explained. The essay, or at least its first part, constitutes a psychology of argument, a living logic. It is thus very close to one of Pascal's chief preoccupations, the art of persuasion, the *esprit de finesse*, the nature of proof, the relation between the geometrical (or logical) and the human. And it constitutes a wonderful pathology of errors in argument, not just logical fallacies but the profound psychological defects which underlie them. Again we find the insistence on order and relevance (an anticipation of the rules of Descartes), an order which is found above all in unsophisticated persons:

L'ordre qui se voit tous les jours aus altercations des bergiers et des enfans de boutique, jamais entre nous.[1]

and on the necessity of recognising the truth, even in the mouth of one's opponent:

Je festoye et caresse la verité en quelque main que je la trouve, et m'y rends alaigrement, et luy tends mes armes vaincues, de loing que je la vois approcher.[2]

It will be apparent from these quotations that logical argument is a moral question, and at one point Montaigne even speaks of verbal crimes:

Nos disputes devoint estre defandues et punies come d'autres crimes verbaus. Quel vice n'esveillent elles et n'amoncellent, tousjours regies et comandées par la cholere! ... Nous n'aprenons à disputer que pour contredire, et, chacun contredisant et estant contredict, il en advient que le fruit du disputer c'est perdre et aneantir la verité.[3]

Indeed the whole essay is in a way concerned with problems of intellectual morality. Thus logic flows into ethics and once again we see the impossibility of constructing artificial barriers. More broadly, Montaigne's living and natural logic, based on directness of understanding rather than on formulae, 'On ne faict poinct tort au subject, quand on le quicte pour voir du moyen de le traicter; je ne dis pas moyen scholastique et artiste, je dis moyen naturel, d'un sain entendement',[4] anticipates the efforts made in the following century, especially by Bacon and Descartes, to create a new anti-scholastic logic to deal with scientific discovery rather

1 III, viii: EM iii, 179; TR 903(*c*).
2 III, viii: EM iii, 178: TR 902(*b*).
3 III, viii: EM iii, 180; TR 904(*c*).
4 III, viii: EM iii, 180; TR 904(*b*).

than with mere deduction from principles universally and unquestioningly accepted. Most important from this point of view is Montaigne's mockery of the scholastic refusal to debate with those who deny the principles.[1] It would be wrong to exaggerate his contribution to the great movement of scientific thought which was to follow so soon after his death, but we have had evidence of his influence on Pascal's logic and, though Descartes's famous rules of method are not the same as Montaigne's precepts, there is a clear affinity in the way they both substitute common sense for technicalities and formalism.

From the point of view of Montaigne himself, however, the most important aspect of the attack on traditional logic is its sceptical orientation. The undermining of the concept of definition offers an outstanding example: if nothing can be defined, nothing can really be known. An examination, however cursory and amateurish, of his epistemology takes us still further in the same direction and shows that common sense is by no means the whole of his philosophy. When we begin to look and think, everything is surprising, knowledge of anything is vague and doubtful:

> Considerons au travers de quels nuages et commant à tastons on nous meine à la connoissance de la pluspart des choses qui nous sont entre mains: certes nous trouverons que c'est plustost accoustumance que science qui nous en oste l'estrangeté.[2]

In fact a group of important essays in Book I may be said (though this does not exhaust their meaning) to deal with obstacles to knowledge, forces inside or outside ourselves which prevent us from seeing things as they really are. They are *De la force de l'imagination* (I, xxi), *De la coustume* (I, xxiii), and *Divers evenemens de mesme conseil* (I, xxiv). Imagination and custom obviously distort and falsify our vision of things; the last of the three has for its real subject fortune or luck, a third power which hinders rational calculation and an ordered knowledge of events. To these may perhaps be added *Du pedantisme* (I, xxv), since false or irrelevant learning is also an obstacle, and even *De l'inconstance de nos actions* (II, i), which, as we have seen, shows personality as essentially unknowable. It will be noticed that all of these, with the possible exception of *Du pedantisme,* are dated

---

[1] II, xii: TR 522.
[2] I, xxvii: EM i, 233; TR 178(a).

by Villey about 1572 and so well before the 'sceptical crisis' of 1575–6.

It is, however, about 1576 (if Villey's dating is right) and in the *Apologie* that the subject receives its fullest treatment. The variability of human judgement and the impossibility of agreement prove that truth is unattainable:[1] this is a main direction of argument. With it goes the critique of the reliability of the senses,[2] following standard lines with many borrowings from Sextus Empiricus and quotations from Lucretius and many stock examples like the bent oar in the water or the taste of wine to a sick man, but also with some original and powerful observations, especially at the end. Montaigne deals succinctly with those who appeal, like Dr Johnson with his stone, to simple practical experience:[3] in spite of his professions of common sense he is not content with appearances and always tries to push beyond. Nothing can be known except through the faculties of the observer,[4] he is dependent on his senses, and as they are unreliable 'toute la science du monde s'en va necessairement à vau-l'eau'.[5] If it is argued that the senses can know things by resemblance, he asks (following Sextus Empiricus) what guarantee there can be of the resemblance since these resembling objects are themselves unknown:

> Tout ainsi comme, que ne cognoit pas Socrates, voyant son pourtraict, ne peut dire qu'il luy ressemble.[6]

The *Apologie* thus concludes with the impossibility of knowing anything in any way which can be called philosophically valid. It should be added that though the Third Book and the later additions do not return to the subject in detail, passing references suggest that there is no contradiction. Thus things may perhaps have intrinsic qualities but it is the soul or psyche which gives them the shape that is familiar to us:

> Les choses ... ont peut estre leurs pois et mesures et conditions; mais au dedans, en nous, elle les leur taille comme elle l'entant.[7]

It will be seen that this position is not only a reflection of Sextus

[1] II, xii: TR 545(*a*).
[2] II, xii: TR 569–86.
[3] II, xii: TR 522–3(*a*).
[4] II, xii: TR 571(*a*).
[5] II, xii: EM ii, 363; TR 583(*a*).
[6] II, xii: EM ii, 366; TR 585(*a*).
[7] I, l: EM i, 388; TR 290(*c*).

Empiricus and the sceptics but also an anticipation of Descartes's universal doubt. We cannot help asking whether Montaigne also foresees the *cogito*, the argument whereby Descartes extricates himself from the apparently inescapable traps of scepticism and builds up a new certainty. He does say of the Pyrrhonian sceptic: 'Il a un corps, il a un ame';[1] but he does not follow up the implications of the admission, and in any case this is an interpolation. Later in the *Apologie* he comes closer. If the soul knew anything it would be itself and if it knew anything outside itself it would be its body:

> Or il est vray-semblable que, si l'ame sçavoit quelque chose, elle se sçauroit premierement elle mesme; et, si elle sçavoit quelque chose hors d'elle, ce seroit son corps et son estuy, avant toute autre chose.[2]

This is essentially the Cartesian position, but the dubitative form is very different from the firmness of 'Je pense donc je suis', and when we look at the context we see that Montaigne is using even this in support of scepticism: again he does not perceive the full consequences.

Logic and epistemology are thus fundamental to the scepticism which we can now approach more directly. Montaigne's scepticism has behind it a long tradition; its relation to the philosophies of antiquity, to its Renaissance precursors and contemporaries, have been fully studied.[3] Here we can only give a brief account, concentrating on the intrinsic place of scepticism in the book while trying to avoid errors of interpretation which might arise if we remained wholly unaware of the wider philosophical background. We have already seen that scepticism enters the work from an early stage, with the group of essays concerned with obstacles to knowledge. Even the earliest essays, the mere compilations as they seem, already strike the note of uncertainty: the first one of all is *Par divers moyens on arrive à pareille fin*, and soon afterwards comes *Comme l'ame descharge ses passions sur des objects faux quand les vrays luy defaillent* (I, iv). The first reference to Pyrrho

---

1 II, xii: EM ii, 231; TR 486(*c*).
2 II, xii: EM ii, 309; TR 543(*a*).
3 See especially Busson, *Le rationalisme dans la littérature française de la Renaissance*, new ed., 1957; Popkin, *The history of scepticism from Erasmus to Descartes*, 1960; Hallie, *The scar of Montaigne*, 1966.

occurs in *Que le goust des biens et des maux*,[1] again an early essay, though this could conceivably be a later interpolation.

However, it is again in the *Apologie* that we find something like a sustained and systematic exposition, mainly based on Sextus Empiricus, of Montaigne's Pyrrhonian scepticism. He distinguishes three classes of philosophers: those who know (including the Stoics and Epicureans); those who think the truth cannot be found (the Academics); and those who are still seeking (the Pyrrhonians, of course).[2] It is hardly necessary to point out that philosophy is still conceived entirely in terms of antiquity: this is the only philosophy really known to Montaigne and no doubt to most of his generation. In the presentation of the Pyrrhonian case which follows we cannot but admire his gift for the simple, lively, concrete and accurate elucidation of difficult ideas. The profession of the Pyrrhonians is to oscillate, to doubt and to seek, to be assured of nothing. Of the three actions of the soul, the imaginative, the appetitive and the consenting, they accept the first two but 'la derniere, ils la soustiennent et la maintiennent ambigue, sans inclination ny approbation d'une part ou d'autre, tant soit-elle legere'.[3] This, incidentally, sums up his own attitude pretty well. The attitude of ataraxia or calm indifference enables them to maintain any proposition with equanimity. If you tell them that snow is black they will say that it is white, if you conclude that it is neither, they will say that it is both, and so on. Their sacramental word is ἐπέχω, translated by Montaigne as 'je soustiens, je ne bouge', perhaps more accurately 'I stay' or 'pause', which leads them to a perfect and total suspension of judgement.[4] How deeply he is himself impregnated with these principles, how much they colour his writing even when he is not specifically concerned with philosophical questions, it is hardly necessary to emphasise. His own version is the medal he had struck with the famous device 'Que sçay-je?'[5] The interrogative form puts the Pyrrhonian position even better than ἐπέχω: even to say that one doubts is too strong and the question is proof against any dogmatism. Two medals have survived with the date 1576, which confirms Villey's dating for the *Apologie* and the

---

[1] I, xiv: TR 54(*a*).
[2] II, xii: TR 482.
[3] II, xii: EM ii, 226; TR 482(*a*).
[4] II, xii: TR 485(*a*).
[5] II, xii: EM ii, 262; TR 508(*b*).

'sceptical crisis'. And apart from these Pyrrhonian passages the greater part of the *Apologie* is composed under their influence: not only the critique of the senses but also the method of exposing the absurdity of philosophical systems by simply juxtaposing them without comment (an almost Voltairean technique).

Villey is therefore right in regarding the *Apologie* as the culminating point of Montaigne's scepticism. In so far, however, as he makes of it a self-contained stage in the evolution of the *Essais* (this is to simplify his view somewhat), then reservations are necessary. The Third Book is much less occupied with formal philosophical problems, but the same general attitude persists. 'Que sçay-je?' is amplified and endowed with greater practical relevance in *Des boyteux*:

(*b*) J'ayme ces mots, qui amollissent et moderent la temerité de nos propositions: A l'avanture, Aucunement, Quelque, On dict, Je pense, et semblables. Et si j'eusse eu à dresser des enfans, je leur eusse tant mis en la bouche cette façon de respondre (*c*) enquesteuse, non resolutive: (*b*) Qu'est-ce à dire? Je ne l'entends pas, Il pourroit estre, Est-il vray?[1]

We are reminded of Eliot's

And his conversation, so nicely
Restricted to What Precisely
And If and Perhaps and But.

except that 'nicely' and 'restricted' suggest a primness which is foreign to Montaigne. At any rate we have in the passage quoted a statement about style which is also a statement about character and a statement about scepticism which is also a statement about education: such interferences will by now be recognised as typical of Montaigne. Or again, defending his interest in Roman history in *De la vanité*, he remarks that 'les choses presentes mesmes, nous ne les tenons que par la fantasie',[2] which implies the whole critique of knowledge set out in the *Apologie*. Or, turning scepticism as often against himself:

Moy qui suis Roy de la matiere que je traicte, et qui n'en dois conte à personne, ne m'en crois pourtant pas du tout [entirely].[3]

And by a customary reversal he also turns scepticism against

[1] III, xi: EM iii, 314; TR 1007.
[2] III, ix: EM iii, 273; TR 975.
[3] III, viii: EM iii, 203; TR 922.

scepticism itself, a trick not at all inconsistent with Pyrrhonian principles. Thus in another essay whose title is itself a proclamation of scepticism, *C'est folie de rapporter le vray et le faux à nostre suffisance* (according to Villey at least partly of 1572 and therefore another instance of early scepticism), he argues that if we do not accept improbable reports, we cannot reject them either:

> Il faut juger avec plus de reverence de cette infinie puissance de nature et plus de reconnoissance de nostre ignorance et foiblesse. Combien y a il de choses peu vray-semblables, tesmoignées par gens dignes de foy, desquelles si nous ne pouvons estre persuadez, au moins les faut-il laisser en suspens: car de les condamner impossibles, c'est se faire fort, par une temeraire presumption, de sçavoir jusques où va la possibilité.[1]

The whole essay revolves round this theme. Its importance lies in the fact that scepticism can be used not only to attack established opinions but also to support them, and our interpretation of Montaigne's attitude to religious or political authority is bound to give weight to passages like this.

With scepticism goes naturally enough the praise of ignorance. We have already encountered this when dealing with the question of books and learning, but we should now briefly consider ignorance as a positive value. This is perhaps the central thread of the *Apologie* (ironically since Sabunde himself regarded ignorance as evil),[2] culminating in a quotation from St Paul (one of the rare biblical quotations), followed by reference to Spartan illiteracy and the ignorance of the American Indians. He proceeds to show that innocence goes with ignorance, cleverness with malice:

> L'incivilité, l'ignorance, la simplesse, la rudesse s'accompaignent volontiers de l'innocence; la curiosité, la subtilité, le sçavoir trainent la malice à leur suite; l'humilité, la crainte, l'obeissance, la debonnaireté (qui sont les pieces principales pour la conservation de la societé humaine) demandent une ame vuide, docile et presumant peu de soy.[3]

We can see here once more a convergence of themes: not only scepticism and disdain for learning, but also primitivism, the noble savage, and political conservatism. In this respect there is

---

[1] I, xxvii: EM i, 234; TR 179(*a*). See also the interpolation which follows.
[2] *Œuvres complètes*, ed. Armaingaud, ix, 243.
[3] II, xii: EM ii, 220; TR 477(*a*).

really no serious sign of evolution. The Third Book and the later additions continue to praise ignorance, in a less systematic way but much more vigorously and pungently. Thus in the *Apologie* he is arguing that Aristotle and Varro were no better off for all their learning, a fairly abstruse historical point. In 1588 he adds a personal reflection which carries a great deal more moral and human weight:

> J'ay veu en mon temps cent artisans, cent laboureurs, plus sages et plus heureux que des recteurs de l'université, et lesquels j'aimerois mieux ressembler.[1]

In the Third Book he goes further still:

> Est-ce pas ce que nous disons, que la stupidité et faute d'apprehension du vulgaire luy donne cette patience aux maux presens et cette profonde nonchalance des sinistres accidens futurs ? ... Pour Dieu, s'il est ainsi, tenons d'ores en avant escolle de bestise.[2]

To keep a school of stupidity is a paradoxical aim for one of the most intelligent of writers, but it none the less represents an essential element in Montaigne. In a final addition to the last essay, *De l'experience,* he gives us what may be his last word on the subject. Philosophy is idle curiosity and ignorance is the best refuge, all summed up in a metaphor which has become famous:

> O que c'est un dous et mol chevet, et sain, que l'ignorance et l'incuriosité, à reposer une teste bien faicte.[3]

Nevertheless there may be a difference between these sallies of the Third Book and the earlier statements, not in content but in emphasis and context. There is less passion to prove, less logic about it, more genuine indolence: but above all praise of ignorance is less firmly attached to social conservatism, much more a contributory factor to the moral liberation of which we have spoken. We must look not only at Montaigne's arguments but also at the way in which he uses them.

But if he is a sceptic who believes that ignorance is the happiest state, he is also a rationalist who uses reason and learning to prove the inadequacy of reason and learning, and this is the next contradiction we have to consider. Admittedly it is a contradiction common to all sceptics, at least of a conscious kind, and scepticism

---

[1] II, xii: EM ii, 205; TR 466(*b*).
[2] III, xii: EM iii, 343; TR 1029(*b*).
[3] III, xiii: EM iii, 372; TR 1050-1(*c*).

and rationalism are perhaps not fundamentally opposed. I have already quoted 'la semance de la raison universelle empreinte en tout home non denaturé'.[1] Earlier he says that it is difficult to assign limits to the avid curiosity of the human mind.[2] He may regret this but he cannot get away from it: it is in fact one of the central data of the *Essais*. Less equivocally:

> C'est, disoit Epicharmus, l'entendement qui voyt et qui oyt, c'est l'entendement qui approfite tout, qui dispose tout, qui agit, qui domine et qui regne: toutes autres choses sont aveugles, sourdes et sans ame.[3]

This was said by Plutarch, but it has none the less an important and perhaps neglected place in Montaigne's thought. He may have only a moderate esteem for learning but he rates intelligence very high in spite of his attacks on reason. Similarly, though he may not quite know what it is, he has a high regard for truth. On the one hand truth is elusive:

> Car nous sommes nais à quester la verité; il appartient de la posseder à une plus grande puissance.[4]

but on the other:

> Le premier traict de la corruption des mœurs, c'est le bannissement de la verité.[5]

> La voye de la verité est une et simple, celle du profit particulier et de la commodité des affaires qu'on a en charge, double, inegalle et fortuite.[6]

These bold and direct statements contrast with some of the twists and paradoxes of the sceptic, but they fit in very well with the emphasis on truth in the self-portrait and in the moral system. They must not be forgotten. However, generally speaking truth is hard to distinguish from lies and reason is an uncertain prop. The matter is perhaps best summed up in a passage from the *Apologie*:

> ... la raison va tousjours, et torte, et boiteuse, et deshanchée, et avec le mensonge comme avec la verité. . . . J'appelle tousjours raison

---

[1] III, xii: EM iii, 354; TR 1037(c). Cf. p. 153 above.
[2] II, xii: TR 543(a).
[3] I, xxvi: EM i, 197; TR 151(a).
[4] III, viii: EM iii, 183; TR 906.
[5] II, xviii: EM ii, 455; TR 649(a).
[6] III, i: EM iii, 9; TR 773.

cette apparence de discours que chacun forge en soy: cette raison . . . c'est un instrument de plomb et de cire, alongeable, ployable et accommodable à tous biais et à toutes mesures.[1]

The view of human reason expressed in the last clause corresponds exactly to the sinuousness of Montaigne's own mind. Not only in the *Apologie* but throughout the *Essais* reasoning of the subtlest kind is employed to weaken our confidence in reason or at least to show that reality is much more complex than the simplifications of abstract reason will allow. There are no doubt two types of mind, those which perceive similarities and those which perceive differences. Montaigne appears to belong to the latter class:

Je n'ay rien à dire de moy [he might have added of anything], entierement, simplement, et solidement, sans confusion et sans meslange, ny en un mot. *Distingo* est le plus universal membre de ma logique.[2]

The finest example of this tendency to distinguish, when applied philosophically, and a further proof of the continued scepticism of the Third Book, is the opening of *De l'experience,* from which I have already quoted the passage on definitions. The trouble, as so often, from the point of view of orderly exposition is that the argument is at once philosophical, linguistic, legal, political, literary. At the risk or arbitrary division, and distinguishing in a way unlike Montaigne's own, it seems best to leave these other aspects aside for the moment. And unfortunately for consistency (ours not his) we find that he does perceive the similarities as well as the differences, that he is impatient of merely artificial and sophistical distinctions. After the passage already quoted he recounts the answer given by Memnon (Meno) to Socrates, who had asked him what was virtue:

Il y a, fit Memnon, vertu d'homme et de femme, de magistrat et d'homme privé, d'enfant et de vieillart. – Voicy qui va bien! s'escria Socrates: nous estions en cherche d'une vertu, en voicy un exaim.[3]

This is just a story from Plutarch, though particularly apt. What follows is much more interesting and reveals a perfect balance between the principle of identity and the principle of difference.

[1] II, xii: EM ii, 314–5; TR 548(*a*).
[2] II, i: EM ii, 6; TR 319(*b*).
[3] III, xiii: EM iii, 367; TR 1046.

(b) Comme nul evenement et nulle forme ressemble entierement à une autre, aussi ne differe nulle de l'autre entierement. (c) Ingenieus meslange de nature. Si nos faces n'estoint semblables, on ne sçauroit discerner l'home de la beste; si elles n'estoint dissemblables, on ne sçauroit discerner l'home de l'home. (b) Toutes choses se tiennent par quelque similitude, tout exemple cloche, et la relation qui se tire de l'experience est tousjours defaillante et imparfaicte; on joinct toutesfois les comparaisons par quelque coin.[1]

The important interpolation of the Bordeaux Copy comes from St Augustine. The slightly obscure final sentence seems to be antithetical, like the first: all things are connected by some similarity *but* every example limps,[2] that is to say cannot truly represent the class it exemplifies because it is unique and different from all the other members of the class. We have here another obstacle to knowledge, another epistemological hazard. More than this, it is the whole life of the mind which is here characterised, since all the operations of intelligence can be reduced to these two. None the less there is here also some advance beyond scepticism: although the classificatory machinery which is necessary to thought and which is built into language is shown to be radically vitiated, yet to some extent it works. The resemblances and the differences are perceptible, the example limps but it is not therefore wholly false or misleading, there is a point at which it fits. Montaigne here shows himself capable of grasping synthesis as well as analysis, and indeed, as so often, the general statement about the processes of thought applies also to the method of the *Essais*.

In the last sentence of the quotation we read of 'la relation qui se tire de l'experience'. Experience is the subject of the last essay and, not for this reason alone, it occupies a key position in Montaigne's scheme.[3] Of the three possible senses (act of experiencing, long experience, experiment) all appear to be present, though with different frequencies. At the beginning of the essay experience, and this is what gives it its significance in our present context, is opposed to reason as a means of attaining truth. It is a weaker and less worthy means (ironical perhaps?) but not to

1 III, xiii: EM iii, 367; TR 1047.
2 This is the scholastic adage 'omnis similitudo claudicat': see C. E. Clark, 'Montaigne and the imagery of political discourse in sixteenth-century France', *French studies*, xxiv (1970), 338.
3 For a full analysis of the essay and the meaning of the word see W. G. Moore, 'Montaigne's notion of experience' in *The French mind*, 1952.

be disdained for all that. The difference seems to be that reason proceeds by the systems of classification which we have just discussed and which have been found imperfect though not useless, experience by the direct perception of reality without systematisation. We see at once that the emphasis on experience is thus a natural consequence of intellectual scepticism, of the rejection of metaphysical systems and formal logic. In the facts of life, in the widest sense, it is possible to find the reality which is inaccessible to ratiocination and *a priori* dogmatism. It is thus no accident that a great part of the essay is taken up, as we have seen, with apparently footling details of everyday life at its most trivial. Experience, of the self and the world, comes in the end to mean more than philosophical speculations, even sceptical ones. This is experience in the first sense, but it is also, at two points in the essay,[1] associated with memory and thus with the second sense. The *Essais* form a register of a long experience of life and we are reminded once again of the flexibility of the time-scale and Montaigne's way of moving backwards and forwards along it.[2] Finally, and by the way, we may note that Sabunde too lays stress on experience, though there were many other possible sources:

L'experience est maistresse de toute science: ce qu'elle nous apprend est en bon escient bien certain.[3]

An important feature of experience as opposed to pure reason is that it is to a substantial degree corporal or physical. For Montaigne thought is a physical activity and what he thinks is expressed largely in physical terms:[4]

C'est tousjours à l'homme que nous avons affaire, duquel la condition est merveilleusement corporelle.[5]

Il n'est rien plus vray-semblable que la conformité et relation du corps à l'esprit.[6]

This no doubt affords one more explanation of why Montaigne scarcely figures among philosophers. It is not just that he argues in the abstract the influence of bodily processes on thought, which is what materialists and even perhaps existentialists may be

1 TR 1051, 1071.
2 Cf. p. 101 above.
3 *Œuvres complètes*, ed. Armaingaud, x, 2.
4 Cf. Moore, 'Montaigne's notion of experience', p. 49.
5 III, viii: EM iii, 186; TR 909.
6 III, xii: EM iii, 351; TR 1035.

held to do, but that his own thinking is at every point vivified or contaminated (whichever one prefers) by the pressure of sheer physical life. It also explains why he thinks so much in metaphors and images ('pensée, image, chez lui, c'est tout un', as Sainte-Beuve says): [1] an abstract idea is expressed by a concrete analogy. This is of course anathema to a professional philosopher, always struggling against the corrupting influence of rhetoric and poetic language. Yet one sometimes wonders whether metaphor and image are quite the right words. In the description of the passing of a stone and life passing with it, [2] the comparison of life to an excrement is a formal simile but when we look at the whole sentence it is difficult to resist the conclusion that the image is literal, that the stone is part of his life, and that his life is being evacuated just as he says. At any rate the literal and figurative elements are so entangled as to be scarcely separable. Again when he speaks of his personal vocabulary for dealing with time: 'je passe le temps, quand il est mauvais et incommode; quand il est bon, je ne le veux pas passer, je le retaste, je m'y tiens', [3] the mental gripping of time as it passes seems to be a physical action and we are reminded of words like apprehension and the probably metaphorical character of all attempts to represent mental activity in words. A last example shows the problem itself under discussion (a typical complication):

> Puisque c'est le privilege de l'esprit de se r'avoir de la vieillesse, je luy conseille, autant que je puis, de le faire. . . . Je crains que c'est un traistre: il s'est si estroittement affreré au corps qu'il m'abandonne à tous coups pour le suyvre en sa necessité. . . . J'ay beau essayer de le destourner de cette colligeance, et luy presenter et Seneque et Catulle, et les dames, et les dances royales; si son compagnon [the body] a la cholique, il semble qu'il l'ait aussi. . . . Il n'y a poinct d'allegresse en ses productions, s'il n'en y a quand et quand au corps. [4]

The union of mind and body is here presented in a characteristic combination of humour and splendour of language: once again it is not easy to see where imagery ends and literal statement begins since what is being conveyed is the actual physical effect of bodily conditions on intellectual operations.

All this anticipates the discussion of Montaigne's imagery in

[1] *Port-Royal*, ed. Doyon and Marchesné, iii, 54.
[2] p. 63 above.
[3] III, xiii: EM iii, 424; TR 1091.
[4] III, v: EM iii, 73; TR 821.

general, but it is necessary for an understanding of his philosophical as well as his stylistic originality. The examples discussed were all from the Third Book. As usual, however, if the fully appropriate linguistic form is a late achievement, the statement of the principle of unity occurs from an early stage. Thus in the *Apologie* he observes that if apoplexy extinguishes the light of intelligence, even a cold must dim it; consequently, as we have seen, the body being always subject to such minor disturbances, the judgement is hardly ever in complete control (another sceptical argument).[1] The implications here are materialistic, and though he is careful most of the time to allow for the Christian distinction between body and soul these implications are strengthened in the Third Book, especially at the end of *De l'experience* where he stresses the insipidity of meditations divorced from physical experience.[2] The balance between body and mind (or soul) is maintained to the end, but it is increasingly tilted in favour of the body.

The emphasis on experience and the primacy of physical sensation, the rejection of *a priori* systems, point towards something else which is empiricism. The opposition of experience to reason as a means of attaining truth suggests the empiricism of later philosophers, though of course Montaigne is far from wanting to turn it into any sort of philosophical system. This in its turn raises the question, which we have already touched on briefly, of his relation to the impending scientific revolution. We have noticed his awareness of Copernicus and his interest in cosmological theories. On the whole however, he is pre-eminently a humanist as opposed to a scientist. The literary background, the very lack of system in his observations, above all the credulity with which he will accept any report, however improbable, for its exemplary value, are all remote from scientific ways of thinking. Scepticism of the Pyrrhonian kind, though a necessary precondition of scientific method, can only lead if persisted in to the blocking of scientific advance. We can indeed see in him some signs of the divorce between science and humanism, now called the two cultures, which perhaps only becomes apparent in the following century. When he says '(*a*) Ces gens qui se perchent à chevauchons sur l'epicycle de Mercure, (*c*) qui voient si avant dans le ciel, (*c*)

---

[1] II, xii: TR 548(*a*). Cf. p. 108 above.
[2] III, xiii: TR 1095.

ils m'arrachent les dens',[1] and goes on to ask how, if they do not know themselves, they can know the causes of the ebb and flow of the Nile, he is expressing a typically humanistic disgust with the technicalities of science and anticipating Boileau's lines in which the opposition becomes fully evident:

> Je songe à me connaître, et me cherche en moi-même. . . .
> Que, l'astrolabe en main, un autre aille chercher
> Si le soleil est fixe ou tourne sur son axe;
> Si Saturne à nos yeux peut faire un parallaxe;
> Que Rohaut vainement sèche pour concevoir
> Comment, tout étant plein, tout a pu se mouvoir. . . .[2]

In the same spirit he makes fun of the atomic theory of Epicurus, asks why atoms have never formed a house or a shoe, and advances an argument (possibly from an ancient source) which has had considerable success since, that any number of Greek letters mixed up at random would never make an *Iliad*[3] (the monkey and the typewriter in fact). This is not on the whole one of his happier intuitions: however, we must not overlook the fact that he was mostly confronted with pseudo-scientists.

This is perhaps particularly true of the science with which he had most to do and to which he devotes most attention, medicine. As so often, though references to the subject are scattered through the *Essais*, one essay, *De la ressemblance des enfans aux peres*, is concentrated on it. It is a strong attack on medicine as practised in antiquity and in Montaigne's own time. The technique is that of the *Apologie*: conflicting beliefs and doctrines are juxtaposed in such a way as to make them all look absurd. However, the note of personal involvement, as might be expected, is very much stronger. Medicine is included among the vain, supernatural and fantastic arts. The picture he gives of doctors is in its essentials the same as Molière's:

> leur irresolution, la foiblesse de leurs argumens, divinations et fondements, l'apreté de leurs contestations, pleines de haine, de jalousie et de consideration particuliere. . . .[4]

Their remedies, the left foot of a tortoise, lizard's urine, elephant's dung, are as absurd as they are, and he adds 'telles autres singeries qui ont plus le visage d'un enchantement

---

[1] II, xvii: EM ii, 411; TR 617.
[2] Épître V, 26–32.
[3] II, xii: TR 526–7.
[4] II, xxxvii: EM ii, 592; TR 749.

magicien que de science solide'.[1] Here we can detect the expression of a genuinely scientific frame of mind and incidentally the use of the word 'science' in something like its modern sense. Medicine was, it is true, the butt of many satirists (Erasmus's *Praise of folly* and Jacques Tahureau's *Dialogues* are two examples) but Montaigne is far from following a stereotyped pattern. And in spite of his adherence to the theory of humours,[2] hardly avoidable in the contemporary climate of medical opinion, what emerges is great independence of mind, a refusal to be taken in by jargon, an interest in new theories (Paracelsus particularly),[3] a good deal of direct observation of his own disease, as we have seen, and a number of suggestions which point to later discoveries. In the last category may be cited the notion (probably from Plato) that diseases have an organic life like animals;[4] a strong and very interesting plea for specialisation in medicine;[5] the idea that doctors actually create illnesses[6] (what are now called iatrogenic diseases). More important than all these is the attitude expressed in his remarks on Galen:

Ils cognoissent bien Galien, mais nullement le malade.[7]

On ne demande pas si Galen a rien dit qui vaille, mais s'il a dit ainsin ou autrement.[8]

The rejection of Galen, the great classical authority, in favour of observation of the patient, the principle of *nullius in verba*: it does appear after all that he grasps the central principles of modern science.

Similar conclusions can be drawn from his treatment of the occult sciences. Disbelief in astrology, alchemy, prognostications and so on was nothing new in itself: Tahureau again devotes considerable energy to demolishing them, very successfully, and Ronsard dismisses alchemy as vanity.[9] At the same time faith in them was still widespread, and not only among the uneducated:

[1] ibid.
[2] e.g. II, xi: TR 408; II, xii: TR 549; I, xxxviii: TR 230. But the last is prudently qualified by 'ils disent'.
[3] II, xii: TR 554; II, xxxvii: TR 751.
[4] III, xiii: TR 1066(c).
[5] II, xxxvii: TR 754(c).
[6] II, xii: TR 470; II, xxxvii: TR 745.
[7] I, xxv: EM i, 179; TR 138(a).
[8] II, xii: EM ii, 279; TR 521(a).
[9] Ode to Pisseleu: *Œuvres*, ed. Laumonier, ii (1914), 3.

Bodin admits, if cautiously, the influence of the planets on the character of peoples.[1] Montaigne's place is, as we should expect, with the advocates of good sense and though his position is not in itself original he puts it with great vigour. He sends the whole crew packing in a splendid if loaded enumeration:

... il n'est rien creu si fermement que ce qu'on sçait le moins, ny gens si asseurez que ceux qui nous content des fables, comme Alchimistes, Prognostiqueurs, Judiciaires [astrologers], Chiromantiens, Medecins, *id genus omne*.[2]

The inclusion of doctors must have given him considerable pleasure. But he uses serious arguments as well. Thus prognosticators must hit the truth sometimes simply by chance. Much more penetratingly, their language is so vague and obscure that posterity can fit it to any situation:[3] he mentions Joachim's prophecies of the lives of the popes and it would apply very well to Nostradamus. In the same essay he partly anticipates Fontenelle on the subject of pagan oracles, remarking that they had ceased to function well before the coming of Christ, contradicting the traditional Christian version.[4] It is only fair to add that there are passages in which he appears to accept the influence of the stars on human life,[5] but they are mainly confined to the *Apologie*, are highly literary with classical quotations, and can be taken as part of the sceptical playing with ideas which characterises that essay.

We can now return to the main line of his scientific interests with a slightly different conception of his relation to the general movement of inquiry in science. This relation is admirably, if grudgingly, summed up by Michelet: '... son doute n'est que le doute provisoire qui rendra la science possible'.[6] Again and again he returns to the theme of *nullius in verba*, the principle that no man's word can be taken on trust, that no human authority, however eminent, can prevail against the authority of fact: 'car la verité ne se juge point par authorité et tesmoignage d'autruy'.[7] In *De l'exercitation* the principle has a more direct application to science when he defends himself by an analogy for talking about himself:

[1] *Methodus*, tr. Mesnard, p. 94.
[2] I, xxxii: EM i, 282; TR 213–4(*a*).
[3] I, xi: TR 44–5(*b,c*).   [4] I, xi: TR 42.
[5] e.g. II, xii: TR 428–9(*a*).
[6] *Histoire de France*, x, 399.
[7] II, xii: EM ii, 233; TR 487(*a*).

Qui me desfand d'en parler selon mon sens, experiance et usage, qu'il ordone à l'architecte de parler des bastimans non selon soi, mais selon son voisin; selon la sciance d'un autre, non selon la siene.[1]

Everyone should write of what he knows and that only. Thus a topographer who has been to Palestine should not take this as a justification for telling stories about the rest of the world (almost certainly aimed at Thevet). And it is much more useful for someone who knows a river or a spring really well to describe that than to attempt a complete treatise of physics[2] (*physique* is used here in its earlier sense of 'natural science'). Montaigne is seen here at his most scientific. He is distrustful of words which correspond to no observable fact, like quintessence, 'car quinte essence n'est autre chose qu'une qualité de laquelle par nostre raison nous ne sçavons trouver la cause'.[3] This is very much the tone of Descartes and not far removed from the argument of Pascal in his writings on the vacuum. For words he would substitute observation. Thus he examines and describes the contents of a goat's stomach; having found stones in it he concludes that the belief in goat's blood as a cure for the stone is unfounded. He adds: 'Ce n'estoit pas tant pour la creinte de l'advenir, et pour moy, que j'estoy curieux de cette experience.'[4] The word *experience* here, as on several other occasions in *De la ressemblance des enfans aux peres*, can only mean 'experiment' and we have here a true if elementary manifestation of the experimental spirit, which cannot but remind us of Bacon's fatal last experiment, the stuffing of a chicken with snow. Similarly, as we noticed in *Des boyteux*,[5] he exposes the widespread human practice of inquiring into the causes of things which do not exist: 'Comment est-ce que cela se faict? – Mais se fait il? faudroit il dire.'[6] Reason is once more opposed to truth, and we can see how his scepticism and empiricism are leading him towards the standards of the scientific age:

... les hommes, aux faicts qu'on leur propose, s'amusent plus volontiers à en cercher la raison qu'à en cercher la verité: ils laissent la les choses, et s'amusent à traiter les causes.[7]

[1] II, vi: EM ii, 60; TR 359(c).
[2] I, xxxi; TR 203(a).
[3] II, xxxvii: EM ii, 607; TR 762(a).
[4] II, xxxvii: EM ii, 604–5; TR 759–60(a).
[5] p. 104 above.
[6] III, xi: EM iii, 309; TR 1004.
[7] III, xi: EM iii, 309; TR 1003.

This is exactly the point of Fontenelle's story in the *Histoire des oracles* about the child who grew a golden tooth. Both Fontenelle and Montaigne can be contrasted with Bodin, who, remarking that Aristotle denies the importance of numbers, demands to know why then a seventh son can cure scrofula.[1] It may be observed, incidentally, that in spite of his playfulness and Bodin's seriousness, there is far less nonsense in Montaigne than in Bodin.

It seems established therefore that his scepticism, however frivolous and at times credulous, points to the scientific method, and it seems likely that he exercised a direct influence on its development through Descartes and Pascal and perhaps even Bacon. However, some of his speculations go deeper than the empirical testing of facts, important though that is. The positive side of the scientific attitude comes out in the statement that 'les hommes sont tous d'une espece, et sauf le plus et le moins, se trouvent garnis de pareils outils et instrumens pour concevoir et juger'.[2] Again we can perceive here something of the insistence of Descartes and Malebranche on the universality of intelligence and hence of the solutions to scientific problems. In the *Apologie* a Bordeaux Copy interpolation, replacing a fairly banal sentence, seems to imply the principle of scientific determinism:

> C'est une mesme nature qui roule son cours. Qui en aroit suffisemment jugé le present estat, en pourroit seurement conclurre et tout l'advenir et tout le passé.[3]

But scepticism has perhaps the last word. In the same essay he affirms that science and philosophy do not tell us the truth but the best they can think of: the epicycles, eccentrics and concentrics of the astronomers (whom he calls astrologers) have no real existence but are simply an aid to interpreting the movement of the stars.[4] All this is very close to the recent concept of models in science, not an exact picture of reality but an approximate representation of how it might be thought to work. When he says that nothing can be established with certainty, 'et le jugeant et le jugé estans en continuelle mutation et branle',[5] he may be pointing

---

[1] *Methodus*, tr. Mesnard, p. 226.
[2] I, xiv: EM i, 59; TR 50(*a*).
[3] II, xii: EM ii, 179; TR 445(*c*).
[4] II, xii: TR 518.
[5] II, xii: EM ii, 366; TR 586. This statement occurs in the conclusion of the *Apologie*, which as we have seen is largely borrowed. However, the statement itself does not appear in the sources quoted by Villey.

towards relativity in its scientific as well as its more general sense, though the details are indeed very different. However that may be, Montaigne's scepticism is clearly more in tune with the doubts of recent science than with the confidence of the great period which immediately followed him. In a way he may be said to jump across the intervening period to anticipate some of the problems in the modern philosophy of science, which has come up against just the sort of difficulty he loves to expound. This does not alter the fact that by his empiricism and attack on merely verbal authority he helps to lay the foundations for the discoveries of the seventeenth century. We cannot help feeling as we read him, in spite of his attacks on science, that the scientific spirit stands poised on the verge of a major renewal. His attitude, with scepticism and confidence now fused, is best summarised in what is also a marvellously expressed formulation of all scientific endeavour:

L'admiration est fondemant de tout philosofie, l'inquisition le progrez, l'ignorance le bout.[1]

By *admiration* he means the initial curiosity which sets the process in motion.

Scepticism thus leads in one direction to experience, empiricism and scientific method. But it also leads, though not at all inconsistently, in a quite different direction which is even more important for Montaigne's thought as a whole. This is the group of related ideas which may be designated as primitivism, relativism and diversity. Each, it will be readily seen, implies a sceptical basis: primitivism or the questioning of civilised values; diversity or the rejection of unitary explanations of the world; relativism or the rejection of absolute standards (and for that matter of local ones as well). Of course this argument does not necessarily mean priority in time: it could just as well be maintained that scepticism springs from these fundamental attitudes of mind.

The foundation of his primitivism lies in his concept of nature. The subject is a familiar one and here only the briefest summary is required. In particular an interesting article by Alexandre Micha shows that much of Montaigne's thought turns on the opposition between art and nature and he groups the related themes in pairs (in each case art comes first and in each case nature is preferred): civilisation: savages; knowledge: ignorance; pseudo-philosophy:

[1] III, xi: EM iii, 314; TR 1008(c).

the way of nature; laws: conscience; theological religion: personal religion; imagination and reasoning: reality; the artificial, fixed self: the moving self; the front shown to the world: the *arrière-boutique*; assumed attitudes: naïveté; Ciceronianism: conversational style.[1] Not all of these pairs are equally convincing but this is a serious attempt to perceive a principle of unity. Of course almost any aspect we choose to pick on can be used in the same way to form a central axis: the mobile complexity and at the same time the unity of Montaigne's constellation of themes are such that a bearing taken in any direction may persuade us that we are looking at the centre. None the less all thoughtful attempts of the kind throw light on some part of the work and help us to a better understanding of the whole, and we can say that an acceptance of all that is natural and the decided rejection of what is artificial dominates Montaigne's thinking in a number of areas, not all of them immediately connected with the art-nature antithesis. One merit of Micha's outline is that he illustrates Montaigne's use of 'nature' by showing it in various concrete situations instead of trying to arrive at a formal definition of one of the most difficult of all words to define. When we are dealing with Montaigne the difficulty is much greater because of his essentially antithetical way of proceeding: we must not (of course) assume, and we have already seen evidence to the contrary, that he is always against art and civilisation.

There are two or three essays in which the concept of nature is especially prominent. One is the *Apologie*, where natural ignorance is opposed to ambitious speculation, certainly, but where also nature is presented as the supreme good and as the animating power of the universe, *natura naturans*. This clearly owes much to his classical sources, particularly Lucretius.[2] In *De la ressemblance des enfans aux peres*, again, the artifices of medicine are compared unfavourably with 'la puissance et uberté de nature', which we have abandoned for something much less reliable:

Je me deffie des inventions de nostre esprit, de nostre science et art, en faveur duquel nous l'avons abandonnée et ses regles, et auquel nous ne sçavons tenir moderation ny limite.[3]

---

[1] A. Micha, 'Art et nature dans les "Essais"', *BSAM*, II, 19 (Jul.–Dec. 1956).

[2] Cf. Gracey, *Montaigne et la poésie*, p. 85.

[3] II, xxxvii: EM ii, 586; TR 744(*b*).

This is no doubt a reflection which is not limited in its application to Montaigne's own time. But it is in the Third Book and most of all in *De l'experience* that nature come to dominate his outlook. In *De la phisionomie* he himself speaks of 'nous autres natural-istes',[1] using a recent word which places him as someone who follows nature and regards this as his principal distinguishing characteristic. In *De l'experience* nature is considered above all as a guide to morals and actions, as the guarantee or guarantor of the recipe for living which we discussed in the last chapter. In a well-known sentence: 'Nature est un doux guide, mais non pas plus doux que prudent et juste.'[2] Still more striking in the last additions to the essay is the recurrence of the adverb *naturelle-ment,* which stresses nature not just as a superhuman force but as a way of performing human actions:

> ... celuy qui a l'heur de sçavoir s'emploier naïfvemant et ordonée-ment, c'est à dire naturellement.[3]
> (*b*) Il n'est rien si beau et legitime que de faire bien l'homme et deuëment, ny science si ardue que de bien (*c*) et naturellement (*b*) sçavoir vivre cette vie.[4]

Nothing could put the point more effectively than this brief inter-calation, identifying natural with good behaviour. The supremacy of nature is a gradual discovery of the *Essais,* but it reaches its culminating point in the closing pages of *De l'experience.*

Before we move further towards primitivism there is another pair which might be added to Micha's list, man and animal. We have already seen something of Montaigne's feeling for animals and the whole natural creation, but he uses them also as part of his sceptical assault on the pride of human reason. Clearly animals can be held to follow nature more closely than even the simplest of men. They are in fact, according to Montaigne, equal and in many ways superior to man. This argument, partly paradoxical, is, however, chiefly confined to the *Apologie,* of which it forms a main plank, and to the immediately surrounding essays. It is moreover largely derivative: it owes a great deal (sometimes almost verbatim) to Plutarch's 'Que les bestes brutes usent de la raison' from Amyot's translation of the *Moralia,* and Sextus

---

[1] III, xii: EM iii, 350; TR 1034(*c*).
[2] III, xiii: EM iii, 427; TR 1094(*b*).
[3] III, xiii: EM iii, 372; TR 1050(*c*).
[4] III, xiii: EM iii, 422–3; TR 1091.

Empiricus uses the intelligence of animals as a sceptical argument. Some of the tales Montaigne takes from his classical models on this subject are quite astonishing. Thus the life of the halcyon, whose nest is described with a wealth of detail, surpasses all human cogitation (as well it might), and there is the tunny: 'En la maniere de vivre des tuns, on y remerque une singuliere science de trois parties de la Mathematique [astrology, geometry, arithmetic].'[1] This is going a little far, even for Montaigne (in fact both examples are from Plutarch). We may admit that a sort of fabulous poetry emerges from these tall stories. But if he owes much to the classics he owes little to to Sabunde, who traces a ladder of beings from the lowest animals to man and concludes that man with his free will is immeasurably superior.[2] Once more, and here more than anywhere, we are struck by the irony that this devastating essay purports to be an apologia for Sabunde and his views. The *Dialogues* of Bruès also devote considerable attention to the relative intelligence of men and animals. We are in fact confronted with a philosophical commonplace and it is hardly necessary to stress the importance of the problem in Descartes, who takes the opposite view to Montaigne's. But though there is nothing new in the argument that animals are at least as rational as men and morally superior, he puts it with liveliness and mordant humour. Of all animals the monkey is the ugliest and resembles man the most; man alone, says Ovid (followed by many others), has an erect stature and looks towards heaven, to which Montaigne replies that the camel (a rather extraordinary choice) and the ostrich are even more erect and heaven-gazing.[3] More seriously, animals must work by reason not instinct (he does not actually use the word at this point but several periphrases for it); then, with a typical lawyer's argument, he adds that even if they do work by instinct they are still superior because this proves they are closer to nature.[4] Man possesses imaginary advantages, knowledge, reason, honour; animals possess real ones, peace, security, innocence, health.[5] This seems pretty wide of the mark, but it illustrates his scale of values, not only at this stage. The animal argument of the *Apologie* ends:

[1] II, xii: EM ii, 195; TR 458–9(a).
[2] *Œuvres complètes*, ed. Armaingaud, ix, 6–7; cf. also Frame, *Biography*, p. 104.
[3] II, xii: TR 463.
[4] II, xii: TR 437.
[5] II, xii: TR 464(a).

cc n'est par vray discours, mais par une fierté folle et opiniatreté, que nous nous preferons aux autres animaux et nous sequestrons de leur condition et societé.[1]

It will be seen that this argument is not meant to be taken too solemnly. However, it is repeated very briefly in *De la phisionomie* and here the lessons which man can learn from animals, especially that of following nature, are formulated without paradox.[2] And even through the string of absurd anecdotes of the *Apologie* pierces his genuine love of animals, a lesson of humility as in the last passage quoted, and again a feeling for the unity of nature. His preoccupation with animals is part of his total preoccupation with life.

We have already seen in chapter 5 the impact of America on Montaigne's sensibility and the sympathy and admiration evoked in him by descriptions of its native peoples and their melancholy history. Not only in America but in Europe also he prefers the simplicity of natural men to those who have been corrupted by artifice, even, to take an example we have discussed, in the logic of shepherds as opposed to the logic of the sophisticated. If, as we have seen, he is aware of the possibility of scientific progress, he more generally situates happiness in the past. In criticising medicine he observes that the earliest ages were without it: 'Il n'est nation qui n'ait esté plusieurs siecles sans la medecine, et les premiers siecles, c'est à dire les meilleurs et les plus heureux.'[3] That was from 1580, but the same note is struck in *De l'experience* about laws, equally absent in the golden age and in the New World.[4] However, Montaigne's primitivism is most monumentally characterised in what is perhaps, thanks in part to Shakespeare, the best-known passage in the *Essais*, and it requires fuller consideration. He is regretting, in *Des cannibales*, the fact that Lycurgus and Plato had not been able to see the nations of the New World and compares them with their ideal republics:

C'est une nation, diroy je à Platon, en laquelle il n'y a aucune espece de trafique; nulle cognoissance de lettres; nulle science de nombres; nul nom de magistrat, ny de superiorité politique; nul usage de service, de richesse ou de pauvreté; nuls contrats; nulles successions; nuls partages; nulles occupations qu'oysives; nul respect de parenté

[1] II, xii: EM ii, 204; TR 465.
[2] III, xii: TR 1026–7.
[3] II, xxxvii: EM ii, 587; TR 745(a).
[4] III, xiii: TR 1043.

que commun; nuls vestemens; nulle agriculture; nul metal; nul usage de vin ou de bled. Les paroles mesmes qui signifient la mensonge, la trahison, la dissimulation, l'avarice, l'envie, la detraction, le pardon, inouies. Combien trouveroit il la republique qu'il a imaginée, esloignée de cette perfection.[1]

We shall notice in particular the absence of trade, letters (in conformity with so much else in the *Essais*), mathematics, a governing class, wealth and poverty, law, family, clothes, agriculture, and mining (which may be said to stand for what we now call industry). The political consequences of this series of negations will have to be examined later. For the moment it can be said that, apart from religion, it denies every basic institution of European society. Gonzalo, who speaks these words translated in *The Tempest*, is partly a figure of fun: the full impact is softened by the dramatic form. Here there is no such counterbalancing commentary to mute the force of the hammer-like negatives. Of course, as usual, it would be wrong to suppose that this diatribe is wholly (perhaps even partly) original. Almost every item can be traced back to a long tradition: we can find similar marks of primitive existence in the classical poets who wrote of the golden age and in many sixteenth-century travel writers.[2] It would be tedious to give a list of examples and one may suffice. Gomara says that '... ces Indiens n'avoient aucuns vestemens, ni lettres, ni monoies, ni fer, ni grain, ni vin ...'.[3] These are clearly the elements of a large part of Montaigne's list. However, Gomara is recording the astonishment of Ferdinand and Isabella at this news; it is a far cry from Montaigne's enthusiasm. Still, this is not true of all cases. In what then does Montaigne's originality lie? Partly in the fact that he brings everything together, partly in the power of his language. The two combined, and the influence on Shakespeare, make of this a key passage in the formation of the myth of primitivism and the noble savage. But there is inevitably a serpent in this Eden, as I have suggested earlier. We, the Europeans, have ruined the ideal world of America by our baseness, cruelty and greed:

---

[1] I, xxxi: EM i, 270; TR 204(*a*).

[2] See Atkinson, *Les nouveaux horizons*, pp. 140–1; Armstrong, *Ronsard and the Age of Gold*, *passim*. Dr Armstrong is particularly interesting on the absence of metals and mining in traditional pictures of the Golden Age.

[3] *Histoire generale des Indes occidentales*, 1584, f. 24ᵛ. Cf. Atkinson, *Les nouveaux horizons*, p. 141.

Bien crains-je que nous aurons bien fort hasté sa declinaison et sa ruyne par nostre contagion, et que nous luy aurons bien cher vendu nos opinions et nos arts.[1]

This is already the theme of Diderot and the *Supplément au Voyage de Bougainville*, with all its consequences for European Romanticism and the development of European attitudes to exotic peoples. The topic itself is of such high general importance that we are in danger of neglecting its place in our immediate context. Obviously primitivism represents one more side of Montaigne's scepticism, his *Umwertung aller Werte*, his undermining of established values and prejudices, his preference for the natural over the artificial.

It can also be subsumed under a wider heading, that of his relativism. His is the opposite of the mind which accepts the local conditions of life, the 'regles de sa parroisse', as eternally valid laws. Everything is seen in relation to everything else, books (and this is another of their functions) enable him to survey the customs of the whole known world and compare them with those of his country or his parish. We have already seen how he studies customs from an anthropological viewpoint, lists widely varying sexual practices, or looks at different national *mores* with a benign cosmopolitanism. But his conception of custom goes deeper than this. In *De la coustume* he quotes Cicero's 'Consuetudinis magna vis est'[2] and the theme is taken up again in *De l'experience* (with further illustrations of variety):

C'est à la coustume de donner forme à nostre vie, telle qu'il luy plaist; elle peut tout en cela: c'est le breuvage de Circé, qui diversifie nostre nature comme bon luy semble.[3]

There is a characteristic ambiguity here: the reference to Circe's potion suggests something rather sinister, but we are not told specifically whether this decisive influence of custom on all our actions is good or bad. Mostly in the *Essais* it seems to be on balance bad, for two reasons: it is an obstacle to pure knowledge, rational morality, just laws; and it encourages a misplaced arrogance and bigotry in those who think their customs a universal rule. Some of the examples he uses appear crude or disgusting, like the nobleman (identified with the Duc de La Rochefoucauld)

[1] III, vi: EM iii, 158–9; TR 887.
[2] I, xxiii: EM i, 138; TR 107(*c*).
[3] III, xiii: EM iii, 381; TR 1058.

who always blew his nose with his hand and argued that this was better than wrapping up this 'salle excrement' in fine linen and carefully preserving it on our persons.[1] Of course the feeling of disgust is deliberately provoked: the point is to upset us and our prejudices, to show that not only our actions but our most deep-rooted attitudes are determined by traditional forms which have no foundation in reason. The true face of things is concealed from us by habit;[2] it is custom which makes things seem impossible, though in fact they are not (in this case going naked).[3] Instead of treating as barbarians those whose customs are different from our own we should judge everything according to reason and not according to vulgar opinions.[4] This position finds still more powerful expression a little further on in *Des cannibales*:

> ... chacun appelle barbarie ce qui n'est pas de son usage; comme de vray il semble que nous n'avons autre mire de la verité et de la raison que l'exemple et idée des opinions et usances du païs où nous sommes. Là est tousjours la parfaicte religion, la parfaicte police, perfect et accomply usage de toutes chose.[5]

We have here a profoundly subversive principle, capable of dissolving any traditionally established system, and it is easy to perceive the affinity at such points between Montaigne and the eighteenth-century *philosophes*. In fact the basic device of discrediting one's own institutions by bringing in an outside observer, as in Montesquieu, is already clearly visible in Montaigne's cannibals. It is true, once again, that the use of variations in behaviour to buttress scepticism is far from new: it is one of the main points in the system of Sextus Empiricus.[6] In the sixteenth century Tahureau, for example, maintains the superiority of reason over custom.[7] As usual, Montaigne's originality lies in the vigour of argument, in the unexpectedness of particular observations, and above all in the whole complex of related attitudes. It emerges more precisely from a comparison with his contemporary Chauveton, on the sale of wives among the American Indians:

> Cependant toutes les fantasies, coustumes, ou loix humaines ne

---

[1] I, xxiii: TR 109(c).
[2] I, xxiii: TR 115(a).
[3] I, xxxvi: TR 222(a).
[4] I, xxxi: TR 200(a).
[5] I, xxxi: EM i, 268; TR 203(a).
[6] On this see Popkin, *The history of scepticism*, p. 51.
[7] *Dialogues*, ed. Conscience, p. 48.

peuvent preiudicier à l'ordonnance de Dieu, qui en ha disposé autrement. . . .[1]

This is a note which is strikingly absent from Montaigne's treatment of the question: he never, I think, judges variable custom by divine law.[2]

But what he does, and here we come up against one of the major contradictions, is to exalt custom and put it forward as the supreme, the only safe, rule of conduct. The full title of I, xxiii is *De la coustume et de ne changer aisément une loy receüe*, and throughout the *Essais* we find the same stress on the necessity, or at least the advisability, of conforming to the custom of the country in which one happens to have been born. How this contradiction can be resolved, if it can, is the subject of another chapter. In the meantime, an interesting point is raised by Mr Imbrie Buffum, who claims that an analysis of the additions to *De la coustume* shows an increasing emphasis after the return from Italy on the usefulness of custom rather than its absurdity.[3] One weakness in the argument is that he takes Montaigne's adaptability on the journey as evidence of a move towards conservatism, when the exact opposite is more plausible. Montaigne's adoption of an Italian way of life is called the triumph of custom, but it is rather the defeat of custom, the proof that all customs are equally indifferent. At any rate the *Journal du voyage* itself is strongly coloured by this view, as we have partly seen. Nothing angers him more than displays of national prejudice: 'chacun ne sçachant gouster que selon l'ordonnance de sa coutume et de l'usage de son village.'[4] And some of the most far-reaching observations on the fragile basis of custom are inserted in the *Essais* after 1581, for example in *De la coustume* itself: 'Les loix de la conscience, que nous disons naistre de nature, naissent de la costume.' Now not only the customs of particular countries but the whole natural and moral law are subjected to the dissolving effect of relativity. What follows comes indeed very close to Durkheim's 'Dieu est la société':

chacun aiant en veneration interne les opinions et meurs approuvées et receues autour de luy, ne s'en peut desprendre sans remors, ny s'y appliquer sans applaudissement.[5]

1 *Histoire nouvelle*, 1579, p. 24.
2 A possible exception is II, xxx: TR 691(c).
3 *L'influence du voyage de Montaigne*, pp. 106–13.
4 *JV*: TR 1170.
5 I, xxiii: EM i, 146; TR 114(c).

Our conscience with its remorse and self-congratulation is thus only a reflection of the prejudices of the society in which we live. How far this contradicts the erection of conscience into supreme moral authority, which I discussed earlier, is hard to say: as these are the laws of conscience there is perhaps still a place for the internal court which is uncorrupted by local laws. Though this remains one of Montaigne's most devastating reflections, our view may be confirmed by another interpolation:

> Nous apelons contre nature ce qui avient contre la costume: rien n'est que selon elle [nature], quel qu'il soit. Que cette raison universelle et naturelle chasse de nous l'errur et l'estonement que la nouvelleté nous apporte.[1]

In the end it is possible to appeal to nature and universal reason against the customs and prejudices masquerading under their name.

With relativity of customs we should perhaps mention, because of its importance in the history of ideas though it is not very original and occupies no large place in Montaigne, the notion that variations of climate determine the character, temperament and genius of different peoples. The form of our being, he says, depends on air, climate and terrain, not only physically but intellectually and morally as well.[2] This looks forward to Montesquieu; among Montaigne's precursors here are Louis le Roy, Belleforest, and above all Bodin.[3]

Relativism itself is again but one aspect of a larger whole, diversity and multiplicity. We have already looked at many examples of his acute awareness of the infinite proliferation of reality and the infinite differences between things, the distinctions that can be made between objects or opinions which appear to be similar, but we have not yet considered it by itself, as a central part of his outlook. We saw too that his is the type of mind that perceives differences rather than resemblances and then that he perceives resemblances as well, achieving a balance between analysis and synthesis.[4] But in the last resort we have to admit that the differences are more characteristic and that 'Distingo est le plus universel membre de ma logique' sums it up very well. His way of dealing with the sophistry most familiarly represented by Buridan's

---

[1] II, xxx: EM ii, 515; TR 691(*c*).
[2] II, xii: TR 559.
[3] On this see Atkinson, *Les nouveaux horizons*, pp. 268, 406 ff.
[4] See above, pp. 178–9.

donkey, though he chooses classical rather than scholastic examples, is wholly typical (the donkey placed between two exactly equal bundles of hay would die of hunger). Montaigne replies with superb common sense that two things never are equal, there is always some difference, however slight.[1] And so he can say with justice:

> Pour me sentir engagé à une forme, je n'y oblige pas le monde, come chacun faict; et crois et conçois mille contreres façons de vie; et, au rebours du commun, reçois plus facilement la differance que la ressamblance en nous.[2]

There is here a declaration of tolerance which links up with the relativism and cosmopolitanism we have just been discussing, but it also points to the philosophical reflections at the beginning of *De l'experience*:

> La consequence que nous voulons tirer de la ressemblance des evenemens est mal seure, d'autant qu'ils sont tousjours dissemblables: il n'est aucune qualité si universelle en cette image des choses que la diversité et varieté. . . . La dissimilitude s'ingere d'elle mesme en nos ouvrages; nul art peut arriver à la similitude.[3]

This takes us at once to the heart of this essay and no doubt of the *Essais* generally. Diversity is not just something that happens to exist, it is the universal principle of existence. Diversity is indeed a continual refrain and examples could be adduced more or less indefinitely. It is certainly not necessary to wait for the Third Book and the Bordeaux Copy, though the earlier references hardly treat the subject at the same deep level. Apart from man as 'un subject merveilleusement vain, divers et ondoyant' in the first essay, one might quote: 'le monde n'est que varieté et dissemblance',[4] or the words which close the edition of 1580:

> Et, a l'advanture, ne fut il jamais au monde deus opinions entierement et exactement pareilles, non plus que deux visages. Leur plus propre qualité, c'est la diversité et la discordance.[5]

Again we can perceive the close connection between diversity and scepticism.

[1] II, xiv: TR 595.
[2] I, xxxvii: EM i, 299; TR 225(c).
[3] III, xiii: EM iii, 360–1; TR 1041–2.
[4] II, ii: EM ii, 10; TR 321(a).
[5] II, xxxvii: DB ii, 364.

One consequence of this sense of diversity is the rejection of any systematic classification of human behaviour for the limitless chaos of reality. Thus he says that he is able to reveal to his friends the inner workings of their minds but 'non pour renger cette infinie varieté d'actions, si diverses et si descoupées, à certains genres et chapitres, et distribuer distinctement mes partages et divisions en classes et regions cogneuës'.[1] We are here approaching the form of the *Essais*. It is often said, and we have seen evidence of its truth, that he anticipates the psychological analysis of the classical writers of the seventeenth century, but he is very far indeed from the psychology of types and genres which is laid down by Boileau and practised by, for instance, Molière or La Bruyère. However, we can go further than this, and his characteristic mode of thought may perhaps emerge, by contrast, from a passage in his translation of Sabunde:

Au reste d'autant que le nombre ternaire revient mieux que nul autre à Dieu trine en personnes ... il a distribué en trois la nature spirituelle creée et la trouppe angelicque, comme il a faict aussi le reste. Car nous voyons l'universelle unité de la creation estre divisee en trois pieces generales, des choses simplement corporelles, simplement spirituelles et mixtes: et la simplement corporelle, à laquelle la simplement spirituelle se doit analogicquement rapporter, estre encore sousdivisee en trois membres.[2]

These divisions and subdivisions, which go on for quite a long time, are the antithesis of Montaigne's method: not for him the *a priori* assumptions and artificial symmetry of ternary thinkers. It might even be suggested that his characteristic way of thought was partly provoked by reaction against Sabunde. And before we dismiss this passage as merely the ratiocination of a very obscure scholastic theologian, we might reflect that, with all their genius, the fundamental *modus operandi* of Pascal, Victor Hugo, Hegel or Marx is not so very different. Reality in Montaigne is never distorted by the need to impose upon it a rigidly consistent or monolithic or tripartite vision of the world. This is not the least of his lessons.

But the acceptance of inconsistency, of the multifariousness

1 III, xiii: EM iii, 376; TR 1053–4.
2 *Œuvres complètes*, ed. Armaingaud, x, 68.

of reality, inevitably involves the sort of contradiction we have frequently come across. Again contradiction is not just something that happens through inadvertence, to be explained away if possible, it constitutes another central principle of the *Essais*. As M. Baraz asks, tentatively but pertinently:

> Ceci est paradoxal et contradictoire, mais l'intuition fondamentale de Montaigne n'est-elle pas précisément celle de la coexistence des contraires ?[1]

There are a number of fundamental intuitions in Montaigne, but we can agree that this is certainly one of them. He says it himself as usual: the doctors he is attacking 'ne me sçauroient fournir proposition à laquelle je n'en rebatisse une contraire de pareille force'.[2] Apart from the pervasiveness of the theme everywhere, several essays are specifically devoted to it. Thus *Comme nous pleurons et rions d'une mesme chose* (I, xxxviii) is important for its study of the multiplicity of human passions and motives, double reactions and contradictory feelings. In *Nous ne goustons rien de pur* (II, xx) everything is shown to be mixed: pleasure and pain, sadness and joy, virtue and vice, justice and injustice. *Des vaines subtilitez* (I, liv) starts with the vain subtleties of the title, but goes on to something much more significant: extremes meeting, things hanging together by their opposites, and ternary groupings of the type a – b – a (peasants are good and so are philosophers, it is the people in between, and Montaigne includes himself, who cause all the trouble in the world). The last is the form of reasoning taken up and cultivated by Pascal, who clearly derived it from this essay: although Montaigne is not given to symmetry and ternary arguments, we see that he can do it when he wants to. Finally he applies the method to the *Essais* themselves (they will appeal neither to ordinary minds nor to outstanding ones but will eke out an existence between the two). This ingenious system shows a way of reconciling many of the apparent contradictions in his thought. In the end, however, his contradictions are a reflection of the contradictory nature of reality, as well as of the changing self. He is indeed justified in saying that he

---

[1] *L'être et la connaissance selon Montaigne*, 1968, p. 176, n. 20.
[2] II, xxxvii: EM ii, 600; TR 755(*b*).

contradicts himself but not truth. Scepticism itself is not so much a stage he passes through as an attitude which irradiates all that he writes. At the same time it is only part of the whole complex of attitudes, an instrument rather than his ultimate view of truth.

9

Montaigne and Religion

NO question connected with Montaigne has given rise to such extraordinarily divergent views as his attitude to religion. One extreme is Sainte-Beuve's unforgettable picture of the concealed free-thinker, of Pascal passing between the pillar of stone (Epictetus) and the pillar of smoke (Montaigne), of Montaigne leading his reader through the labyrinth of opinions, bearing a lamp which he then blows out with a chuckle.[1] Beyond the extreme point stands Armaingaud, who argued that everything in the *Essais* which seemed to mark the acceptance of orthodox Catholicism was a mere device of prudence and that underneath this mask we find an apology for atheism. Gide largely follows the same line. Not surprisingly there has been a strong reaction against a theory which means that a great deal of the *Essais* is no more than camouflage, not to be taken seriously, and the general consensus of recent work has moved to the other extreme, suggesting that Montaigne was really an excellent Christian and Catholic after all.[2] The reaction has been considerably reinforced by R. H. Popkin's *History of Scepticism* (1960), which shows convincingly that the Pyrrhonian scepticism of the *Apologie* was not an isolated phenomenon but a powerful weapon much used by Catholic controversialists and missionaries in their struggle against Protestantism. Why this weapon should be particularly favourable to the Catholic side is fully explained by Popkin; the question is hardly relevant here. In spite, however,

[1] *Port-Royal*, ed. Doyon and Marchesné, iii, 13–14, 52.
[2] See for example Müller, *Montaigne*, 1965 (in the series 'Les écrivains devant Dieu'). The fullest and most balanced account is Dréano, *La religion de Montaigne* (1969). Also important is Busson, *Le rationalisme dans la littérature française de la Renaissance* (revised ed., 1957).

of such weighty arguments there are some grounds for thinking that the reaction has gone too far.

One thing that need not trouble us much is the evidence from Montaigne's life. Virtually all of it goes to prove that he was in every external action a devout Catholic and was always taken to be so: the pilgrimage to Loretto and the edifying death are only two of them. To penetrate beyond external actions we can only turn to the *Essais* and to some extent the *Journal du voyage,* in fact from the life to the work. However, the question whether he was in his heart of hearts a good Catholic or Christian is not quite the one we are concerned with and is in any case hardly soluble without more than human insight. What we have to decide if possible is the meaning of the work as it stands, what it says rather than what its author intended to say or what his contemporaries said: we have seen that though the man and the work are consubstantial they are not identical. Such an inquiry is obviously fraught with difficulties and the separation cannot be maintained with total rigour.

But before we proceed further it will be as well to look at Montaigne's method of argument in dealing with dangerous subjects: from all that has been said we shall not expect him to speak directly and unambiguously. It must be emphasised that what follows applies for the most part as much to his treatment of political, juridical and social questions as to religious and should therefore be taken in relation to the next chapter as well as this one. First of all he denies his competence to discuss theological matters:[1] he exaggerates his ignorance, and we have observed the keen interest he took in the subject on his journey,[2] but it must always be borne in mind that we are not dealing with the words of a professional theologian. Then, at length in two passages of *Des prieres* but more briefly at several other points, he makes a declaration of humble submission to the authority of the Church. In the first he says that he puts forward only unformed fancies, not to establish the truth but to seek it, and submits them to the judgement of those who have to regulate not only his actions and writings but his thoughts (this seems to be going a little far). In an addition which follows he disavows anything which goes against 'les sainctes prescriptions de l'Eglise catholique, apostolique et Romeine, en la quelle je meurs et en la quelle je suis

[1] e.g. II, xii: TR 417; II, 16: TR 602.
[2] p. 23 above.

nai'.[1] The conclusion (in the original edition) is that, subject always to the censorship of the authorities 'qui peut tout sur moy' (an important statement as we shall see), he rashly engages in talk on all sorts of topic. The second declaration is entirely in the Bordeaux Copy and follows the same lines, in a way even more firmly:

Je propose les fantasies humaines et mienes, simplemant come humaines fantasies ... matiere d'opinion, non matiere de foi; ce que je discours selon moi, non ce que je croy selon Dieu, comme les enfans proposent leurs essais: instruisables, non instruisans; d'une maniere laïque, non clericale, mais tres religieuse tousjours.[2]

He writes as a layman but always religiously. It is right to give the fullest weight from the start to these key statements, which suggest that any apparent deviation from orthodoxy is due to ignorance or a fondness for playing with ideas. And they are confirmed by a number of other remarks, including the admission that he often maintains a point of view which is not his own just for amusement and practice in arguing[3] (this is two-edged of course). More significant is a well-known and culminating passage, also in the *Apologie,* where he suddenly reveals that the whole array of sceptical arguments accumulated at such length is no more than a trick, the ultimate resource of a fencer, 'ce dernier tour d'escrime':

C'est un coup desesperé, auquel il faut abandonner vos armes pour faire perdre à vostre adversaire les siennes, et un tour secret, duquel il se faut servir rarement et reservéement.[4]

All this fits in extremely well with Popkin's view of scepticism used as a weapon in the defence of Catholicism.

At the same time there are other passages with very different implications. When we speak of going to the stake for something, it is a metaphor; when Montaigne does, it may well be a reality. This reflection gives point to observations like:

Tant y a qu'en ces mcmoires, si on y regarde, on trouvera que j'ay tout dict, ou tout designé. Ce que je ne puis exprimer, je le montre au doigt.[5]

1 I, lvi: EM i, 408; TR 303(*c*).
2 I, lvi: EM i, 416; TR 308–9(*c*).
3 II, xii: TR 549. Cf. p. 102 above.
4 II, xii: EM ii, 304; TR 540(*a*).
5 III, ix: EM iii, 254; TR 961.

A very pertinent quotation from Lucretius follows, hinting at hidden meanings.

> Joint qu'à l'avanture ai je quelqu' obligation particuliere à ne dire qu'à demi, à dire confuséement, à dire discordemment.[1]

Again, expressed with fitting obscurity, there appears the intention of disguising thoughts rather than revealing them openly. Examples of such asides, which might easily pass unnoticed, could be multiplied, especially in the later stages. One goes into more detail, though it is still cryptic enough:

> Et combien y ai je espendu d'histoires qui ne disent mot, les quelles qui voudra esplucher un peu ingenieusement, en produira infinis essais. Ny elles, ny mes allegations [quotations] ne servent pas tousjours simplement d'exemple, d'authorité ou d'ornement ... Elles portent souvant, hors de mon propos, la semance d'une matiere plus riche et plus hardie, et sonent à gauche un ton plus delicat, et pour moi qui n'en veus exprimer davantage, et pour ceus qui rencontreront mon air.[2]

The word *hardie* is particularly striking. All these passages, and they converge with many others, end by forming a pattern, a refrain. They constitute an invitation, all the more pressing because it is veiled, to read between the lines, to explore the secret meaning of the *Essais*. In the light cast by them the Armaingaud position no longer looks quite so absurd. At any rate it is no use approaching Montaigne with the idea that everything is as it seems on the surface.

Among the devices which may serve to convey hidden meanings an obvious one, suggested in the last passage, is quotation. Separated by a short interval in the *Apologie* come two from Lucretius, the familiar

> Tantum relligio potuit suadere malorum![3]

and

> sæpius olim
> Relligio peperit scelerosa atque impia facta.[4]

The first is applied to the human sacrifices of the Mexicans, the second to ancient Greece, but it was really not possible, for the

[1] III, ix: EM iii, 272; TR 974(c).
[2] I, xl: EM i, 326; TR 245(c).
[3] II, xii: EM ii, 254; TR 502(c).
[4] II, xii: EM ii, 256; TR 503(a).

first quotation especially, to avoid drawing the parallel with contemporary France and its ferocious wars of religion. The throwing together of the opinions of different philosophers, especially on such problems as the immortality of the soul, is at least potentially anti-Christian, as we can perhaps see in Bayle. A further complication is that it is often difficult to distinguish Montaigne's exposition of ancient philosophers from his own arguments, another element of disguise. To see the same process on a smaller scale we might look at a passage where he is arguing that belief in eternal life ought to produce more effect than it does:

Je veuil estre dissout, dirions nous, et estre aveques Jesus-Christ. La force du discours de Platon, de l'immortalité de l'ame, poussa bien aucuns de ses disciples à la mort, pour joïr plus promptement des esperances qu'il leur donnoit.[1]

Is this an example of the Voltairean technique of irony by juxtaposition? The whole point about Montaigne is that we can't be sure. Finally, we should keep, as always, a careful watch on interpolations and deletions. Thus at the beginning of *Coustume de l'isle de Cea*, in the 1580 edition, he says : 'Mon cathedrant, c'est l'authorité de la sacrosainte volonté divine . . .'.[2] In the Bordeaux Copy *sacrosainte* is deleted. This may or may not be significant, but the deletion is not recorded in Thibaudet and Rat or the ordinary non-critical editions. It does not follow that we must necessarily adopt an anti-Catholic or anti-Christian interpretation of all or any of these examples: they serve to show none the less what Montaigne might mean by his veiled hints.

Though we are concerned with the book rather than the man, it is obviously impossible to decide the religious significance of the *Essais* without reference to external evidence, to systems of belief and to the official reactions of the Church. Two external facts of this kind mark the limits of the problem. As we saw in the introduction, the *Essais* were passed with minor objections by the papal censor in Rome in 1581 and placed on the Roman Index in 1676, 'ubicunque, et quocunque idiomate impressus'.[3] There

---

[1] II, xii: EM ii, 149; TR 422(a).
[2] II, iii: DB i, 285.
[3] They had already been placed on the Spanish Index, 'hasta que se expurgue', at least as early as 1640 (*Librorum expurgandorum . . . novissimus index*, Madrid, D. Diaz, 1640, p. 795). I am indebted to Professor E. M. Wilson for the suggestion which led to this discovery.

was clearly a change of mind or rather, as I suggested, the book had changed its meaning in new circumstances or its latent meaning had only gradually been drawn out. At any rate, the placing of the book on the Index, partly the result of Jansenist pressure (though this could hardly account for Spain), shows that the ecclesiastical authorities themselves found something dangerous in it. The first encounter with the Roman censorship is described in the *Journal du voyage*. The actual reading, says Montaigne, must have been done by some French friar because the dignitary responsible for censorship, the Maestro del Sacro Palazzo, knew no French. The *Journal* gives a list of six objections. One was the recurrent use of the word 'fortune': this could imply a random organisation of the world and a disbelief in Providence; Machiavelli's use of the word might well have made the Church sensitive to it. Then Montaigne had named heretical poets: the *Journal* does not specify, but Beza and Buchanan were two. He had defended Julian the Apostate: this was in *De la liberté de conscience*. He had said that anyone engaged in prayer must be free of all vicious inclination: this was in *Des prieres*.[1] The last is the most substantial theological point. Montaigne's error was in all probability due to theological ignorance, not to any subversive intention, but it perhaps indicates none the less a fundamental misunderstanding of Christianity, a pagan-philosophical approach.[2] He had said that any punishment beyond simple death was cruelty: this was in *De la cruauté*. Finally, he had said that a child should be brought up to do anything: this refers to *De l'institution des enfans* and the educational and moral principles we have already discussed.[3] In the last objection the censor was on the brink of making some grave discoveries about Montaigne. With this exception, however, and possibly the one about prayer, the objections are all trivial and marginal: the whole affair was conducted in a friendly way and no one took it very seriously. There was no apparent reason why anyone should, nor is there any reason to suppose that the reading was more than cursory: it is a mistake to think that censors are always efficient. It must be remembered too that only the first two books were read, though even in them there is a great deal that a vigilant censor might have seized on. The great question is what the author did about it.

[1] I, lvi: TR 304(*a*).
[2] A point well made by Busson, *Littérature et théologie*, 1962, pp. 70–4.
[3] On all this see *JV*: TR 1228–9; also 1240.

Attacking the liberal view of Montaigne, Edward Williamson writes: 'When the Vatican suggested modifications they were promptly made.'[1] In fact, in spite of his many protestations of devotion and submission to the rulings of the Church, he made no corrections at all and even boasts of it:

> Et ne conceday pas au magistrat mesmes qu'il eut raison de condamner un livre pour avoir logé entre les meillurs poëtes de ce siecle un heretique.[2]

It is true that, as usual, he has a loophole, and there is a possible justification for his disobedience. In his final interview with the Maestro del Sacro Palazzo he was told that he could use his own judgement in deciding what changes to make. Still, the fact that he made none, and the whole episode, must count against a wholly orthodox interpretation of the *Essais*. The reasons for the decision of 1676 are not known: they must have sprung from a much fuller view of his whole religious and moral position.

Certainly the evidence of acceptance of religious belief that can be derived from the *Essais* is overwhelming in quantity and impossible to explain away merely as prudent disguise, though inevitably some of it is difficult to interpret both because of the intricacy of all theological questions and because of Montaigne's peculiar mode of thought. He does not quote the Bible much, though he does quote it: but Ecclesiastes is probably his favourite book, which must seem slightly suspect; and when he cites Leah, Rachel and Sarah in support of his praise of polygamy among the American Indians,[3] we may wonder whether this ranks as evidence of piety. Or when he says that if we had real faith we could move mountains, is this an expression of simple trust or of profound irony? Augustine is quoted quite often, Aquinas once or twice. More interestingly, St Charles Borromeo is the subject of an admiring and moving sketch,[4] though of course to admire a saint is not necessarily to be religious oneself and it may be surmised that the motive force here is aesthetic or anthropological rather than strictly religious. As has often been pointed out, references to Christ are extremely few and even then tend to be

---

[1] 'On the liberalizing of Montaigne: a remonstrance', *French review*, xxiii (1949).
[2] III, x: EM iii, 292; TR 990(*c*).
[3] I, xxxi: TR 211(*c*).
[4] I, xiv: TR 61–2(*b*).

to his humanity alone[1] or to be thrown in pell-mell with other examples.[2]

Against such considerations we must set many expressions of unstudied faith which mostly occur in contexts which seem to rule out deception or irony. Some of the arguments of *Des prieres* may be theologically dubious, but it is difficult to resist the deep simplicity of his attachment to the Lord's Prayer,[3] which he mentions or quotes on several other occasions. Of course it could always be argued that, like the sign of the cross which he also likes making, especially when he yawns,[4] this is no more than a mechanical habit. But at times he goes much further than this. At the end of the same essay (in 1580) he writes:

> Il n'est rien si aisé, si doux et si favorable que la loy divine: elle nous appelle à soy, ainsi fautiers et detestables comme nous sommes; elle nous tend les bras et nous reçoit en son giron, pour vilains, ords et bourbeux que nous soyons et que nous ayons à estre à l'advenir.[5]

It is impossible here to deny the specifically Christian character of the sentiment expressed, though even here a reference to Plato is inserted in the Bordeaux Copy and the essay ends in 1588 with a quotation from Horace which is entirely pagan in feeling. Still, there are a number of passages where he establishes a distance between pagan and Christian virtue. Thus Plato is great but with only a human greatness;[6] the virtues of Socrates and Cato are useless because they have not known the true God.[7] The latter, certainly contradicted by a great deal that he says elsewhere, especially about Socrates, is from the first edition. The last sentence of the *Apologie*, however, was added in the Bordeaux Copy and so must represent a final thought (it refers to Seneca): 'C'est à nostre foi Chrestiene, non à sa vertu Stoïque, de pretandre à cette divine et miraculeuse metamorfose.'[8] We can, if we wish, dismiss this as an additional precaution but if so it seems unnecessary as all four editions had appeared without it and without causing any trouble.

With these criticisms of pagan virtue is associated a strong

---

1 I, xx: TR 83.
2 I, xiv: TR 60.
3 I, lvi: TR 303.
4 I, lvi: TR 304.
5 I, lvi: EM i, 419; TR 311(*a*).
6 II, xii: TR 423(*b*).
7 II, xii: TR 425(*a*).
8 II, xii: EM ii, 370; TR 589(*c*).

attack on atheism, also in the Bordeaux Copy.[1] One remark could be applied to those, like Armaingaud, who would force him into an anti-religious mould: 'un atheiste se flate à ramener tous autheurs à l'atheisme: infectant de son propre venin la matiere innocente.'[2] Whatever view we take of his religion, he cannot be made into an atheist. His frequent references to God need to be treated with caution: for the moment we are concerned only with those which seem to have a definitely Christian colouring. Thus one of his pleadings in defence of the body is supported by the Christian conception that body and soul are united and that divine justice rewards or punishes both together.[3] When he opposes God to Satan[4] or speaks of 'Dieu tout-vivant et tout-puissant',[5] Christian doctrine or phraseology are clearly apparent. In many cases God and grace are mentioned together, in the Third Book as well as in the first two. At one point near the end of *De l'experience* they are ingeniously introduced into an argument which seems wholly pagan, epicurean and hedonistic. The soul

> mesure combien c'est qu'elle doibt à Dieu d'estre en repos de sa conscience et d'autres passions intestines, d'avoir le corps en sa disposition naturelle, jouyssant ordonnéement et competamment des functions molles et flateuses par lesquelles il luy plait compenser de sa grace les douleurs de quoy sa justice nous bat à son tour. . . .[6]

This achieves a synthesis which is not too far removed from the devout humanism of St Francis of Sales and his school. In the same way there is a reference to original sin even in *Sur des vers de Virgile*.[7] And in a late addition to the *Apologie* he advances an argument which may contain the germ of Pascal's wager:

> Est il si simple entandemant, le quel aiant d'un coté l'object d'un de nos vicieus plaisirs et de l'autre en pareille conoissance et persuasion l'estat d'une gloire immortelle, entrat en troque de l'un pour l'autre?[8]

The word *troque* is particularly noteworthy, though of course there is none of Pascal's mathematical apparatus. It is true that

---

1 II, xii: TR 423(*c*).
2 II, xii: EM ii, 154; TR 425(*c*).
3 II, xvii: TR 623(*a*).
4 I, lvi: TR 310(*a*).
5 II, xii: EM ii, 208; TR 468(*a*).
6 III, xii: EM iii, 425; TR 1092–3(*b*).
7 III, v: TR 856.
8 II, xii: EM ii, 148; TR 421(*c*).

the final phrase is somewhat ambiguous, but the context hardly permits doubt about the genuineness of the argument.

However, what is closest to Christian doctrine in the *Essais* is perhaps the insistence on the virtues of humility, obedience and ignorance, though here again it is not always easy to distinguish between them and the Pyrrhonian scepticism we have already discussed. It may be artificial to attempt any such distinction if we think that scepticism is solely a weapon in the defence of orthodoxy: but this position can scarcely be maintained in a rigorous form. The object of the *Apologie* is stated at the outset to be to lay low human pride and reason, 'leur faire baisser la teste et mordre la terre soubs l'authorité et reverance de la majesté divine'.[1] Though it remains to be seen whether the object is achieved, we are bound to some extent to read the whole essay in the light of this declared purpose. Curiosity and the thirst for knowledge are said to have been the first ruin of mankind and the way to eternal damnation.[2] The curiosity Montaigne himself displays throughout the *Essais* need not be regarded as contradicting this. The apostles were simple and ignorant, and it is ignorance not knowledge that leads us to God.[3] Only humility and submission can make a good man.[4] This is far from the whole of Montaigne's story but we must not forget that he said it. It will be noticed that all these arguments are from the *Apologie* and from 1580. However, there is at any rate one addition in the Bordeaux Copy which confirms them, in perhaps even stronger terms:

> Gens qui jugent et contrerollent leurs juges ne s'y soubmettent jamais deuëment. Combien, et aux lois de la religion et aux lois politiques, se trouvent plus dociles et aisez à mener les esprits simples et incurieux, que ces esprits surveillants et pædagogues des causes divines et humaines![5]

But this is moving away from religious to political considerations. The fact that it touches not only Montaigne himself but the whole design of the *Essais* (with their emphasis on judgement) may lead us to consider the possibility that in the context of the whole work it should be interpreted in a not wholly laudatory sense. However that may be, there is no doubt that the attack on human

[1] II, xii: EM ii, 154; TR 426(*a*).
[2] II, xii: TR 478(*a*).
[3] II, xii: TR 479–80(*a*).
[4] II, xii: TR 467(*a*).
[5] II, xii: EM ii, 231; TR 486(*c*).

presumption in the *Apologie*: 'O cuider! combien tu nous empesches',[1] is given a strong impulsion towards religious orthodoxy. And the misery of man, which we have examined from the point of view of Montaigne's pessimism, is employed to convey in Pascalian terms (as usual the coincidence is due to direct influence) the separation from God and the fall from grace:

> Considerons donq pour cette heure l'homme seul, sans secours estranger, armé seulement de ses armes, et despourveu de la grace et cognoissance divine, qui est tout son honneur, sa force et le fondement de son estre.[2]

So far we have been considering what appears to be Christian in Montaigne. His Catholicism can best be defined, since his references to such topics as grace are too general for accurate assignment to any theological system, in terms of his attitude towards the Reformation. Apart from his professions of obedience to ecclesiastical authority, one or two passages go further. In the *Apologie* he not only denounces departures from the way of Christian truth but also from 'la voye tracée et battuë par l'Eglise'.[3] In *C'est folie de rapporter le vray et le faux à nostre suffisance* he criticises Catholics who give way on even the smallest points of faith.[4] If this passage were taken in isolation we should have to conclude that he is not just a Catholic but an adherent of the most intransigent wing of the Catholic party. Of course the passage is early, and here again the presence of an evolutionary factor cannot be ignored. But expressions of hostility to Protestantism are by no means confined to the early stages. He speaks of the errors of Wycliffe,[5] attacks Luther for the divisions he has created,[6] and an unnamed man (who must be Beza) for offering with one hand beautiful and licentious verses and with the other 'la plus quereleuse reformation theologienne de quoy le monde se soit desjeuné il y a long temps'.[7] He refers, significantly, to 'la Religion pretendue reformée',[8] the standard Catholic appellation of the reformed church. The strongest denunciation, among many, comes in *De la phisionomie*, where he doubts whether there is

1 II, xii: EM ii, 220; TR 478(*c*).
2 II, xii: EM ii, 155; TR 427(*a*).
3 II, xii: EM ii, 252; TR 501(*a*).
4 I, xxvii: TR 180–1(*a*).
5 I, iii: TR 21(*b*).
6 III, xiii: TR 1046(*b*).
7 III, ix: EM iii, 263; TR 967(*b*).
8 II, xxxii: EM ii, 526; TR 699(*a*).

any reformer 'à qui on aye en bon esciant persuadé qu'il aloit
vers la reformation par la derniere des difformations, qu'il tiroit
vers son salut par les plus expresses causes que nous ayons de
tres certeine damnation . . .'.[1] Sometimes he moves from the
general to the particular and deals with specific points at issue: thus
he argues that Protestantism must lead to atheism because once
doubt has crept in there is no stopping it.[2] He criticises frequently
and with particular severity the Protestant reliance on the Bible,
and one of the reasons he gives, based on diversity, is characteristically penetrating:

> Et ceux là se moquent, qui pensent appetisser nos debats et les
> arrester en nous r'appellant à l'expresse parolle de la Bible. D'autant
> que nostre esprit ne trouve pas le champ moins spatieux à contreroller
> le sens d'autruy qu'à representer le sien, et comme s'il y avoit moins
> d'animosité et d'aspreté à gloser qu'à inventer.[3]

He objects to the diffusion of the Bible in different languages (who
is qualified to judge a translation into Basque or Breton?),[4] and
above all among the common people, shopboys, artisans, women
and children. This was the usual Catholic line (for instance in the
preface of the Louvain Bible of 1550) and it is clearly anti-
democratic. Incidentally it tends to confirm the Marxist theory of
the class origins of the Reformation. An objection which perhaps
springs from a deeper personal and temperamental cause is that
the Protestants have tried to build a purely contemplative and
immaterial religion, an attempt that was bound to fail precisely
because of the corporal nature of man.[5] But the most fundamental objection of all, often voiced, is no doubt on the score of
innovation alone.[6] Nor can we entirely overlook, though this is
external evidence, the fact that many of Montaigne's friends, including La Boétie, the Jesuit Maldonatus (the *Journal du voyage*
praises the Jesuits highly), Florimond de Raemond and Mlle de
Gournay, were prominent on the Catholic and even the extreme
Catholic side.

Against this there is very little that could be interpreted as
ideological sympathy for the Protestants. Montaigne says in *Des*

[1] III, xii: EM iii, 331; TR 1020(*c*).
[2] II, xii: TR 416(*a*).
[3] III, xiii: EM iii, 361; TR 1042(*b*).
[4] I, lvi: TR 306(*b*).
[5] III, viii: TR 909(*b*).
[6] e.g. I, xxiii: TR 118(*b*).

prieres that in his youth he might have been tempted by the dangers of embracing the Protestant cause and he praises them for not using the name of God in ordinary conversation:[1] this is about all. But he does feel a human sympathy which comes out especially in his comments on the religious wars. Here he shows considerable impartiality, implying that there is a right side but that its motives and conduct are discreditable.[2] Coligny's French soldiers had contributed to pay for his foreign auxiliaries: such ardent devotion, Montaigne says, could hardly have been found on the Catholic side.[3] In a Bordeaux Copy addition he suggests, in a veiled way, that if the Protestants are bad the League are worse:[4] this is what one might expect from his association in his later years with the party of the Politiques or moderate Catholics. On the whole he is much harsher in his strictures on the Catholics, who disfigure their righteous cause by violence, vengeance and greed.[5] Montaigne told de Thou at Blois in 1588 that he had acted as an intermediary between Guise and Henry of Navarre and that religion for both was only a pretext to serve political ends.[6] He was and could be under no illusion about the religious sentiments of the belligerents, especially the Catholics. This does not much affect the question of the genuineness of his adherence to the old faith, but it does help to explain a certain lukewarmness: 'Hors le neud du debat [the theological question], je me suis maintenu en equanimité et pure indifference.'[7] Here we can see a clear statement of the neutralism of the Politiques, whose Catholicism did not prevent them from seeking a political rather than a religious solution to the troubles.

With a few reservations (important ones admittedly) we have discovered a formidable case for the presence of a Christian purpose in the *Essais* and an even stronger, in fact almost overwhelming, one for Montaigne's adherence to Catholicism. We must now turn to the evidence on the other side which is much more difficult to assess: statements in favour of orthodoxy could

---

1 I, lvi: TR 305(c), 309(a).
2 II, xii: TR 419–20(a).
3 II, xxxiv: TR 720(a).
4 III, x: TR 991(c).
5 II, xix: TR 651(a); I, liv: TR 299(b).
6 See Françon, *BSAM*, IV, 18 (1969), pp. 34–5. Montaigne's admirer Pierre de l'Estoile expresses a very similar view of the motives of the Ligueurs (*Journal, passim*).
7 III, x: EM iii, 291; TR 989(b).

be made openly and boldly, any doubts could hardly be expressed except by ambiguities, hints and allusions.

One feature which by its cumulative effect tells against Christianity is obviously the classical background of the *Essais*. The *Apologie* in particular contains an enormous number of borrowings. This detracts from its originality but the extensive survey of the freedom of Greek thought contrasts sharply with the dogmatism of the Catholic Church and is liberating in itself. Though Montaigne is here the heir of the tradition of humanistic scholarship and owes an enormous debt to the many translators and compilers, it might almost be said that he is the first to put the dangerous speculations of the philosophers in a universally accessible form. It is not at all easy to sum up the general impression given by the essay. Some incidental remarks are highly damaging. To give a few examples, he reports (in the Bordeaux Copy) the legends surrounding Plato's birth and goes on:

> Combien y a il, es histoires, de pareils cocuages procurez par les Dieus contre les povres humains? et des maris injurieusement descriez en faveur des enfans?[1]

Now there are so many instances in mythology of men cuckolded by the gods that it is not necessary to read more into the passage; yet the parallel with the birth of Christ is so close as to be nearly inescapable. It may be objected that this is an anachronistic reading: Montaigne was not Voltaire or a philosopher of the Enlightenment. We have at any rate a characteristic ambiguity; there can be no doubt about the ammunition which questions like these provided for later generations. Or again there is the story of Stilpon who was asked whether the gods rejoice at the honours and sacrifices we offer them: 'Vous estes indiscret, respondit il; retirons nous à part, si vous voulez parler de cela.'[2] This, following a quotation from St Paul, is a gloss on an argument slightly suspect in itself: the divine nature is so far removed from our abjectness that there can be no correspondence or similitude between the two. The story may mean nothing, but it suggests that Montaigne too could say a great deal more if he whispered in our ear. He asks, again, how the gods can reward and punish men for actions which these same gods have inspired or could have prevented:[3] we have here the most familiar of all difficulties

---

[1] II, xii: EM ii, 269; TR 513(c).
[2] II, xii: EM ii, 256; TR 504(c).
[3] II, xii: TR 500(a).

H

in the Christian theodicy and it seems impossible not to draw the parallel. He even produces (probably from Cicero) a satirical summary of the arguments for the existence of God, including two of the stock Christian proofs, the argument from perfection and the argument from design:[1] the intention is no doubt only to mock the speculations of the philosophers ('enfle toy, pauvre homme') but some of the mockery is bound to be transferred to Christian theology, whatever the intention.

Scepticism then can be directed against religion as well as used to support it, or at least gives that impression. The same is more especially true of custom and relativism, where the ambiguity of his observations is even more pronounced. When he says that we pray by usage and custom and that it is all no more than outward show,[2] it is possible to conclude that this is a bad state of affairs which ought to be put right. We cannot be nearly so confident about a well-known crux, the passage in the *Apologie* where he says that we accept our religion because it is the custom of our native country and follows with the interpolation: 'Nous sommes Chrestiens à mesme titre que nous sommes ou Perigordins ou Alemans.'[3] This can be read as meaning that we are Christians only from tradition and ought to be ashamed of ourselves for not having a more lively faith, an interpretation which is supported by the immediate context, especially the sentence: 'Ces considerations la doivent estre employées à nostre creance, mais comme subsidiaires: ce sont liaisons humaines.' But the interpolation detaches itself from this sentence in a way which is impossible to ignore. And in the context of the *Essais* as a whole, with their continual emphasis on custom as a force which deadens reason, on the absurdity of turning our local customs into universal laws, it implies that religion, including our own, is a mere local accident. If we look at what Montaigne says rather than attempting to discover what he meant to say, this is a terrible blow to Christianity or at least to its claims to a unique status among religions. The blow, but also the element of ambiguity, is weaker in the statement that any opinion is powerful enough to make martyrs, with examples of Turks who have refused baptism: 'Exemple de quoi nulle sorte de relligion n'est incapable.'[4] This is in a way obvious;

[1] II, xii: TR 511–2.
[2] I, lvi: TR 304(*a*).
[3] II, xii: EM ii, 149; TR 422(*b*).
[4] I, xiv: EM i, 62; TR 53(*c*).

Montaigne and Religion

but the relativity of the standpoint is sufficient to shake the belief that the Christian religion has a monopoly of genuine martyrs.

With relativism goes, so closely as to be almost inseparable from it, the political view of religion, summed up by Gibbon when he said that the numerous Roman religions were considered 'by the people as equally true; by the philosopher as equally false; and by the magistrate as equally useful'. Montaigne was a magistrate, and we have here one key, perhaps the most important, to his religious thought. Thus he says that the Christian religion has all the marks of extreme justice and utility (the word that matters in this argument), none more so than its recommendation of obedience to established authority; he goes on to admire the divine wisdom which 'pour establir le salut du genre humain... ne l'a voulu faire qu'à la mercy de nostre ordre politique...'.[1] This sounds all right, though the continuation (the injustices of the political order and the rivers of blood which have flowed to maintain it) might be taken as ironical. But the argument is in the end (as we see from the way it is used by Voltaire or Maurras) profoundly antagonistic to religion: usefulness of this kind is hardly compatible with truth. This becomes clearer when we look at another remark:

Ce moyen [false beliefs] a esté practiqué par tous les Legislateurs, et n'est police où il n'y ait quelque meslange ou de vanité ceremonieuse ou d'opinion mensongere, qui serve de bride à tenir le peuple en office.[2]

Christianity is not mentioned, and a reference to 'religions bastardes' might be held to exclude it, but again the parallel forces itself on the reader. It is easy to understand those who, like Sainte-Beuve and Gide, have thought Montaigne to be a Catholic but not a Christian. He speaks more openly when he condemns contemporary Christians and their violence (the argument is not fundamentally different, though the angle of vision has changed):

Il n'est point d'hostilité excellante come la chrestiene. Notre zele faict merveilles, quand il va secondant nostre pante vers la haine, la cruauté, l'ambition, l'avarice, la detraction, la rebellion.[3]

Here again there is ambiguity: an immediate interpretation

1 I, xxiii: EM i, 154; TR 119(b).
2 II, xvi: EM ii, 404; TR 613(a).
3 II, xii: EM ii, 148: TR 421(c).

217

suggests that, though this is what happens, it is contrary to true Christianity. But again the reader is left wondering why the true religion of love should produce these effects more than any other, and again a terrible blow has been struck. Even more terrible is the comparison introduced into the *Apologie* in 1588: 'comparez nos meurs à un Mahometan, à un Payen; vous demeurez tousjours au dessoubs.'[1] So far, though that 'always' is devastating enough, the usual explanation remains open and is supported by the following sentence: our religion is superior and therefore we ought to amend ourselves. But at this point the Bordeaux Copy introduces another interpolation which simply knocks this defence away:

> Toutes autres apparances sont communes à toutes relligions: esperance, confiance, evenemans, ceremonies, pœnitance, martyres. La marque peculiere de nostre verité devroit estre nostre vertu. . . .

Thus the *only* test of a religion is now conduct, and he has just shown that Christians are inferior in this respect to all Mohammedans and pagans. The reference to 'events' is particularly disturbing: it looks as if this must include all the historical evidence for Christianity, including the Incarnation and Resurrection. A passage like this cannot destroy all the arguments on the other side, but it too has to be given full weight.

The treatment of miracles is a special case which demands separate attention. We are at once confronted with the same difficulties and ambiguities. One essay, *C'est folie de rapporter le vray et le faux à nostre suffisance*, exemplifies the turning of scepticism against scepticism and makes a qualified plea for the acceptance of miracles because to reject them is to assume a knowledge of the limitations of God and nature which we do not possess. He gives a list of miracles guaranteed by the authority of St Augustine, which he regards as sufficient in itself.[2] More profoundly, and more in accordance with his usual modes of thought, he argues that we call monsters or miracles anything that goes beyond our reason, which is in fact custom, what we are used to: but once the scales of habit are removed from our eyes everything is extraordinary. Here the usual double edge is beginning to appear: on the one hand the fact that something is against reason is no final argument against its happening; on the other, if everything is miraculous then really nothing is (but this last is a conclusion he

1 II, xii: EM ii, 145; TR 419(*b*).
2 I, xxvii: TR 180(*a*).

does not draw at this point). The same argument can be given a totally different twist, as it is in a late addition to *D'un enfant monstrueux* (another significant title):

Ce que nous apelons monstres, ne le sont pas à Dieu, qui voit en l'immansité de son ouvrage l'infinité des formes qu'il y a comprinses ... De sa toute sagesse il ne part rien que bon et commun et reglé; mais nous n'en voïons pas l'assortimant et la relation.[1]

Incidentally this reminds us of one of Baudelaire's prose poems.[2] But under the very pious phraseology there lurks a highly unorthodox idea: that the universality of the divine laws excludes happenings against nature and that the apparently unnatural or supernatural is always susceptible of a rational explanation, or would be if we could see it. This is the view of the world which we find in the system of knowledge prefixed to the *Encyclopédie* and which attains its full development in the eighteenth century. Miracles are not specifically mentioned, but other essays show that the same principle applies to them: 'Les miracles sont selon l'ignorance en quoi nous somes de la nature, non selon l'estre de la nature.'[3] This could no doubt be given an orthodox construction, but it suggests that if we knew more we could find a natural explanation for any miracle. In *De la force de l'imagination*, after saying that some people attribute the stigmata of St Francis to the power of the imagination (and not contradicting them), he goes on:

Il est vray semblable, que le principal credit des miracles, des visions, des enchantemens, et de tels effects extraordinaires, vienne de la puissance de l'imagination agissant principalement contre les ames du vulgaire, plus molles. On leur a si fort saisi la creance, qu'ils pensent voir ce qu'ils ne voyent pas.[4]

The expression is prudent but the thought is powerfully destructive. It is not surprising that the reference to miracles was suppressed in Mlle de Gournay's 1595 edition. In *Des boyteux*, one of the latest essays, he moves from the philosophical to the practical level, showing from his own experience ('J'ay veu la naissance de plusieurs miracles de mon temps')[5] how stories of miracles grow

---

[1] II, xxx: EM ii, 515; TR 691(*c*).
[2] *Mademoiselle Bistouri* in *Le spleen de Paris*.
[3] I, xxiii: EM i, 141; TR 110(*c*).
[4] I, xxi: EM i, 124; TR 97(*a*).
[5] III, xi: EM iii, 310; TR 1004(*b*).

and spread: the first to start them senses opposition and invents bits to cover up the weak points; later, people think it an act of charity to pass on the good news and do not hesitate to add their own embellishments. This brilliant and ruthless analysis, so like the work of the *philosophes* in its pure rationality, is directed at prodigies of various kinds rather than at specifically Christian miracles but again it is impossible not to make the connection. In all these cases it may be urged that only false miracles are affected, while the true remain intact, but the attitude and the method alike tend to discredit all belief in the miraculous. He gathers it all together in characterising his own cast of mind:

> Jusques à cette heure, tous ces miracles et evenemens estranges se cachent devant moy. Je n'ay veu monstre et miracle au monde plus exprès que moy-mesme.[1]

His scepticism really extends to all manifestations of the supernatural.

Another group of topics, repentance, death (including suicide), the soul and the after-life, may be dealt with more briefly, partly because they have been very fully discussed by others, partly because we have already considered death at some length. Montaigne's theory of repentance is naturally concentrated in *Du repentir* and as far as religion is concerned two main points emerge from that remarkable essay: it is impossible to repent of faults which are inherent and constitutional; repentance brought on by age and weakness is without value. In a roundabout way he admits that he does not repent: he is as he is and could not have behaved otherwise;[2] if he had to live his life again he would not change it.[3] This was one of the principal charges levelled at Montaigne by Pascal and the Jansenists. However, in this case it may be admitted that he is describing his personal reactions rather than laying down a rule of general application, and *Des prieres* suggests a more orthodox view. For his own salvation the question is no doubt of the highest importance; for the religious significance of the work its place is a minor one. The Stoical attitude to death of the early essays, though not Christian, is, as we saw, reconcilable with Christianity. The gradually developing acceptance of death as a natural occurrence not worth bothering about is another

---

[1] III, xi: EM iii, 313; TR 1006(*b*).
[2] III, ii: TR 791.
[3] III, ii: TR 794(*c*).

matter, and again draws Pascal's savage though not quite accurate condemnation: 'il ne pense qu'à mourir lâchement et mollement par tout son livre'.[1] Most serious is perhaps the preference for a sudden (and therefore unprepared and unshriven) death.[2] It is certainly striking that in these cases he does not seem at all perturbed by the thought of death without the sacraments. However, we are still in the realm of the personal. His views on suicide have a wider bearing. The essay *Coustume de l'isle de Cea* presents an even closer union than usual between form and content. The original version has a sort of see-saw movement from one point of view to the other. The numerous later additions which obscure these relatively simple lines serve to muddle the reader and perhaps put him off the scent. It is difficult none the less to avoid the conclusion that Montaigne is making an apology for suicide, at least in certain circumstances, or at least for toleration of it. Some asides in other essays perhaps speak more clearly, as in *De la cruauté* where Cato's suicide is described as a noble action[3] or in *De juger de la mort d'autruy*, the whole atmosphere of which is very pagan, where examples of suicide are given with no hint of disapproval, indeed with strong hints of the opposite. Even in the *Journal du voyage*, usually more conformist, two remedies are suggested for great pain, to bear it humanly or to end it bravely and swiftly.[4] The approval of suicide, however cautiously expressed as a rule, is one of the themes in the *Essais* which show the influence of antiquity most clearly and which are most opposed to Christian doctrines. It should be added that the majority of the examples quoted are from Book II and that in the Third Book, where the emphasis is on life, the subject has ceased to obtrude.[5]

On the central question of the immortality of the soul it is equally difficult to pin him down. Expressions of belief are numerous, for example: 'La mort est origine d'un' autre vie.'[6] But statements of the contrary are at least as numerous though, as we should expect, more equivocal. They occur mostly in the

---

[1] *Pensées*, ed. Lafuma, 1951, i, 393.
[2] e.g. II, vi: TR 357; II, xiii: TR 592.
[3] II, xi: TR 403.
[4] TR 1311.
[5] Pierre Barrière has suggested that suicide is the dominant theme of Book II (*Montaigne gentilhomme français*, pp. 146–8). This is an exaggeration, though an interesting one.
[6] I, xx: EM i, 114; TR 90(c).

Apologie and again mostly in the exposition and criticism of the ideas of ancient philosophers. Thus Plato's view of immortality is attacked in a very subtle argument, but the objections made against him are equally applicable to the Christian view.[1] When Montaigne says: '. . . . ce qui se recite des enfers et des peines futures est feint',[2] he is quoting Plato's hostile summary of certain philosophers who denied immortality but it looks as if in a most oblique way he is making their opinion his own. At any rate it is impossible to ignore the interferences with his religous thinking which are set up by his familiarity with pagan antiquity.

One argument he uses raises a wider question. Belief in the immortality of the soul is clear and just but philosophers have not been able to establish it by human force. It is a good thing that we should be beholden to God for the gift of this truth.[3] He continues in the Bordeaux Copy:

> Confessons ingenuement que Dieu sul nous l'a dict, et la foi: car leçon n'est ce pas de nature et de nostre raison.[4]

This sounds very dangerous and though he goes on to say that the more we attribute to God the better Christians we are, the damage has already been done. With the insistence on the feebleness of all human arguments for immortality we are confronted with the problem of Montaigne's fideism.[5] Fideism, the separation of faith and reason, is typified by the argument just discussed. When it is genuine, that is to say when faith really is exalted and reason abased, it is usually regarded as at least dubiously orthodox because it strikes at the root of the system of rational theology of which Aquinas was the great constructor and which has become the main line of Catholic doctrine. Incidentally Sabunde occupies an extreme rationalist position and once again we can only wonder at the peculiar character of this apologia for him. But fideism is not always genuine, and it can turn into a convenient way of conducting rational attacks on Christian tenets by saying what Montaigne says here: human reason shows this to be impossible or highly doubtful, faith tells us that it is true. But the acknowledgement to faith need be no more than perfunctory. This was

---

[1] II, xii: TR 498–500.
[2] II, xii: EM ii, 150; TR 423(c).
[3] II, xii: TR 535–6.
[4] II, xii: EM ii, 298; TR 536(c).
[5] See particularly Janssen, *Montaigne fidéiste*, 1930; also Busson, *Rationalisme*, and *Littérature et théologie*.

almost certainly the case with Pomponazzi and the Paduan school in the early sixteenth century. In a time of intellectual and spiritual crisis fideism offers a way round to believers who can reject rational arguments because they contradict faith, and to unbelievers who can pursue their rational inquiries undisturbed by the obeisance they are required to make to the superiority of revealed truth. Whether Montaigne exactly fits this picture is rather hard to say. It is certainly a means of reconciling what otherwise might seem insoluble contradictions. To say that he had probably never heard of fideism is obviously no answer: these ideas were so prevalent that he could scarcely remain unaffected by them. But fideism seems to imply a more systematic approach to theology than his. It works best for the *Apologie* and most of the proofs adduced come from it. We are bound to notice the disproportion between the two parts of the defence of Sabunde: the first, that reason can aid faith, takes up about a sixteenth of the essay; the second, that reason is no use anyway, all the rest. The first part is half-hearted (though it shows a surprising grasp of the theological issues),[1] the second is conducted with unflagging enthusiasm. Throughout the second part human reason is gaily demolished even, as we have seen, where important Christian beliefs tend to be demolished with it. He says:

C'est aux Chrestiens une occasion de croire, que de rencontrer une chose incroiable. Elle est d'autant plus selon raison, qu'elle est contre l'humaine raison.[2]

Here we are inevitably reminded of Tertullian's 'certum est quia impossibile est', a two-edged principle indeed and one not far removed from fideism. On the whole we can probably conclude that there is a strong tincture of fideism in the *Apologie* and occasionally elsewhere,[3] but that it cannot provide a key which solves all the difficulties. Whether it is of the believing (but still unorthodox) or unbelieving kind is not yet clear: the answer must depend on a total view of Montaigne's religion.

There are in any case more dangerous methods even than fideism. One of these is comparative religion, an interest in which is an important consequence of Montaigne's relativism. There was

---

[1] See for example the remarks on the relation between reason and grace (TR 425), very close to Pascal.

[2] II, xii: EM ii, 221; TR 478(a).

[3] For example the argument in *Des prieres* that theology and philosophy should be kept separate (TR 308(b)).

nothing new about this interest in itself: practically every travel-
ler reported on the beliefs and rites of the peoples he had visited
and compared them with Christianity, nearly always however to
their disadvantage.[1] The discovery of parallels between Christian
or Judeo-Christian beliefs and those of other religions can of
course be used to undermine established orthodoxies (by suggesting that one myth is much like another) or to strengthen them (by
confirming accounts of events like the Deluge). An example of the
latter is Bodin's comparison of the story of Noah and Ham to that
of Saturn and Jupiter (emasculation of the father).[2] It is naturally desirable to decide which of the two alternatives is present.
But in general the tendency of comparative religion, whatever the
intentions behind it, provided always that it is serious and not a
caricature, is to weaken faith inasmuch as it weakens belief in the
uniqueness of our own religion. It would be pointless (or rather,
though very interesting, too long) to consider all or even many of
the observations on differences and resemblances between
religions which crowd the pages of the *Essais* and the *Journal du
voyage*. The *Journal* illustrates Montaigne's passion for theological
disputation and his curiosity, particularly about non-Catholic
religions. Most noteworthy is probably the vivid description of a
circumcision in Rome: 'la plus antienne cerimonie de religion qui
soit parmy les homes.'[3] There may be an echo of this in the *Essais*
when he remarks that all religions condemn the sex act and many
practise circumcision 'qui en est une punition' (a penetrating
addition in the Bordeaux Copy).[4] In some cases comparison goes
to prove the superiority of Christianity, as when, after listing such
ceremonies and beliefs among the American Indians as circumcision, fasting, crosses, paradise lost, and the deluge, he goes on to
comment: 'Ces vains ombrages de nostre religion . . . en
tesmoignent la dignité et la divinité.'[5] Even here, in the context,
the possibility of irony is not absolutely to be excluded. And such
cases are a minority. More often, though again less explicitly, the
comparison works in the opposite direction. When in 1580 he
mocks the Mohammedan conception of paradise: 'un paradis

---

[1] A possible exception is Guillaume Postel whose exposition of Moham-
medanism in *La republique des Turcs* (1560) is impartial and occasionally
admiring; but there are many statements of the superiority of Christianity.
[2] *Methodus*, tr. Mesnard, p. 320.
[3] TR 1214.
[4] III, v: EM iii, 118; TR 856(c).
[5] II, xii: EM ii, 329; TR 558(b).

tapissé, paré d'or et de pierrerie, peuplé de garses d'excellente beauté, de vins et de vivres singuliers',[1] we cannot help reflecting that, apart from the houris, this could be turned against the Christian heaven, and in fact Montaigne says so himself in the Bordeaux Copy addition which follows. Perhaps the most alarming of many similar observations is the description of the tranquil existence of the Brazilians in a passage (from the Bordeaux Copy) which resembles the one already quoted from *Des cannibales* but with a new and significant item added to the list: 'come gens qui passoint leur vie en une admirable simplicité et ignorance, sans lettres, sans loy, says roy, sans relligion quelconque.'[2] No other conclusion seems possible than that they are happy at least partly because they have no king and no religion. We have seen that this sort of enumeration is something of a commonplace. Montaigne here seems to have been directly inspired by Goulart's *Histoire de Portugal*[3] or the Latin original of Osorius. However, Osorius states the facts only: there is no expression of admiration as in Montaigne. We might also compare Louis Le Roy on the savages of the New World: 'comme les premiers hommes, sans lettres, sans loix, sans Roys, sans republiques, sans ars: non toutefois sans religion',[4] or Léry's indignation when he encounters the Brazilians' lack of religion.[5] It is indeed difficult to explain away the implications of Montaigne's words. Typical of much argument on the subject is Popkin's comment:

> The Christian message is, according to Montaigne, to cultivate a similar ignorance in order to believe by faith alone.[6]

This might be true of the *Apologie* as a whole, it cannot possibly be derived from this passage. In his preoccupation with his own thesis he seems not to notice the extremely subversive consequences of 'sans relligion quelconque'.

One result of relativism and of comparative religion particularly is the development of toleration. Religious tolerance is now generally thought to be a good thing; it was not so in Montaigne's time for the great majority of the warring factions.

[1] II, xii: EM ii, 248; TR 498(*a*).
[2] II, xii: EM ii, 211; TR 471(*c*).
[3] *Histoire de Portugal*, Paris, 1581, f. 46ᵛ.
[4] *De la vicissitude ou varieté des choses*, Paris, 1576, f. 25ʳ; quoted by Atkinson, *Les nouveaux horizons*, p. 349.
[5] *Histoire d'un voyage*, 1578, pp. 262–3.
[6] *The history of scepticism*, p. 47.

In the *Journal du voyage,* in spite of the punctilious observance of Catholic duties, what is most striking is the attitude of tolerant curiosity in the encounters with representatives of other religions. In the essay which deals directly with the subject, *De la liberté de conscience,* he comes to a typically balanced conclusion: there is something to be said for and against it. In any case he treats it as a question of political expediency rather than of high principle. However, the real meaning of the essay is contained in the defence of Julian the Apostate which was criticised by the Roman censor, and perhaps especially in the passing remark about Julian: 'ayant essayé par la cruauté d'aucuns Chrestiens qu'il n'y a point de beste au monde tant à craindre à l'homme que l'homme.'[1] Dislike of superstition and fanaticism is everywhere apparent (except in minor matters like sitting thirteen at table). The characteristic attitude, dismissive but without over-emphasis, without intolerance even of fanaticism, appears in the description of the flagellants: 'Cela ay-je veu souvent et sans enchantement'.[2] However, there are cases where such dry and civilised understatement is inadequate and where tolerance takes on a much more positive value. One is his praise of the Indians for refusing to accept Christianity under threats,[3] and vigorous condemnation of the Spaniards who had boasted of burning 460 Indians alive: 'Seroit-ce pour tesmoignage de leur justice ou zele envers la religion? Certes, ce sont voyes trop diverses et ennemies d'une si saincte fin.'[4] An even better illustration is the story (from Osorius) of the expulsion of the Portuguese Jews,[5] told almost without overt comment but the more deeply moving because the indignation is controlled. It breaks through ('un horrible spectacle') when he recounts how the children were forcibly removed from their parents to be brought up as Christians. Of course Montaigne was not the first to advocate religious tolerance: the name of Castellio immediately comes to mind, and it is put very well by Osorius from a Catholic point of view. But again he may well have been the most influential up to that date. By contrast we might consider the sceptical Bruès on believers in metempsychosis (though a speaker in a dialogue does not necessarily speak for the author):

[1] II, xix: EM ii, 462; TR 654(*a*).
[2] I, xiv: EM i, 73; TR 61(*a*).
[3] III, vi: TR 889–90.
[4] III, vi: EM iii, 164; TR 891.
[5] I, xiv: TR 53(*c*).

'desquels on ne pourroit faire assez cruelle punition ... on ne les devroit permettre vivre plus longuement.'[1]

It seems too that Montaigne's hedonistic morality is not that of Christianity, is indeed fundamentally pagan. Since we have discussed it at some length a brief summary of its religious implications will suffice. The evidence, as usual, is difficult to assess. The preponderance of illustration and argument from ancient sources is not in itself anti-Christian: the same might be said of most Renaissance writers, even those who are indubitably Christian. At the same time the fact that there is so much about antiquity, so little about Christianity, is bound to carry some weight in itself. And much of the evidence is negative in that he does not mention Christian beliefs where he might reasonably be expected to do so. Thus there is nothing wrong, or nothing very much wrong, in a humanistic Christian praising Socrates: we have seen that Erasmus does. But when Montaigne puts him forward in *De la phisionomie* as the supreme exemplar of human perfection without any reference to Christ or the saints, when he says (adapting Cicero but making the thought fully his own): 'C'est luy qui ramena du ciel, où elle perdoit son temps, la sagesse humaine, pour la rendre à l'home',[2] we may well feel that he is substituting earthly wisdom for heavenly, almost in the manner of Voltaire or Goethe. In Cicero the word *caelestia* may possibly refer to heavenly bodies,[3] but the French is at least highly ambiguous. Sometimes paganism is turned explicitly against Christianity. Our religion did more damage to the classics than all the fires of the barbarians: no complete copy of Tacitus has survived the efforts of those who wanted to destroy his work 'pour cinq ou six vaines clauses contreres à nostre creance'.[4] Here speaks the humanist, certainly not an orthodox Christian. As far as morals are concerned he says that in distracting a young prince from thoughts of vengeance he did not advise him to turn the other cheek but showed him the honour and beauty (the aesthetic approach again) of clemency.[5] To turn the other cheek is hardly advice that could be given in a court; it is none the less revealing that the pagan recipe is openly preferred to the Christian. The underlying paganism of the *Essais* is brought to a head in the conclusion of

1 *Dialogues*, ed. Morphos, p. 142.
2 III, xii: EM iii, 324; TR 1015(*c*).
3 *Academica*, I, iv (ed. Reid, London, 1885, p. 109).
4 II, xix: EM ii, 459; TR 651.
5 III, iv: TR 813.

De l'experience and of the whole book. A little way from the end he gives thanks for the beauty of life:

> (*b*) J'accepte de bon cœur, (*c*) et reconnoissant, (*b*) ce que nature a faict pour moy, et m'en agrée et m'en loue. On fait tort à ce grand et tout puissant donneur de refuser son don, l'annuller et desfigurer. (*c*) Tout bon, il a faict tout bon.[1]

There seems to be a characteristic confusion between nature and God. The feeling expressed is religious beyond doubt but it can hardly be called Christian. And at the very end we have the invocation of Apollo, which is almost a prayer, and the quotation from Horace:

> Recommandons la [old age] à ce Dieu, protecteur de santé et de sagesse, mais gaye et sociale:
> > Frui paratis et valido mihi,
> > Latoe, dones, et, precor, integra
> > Cum mente, nec turpem senectam
> > Degere, nec cythara carentem.[2]

In a less prominent position we might dismiss this as poetic ornament; here we cannot ignore the resolutely pagan conclusion.

Passages like these, then, are powerfully stamped with religious experience of a kind which, though coloured by antiquity, cannot be specifically assigned to any single religion. Such experience is likely to lead to deism or pantheism (we need not, as far as Montaigne is concerned, distinguish too sharply between them) and in view of the importance of these systems in the subsequent history of European thought, as well as for their own sake, we ought to ask how far they can be applied to Montaigne. Both have, unlike most institutional religions, the advantage of nearly absolute consistency, and it is tempting to seek in them a possible key to the contradictions. The confusion between God and nature seems to tend towards pantheism. Thus when he observes that to say anything is absolutely false, 'c'est se donner l'advantage d'avoir dans la teste les bornes et limites de la volonté de Dieu et de la puissance de nostre mere nature',[3] it is almost as if there were two equal divinities. A little later in the same essay 'cette infinie puissance de Dieu' in the published editions is changed

---

[1] III, xiii: EM iii, 426; TR 1093–4.
[2] III, xiii: EM iii, 431; TR 1096–7(*b*).
[3] I, xxvii: EM i, 233; TR 178(*a*).

to 'cette infinie puissance de nature' in the Bordeaux Copy,[1] an indication of the greater emphasis on nature in the last stages. M. Baraz defines this side well when he says

> Sa conception de Dieu exclut en principe le surnaturel, les miracles et toute autre représentation anthropomorphe. (Son Dieu ne peut ni récompenser ni punir, car il est l'être même de tout ce qui existe.)[2]

This is borne out particularly by the close of the *Apologie* and its identification of God with being ('nous n'avons aucune communication à l'estre'), though this identification is also present in Sabunde.[3] It is true that the long quotation from Plutarch, 'cette conclusion si religieuse d'un homme payen', where God is presented in magnificent but not at all Christian terms, is followed by the brief statement already quoted, that man can only rise if God assists him and that this can only come about through Christian faith, not through the virtue of the Stoics.[4] But this cannot remove the deistic or pantheistic impression which has already been conveyed. Many other statements point to the remote God of the deists, an incomprehensible power accepting honours from men under any name and in any manner. However, at the point where this idea is most plainly expressed,[5] there is the same ambiguity as in the case of the Plutarch quotation: it is presented as the most probable and excusable among ancient opinions on religion. In general we can say that deistic views are always expounded with great sympathy, that they accord very well with Montaigne's distrust of supernatural explanations and divine interventions in human affairs, and that they are very close to his own deep religious feeling. At the same time they are so hedged in with precautions and are contradicted by so many statements of the necessity for Christian faith that we cannot characterise the *Essais* as deistic without some simplification. There is a strong deistic undercurrent and it is part of Montaigne's influence on the development of free thought in Europe.

We can now see that there were powerful reasons for placing the *Essais* on the Index. Before we try to draw conclusions from the conflicting and confusing evidence we have discussed, there are two aspects of Montaigne's Christianity, closely related, which

---

[1] I, xxvii: EM i, 234; TR 179.
[2] *L'être et la connaissance selon Montaigne*, p. 17.
[3] *Œuvres complètes*, ed. Armaingaud, ix, 24–6.
[4] II, xii: TR 588–9.
[5] II, xii: TR 493.

need to be examined. One is the conservatism which is an extension of the political defence of religion and which we have observed particularly in the attacks on Protestantism. Hatred of innovation, hatred of disturbance, scepticism about the existence of any truth which could justify the upheavals of religious war, all this has a prominent place and offers perhaps the simplest key to Montaigne's religion. In the uncertainty of all things we should follow the observances of the society to which we belong (in any case we are conditioned to do so), without any necessary commitment of belief. Important though this argument is, and it will be the subject of the next chapter, there are too many strands of thought and feeling which cannot be accommodated to it. It is not adequate as a total explanation.

The second, related to the first, is only a minor and incidental theme, but it is one which has since had an important history, the aesthetic approach to religion. In *Des senteurs* Montaigne observes that incense and perfumes have been used in all religions to inspire a mood of contemplation,[1] an example of his sensory awareness as well as of the touches of relativism which produce a cumulative effect even though each may be innocent enough in itself. Two passages in the *Apologie* take the matter further and both are worth quoting, though one at least is well known:

> Mais à peine me feroit on accroire, que la veuë de noz crucifix et peinture de ce piteux supplice, que les ornemens et mouvements ceremonieux de noz eglises, que les voix accommodées à la devotion de nostre pensée, et cette esmotion des sens n'eschauffent l'ame des peuples, d'une passion religieuse, de tres-utile effect.[2]

Here, it will be noted, the argument of utility is joined to that of beauty, the political to the aesthetic. The other passage is still more eloquent and moving, in quite an anachronistic way:

> Il n'est ... ame si revesche qui ne se sente touchée de quelque reverence à considerer cette vastité sombre de nos Eglises, la diversité d'ornemens et ordre de nos ceremonies, et ouyr le son devoticux de nos orgues, et la harmonie si posée et religieuse de nos voix. Ceux mesme qui y entrent avec mespris, sentent quelque frisson dans le cœur, et quelque horreur, qui les met en deffiance de leur opinion.[3]

[1] I, lv: TR 302(*b*).
[2] II, xii: EM ii, 243; TR 494(*c*).
[3] II, xii: EM ii, 355–6; TR 577(*a*).

Although the first of these passages and perhaps the second spring from opposition to Protestant austerity, there is at least a suggestion here of the attitude which we associate with Chateaubriand and which dominated much of nineteenth-century art, that Christianity is less true than beautiful. The response to the vastness and darkness of (obviously Gothic) churches has a quality which can only be called Romantic and again we are forced to conclude that a view of Montaigne that sees him only in historical terms, in relation to his time, is quite insufficient. It seems likely, rash though such claims are, that no one had struck exactly this note before. Erasmus had spoken, but disapprovingly, of the multitudes who go to church to hear the singing and watch the ceremonies.[1] Busson quotes from Sadoletus a description of church services which has some points in common, though again there appears to be a slightly satirical implication and there is nothing about architecture.[2] Ronsard describes how he wears vestments, burns incense, and sings the liturgy,[3] but though there is a hint of aesthetic response it is not explicitly stated. None of them really approaches Montaigne's feeling.

To make sense of these varied reactions we have to bear in mind the mobility of Montaigne's thought and his aim of registering the truth of the moment. As he says, the writings of the ancients manipulate him at their pleasure and he believes – for the moment – everything they say, however contradictory.[4] With this goes inseparably his receptivity to all or most possible ideas, religious or irreligious. It is thus no use seizing upon isolated remarks and supposing that they reveal the whole truth about him. We should like to pin him down and he is determined not to be pinned down. But we must also take into account the Marxist distinction between the subjective and objective significance of a writer's thought. Subjectively, and even in the context of the controversies of his time, he appears as a defender of the Catholic positions, if a rather wayward one (though it must be admitted that there are places where he seems fully aware of the destructive effect of what he is saying). Objectively, his curiosity and liberty of mind have led him to entertain, perhaps only

---

[1] *Moriae encomium*, Strasburg, 1511, H2ᵛ.

[2] *Littérature et théologie*, p. 54.

[3] Armstrong, *Ronsard and the Age of Gold*, p. 181. The reference is to *Œuvres*, ed. Laumonier, xi, 146–8.

[4] II, xii: TR 553(a).

momentarily, many explosively anti-Christian ideas which furnished ammunition for several generations of free-thinkers. A parallel might be drawn with the *Provinciales*, though at least Pascal's own position is unmistakably clear. Attachment to the established religion for political reasons, as part of a general conservatism, is strongly marked. But this in itself is almost an anti-Christian argument: at least it distracts attention from what is fundamental in the Christian faith and to defend a religion because it is old seems to imply that it cannot be defended because it is true. The mysteries, the central dogmas of Christianity, seem to leave him emotionally indifferent (which does not exclude intellectual curiosity about them). How he feels is summed up when he says that like the old woman in the story he would if necessary carry one candle to St Michael and another to his snake.[1] This does not mean that he is irreligious, but the deeper religious feelings expressed in the *Essais* are mostly philosophical (deistic), at least in tendency, and aesthetic. He is the very opposite of the *anima naturaliter christiana*, though Thibaudet surprisingly puts him in this category.[2] The *Essais* are like the tower: the chapel is there and is visited from time to time but the main room is the library where the pagan authors of antiquity stand on their five rows of shelves, dominating the building and the book. To speak of Montaigne's mind as divided into watertight compartments is too rigid; but it is true that he presents in an acute form the dichotomy of post-Renaissance Europe, between Christian religion and classical culture, a dichotomy which has lasted almost to our own time. In him classical humanism, relativism, scepticism, indifference, combine to produce his most positive contribution to religious thought, the toleration which released western man from at least one source of savagery and fanaticism.

[1] III, i: TR 769. The story is in Henri Estienne's *Apologie pour Hérodote* of 1566 (R. Trinquet, 'Note sur saint Michel et son serpent', *BSAM*, II, 18 (1956), 45). But it is found earlier in Calvin (*Traité des reliques*, ed. Autin, 1921, p. 196).

[2] *Montaigne*, p. 334.

10

The Conservative
and the Revolutionary

THAT Montaigne was a conservative is incontrovertible, a commonplace indeed.[1] We have seen the decisive place his conservatism occupies in his religious thought, as well as his emphasis on custom and the need to follow it. But it permeates his whole outlook and way of thinking, from small matters to great.

> Je suis desgousté de la nouvelleté, quelque visage qu'elle porte, et ay raison, car j'en ay veu des effets tres-dommageables.[2]

> ... il n'est aucun si mauvais train, pourveu qu'il aye de l'aage et de la constance, qui ne vaille mieux que le changement et le remuement.[3]

These are the central statements, and it would be difficult to go further in extreme attachment to the *status quo,* whatever its faults. He condemns new fashions in dress, long hair for men, padded doublets, appearing in public without a sword: superficial though they are, these errors suggest that the foundations are cracking.[4] It is easy to recognise here one of the basic symptoms of the conservative temperament which seeks to rationalise a dislike of quite harmless novelties. All the same there is an important reservation even in this respect: the sensible man follows custom in externals but internally preserves his own liberty of judgement.[5] But principally conservatism has to do with political

---

[1] For a detailed study see Frieda S. Brown, *Religious and political conservatism in the Essais of Montaigne,* 1963.
[2] I, xxiii: EM i, 152; TR 118(*b*).
[3] II, xvii: EM ii, 441; TR 639(*a*).
[4] I, xliii: TR 261(*b*).
[5] I, xxiii: TR 117.

(as well as religious) affairs. It is the rule of rules and law of laws that everyone should follow those of the place where he finds himself.[1] One consequence of this, though still highly conservative in the strictest sense, is the opposite of reactionary or counter-revolutionary: it is folly to want another system of government if one lives under a monarchy but also to seek the government of a few in a popular state.[2] Evidently these views are to a large extent inspired by his experience of the Wars of Religion. It is wicked, he says, to risk certain evil for an uncertain good,[3] again a universal conservative tenet. And change brings not only disorder but tyranny, 'guarir les maladies par la mort'.[4] Incidentally this important passage is from the Third Book: though references to custom in it are fewer, there is no sign that the fundamentally conservative attitude has altered. Those who start revolutions are the first to be destroyed by them: 'Le fruit du trouble ne demure guiere à celluy qui l'a esmeu, il bat et brouille l'eau, pour d'autres pescheurs.'[5] All this reveals considerable penetration and indeed prescience, a capacity for inferring universally valid laws from history and observation. Theoretical Utopias and for that matter political theory in general are intellectually entertaining but practically useless because it is impossible to ignore existing forms and customs.[6] Once again we find the complexity of reality opposed to the simplifications of systematic thinkers. And this has considerable bearing on the bold statements which seem to be anything but conservative: we might be entitled to conclude that in these cases Montaigne is playing with ideas for his and our amusement.

Unfortunately this all-pervading conservatism appears to be in contradiction with the even more fundamental principle of change and movement as the universal law of all things. It seems at first sight extraordinary that the writer who has most fully incorporated change into the very substance of his writing and has treated his writing as a reflection of the moving world should be so strongly opposed to change on the political and social plane. However, though the two poles are characteristic of Montaigne's antithetical approach to truth, the contradiction is only apparent. It

[1] ibid.
[2] III, ix: TR 934.
[3] I, xxiii: TR 119.
[4] III, ix: EM iii, 221; TR 935.
[5] I, xxiii: EM i, 152; TR 118(c).
[6] III, ix: TR 934.

might indeed be argued that one leads inevitably to the other. The finely adjusted sensitivity to all the manifestations of flux naturally produces a more than normal desire for stability, the need for some fixed point or some fixed values. We have already seen how this works on the psychological level (in *De l'inconstance de nos actions* recognition of universal fluidity of personality, admiration for constancy as an ideal), but it can be applied generally. A crucial passage in the *Apologie* explains this with the utmost clarity:

> Or de la cognoissance de cette mienne volubilité j'ay par accident engendré en moy quelque constance d'opinions, et n'ay guiere alteré les miennes premieres et naturelles. Car, quelque apparence qu'il y ait en la nouvelleté, je ne change pas aisément, de peur que j'ay de perdre au change. Et, puis que je ne suis pas capable de choisir, je pren le chois d'autruy et me tien en l'assiette où Dieu m'a mis. Autrement, je ne me sçauroy garder de rouler sans cesse.[1]

Thus the fixed point is external authority to which he must cling if he is to avoid the dizzy motion created by his own instability. A few sentences further on he argues that we should distrust any new doctrine because its contrary was previously in vogue and it may itself be reversed in the future; in this way relativism and mobility are used directly to support conservatism. Elsewhere the same idea is expressed by the image of the peg and the wheel:

> de nos loix et usances, il y en a plusieurs barbares et monstrueuses: toutesfois, pour la difficulté de nous mettre en meilleur estat et le danger de ce crollement, si je pouvoy planter une cheville à nostre roüe et l'arrester en ce point, je le ferois de bon cœur.[2]

The hypothetical construction is vital: he would like to stop the movement but cannot. There is thus no contradiction between Montaigne's conservatism and his mobility. Nevertheless his conservatism is already beginning to appear in a different light. It is nothing like the complacent, limited and stationary position which the word often suggests. On the contrary, it is what seems at times an almost desperate effort to impose order and stability on a situation which is totally unstable.

Moreover the basic attitude itself is subject to serious qualifications. We have already discussed custom in connection with

[1] II, xii: EM ii, 321; TR 553(*a*). On this question cf. Thibaudet, *Montaigne*, pp. 301, 307–8.
[2] II, xvii: EM ii, 441; TR 639(*a*).

knowledge and relativism and have seen that, though it is to be followed, it has no status other than that of existing. We have glanced at the title of *De la coustume et de ne changer aisément une loy receüe*, itself a proclamation of conservatism (though the reservation of *aisément* is not to be ignored). The essay is, however, in many ways a critique of custom and the acceptance of established ways of doing things. It must be remembered to begin with that custom is in continuous motion like everything else:[1] it is therefore a tottering foundation for any political or social system. It is tyrannical and rules by prejudice, being so deeply ingrained in us that it usurps the place of reason.[2] On one occasion when he set out to defend a particular usage and tried to get to the bottom of it, Montaigne found its origins so weak that he was almost disgusted by what he was supposed to be advocating.[3] This anticipates, and no doubt influences, one of Pascal's most far-reaching political reflections:

L'art de fronder, bouleverser les états est d'ébranler les coutumes établies en sondant jusque dans leur source, pour marquer leur défaut d'autorité et de justice.[4]

In Pascal this could be taken for a warning, in Montaigne hardly: his attitude here is at least potentially subversive. A little later he generalises this disgust in an even stronger statement:

Qui voudra se desfaire de ce violent prejudice de la coustume, il trouvera plusieurs choses receues d'une resolution indubitable, qui n'ont appuy qu'en la barbe chenue et rides de l'usage qui les accompaigne; mais, ce masque arraché, rapportant les choses à la verité et à la raison, il sentira son jugement comme tout bouleversé, et remis pourtant en bien plus seur estat.[5]

He in fact overthrows all our judgements and prejudices, even though, as we see in the last phrase, he manages to draw a conservative conclusion none the less: again we are reminded of Nietzsche and the *Umwertung aller Werte*. The rule of following custom is itself demolished, admittedly as part of the sceptical exercise of the *Apologie*.[6] His idea of custom then is very different

1 Cf. I, xlix: TR 285(*a*).
2 I, xxiii: TR 106, 114.
3 I, xxiii: TR 115(*a*).
4 *Pensées*, ed. Lafuma, 1951, i, 53.
5 I, xxiii: EM i, 149; TR 116(*a*).
6 II, xii: TR 562-3.

from the placid routine which some critics might lead one to attribute to him. It can only be understood against the background of the instability and precariousness of everything. His defence of conservatism is accompanied at every step, is organically and inextricably mingled with, a critique of conservatism which is at least as deeply felt and is much more powerful in its expression and influence. This is a more difficult contradiction to resolve than the first, and before we attempt to do so, or to inquire whether it is necessary, it will be as well to examine his views on specific political questions, especially those where conservatism is exposed to practical tests.

His conception of the state as a political form, irrespective of the actual type of government is, as we should expect, organic and complex. In *De la coustume*, arguing that the alteration of a settled law is bound to do more harm than good, he says that a society (*police*) 'c'est comme un bastiment de diverses pieces jointes ensemble, d'une telle liaison, qu'il est impossible d'en esbranler une, que tout le corps ne s'en sente.'[1] His feeling for the infinite diversity and unity of life comes out in his political theory as everywhere else: it is the opposite of Descartes's preference for a city rationally designed by a single engineer over one that has grown unplanned through the centuries.[2] The idea is more fully worked out in *De la vanité*, and slightly modified. The whole body politic is still affected by even minor changes, but its complete overthrow is very difficult indeed:

En fin je vois par nostre exemple que la societé des hommes se tient et se coust, à quelque pris que ce soit. En quelque assiete qu'on les couche, ils s'appilent et se rengent en se remuant et s'entassant. . . .[3]

This line of thought (partly influenced by Plato) implies a view of the nature of society which is perhaps more convincing than that of more ambitious political philosophers. Montaigne is not swayed here by the superficial appearances of contemporary events, the prevailing anarchy, of which he is fully aware of course, but goes beyond them to the underlying tenacity of social structures (of which we have had many recent examples). The difficulty is that there now appears to be political stability after all:

---

[1] I, xxiii: EM i, 151; TR 118(*a*). On this and similar passages see the interesting remarks in Clark, 'Montaigne and the imagery of political discourse in sixteenth-century France'.
[2] *Discours de la méthode*, ed. Gilson, Paris, 1947, pp. 11–12.
[3] III, ix: EM iii, 218; TR 933.

states and societies are not eternal but they are nearly indestructible. Consistency is saved in this case by the verb *se coust* (literally 'sews itself together') which conveys the idea of motion: stability itself is part of organic life. We have here in fact a variation on 'la constance mesme n'est autre chose qu'un branle plus languissant'.[1] Before we go further we thus have another complication to bear in mind, the understanding of the organic nature of society which cannot be reduced to simple rules.

His attitude to monarchy is that of a loyal subject who owes obedience to the king because he is king, but there is a marked lack of enthusiasm, more particularly perhaps in the later stages.

Je regarde nos Roys d'une affection simplement legitime et civile: ny esmeue ny desmeue par interest privé.[2]

All submission is due to them except that of reason:

Ce que j'adore moy-mesmes aus Roys, c'est la foule de leurs adorateurs. Toute inclination et soubmission leur est deuë, sauf celle de l'entendement. Ma raison n'est pas duite à se courber et flechir, ce sont mes genoux.[3]

Obedience is owed to their office but esteem only to their virtue.[4] Thus independence of judgement is not sacrificed and loyalty is limited by a powerful right of criticism (the idea of external submission only is again developed and reinforced by Pascal). Kings are the companions and not the masters of law:[5] there is nothing very revolutionary about this in the sixteenth century, especially for a member of a Parlement, but it shows that conservatism in Montaigne is far from a blind belief in absolutism. One essay, *De l'inequalité qui est entre nous*, deals with the question in rather more detail, though it is disappointing in the sense that it hardly treats the broad subject suggested in the title. The main theme is the paradoxical one of the disadvantages of kingship and the effect is predominantly conservative: kings are to be pitied rather than envied. At the same time there is another side, a robust humour, a refusal to be taken in, and deep down the essay deals a blow, if a minor one, at the mystique of monarchy. So far then there is nothing seriously at variance with a conservative outlook,

1 Cf. p. 109 above.
2 III, i: EM iii, 4; TR 769(*c*).
3 III, viii: EM iii, 192; TR 913.
4 I, iii: TR 19(*c*).
5 I, iii: TR 18(*b*).

but this conservatism includes a strongly independent and critical note.

Independence with regard to supreme political authority is partly conditioned by social class and it is therefore important to determine not so much what class Montaigne belonged to, which is a biographical question, but what class he spoke for. On the first point, as we have seen, he was a rich country gentleman, very proud of his recent and undistinguished nobility and anxious to present himself as a member of the *noblesse d'épée* rather than the *noblesse de robe*. He was also the descendant of a long line of merchants, and the pattern of their history, the move from the town to the country, was wholly typical of the famous rise of the bourgeoisie. Eyquem de Montaigne has very much the ring of Chardon de Rubempré or Stoke d'Urberville, to mention only fictional examples. The Jewish antecedents on the maternal side, perhaps concealed, perhaps forgotten, may or may not be important (it is certainly intriguing to speculate whether in the terrible description of the Portuguese Jews and the forced conversions he knew that he was talking about the fate of his own ancestors). This sort of independence was no doubt the prerogative of the nobility. So Montaigne gives a vivid picture of the life of a Breton squire, remote from the court (he holds a court of his own), almost untouched by the royal authority (he hears the king's name mentioned once a year as if he were the Shah of Persia). A French nobleman, if he abstains from court service, is as free as the Doge of Venice.[1] This was not quite Montaigne's own situation because of his involvement in political affairs, but it suggests the world from which he sprang. This world was by its nature essentially conservative. None the less there is a case for considering Montaigne to be the first of the great modern bourgeois writers, for thinking that his distant origins were more important than his present situation.[2] He has a great deal in common with Flaubert, Gide or Proust, or for that matter with James or Forster. Financial independence is the first thing. Partly a consequence of this is individualism, the lack of any strong feeling of class solidarity. Just as he criticises his compatriots in Italy, so, as we have seen, he criticises the members of the nobility who

[1] I, xlii: TR 257(*b*).
[2] For Montaigne as bourgeois see Barrière, *La vie intellectuelle en Périgord*, p. 119. Thibaudet's suggestion that he is an Orleanist bourgeois of 1840 like Guizot or 1871 like Thiers (*Montaigne*, p. 322) is one of his far-fetched parallels and quite off the point.

surround him and their semi-barbarous immersion in war and hunting. The self-portrait may be the first major expression in European literature of the individualism which has been associated with the middle class. With it goes the independence of judgement which we have seen at work even when his protestations of submission and humility are most convincing. More important, however, than individualism in the abstract are the liberalism which above all was to express the bourgeois ethos, at least in the period of ascension, and its manifestations in a series of attacks on some of the fundamental positions of absolutism, itself hardly yet fully established.

The centre of both liberalism and individualism is no doubt the supreme value of a man in himself apart from all considerations of rank. When Montaigne speaks of the man who is indifferent to death and whose soul is tranquil (significantly in *De l'inequalité qui est entre nous*), 'un tel homme est cinq cens brasses au dessus des Royaumes et des duchez: il est luy mesmes à soy son empire',[1] he is adapting Stoicism to modern circumstances (this is an early essay). But the influence of antiquity does not detract in the slightest from the liberalism: it is hardly necessary to stress the influence of Stoicism on liberal and republican thought, especially in the eighteenth century. Liberalism, individualism, scepticism about monarchy, bourgeois humour (possibly) converge in the remark that it is not a notable convenience for a sensible man to have 'une vingtaine de contrerolleurs à sa chaise percée', or to be served by someone who has won great battles rather than by a well-trained valet.[2] Already we have the satirical tone of Montesquieu or Voltaire on the hangers-on of courts, though here the emphasis is on inconvenience rather than expense. There is criticism of royal extravagance too.[3] But though retrenchment, the contrast between the ostentation of the absolute monarch and middle-class thrift, was a not unimportant part of the liberal programme, it is obviously no more than a passing thought in Montaigne. His attitude to freedom of opinion is of greater consequence. He criticises, if mildly, the burning of books,[4] and much more powerfully the use of force to impose opinions:

Il n'est rien à quoi communement les hommes soient plus tendus

---

[1] I, xlii: EM i, 335; TR 252(*a*).
[2] I, xlii: EM i, 342; TR 257(*a*).
[3] e.g. III, vi: TR 880(*c*).
[4] II, viii: TR 381.

qu'à donner voye à leurs opinions: où le moyen ordinaire nous faut, nous y adjoustons le commandement, la force, le fer, et le feu.[1]

Again we feel a premonition of Voltaire. Such statements, vigorous though they are, have to be set against the much more numerous recommendations of ignorance, obedience and submission. There is indeed no necessary incompatibility. Humility in accepting the opinions of higher authority matches humility in abstaining from the forcible imposition of our opinions when we are in authority ourselves: they are two sides of the same coin. None the less the first fits best into a conservative framework, the second into a liberal.

Beyond this there is the hatred of tyranny and the praise of liberty in general. I have already quoted in another context the remark about La Boétie:

Et sçay d'avantage que, s'il eut eu à choisir, il eut mieux aimé estre nay à Venise qu'à Sarlac; et aveq raison.[2]

The last phrase, as we saw, is an addition of 1582: in the meantime Montaigne had been to Venice and admired its political organisation, as he says several times in the *Journal du voyage*. The whole sentence is a fairly strong affirmation of republican feeling, though he goes on to quote another maxim of La Boétie's on the duty of obeying the laws of one's own country. As usual the two sides are given, and his friend clearly influenced both. With his praise of liberty and republican leanings at least, we can contrast Bodin's balanced but finally unfavourable view of Venice, enthusiastic devotion to hereditary monarchy, and belief that the object of the state is not liberty but regulated life.[3]

The presence of a liberal strand in Montaigne's political thought is therefore undeniable (and further examples will confirm this). The question now arises how far liberalism inclines towards democracy.[4] It must be admitted, I think, that his democracy is largely a matter of sentiment rather than of political organisation. He frequently expresses sympathy and admiration for the mass of people and peasants especially. There is no differ-

[1] III, xi: EM iii, 311; TR 1005.
[2] I, xxviii: EM i, 254; TR 193.
[3] *Methodus*, tr. Mesnard, pp. 268 ff. His private views, however, appear to have been different: cf. the praise of Venetian liberty in *Colloquium Heptaplomeres*, ed. Noack, 1857, p. 1.
[4] The most persuasive case for a democratic Montaigne is perhaps to be found in Frame, *Montaigne's discovery of man*.

ence between king and peasant, rich and poor, except in externals,[1] or, in a celebrated phrase, the souls of emperors and cobblers are cast in the same mould.[2] His father had put him out to nurse with poor people in a neighbouring village with the object 'de me ralier avec le peuple et cette condition d'hommes qui a besoin de nostre ayde; et estimoit que je fusse tenu de regarder plutost vers celuy qui me tend les bras que vers celuy qui me tourne le dos'.[3] Altogether he has the keenest sense of responsibility towards the poor; but this is really paternalistic ('besoin de nostre ayde') rather than democratic. When he remarks that virtue is rare among the noble and rich[4] he is only uttering a commonplace of Christian thought. Moments of irritation with *le vulgaire*[5] are compensated by an interpolation in the *Apologie* of which Professor Frame makes a great deal:

(a) Il en adviendroit par là que tout le vulgaire, et (c) nous somes tous du vulguere, (a) auroit sa creance contournable comme une girouette.[6]

But Machiavelli says almost exactly the same thing, 'e nel mondo non è se non vulgo',[7] and it would hardly occur to anyone to call him democratic on that account. And there are many references to the dangers of allowing the majority of people to decide what is right in matters of law and religion: only a few can be trusted to exercise judgement freely.[8] The attack on oratory in *De la vanité des paroles* is associated with an unfavourable comparison between democracy and monarchy: no orator of renown emerged from Macedon or Persia, whereas they flourished in Athens and Rome.[9] This suggests a deep distrust of the whole democratic process. However, there are a few passages where democracy appears in its full political sense and is regarded with sympathy. Most of them turn on the question of equity, which contains also the principle of equality.[10] Thus in denouncing some injustice committed by the people of Athens:

[1] I, xlii: TR 252.
[2] II, xii: TR 454.
[3] III, xiii: EM iii, 408; TR 1079.
[4] II, xxxv: TR 724.
[5] e.g. I, li: TR 293; II, xvi: TR 607; II, xxvii: TR 672.
[6] II, xii: EM ii, 323; TR 554.
[7] *Il principe*, ed. Lisio, 1942, p. 106.
[8] e.g. II, xii: TR 467, 541.
[9] I, li: TR 293.
[10] I, xx: TR 92(c).

A peu que je n'entre en haine irreconciliable contre toute domination populere, quoi qu'elle me semble la plus naturelle et æquitable. . . .[1]

The two sides of this preamble are equally important. Similarly

les polices où il se souffre moins de disparité entre les valets et les maistres, me semblent les plus æquitables.[2]

He admits democracy as a possible form of government, and as theoretically right, though his conservative instincts hardly allow him to argue for it in practical terms. This is not really enough to make him a democrat, though he explores the idea of democracy as he does nearly all major ideas. It looks so far, therefore, as if his liberalism is of the aristocratic or paternalist kind. But before we can decide this finally we must look at his views on some more particular topics.

We have already come upon war in several connections and noted his personal pleasure in it as well as his revulsion from its horrors (the usual ambiguity or perhaps rather the usual truthfulness in rendering the feeling of the moment). Observations on the conduct of war, on strategy and tactics, are numerous, and, though this is a side of him which has not appealed much to modern readers, Mlle de Gournay has some right to ask 'quelle escole de guerre et d'estat est-ce que ce livre?'[3] We need not pursue the question of Montaigne as military expert but his observations on the effects of artillery and musketry are worth noting, with the prediction of the invention of the tank.[4] However, what matters now is his basic moral attitude, and in this respect it is possible to speak without reservations. In spite of the superficial attractions of the military life, he condemns war, its stupidity and futility, 'cette maladie humaine',[5] which threatens the very existence of the species: 'la science de nous entre-desfaire et entretuer, de ruiner et perdre nostre propre espece.'[6] There is nothing original about detestation of war (Rabelais is an obvious sixteenth-century example, with a similar combination of enjoyment and disapproval) nor is it exactly incompatible with conservatism, since war is one of the greatest

---

[1] I, iii: EM i, 21; TR 23(c).
[2] III, iii: EM iii, 44; TR 799(c).
[3] *Essais*, 1595, Preface, ẽ3ᵛ.
[4] II, ix: TR 385(a).
[5] I, xxxi: EM i, 275; TR 208(a).
[6] II, xii: EM ii, 187; TR 452.

threats to settled society. Still, a typical conservative tends to include war as part of what is to be conserved, and pacifism, or a pacific attitude at least, is an essential ingredient of classical liberalism.

Much more important, indeed central to the book as we have already suggested, is the sustained attack on colonialism. We have considered America as part of Montaigne's world-view, as a key-point in his moral relativism, as a stage in the growth of the European myth of the noble savage. Its political implications are mostly negative: it is not now the goodness of the Indians but the wickedness of their oppressors which is in the forefront. In *Des cannibales* the stress was on the first, in *Des coches* it is on the second, and Montaigne perhaps never surpasses the eloquence of the denunciations this essay contains. The ferocious contempt and pitying indignation of the account of the torturing of the King of Mexico is one of the most powerful examples.[1] Almost better, is the scathing picture of Spanish greed and the genocide it inspired:

Qui mit jamais à tel pris le service de la mercadence et de la trafique? Tant de villes rasées, tant de nations exterminées, tant de millions de peuples passez au fil de l'espée, et la plus riche et belle partie du monde bouleversée pour la negotiation des perles et du poivre: mechaniques victoires.[2]

The understanding of the economic motivation of the Spanish conquest is everywhere apparent (not that he was the first to think of this). To call it pre-Marxist would be an exaggeration, but there is a hint of it. Incidentally we see once again that there are limits to his moderation and tolerance, that he is capable of loftiness of thought and language. Attacks on the aims and methods of Spanish colonisation were of course by no means new, but, apart from the great name of Las Casas, they were mostly the instruments of Protestant propaganda (Chauveton is an example we have come upon). It might indeed be asked whether Montaigne is not also actuated by a political motive, the resentment of the *politiques* at Spanish intervention in the French civil wars. There are occasional signs of a special animosity against Spain, which might be contrasted with Bodin's praise of the Spanish conquest.[3]

[1] III, vi: TR 891.
[2] III, vi: EM iii, 161; TR 889.
[3] *Methodus*, tr. Mesnard, p. 260.

But these are trivial. What distinguishes Montaigne and lifts him above the sectarian spirit of the main line of anti-Spanish propaganda is his appeal to a general and common humanity. A Protestant like Léry speaks objectively about the Indians and praises their charity;[1] their lack of religion, however, forces him to speak of them in tones of pitying superiority. Montaigne says:

Quelle reparation eust-ce esté, et quel amendement à toute cette machine, que les premiers exemples et deportemens nostres . . . eussent appelé ces peuples à l'admiration et imitation de la vertu et eussent dressé entre eux et nous une fraternele societé et intelligence![2]

Human brotherhood, not missionary condescension, is his directing force. In this essay there can be no question of merely playing with ideas. The treatment of colonialism shows him at his most liberal and also at his most prescient. Only now perhaps can we fully realise to what extent he has grasped the most terrible problem of European civilisation, the repercussions of which continue to shape our lives.

The main plank of Montaigne's conservatism is then the principle that we should obey the laws of the country we live in and not try to change them. And this is not only true of him: conservatism, law and legality generally go hand in hand. It is therefore necessary to look a little more closely at his treatment of law. We need not take too seriously his passing digs at lawyers, similar to those against doctors though less numerous. When he tells the very funny story of the judge who after delivering a particularly tangled and inept judgement was heard muttering in the *pissoir* 'non nobis, Domine, non nobis, sed nomini tuo da gloriam',[3] this is no more than the irreverence which springs from familiarity. Some illustrations go rather deeper, like the remark that from the paper on which he has just written the condemnation of an adulterer the judge (generalised) tears a piece to write a note to another judge's wife: the hypocrisy and double-think inseparable from any judicial system are perfectly caught. What follows is even more disturbing: 'Et tel condamne des hommes à mourir pour des crimes qu'il n'estime point fautes.'[4] Judges are biased not only by major influences, friendship, kinship, beauty,

---

1 *Histoire d'un voyage*, 1578, pp. 321–3.
2 III, vi: EM iii, 161; TR 888.
3 III, x: EM iii, 305; TR 1000.
4 III, ix: EM iii, 262; TR 967.

vengeance, but by chance inclinations and irrational favour[1] (again we are bound to admire the delicacy and subtlety of his penetration of motive). But we are still dealing with superficial blemishes and though the association of law with justice has taken some hard knocks the main principle is not seriously affected. Judicial errors are more disquieting: Montaigne notices the condemnation of innocents and executions based on false confessions.[2] But scattered through the *Essais* there are more far-reaching criticisms than these. They follow the lines of relativism we have already discussed. Local laws are partial and bizarre when confronted with the true justice of natural law which must present the same face everywhere.[3] Of course he also denies the possibility of discovering true justice and natural law,[4] but in the process of argument respect for the laws of the country has been gravely weakened.

However, all this is no more than skimming the surface in comparison with the lengthy examination of the very notion of law at the beginning of *De l'experience*. We have already considered the general course of the argument and its application in other spheres than that of law. The main point, which proceeds from the observations on identity and difference, is the difficulty of conciliating general principles and concrete cases. This is indeed the central difficulty of law and administration (not to speak of moral theology) and perhaps of all intellectual activity. It may seem obvious but one wonders whether anyone but Montaigne has said it, at least in quite this way. No laws can be devised which will account for all individual cases and however varied the law each case will have its own peculiarities. Thus multiplying laws is useless and it is best to have a few simple general principles.[5] There are more laws in France, he goes on to say, than in the rest of the world put together. Though he probably got this from Bodin, it further weakens the conservative position of total respect for the law; in fact it anticipates the work of the Revolutionaries and Napoleon. The whole argument is summed up in 'Il y a peu de relation de nos actions, qui sont en perpetuelle mutation, avec les loix fixes et immobiles'.[6] Laws by definition are fixed, human

1 II, xii: TR 548.
2 e.g. III, xi: TR 1009.
3 e.g. II, xii: TR 562; III, i: TR 773; III, v: TR 858.
4 II, xii: TR 563–5.
5 III, xiii: TR 1042.
6 III, xiii: EM iii, 362; TR 1042.

actions will never conform to them. The legal and political argument thus joins the central argument of the *Essais*, uniqueness of the self, mobility and relativism. There follows in the same spirit a still deeper analysis of legal methods and language, difficult to summarise, partly because it is linguistic as well as legal.[1] Lawyers have made such strenuous efforts to remove doubt from their language by weighing and subdividing each clause that they have produced the opposite result: like children playing with quicksilver (an image I have quoted before), the more they try to push their material into set moulds the more it runs away. Though he is talking about law the implications extend to the nature of language and all human communication. The doubts which arise from these methods call for commentaries to clear them up, these commentaries for more commentaries, and so on for ever:

Il y a plus affaire à interpreter les interpretations qu'à interpreter les choses, et plus de livres sur les livres que sur autre subject: nous ne faisons que nous entregloser.[2]

This had already been said by, among others, Erasmus[3] but Montaigne goes much deeper than a mere joke about pedantic addiction to glosses. It is true that, as with examples, laws do work in a roundabout sort of way: 'Ainsi servent les loix, et s'assortissent ainsin à chacun de nos affaires, par quelque interpretation destournée, contrainte et biaise',[4] an oblique statement wholly characteristic of his mode of thought. The argument, however, concludes in a more forthright manner. The justice that governs us is so full of contradiction and error that it is no more than proof of human imbecility: 'Combien ai-je veu de condemnations, plus crimineuses que le crime?'[5] At this point practically nothing is left of the respect for law, now shown to be radically unjust, foolish and ultimately perhaps impossible. If we ask why then we should obey such laws Montaigne replies:

Or les loix se maintiennent en credit, non parce qu'elles sont justes, mais parce qu'elles sont loix. C'est le fondement mystique de leur authorité; elles n'en ont poinct d'autre.[6]

1 III, xiii: TR 1043–5.
2 III, xiii: EM iii, 365; TR 1045.
3 *Moriae encomium*, Strasburg, 1511, E8ᵛ
4 III, xiii: EM iii, 367; TR 1047.
5 III, xiii: EM iii, 368; TR 1048.
6 III, xiii: EM iii, 370; TR 1049.

I

The conservative position is maintained on the surface but the underlying argument is profoundly subversive (as it is also in Pascal who again follows it closely). Nowhere more than in his treatment of law do we see how infinitely unstable are the foundations on which his conservatism rests.

Of the particular questions which are connected with law and which reflect his legal experience one of the most striking is witchcraft. He was writing nearly at the peak of one of the great waves of belief in witchcraft and persecution of witches, the sort of collective panic which is difficult to resist. There is not space here to give even a short history of this extraordinary phenomenon which affected Catholic and Protestant countries alike, or to consider its causes, a subject of much controversy.[1] It is, however, important to remember that it was not merely an outbreak of popular superstition but the object of grave study by lawyers who trained on it their usual battery of precedents and case-law. Bodin's *De la demonomanie des sorciers,* published in the same year as the first edition of the *Essais,* is no doubt the best-known example. After Montaigne's death Pierre de Lancre, also a member of the Bordeaux Parlement, stated categorically that in 1609 the devil had held session almost in the heart of the city.[2] The list of those who expressed belief in the reality of witchcraft would be a very long one: it would include even the scientific Paré and the un-fanatical L'Estoile.[3] Montaigne brings to the question his habitual combination of cool detachment with regard to manifestations of the supernatural and controlled indignation at wickedness and cruelty. His remarks on witchcraft, apart from passing references, are entirely contained in *Des boyteux* and form the real core of the essay, a core which, as we have seen, is enveloped in a number of other themes including the lame girls. Of all the essays it is perhaps, though this is a large claim, the most devastating for its criticism of commonly held and ferocious beliefs. It is equally remarkable for the vigour of its denunciation and the subtlety with which denunciation is presented and camouflaged. After the long

[1] For an excellent survey see H. R. Trevor-Roper, *The European witch-craze of the 16th and 17th centuries,* 1969. He does not give sufficient weight to Montaigne, probably the most important figure to have dealt with the question at this time, brief though his comments are (and perhaps the more effective for their brevity).

[2] *Tableau de l'inconstance des mauvais anges et demons,* Paris, 1612, ẽ1ᵛ.

[3] On Paré see Villey, *Sources et évolution,* ii, 362; L'Estoile, *Journal,* 26 February 1587.

preamble we have already studied he begins by saying that the witches of his neighbourhood run the risk of their lives whenever a new author gives body to their dreams (this would apply very well to someone like Bodin). God has said that witches exist and God must be believed, but only He can tell who is or is not one.[1] This restriction on the meaning of the words of Scripture includes not only judges but witches, who cannot be believed against themselves (an extension of his views on the unreliability of confessions). What follows, an examination of the actual evidence put forward in such cases, is still sharper:

Certes je ne m'en croirois pas moy mesme. Combien trouvé-je plus naturel et plus vray-semblable que deux hommes mentent, que je ne fay qu'un homme en douze heures passe, quand et les vents, d'orient en occident? Combien plus naturel que nostre entendement soit emporté de sa place par la volubilité de nostre esprit detraqué, que celu, qu'un de nous soit envolé sur un balay, au long du tuiau de sa cheminée, en chair et en os, par un esprit estrangier?[2]

In politics as in religion scepticism and the questioning spirit can be used on the side of conservatism and established opinions, but they can be used on the other side too, and such is the case here. These questions clearly go beyond the immediate subject of witchcraft and can be employed (as similar questions were to be from Bayle and Fontenelle onwards) against the whole apparatus of the supernatural. That they are buttressed at this moment by a prudent quotation from St Augustine only reinforces the point. Now comes an account of an interview he had had with a group of prisoners accused of witchcraft. He gives them close and unprejudiced attention (typical of his scientific side) and concludes:

En fin et en conscience, je leur eusse plustost ordonné de l'ellebore que de la cicue [the remedy for madness rather than the hemlock of the death-sentence].[3]

This is exactly the humane and enlightened tone we associate with the eighteenth century rather than the sixteenth (the reference to hemlock is of course just another instance of his way of thinking in classical terms). Even more far-reaching are the general conclusions he draws:

[1] III, xi: TR 1008.
[2] III, xi: EM iii, 316; TR 1009.
[3] III, xi: EM iii, 317; TR 1010. For earlier examples of this argument see Trevor-Roper, n.56.

A tuer les gens, il faut une clarté lumineuse et nette; et est nostre vie trop réele et essentielle pour garantir ces accidens supernaturels et fantastiques.[1]

Apres tout, c'est mettre ses conjectures à bien haut pris que d'en faire cuire un homme tout vif.[2]

The usual moderation and understatement are here, but in the second case understatement used with almost Voltairean effect, a high value indeed to set on conjecture, irony as annihilation. In the first sentence we catch a glimpse of a rather different Montaigne from the one who has been most often present to us: all ambiguity is abandoned in this luminous clarity and the effect is almost as if a mask had been dropped. There are few statements more important for the history of modern Europe than these at the climax of *Des boyteux*. Of course Montaigne was not the first or the only one to express disbelief in witchcraft. The name of the German physician Johannes Wier (or Weyer) is outstanding,[3] and Busson observes that other members of the Bordeaux Parlement, including the president Lagebaston, shared Montaigne's scepticism.[4] Castellio had said that religious truth was too uncertain to justify the killing of heretics.[5] But Castellio was a Protestant controversialist, Wier an obscure medical writer, opinions privately uttered in Bordeaux could not have much impact. It was, we may assert, largely through Montaigne, the force of his language and the diffusion of his book, that principles of humanity and plain sense produced the reaction which gradually triumphed in the course of the following century.[6]

Closely akin to the remarks about witchcraft is the attack on judicial torture and cruel laws in general. Though two essays (*De la conscience* and *De la cruauté*) carry the spearheads of this attack, there are many supporting thrusts elsewhere. We have seen that the designation of any punishment beyond simple death as cruelty was one of the points to which the Roman censor took

[1] III, xi: EM iii, 316; TR 1009.
[2] III, xi: EM iii, 317; TR 1010.
[3] *De praestigiis daemonum*, Basle, 1564.
[4] *Littérature et théologie*, p. 18.
[5] Popkin, *The history of scepticism*, p. 10.
[6] I am aware that this interpretation of *Des boyteux* is slightly different from the one I put forward in speaking of its form (p. 104 above): there natural and organic development from one theme to another, here deliberate concealment of dangerous thoughts at the centre of a labyrinth. On reflection it may appear that the two are not mutually exclusive.

objection and that Montaigne did not change it. In fact he says it twice.[1] The second statement is fuller than the first and explains the reason, or at any rate one argument: if someone is not deterred by fear of hanging or beheading, he is not likely to be any more affected by the thought of fire, pincers or wheel. Thus the whole treatment of the subject is set in a context not only of opposition to orthodoxy but of what looks like deliberate defiance. Torture as a preliminary to trial is likewise castigated in *De la conscience*: it is a test of stamina rather than truth (a contention quoted with approval by Pasquier), it can force false confessions as well as true, the guilty are as likely as the innocent to come through successfully.[2] It is easy to recognise here the main heads of the argument employed later by the liberal opponents of cruel punishments. When he seeks justification for torture Montaigne is not able to find very much, and the successive versions of 1580, 1588 and the Bordeaux Copy offer an admirable illustration of the gradual weakening of his ironical defence:

> Mais tant y a que c'est le mieux que l'humaine foiblesse aïe peu inventer.[3]

> Mais tant y a que c'est le moins mal que l'humaine foiblesse aye peu inventer.[4]

> Mais tant y a que c'est, dict on, le moins mal que l'humaine foiblesse aye peu inventer.[5]

The essay ends at this point in 1580. In 1588 a new conclusion drops this judicial approach and launches on a direct and eloquent plea against torture (added, it should be noted, after the Italian journey and the brush with the censor). It may have been inspired by the humanist Vives, but Montaigne is among the very few who took a stand against the growing practice of judicial torture. This was, as with witchcraft trials, not so much a long-established medieval abuse as a development of the sixteenth century (it appears to have been legalised in France by the ordinance of Villers-Cotterêts in 1539).[6] Montaigne does not attack capital punishment itself (which would have been most extraordinary

---

[1] II, xi: TR 410(*a*); II, xxvii: TR 679(*a*).
[2] II, v: TR 348.
[3] II, v: DB i, 302.
[4] MJ iii, 54.
[5] EM ii, 48; TR 349.
[6] Villey, *Sources et évolution*, ii, 366.

then), but it is clear that he dislikes it, sympathises with the victims, and hedges it in as much as he can. The strongest statement occurs at the end of *De la phisionomie*:

> (b) Et lors que l'occasion m'a convié aux condemnations crimineles, j'ay plustost manqué à la justice . . . (c) l'horreur du premier meurtre m'en faict craindre un secont, et la haine de la premiere cruauté m'en faict hayr toute imitation.[1]

It is true, as we have seen and as this example confirms, that hatred of cruelty springs partly from extreme sensibility. We also see now that sensibility is united with reason in a powerful and it might almost be said anachronistic defence of the rights of humanity.

Nowhere, it may be concluded, is Montaigne less conservative than in his attack on the barbarities of the contemporary legal system (not only in France). This is not just because detestation of witch-hunting, torture and cruel punishments is at the centre of the classical liberal position and was to occupy such a large place in the liberal thought of succeeding centuries. It is also because, though a conservative is not someone who believes in witchcraft and torture, yet these things are in a sense at the heart of the conservative position too; at least the defence and maintenance of the repressive power of the state, particularly when used against scapegoats and heretics, whatever form this power may take at a given time. There is perhaps no surer criterion of the distinction between the conservative and liberal frame of mind. In these respects at least Montaigne was probably the earliest of the great liberal thinkers of modern times.

Liberalism is not only a matter of law but also of political morality, and here the question becomes much more complicated, especially as it involves Montaigne's attitude to Machiavellianism. In his interesting book on Mannerism Arnold Hauser says that 'even Montaigne was at heart as much a Machiavellian as Luther or Loyola' and quotes in support from *De l'utile et de l'honneste*: 'vice n'est ce pas, car il [the prince] a quitté sa raison à une plus universelle et puissante raison . . .'.[2] He goes on to argue that Montaigne 'recommends honesty to princes only as the best policy' and that, like Machiavelli, he 'derives his view of ideology from

---

[1] III, xii: EM iii, 359; TR 1040-1.
[2] III, i: EM iii, 14; TR 777.

the relativity of standpoints and values',[1] which is a rather more substantial observation. There are two direct references to Machiavelli in the *Essais*. The purport of the more important of the two is that Machiavelli's arguments are solid but just as easy to attack as to defend:

> Il s'y trouveroit tousjours, à un tel argument, dequoy y fournir responses, dupliques, repliques, tripliques, quadrupliques. . . . les raisons n'y ayant guere autre fondement que l'experience, et la diversité des evenements humains nous presentant infinis exemples à toute sorte de formes.[2]

Machiavelli himself is caught in the suspension of judgement, in the relativity of standpoints and values of which Hauser speaks. The passage suggests that Machiavelli has failed to do justice to the infinite diversity of human experience, that Montaigne contains him as well as his opponents. Two other passages, much more outspoken, seem to be directed at Machiavelli, though he is not named. One denounces those who preach injustice:

> au lieu de peindre la vertu, ils peignent l'injustice toute pure et le vice, et la presentent ainsi fauce à l'institution des princes. . . .[3]

The other, a Bordeaux Copy addition, displays the same indignant tone:

> Ceus qui, de nostre temps, ont consideré, en l'establissement du devoir d'un prince, le bien de ses affaires sulement, et l'ont preferé au souin de sa foi et conscience. . . .[4]

What follows takes us to the heart of the debate, but so far the evidence does not support the idea of a Machiavellian Montaigne.

Still, this is far from the whole story, and if Machiavellianism is an appreciation of the realities of political action, of what is rather than what ought to be, 'da come si vive a come si doverrebbe vivere',[5] clearly Montaigne has many affinities with it.

> Je ne veux pas priver la tromperie de son rang, ce seroit mal entendre le monde.[6]

---

1 Hauser, *Mannerism*, 1965, p. 85.
2 II, xvii: EM ii, 440; TR 638–9. The other reference is II, xxxiv: TR 713.
3 III, ix: EM iii, 268; TR 971.
4 II, xvii: EM ii, 431; TR 631(*c*).
5 *Il principe*, ed. Lisio, p. 92.
6 III, i: EM iii, 9; TR 773.

This cool acknowledgement of the way things are, the refusal to be taken in, is at the root of his political morality (and furnishes another link with the main tradition of French moralists, with La Rochefoucauld, La Fontaine, Chamfort, Stendhal or Alain). After Machiavelli, and anticipating Mandeville, he argues that vices are not merely tolerable from a political and social point of view but actually useful and necessary (thus cupidity drives men on to philosophy, honour and learning).[1] The converse of this, though rather a matter of individual than political morality, is naturally that what appear to be virtues are in fact concealed vices. The passage from the *Apologie* just cited continues:

> (*b*) la prudence de nous conserver et gouverner est esveillée par nostre crainte: et combien de belles actions par l'ambition? combien par la presomption? (*a*) Aucune eminente et gaillarde vertu en fin n'est sans quelque agitation desreglée.[2]

An addition to *Du jeune Caton* strikes a slightly different note:

> Grande subtilité! Qu'on me donne l'action la plus excellente et pure, je m'en vois y fournir vraysemblablement cinquante vitieuses intentions. Dieu sçait, à qui les veut estendre, quelle diversité d'images ne souffre nostre interne volonté![3]

Taken together these two short passages both contain and transcend the whole of La Rochefoucauld. Yes, virtue has vicious roots, but no, virtue is not thereby abolished or even seriously undermined.

This was a digression (all too easy in dealing with Montaigne) but not perhaps an irrelevant one, since the answer he gives to La Rochefoucauld is closely linked with the answer to Machiavelli. Both Machiavelli and Montaigne lay great stress on fortune, a fundamentally un-Christian concept (hence the objection of the Roman censor), but the nature of the emphasis is quite different. Machiavelli's attitude is active: fortune is more powerful than men, but it can be directed. He compares it to a great river in flood, sweeping everything before it; but this does not mean that it is impossible to build dams and embankments beforehand.[4] For Montaigne, on the other hand, and this is consonant with his scepticism and his mobility, fortune rules events and makes

---

[1] II, xii: TR 550.
[2] II, xii: EM ii, 318; TR 550.
[3] I, xxxvii: EM i, 301–2; TR 226(*b*).
[4] *Il principe*, ed. Lisio, p. 138.

prudence otiose (a constant refrain). The moral, and anti-Machiavellian, conclusion he draws is that, since there is no certainty in calculation, the best course is to choose the side which has more justice, to do what is fine and generous.[1] As so often we are struck by the soundness, even nobility, of his moral judgements.

These are, however, peripheral matters. The central question is whether, or how far, it is permissible to engage for political advantage in actions which appear to be positively wicked. Montaigne makes a distinction between private virtue and public life. Conscience, his touchstone as we have seen, is not always a good guide in affairs of state and he himself has found that when he has been involved in politics his own simple virtues were inept and dangerous.[2] He admits the *raison d'état*, as Hauser says: the prince may be forced by a higher reason to abandon what would ordinarily be considered his duty or his good faith.

(b) Le bien public requiert qu'on trahisse et qu'on mente (c) et qu'on massacre.[3]

This sounds Machiavellian enough and is certainly at variance with any naïvely moralistic approach to politics. Even here, though, there is a difference. For Montaigne such actions can only be justified by the most pressing public need.[4] Machiavelli, on the other hand, scarcely makes the distinction between public and private conduct: all that conduces to the advantage of the prince is assumed also to conduce to the well-being of the state, and the supreme value seems to be self-affirmation (or *virtù*). It is partly perhaps the difference between a traditional state, however agitated, and the world of the *condottieri*.

Moreover, I have omitted the very important qualifications which Montaigne adds to the most Machiavellian of the statements quoted. In the one about universal reason he goes on: 'il le falloit faire; mais s'il le fit sans regret, s'il ne luy greva de le faire, c'est signe que sa conscience est en mauvais termes',[5] so that conscience, though not always a trustworthy guide, is still the norm and offences against it are only 'rares et maladifves ex-

1 I, xxiv: TR 127.
2 III, ix: TR 970.
3 III, i: EM iii, 3; TR 768.
4 e.g. III, i: TR 778.
5 III, i: EM iii, 14; TR 777.

ceptions'.[1] For Machiavelli these exceptions are the ordinary condition of political life, and conscience hardly appears in a prince except as pretence. After saying that the public good requires treachery, lying and massacres, Montaigne continues, in a well-known disclaimer: 'resignons cette commission à gens plus obeissans et plus soupples.'[2] It has to be done, but he is not going to be the one to do it. This raises again the charge of his selfishness. But if we follow the sinuosities (a pleasure in themselves) of the argument of *De l'utile et de l'honneste*, we see that he generalises this selfishness, if that is what it is, into a line of conduct for the man of honour, hedging in the permission to act against morality with all sorts of restrictions quite foreign to the spirit of Machiavelli. And at the end Epaminondas and humanity are presented as the supreme standards.

But Montaigne's critique of Machiavellianism goes deeper still. I left unfinished a quotation from *De la præsumption* in which he condemns those who teach princes to put political advantage before faith and conscience. He goes on to say that this might work if one were dealing with a single act of perfidy. But 'on faict plus d'une paix, plus d'un traité en sa vie'.[3] The disadvantages which ensue from a reputation for faithlessness far outweigh the temporary benefits. Machiavelli's schematic account of political behaviour here comes up against Montaigne's massive common sense as well as his feeling for the diversity of life. Montaigne, it is true, is arguing at this point in strictly Machiavellian and pragmatic terms: he expresses no moral revulsion, he just says that it fails in practice. However, the reference to faith and conscience immediately before suggests the presence of concealed indignation, which appears also in the parallel attack on Guicciardini at the end of *Des livres*: Guicciardini's weakness as a historian is that he attributes all actions to low motives, perhaps judging other people by himself[4] (which brings us back again to detraction, motivation, and La Rochefoucauld). Behind all these hostile reactions lies the hatred of lying and cruelty which we have so often noticed and which may stand as a moral absolute for Montaigne, or as near as he gets to it. For Machiavelli extreme cruelty is a legitimate and sometimes laudable means of political

[1] III, i: EM iii, 15; TR 778.
[2] III, i: EM iii, 3; TR 768.
[3] II, xvii: EM ii, 431; TR 631-2(c).
[4] II, x: TR 399.

action. The opposition is clearest in their comments on the same series of events, the expulsion of the Spanish and Portuguese Jews. What Montaigne calls, as we saw, 'un horrible spectacle' is described by Machiavelli with some compassion but with far greater admiration.[1]

Montaigne's character and his moral attitude alike lead him to the strongest declarations of antagonism to the central rules of *Realpolitik*. However, he does make concessions. And he does not deal in abstract moralities but in life, with concrete cases and complex characters. It is here perhaps more than anywhere that we can appreciate the precision of his moral judgement, the way in which deeply held principles underlie the sense of diversity. This balance is especially visible in his general observations on the practical operation of political morality, as in his remarks on the dangers of excessive intelligence which makes men unfitted for the conduct of affairs[2] (not a wholly original view perhaps but he shows exactly why) or in the very telling:

> C'est agir pour sa reputation et proffit particulier, non pour le bien, de remettre à faire en la place ce qu'on peut faire en la chambre du conseil, et en plain midy ce qu'on eust faict la nuict precedente, et d'estre jaloux de faire soy-mesme ce que son compaignon faict aussi bien.[3]

To act for one's own reputation and profit rather than for the general good: this is anathema to Montaigne and the scale of values involved is again highly un-Machiavellian.

In pursuing his meaning along these tortuous paths (an indispensable process) I may have failed to give sufficient weight to the loftiness of reaction and depth of feeling which, as so often, have to be set against balance and moderation.

> (*b*) toutes choses ne sont pas loisibles à un homme de bien pour le service (*c*) de son Roy ny (*b*) de la cause generale et des loix.[4]

It would be difficult to state the case against Machiavelli more soberly and pointedly. Best of all perhaps and most moving is the end of *Comme nous pleurons et rions d'une mesme chose*, when Timoleon has killed the tyrant his brother (a very Machiavellian situation):

---

[1] *Il principe*, ed. Lisio, p. 126.
[2] II, xx: TR 657.
[3] III, x: EM iii, 304; TR 999–1000.
[4] III, i: EM iii, 18; TR 780.

Quand Timoleon pleure le meurtre qu'il avoit commis d'une si
meure et genereuse deliberation, il ne pleure pas la liberté rendue
à sa patrie, il ne pleure pas le Tyran, mais il pleure son frere. L'une
partie de son devoir est jouée, laissons luy en jouer l'autre.[1]

How much better this is in Montaigne than in Amyot![2] What it
shows above all is the complication of political action by human
feeling, a complication which Machiavelli seems to ignore. Of
course Machiavelli is also a complex figure and for the purposes of
this comparison he has no doubt been simplified, though the
simplification corresponds well enough to the view taken of him
in the sixteenth century. Montaigne in these terms is anything
but a Machiavellian at heart. In fact, in spite of the seventeenth-
century theorists of *raison d'état*, of Joseph de Maistre and Balzac,
of Maurras and the Action Française, he may be said to represent
the dominant French tradition in political thought which rejects
Machiavelli and the notion that political good is the same as
political advantage.[3]

In spite of appearances there is no real contradiction between
the liberation of personal morality and the fairly rigorous limitations placed on the exercise of political action: the excesses of
political power are not only wicked in themselves but distract
attention from the essential business of living. A more difficult
question is whether the anti-Machiavellian side of Montaigne is
to be counted as evidence of his conservative or liberal tendencies. In the narrower context of his time it is conservative :
Machiavelli's revolution in political thought was to separate political action from religion and also from morals (a separation which
had no doubt always existed in practice but not in theory). Anti-
Machiavellians were also traditionalists. From a wider viewpoint,
however, when we consider the subsequent history of this argument, it would appear that resistance to unbridled power (as in
Acton's famous dictum) and the moralisation of politics are again
essential features of the classical liberal position. Montaigne's
combination of individual freedom and restraint on political power
(if only moral restraint) is characteristic of this attitude or at
least anticipates it.

So far we have shown that he was, partly, a liberal, but we must
remember that under the absolutist system liberalism was revolu-

---

[1] I, xxxviii: EM i, 308; TR 231(*a*).
[2] Plutarch, *Les vies*, 1565, f. 179.
[3] On this see Chérel, *La pensée de Machiavel en France*, 1935.

tionary. His views on such matters as colonialism, law and punishment, strike at the roots of the established system. The parallel with Voltaire and the *philosophes* may make this point clear. *Des cannibales* goes rather further. I have already quoted the great passage near the beginning of the essay where he holds up for admiration a society without political hierarchy, trade, riches, poverty, family or laws. The essay closes with the Indians he met at Rouen and their surprise at European inequalities of wealth:

> ... ils avoient aperçeu qu'il y avoit parmy nous des hommes pleins et gorgez de toutes sortes de commoditez, et que leurs moitiez [fellow-men] estoient mendians à leurs portes, décharnez de faim et de pauvreté; et trouvoient estrange comme ces moitiez icy necessiteuses pouvoient souffrir une telle injustice, qu'ils ne prinsent les autres à la gorge, ou missent le feu à leurs maisons.[1]

The socialism or communism implied in these statements need not perhaps be taken too seriously. He is accustomed to playing with all possible ideas and the influence of Plato is strongly marked. None the less, he does identify himself with the Indians, at least for the moment, and the communism of *Des cannibales* is in harmony with his general sympathy for the people and his pronouncements in favour of democracy.

We are thus faced with a Montaigne who is at once deeply conservative and radically liberal, even revolutionary, above all subversive. His conservatism, however, is pragmatic only. It is based entirely on the premise that all change runs the risk of producing a worse state of affairs than the present one, however bad it may be. In a sense, the worse it is shown to be, the stronger the argument. He is thus led to question all established values, to reveal the injustices, absurdities and hollowness of all venerated institutions, religious, political and social. He remains a conservative but his conservative position is reached by a circuitous route which takes in all the potentially revolutionary themes which were eventually to find expression in action as well as thought. If we consider Montaigne in himself, especially from the point of view of temperament and personality, we shall no doubt stress his conservative side; if, with the advantage of hindsight, we consider his influence and the later history of his subversive ideas, we shall find that it is the revolutionary side which is uppermost.

---

[1] I, xxxi: EM i, 280; TR 213(*a*).

☙ 11 ☙

The Form of the Essays

IN a sense this is a subject we have already dealt with, at least in part. The form of the *Essais*, individually and collectively, is not something that can be easily separated from the argument or above all from the argumentative procedures, some of which we have studied in some detail. This is particularly true of *le passage*, where movement and the depiction of movement advance together; it is true of Montaigne's logic or of his scepticism and the balanced alternation of arguments it produces in an essay like *Coustume de l'isle de Cea*; it is true of the concealment of the subversive core of an essay under a disguised title, within a series of wrappings, as we have just seen in *Des boyteux*. None the less, though form may not be theoretically separable from content (a question which is far from closed), it is in practice a fruitful way of looking at content. It is virtually impossible to avoid talking about the essay form, and here all the more important not to try, because, as we have seen, Montaigne may be said to have invented it and the creation of a new literary genre is an event of some importance. We may readily concede that he also invented a content to go with it, or that one sprang from the other, or that both proceeded simultaneously, but we ought to look at form a little more systematically than we have done so far.

If we are to believe Montaigne himself the *Essais* have no form and no order. He refers to them variously as 'une galimafrée de divers articles',[1] as 'une marqueterie mal jouinte',[2] most appropriately perhaps as an 'embrouilleure',[3] with its suggestion of the

[1] I, xlvi: EM i, 354: TR 265(*a*).
[2] III, ix: EM iii, 228; TR 941(*c*).
[3] III, ix: EM iii, 271; TR 974(*b*).

tangling of threads. He denies that there is any art in his arrangement (or rather non-arrangement), he glories in the disorder of his examples, and he asserts that the only order is purely fortuitous:

> Que sont-ce icy aussi, à la verité, que crotesques et corps monstrueux, rappiecez de divers membres, sans certaine figure, n'ayants ordre, suite ny proportion que fortuité ?[1]

Such assertions are very numerous, and they confirm the reader's immediate impression. There are others, however, which point in a different direction and reveal a concern with form. When he says 'Mon humeur est de regarder autant à la forme qu'à la substance',[2] he is talking about argument but it might be applied to the *Essais*, as is certainly the case with 'Qu'on ne s'attende pas aux matieres, mais à la façon que j'y done'.[3] This needs interpretation: 'fashion' is by no means only a matter of form and arrangement in a narrow sense; but they are included. In 'J'ayme l'alleure poetique, à sauts et à gambades',[4] the emphasis on disorder is maintained but at any rate a principle of rhythm is introduced. But at the same point in *De la vanité* he puts forward a not inconsistent but ultimately quite different explanation of his lack of order:

> Je m'esgare, mais plustost par licence que par mesgarde. Mes fantasies se suyvent, mais par fois c'est de loing, et se regardent, mais d'une veuë oblique.[5]

This is capital: it suggests that disorder itself follows a deep and hidden plan, that his themes are linked though separated by digressions. Moreover, whatever the apparent disorder, there is an underlying unity which binds all the digressions together:

> Que je commence par celle qu'il me plaira, car les matieres se tiennent toutes enchesnées les unes aux autres.[6]

His ideal of form is therefore a continuous development in which joints and transitions are invisible:

---

[1] I, xxviii: EM i, 238; TR 181.
[2] III, viii: EM iii, 183; TR 906.
[3] II, x: EM ii, 101; TR 387.
[4] III, ix: EM iii, 270; TR 973.
[5] III, ix: EM iii, 269; TR 973.
[6] III, v: EM iii, 116; TR 854. This, curiously, echoes the Sabunde translation: 'Ainsi sont toutes ces pieces enchainees l'une à l'autre' (*Œuvres complètes*, ed. Armaingaud, ix, 153).

Je n'ayme point de tissure où les liaisons et les coutures paroissent, tout ainsi qu'en un beau corps, il ne faut qu'on y puisse compter les os et les veines.[1]

This points to organic as against symmetrical or mathematical form, and it suggests an aesthetic preoccupation which hardly consorts with artlessness. All these remarks are summed up in 'Mon livre est tousjours un':[2] superficial disorder conceals underlying unity. It remains to be seen how far these programmatic statements are realised in the actual structure.

The essay form as practised by Montaigne was, as we have seen, virtually unique in his own time: 'C'est le seul livre au monde de son espece, d'un dessein farouche et extravagant.'[3] The claim was not far-fetched and although the *Essais* have had many imitators and the genre has become established, there is still perhaps no book quite like them. There is a certain superficial resemblance to other kinds of personal writing, but there are also fundamental differences. The *Essais* can be regarded as a sort of autobiography or confession, and parallels with St Augustine or Rousseau are not at all out of place. However, as we saw in discussing the self-portrait, Montaigne's picture of himself, though complete in a sense, is not systematically so. Above all it is not in chronological order and has to be pieced together from scattered touches. The difference between chronological and 'synchronic' presentation has more significant consequences ('synchronic' is not quite the right word but it is difficult to express otherwise the random occurrence of incidents from the life with no reference to a fixed time-scale). The pure autobiographer looks back on his life from a point whence it may be considered as provisionally complete. His tense is the past and there is an inevitable distance, diminishing as he goes on, between the writer and his hero. Distance is likely to lead to falsification, even with total good faith, because maturity and hindsight interpret and arrange the raw material of experience (Rousseau offers outstanding examples). At best there is bound to be some degree of freezing into set patterns. Montaigne's time, on the other hand, is the present and he offers us, as we have seen, immediate experience and thought as he thinks it. The diarist may seem to come closer to the form of the essay, and he certainly gives us his experiences 'de jour en

[1] I, xxvi: EM i, 223; TR 171(a).
[2] III, ix: EM iii, 228: TR 941(c).
[3] II, viii: EM ii, 69; TR 364(a,c).

jour'. Even here, however, whether he is recording external events or inner feelings, the tense is essentially the past, though an immediate past: at the end of the day he writes up his memories of what has happened during it. More important, the jerky movement from day to day precludes unity of form (there may be a unity of personality, of course). Gide's *Journal* in particular manifests this disjointed effect; Kilvert's *Diary*, though more unified, is still a succession of scenes. The notebooks (Baudelaire's *Fusées* or *Mon cœur mis à nu* for example) give us direct thought but disjointedness is even more apparent. Montaigne's essay form has the advantages of immediacy of spontaneous thought and continuity; but also, paradoxically, by the grouping of thought, however loosely, round some sort of central theme, it achieves an aesthetic unity. In some ways the closest parallel is the letter, which is cast in the present and represents immediate impressions; but either it is formal as in Seneca, where the frozen effect is very noticeable, or it is informal, as in Mme de Sévigné, and then the feeling of an aesthetic whole is lost, except in a very lax sense. One of Montaigne's greatest achievements is the reconciliation of these two opposite poles. It is none the less interesting that he contemplated the use of the letter form but rejected it because after the death of La Boétie he had no one to write to and because his hatred of falsehood prevented him from addressing an imaginary correspondent (in other words from adopting the formal epistle).[1] This brings out another vital difference between the essay and the letter: communication with a single person, real or feigned, limits the perspective (Montesquieu's *Lettres persanes* illustrates this very well); Montaigne opens it by addressing himself to mankind in general, or perhaps to himself but because of the presence of the human condition in every man there is not much difference.

Before we examine in more detail the form of the individual essay, one question demands some attention, the order in which the essays are placed.[2] Each essay forms a unity, but so does the work as a whole. This is partly a matter of the literary personality of the author and of the harmony even of disparate and contradictory themes, but there may be more than this. That the Third Book, added in 1588, should be separated from the rest is not

---

[1] I, xl: TR 246(c).
[2] Only a brief outline is possible here; for a fuller discussion see my article, 'L'ordre des *Essais* de Montaigne', *BHR*, xviii (1956).

surprising, but there is presumably some significance in the
original division into two books. At least two attempts have been
made to establish a unity of theme in each book. For Barrière
it is retirement, suicide, and diversion;[1] for Butor (to simplify a
highly complex argument) friendship and La Boétie, the apology
for Julian the Apostate, the opening on to the world.[2] Both these
attempts are illuminating but both are too rigid, there is far too
much that they leave out of account. In a general way we might
say that the first two books are of approximately equal length in
spite of the difference in the number of essays. Book I is mainly
concerned with external matters (the military essays, education,
the cannibals), Book II with philosophical and moral problems
(the *Apologie*, cruelty, conscience). But there are many exceptions
even to this very broad generalisation. It is perhaps more to the
point that the first chapter of Book I (*Par divers moyens on arrive
à pareille fin*) and the first and last of Book II (*De l'inconstance de
nos actions* and *De la ressemblance des enfans aux peres* in its closing words) all stress the theme of diversity.

A more promising, or at least more precise, line of inquiry may
be to trace the connections between succeeding essays. Montaigne,
as we have seen, calls them chapters and though too much importance should not be attached to this it does suggest that they are to
be regarded as parts of a whole and not as separate entities. The
most obvious explanation of their sequence is that they were
arranged in order of composition, and this is Villey's general
argument,[3] though his dating admits of many exceptions. From
our point of view, that of the *Essais* as a single existing work of art,
the question has only secondary importance: what matters is the
order they are in now. Looking at it in this way we find that a
number of essays are unmistakably interconnected. Thus *L'heure
des parlemens dangereuse* (I, vi) simply continues the argument
of *Si le chef d'une place assiegée doit sortir pour parlementer*
(I, v), the two being linked by a conjunction. More interesting is
the case of what may be called the antechamber, where a major
essay is preceded by a minor one which serves as an introduction.
Examples are *Qu'il ne faut juger de nostre heur, qu'apres la mort*
(I, xix) and *Que philosopher, c'est apprendre à mourir* (I, xx), and
even more strikingly *Du pedantisme* (I, xxv) and *De l'institution*

[1] *Montaigne gentilhomme français*, 1948, pp. 143–51.
[2] *Essais sur les Essais*, 1968, *passim*.
[3] *Sources et évolution*, i, 339, 342.

des enfans (I, xxvi). Occasionally we find an appendix instead of
an antechamber, as with *De l'inequalitè qui est entre nous* (I, xlii)
and *Des loix somptuaires* (I, xliii). Adjacent essays are related by
their main theme, for instance *De trois bonnes femmes* (II, xxxv)
and *Des plus excellens hommes* (II, xxxvi), also three, or by
tangential themes, like the conflict between public and private duty
in *Comme nous pleurons et rions d'une mesme chose* (Timoleon,
already mentioned, at the end of I, xxxviii) and *De la solitude*
(I, xxxix), or by keywords (the 'mot en un coin'), like *imposture*
in *Des cannibales* (I, xxxi) and *Qu'il faut sobrement se mesler de
juger des ordonnances divines* (I, xxxii). In ways like these a tangible though not uninterrupted rhythm is built up. Particularly
notable are such groups of related chapters as the military essays
at the beginning of Book I or the magnificent closing series of
Book II, six essays on virtue and heroes (the final essay, *De la
ressemblance des enfans aux peres,* which reiterates some of the
major themes, is not included in the series). In the Third Book
continuity of one kind or another is more marked and may be
regarded as practically unbroken, apart from *De l'experience,*
which again provides a conclusion by summarising and complet-
ing the whole book. The Third Book possesses, moreover, a
definite, almost musical, structure. The first two chapters (*De
l'utile et de l'honneste, Du repentir*) deal with solemn subjects
in a mainly solemn way. The next four chapters are grouped round
the theme of diversion, including *De la diversion* and *Sur des vers
de Virgile,* and the tone becomes correspondingly playful (though
Montaigne's playfulness is also very serious). The turning-point
comes with *Des coches,* which may be thought at once the most
fanciful and the most deeply serious of all. The final group of
seven essays is serious but not solemn: the subjects are grave but
the tone often humorous (*Des boyteux* is a good example). In
spite of the evident unity of the Third Book we might thus regard
it as being composed of three movements.

When we come to the form of the individual essays, we find
that, leaving aside the *Apologie* which is a special case, there
is a tendency for them to grow longer as the work develops, a
tendency sometimes masked by the interpolations. The first essays
of Book I are, as we have seen, very brief, those of the Third Book
mostly very long. This is not a purely mechanical observation,
and Montaigne himself explains its significance:

Par ce que la coupure si frequante des chapitres, de quoi j'usois au comancemant, m'a samblé rompre l'attention avant qu'elle soit née, et la dissoudre ... je me suis mis à les faire plus longs, qui requierent de la proposition et du loisir assigné.[1]

He puts it in terms of the effect on the reader, of attention and leisure; it can also be viewed as a progress towards a more flowing and unified form.

We have noticed the frequent disparity between the title and the real subject of an essay. Again Montaigne also notices it (as does Florio in his preface) and again his admission goes beyond mere statement of the fact:

Les noms de mes chapitres n'en embrassent pas tousjours la matiere; souvent ils la denotent seulement par quelque marque. . . .[2]

This is to be related to the 'mot en un coin' passage in the same essay: both typify Montaigne's oblique and tangential approach to the matters he treats. We have already seen that *Du jeune Caton* is about poetry, *Coustume de l'isle de Cea* about suicide, *Sur des vers de Virgile* about sex, and *Des boyteux* about, chiefly, witchcraft and irrational penal codes. *Des coches* is perhaps the finest example, with its contrast between the triviality of the ostensible subject, which occupies a page or so, and the depth and importance of the real subject. *De la phisionomie* is almost as surprising: the title refers to the physical ugliness of Socrates, which is not reached till almost the end, though the essay opens with a eulogy of his character. Some of these misleading titles are, we know, disguises for dangerous thoughts, but by no means all. From the point of view of form what counts is the mood of play they set up, the surprise effect, the oblique approach, and the counterpoint between title and essay.

The introduction or overture of the essay follows a similar pattern. A good, if simple, example is *Du dormir*. Reason, says the first sentence, commands us to go in the same direction but not always at the same pace. The pulse of virtue itself would beat faster before battle than before dinner. Then comes the sentence which sets the whole essay in motion: he admires great men who in such circumstances have not even lost sleep.[3] With this ingeniously gradual entry we have reached the subject before we

[1] III, ix: EM iii, 272; TR 974(*c*).
[2] III, ix: EM iii, 270; TR 973.
[3] I, xliv: TR 262.

are properly aware of it. The opening of the *Apologie* is rather different: the casual-seeming introduction, both in its scepticism about learning and the moderation with which it is expressed, in fact strikes the keynote of the whole essay. But the personal remarks about the visits of learned men to the château and the difference between his father's generation and his own hardly lead us to expect what is to follow. In a large number of cases an essay begins with a discussion of what he is doing, his method, the characteristics and originality of the book and the self-portrait, thus throwing into relief the involuted nature of the enterprise, the observer observed. In at least one case, *Du dementir*, the introductory remarks about the self-portrait are so long that the actual subject appears as no more than an appendix.

Of the different formal types of essay we should perhaps begin with the clearly articulated logical structure because it is untypical and largely early. A good example is *De l'amitié*. After the usual observations on the *Essais* (in this case their disorder, ingeniously contrasted with La Boétie's mastery of composition) and a narrative account of their meeting and relations, comes the general discussion of friendship, sub-divided into its different kinds (father and son, brothers, with women, marriage, homosexual friendship, ordinary friendship, supreme friendship), and finally the character of La Boétie. This classical construction is, however, animated by great emotional force. Or we may find, very similarly but with less organic unity, composition by blocks as in *Des livres*: after the introduction there are sections on poets, moralists, Cicero, and historians. The most obvious instance of logical structure is of course the *Apologie*, the plan of which has often been summarised. Here it need only be said that the essay falls into two carefully distinguished if utterly disproportionate parts (for reason, against reason) and that the second part is composed of a classified series of sceptical objections to the sovereignty of human reason (animals, the senses, and so on). The order of these objections is not perfectly logical and the whole is shot through with contradiction and paradox; the main lines of structure are none the less clearly apparent. The Third Book produces something quite different but there are two possible examples. *De l'utile et de l'honneste* is closely knit and argued, without digressions, though the argument, as we have seen, is sinuous and it cannot be broken down into blocks. *De trois commerces* (conversation, women, books) exhibits the ternary form of two of the earlier essays, but the order is less rigid, the divisions less marked, and a degree of coagulation has taken place, especially in the first part: in some places indeed it is difficult to decide which of the three he is talking about.

Turning now to more characteristic types, the first, simply an extension of what we have said about titles and introductions, is the indirect entry. A very early and elementary example is *Des menteurs,* which begins, like so many others, with the author, in this case the weakness of his memory; the link with the subject is made by the statement, in the final version nearly halfway through the essay, that those with bad memories should not try to be liars. Much more fully developed is *Des mauvais moyens employez à bonne fin* (about 1578), where the approach is very indirect indeed. He begins by saying that everything is connected; this includes the physical body and the body politic; purging and bleeding the one corresponds to colonisation and war in the other; external war has been suggested as a remedy for civil commotion in France; this seems unjust:

> Toutesfois la foiblesse de notre condition nous pousse souvent à cette necessité, de nous servir de mauvais moyens pour une bonne fin.[1]

There at last we are, but this time more than halfway through. Cases of direct entry also occur, of course, like *De la vanité* and *De l'experience,* but more rarely. The extreme extension of indirect entry is inverted order, where the subject (at least the ostensible subject) is only reached at the very end. We have already seen this in *Des boyteux* and *De la phisionomie.* Another example is *L'histoire de Spurina,* also remarkable for the elusiveness of its subject. The main theme appears to be the control of amorous instincts, which is discussed at the beginning and is illustrated by the brief anecdote about Spurina nearly at the end. But in the middle comes a study of Caesar's character which constitutes the main body of the essay and its principal interest; it is linked to the rest by Caesar's amorous adventures but only just, and this is typical of Montaigne's whole method: 'je me contente du bout d'un poil, pour les joindre à mon propos.'[2]

This last essay exemplifies the binary type, though the sandwich arrangement is unusual. More often the two themes are

[1] II, xxiii: EM ii, 478; TR 664.
[2] II, xxvii: CR iii, 111.

consecutive or there is a continuous to-and-fro movement between them. The first appears in *De l'yvrongnerie* where, after an indirect entry, drunkenness leads to the effect of physical accidents on the mind and the fury inspired by poetry or martyrdom (but this is perhaps rather a case of extension), or *De la conscience* where the topic of conscience is followed by that of torture, the transition being made unobtrusively as usual. The second can be best observed in a mature essay of the Third Book, *De mesnager sa volonté*. Here the two themes, closely connected, are (particular and concrete) his experience as mayor and (general) his refusal to commit himself, to engage his whole being in external pursuits and duties. In treating the second theme he passes continually from the individual to the human condition and back again, so that a second binary movement is superimposed on the first. The essay begins with the general theme and ends with the particular, but more significant is the effortless movement from one to the other. The ternary form of *De trois bonnes femmes, Des plus excellens hommes* and *De trois commerces* we have already considered.

De mesnager sa volonté illustrates a more general feature, the interweaving of themes, which is characteristic of the form of the fully developed essay, whatever its type.[1] The outstanding example among many is *De la vanité*, perhaps the most complex of all and remarkable, even in Montaigne, for the variety of topics introduced. The apparent confusion impelled Grace Norton to argue that there were originally two essays, one on vanity and one on travel, and that Montaigne cut them up and mixed them together.[2] All that need be said about this is that it would have taken some doing; more importantly, *De la vanité* is only an extreme example of his usual manner of proceeding. In fact it seems possible to discern at least eleven major topics, but all in some way interconnected. These are, in order of appearance and numbered for the sake of reference: (i) vanity (generally left in the background but appearing at the beginning and end, a sort of ground-bass); (ii) the state of France and the civil wars; (iii) travel (the most prominent); (iv) household management (closely interwoven with iii and connected with ii); (v) society and politics (a minor theme deriving from ii); (vi) Rome (part of iii but also uniting with i in the final climax); (vii) the composition of the *Essais* (connec-

---

[1] On this see also S. J. Holyoake, 'The idea of "jugement" in Montaigne', *Modern language review*, lxiii (1968), 350–1.
[2] *Studies in Montaigne*, 1904, pp. 61ff.

ted with both i and iii); (viii) obligations (connected with ii and iv); (ix) death (connected with iii); (x) the inconsistency of philosophy; (xi) fortune (both the last connected with i). We should observe especially the alternation of the travel and household themes and the distant recurrences of death, obligations, composition, with vanity the most distant of all. Four of the topics (i–iv) can reasonably be considered as main themes of the essay and these weave in and out of the fabric, threads of different colours composing a unified design. Or we might think of it in terms of strata with vanity as the deepest layer and above it travel which constitutes the principal unifying factor. Thibaudet's comment: '. . . vanité même du discours, qui n'a jamais été aussi décousu, aussi fait de lopins que dans cet important essai',[1] could hardly be further from the truth.

But in spite of the frequency of essays with a binary or ternary arrangement or with numerous interwoven themes, the most characteristic is no doubt the essay with a single central theme, though this may not always be easy to disentangle from the false trails and minor digressions which surround it. A not too complicated early example is *Divers evenemens de mesme conseil* where the central idea, itself typical of Montaigne, is that the same causes produce opposite effects. The interest lies in the slip from one idea to another grouped round this centre: clemency, fortune, honesty, prudence, confidence. More highly developed is *De l'affection des peres aux enfans*, remarkable for its homogeneity and continuous argument, including the later interpolations and with only one brief digression. But within this homogeneity a number of subordinate themes are accommodated (the most suitable age for marriage, the position and authority of women as wives and mothers, the relation of the artist to his works identified with that of the father to his children). In the Third Book *Du repentir* offers an excellent example but the most interesting and complex is *De l'experience* which at first sight seems thoroughly disorganised. Yet it has a plan and a unity, even though the plan is submerged and concealed. The themes can again be enumerated: (i) experience; (ii) identity and difference; (iii) laws; (iv) self-examination; (v) medicine; (vi) Montaigne's disease; (vii) his way of life and habits; (viii) custom; (ix) body and soul; (x) human and inhuman wisdom; (xi) the aim of life ('jouyr

---

1 *Essais*, Bibliothèque de la Pléiade, 1946, p. 915 n.1.

loiallement de son estre'). Experience is clearly the central theme running through the whole essay, which presents various facets of human experience. From this point of view nothing is irrelevant. Identity and laws, as we have seen, belong together as part of the same argument. The themes numbered (v) to (viii) are closely connected and interwoven, both with each other and with the rest (thus the diversity of individual patients in medicine corresponds to the diversity of cases in law). The last three bring the essay to a climax, revealing the significance and unity of the apparently desultory observations and anecdotes which precede: the life of the body is not despicable, it forms the texture of life itself, it is part of thought and of the life of the mind. Beneath all this we now see emerging a logical plan in three parts: the insufficiency of reason and law, which must be supplemented by experience; the study of many kinds of experience, mostly the author's but also humanity's; experience as teaching how life should be lived. At a deeper level still the transcending theme of the essay, the liberation of life from the restrictions of codes and classifications, is thus reflected in its free but unified form.

A particular variant of the central type is the circle. Some care is needed in using what may appear to be spatial metaphors of this kind, but when an argument returns to its point of departure a circular motion can be legitimately invoked. When Montaigne says: 'et doit en outre leur course se manier, non en ligne droite qui face bout ailleurs, mais en rond, duquel les deux pointes se tiennent et terminent en nous par un brief contour',[1] he is talking about human desires, contrasting the insatiability of the miserly or the ambitious with the limited aims of the wise man who brings everything back to himself and his true needs, but he is also suggesting something important about his view of the self and the form of the *Essais* in general. A simple case of circular form is *Toutes choses ont leur saison,* also an example of indirect entry, which begins and ends with Cato the Younger, taking in the subject of the title on the way. A richer and finer example is *Des cannibales,* firmly based on the continuing description of the customs of the Brazilians, from which the revolutionary ideas spring like the spokes of a wheel from its hub. The way in which the circle is closed is particularly noteworthy. The essay begins with Pyrrhus's remark on the civilised discipline of the barbarous

---

[1] III, x: EM iii, 290; TR 988.

Romans and ends with a similar antithesis applied to the Brazilians: 'Tout cela ne va pas trop mal: mais quoy, ils ne portent point de haut de chausses!'[1] But the circular form is not confined to the whole essay; in longer and more complex cases we find circles within circles. We have seen that *De la vanité* begins and ends with vanity. On page 949 (in the Thibaudet and Rat edition) Montaigne gives his reply to those who ask him the reason for his travels; travel had last been mentioned on page 933. We thus have a great circular movement (within the greater circle of the whole essay), bringing us back to its starting-point by way of politics, civil war, the composition of the *Essais*, obligations, and civil war again. This is of course only a momentary resting-place before another movement begins.

So far we have considered the organisation of themes in a general way, assuming the continuity between one theme and another rather than demonstrating it. How one theme is linked to another is the central question in dealing with the form of the *Essais*; it is also a question of detail and almost of style. Before we look at particular devices we might take an outstanding example of almost imperceptible movement from one theme to another, *Des coches*, which has proved more baffling from the point of view of form than any other essay.[2] It has two main themes: kings and royal magnificence; and, as we have seen, the Spaniards in America. To these may perhaps be added fear, which serves as introduction. Coaches seem only vaguely if at all related to these topics. Their function is no doubt partly disguise, and this was perhaps the motive for their introduction, but having been introduced they become an important formal element, a unifying factor (the principal one on the scale of the essay as a whole) and a symbol or at least concrete embodiment of the theme of magnificence. The passage from one theme to the next is secured, as we should expect, by associations of ideas. This will be clear from an outline plan in which the associating or linking words are italicised and the appearances of coaches capitalised. Page numbers (Thibaudet and Rat) are given in order to show the proportions.

876   Authors multiply *causes*
       Causes of blessing sneezes
       Causes of sea-sickness – *fear*

---

[1] I, xxxi: EM i, 281; TR 213.
[2] Cf. my article, 'Baroque elements in Montaigne', *French studies*, viii (1954).

877 Not *fear* in my case
    Fear overcome by great men
878 Absence of *fear* in me due to insensibility not strength
    for I cannot stand for long COACH, litter or boat
878(c) I would give the history of COACHES in war (if I had
    a better memory)
879(c) Examples of COACHES in war
    Early French *kings* travelled in *ox-carts*
879–83 Roman *emperors* drawn in COACHES by strange beasts
    Monarchs should not indulge in vain *expense*
    (developed)
883–5 *Yet* Roman *emperors* did well to give great displays
    (described at length) remarkable for *ingenuity*, not
    merely *expense*
885 *Ingenuity* of ancients compared with *us*
866 *We* have made little progress, our *knowledge* of
    history is very limited
    And our *knowledge* of the *world*
    We have just found another *world*
886–94 Attack on Spanish cruelties in *New World*
894 Retombons à nos COCHES
    COACHES in *New World* (or rather their absence)

Any attempt to epitomise a work of verbal art in this way (and
Des coches resembles a poem) is bound to seem rather absurd,
and the scheme is grossly simplified and deformed, omitting Montaigne's discussions, nuances and brilliant asides. Nevertheless
it may help to show the design of this seamless fabric, with no
interruption of the train of thought, with only one break and that
feigned ('Retombons à nos coches'). Most remarkable of all is the
conclusion which follows this abrupt jerk: instead of coaches the
American Indians had litters borne on men's shoulders, like the
one that carried Atahualpa at Cajamarca. The essay ends with a
simple narration, its grave and mournful cadences all the more
powerful for their understatement and lack of overt emotion:

Ce dernier Roy du Peru, le jour qu'il fut pris, estoit ainsi porté
sur des brancars d'or, et assis dans une cheze d'or, au milieu de sa
bataille. Autant qu'on tuoit de ces porteurs pour le faire choir à bas,
car on le vouloit prendre vif, autant d'autres, et à l'envy, prenoient
la place des morts, de façon qu'on ne le peut onques abbatre, quelque

meurtre qu'on fit de ces gens là, jusques à ce qu'un homme de cheval l'alla saisir au corps, et l'avala par terre.[1]

This is a story that has often been told but perhaps never more movingly. Apart from the emphasis on falling ('choir à bas', 'abbatre', 'avala par terre'), what is notable is the final visual effect, the gold of the litter and the chair echoing the earlier descriptions of the coaches of the Roman emperors, there in a triumphal mode, here in a tragic. More than this, nearly all the heterogeneous themes of the essay are picked up and reunited with astonishing virtuosity: the cruelty of the Spaniards, of course, and the disastrous end of a culture, but also coaches (and the litter of page 878), kings, and magnificence. The contrasted pictures of Heliogabalus in a coach drawn by four naked girls and the Inca on the shoulders of his dying warriors form only one of the distant repetitions that bind the essay together, for all its apparent formlessness. It is in fact made up largely of three extensive borrowings, from Crinitus, Justus Lipsius, and Gomara.[2] The final achievement of unity in diversity (but unity by association, not the unity of logical discourse) is all the more remarkable.

It will have been noticed that in *Des coches* (pages 878–9) the Bordeaux Copy addition on coaches in war, by bringing in the reference to the Merovingian kings and their ox-carts, introduces an easy transition at the one point (apart from the closing *tour de force*) which in the original version was slightly abrupt: the one small flaw has been removed. We have already discussed the general consequences of the numerous interpolations, but it seems desirable to say a little more about their effect on the form, which is considerable. It could be argued that critically we are only concerned with the final version. However, once the fact of interpolation is known it becomes very difficult to ignore, and we have seen that the changing text is no superficial accident but a reflection of Montaigne's innermost character as a writer. And the interpolations have a direct bearing on the question whether in the proper sense the *Essais* have a form at all (though by this time the reader may be convinced that they have). The most usual result is the one we have just observed in *Des coches*: transitions are made, corners are rounded off, detached examples are related to personal and universal experience. A straightforward case,

---

[1] III, vi: EM iii, 167; TR 894.
[2] Villey, *Sources et évolution*, ii, 298.

without the splendour of *Des coches* but in proportion much more extensively enlarged, is the early *De la tristesse,* where a string of anecdotes has been endowed by later accretions with a unified argument. In the next essay, *Nos affections s'emportent au delà de nous,* the long introduction, entirely added in 1588 and the Bordeaux Copy, gives a profound meaning to the title (man's incapacity to live in the present), which is quite absent from the original version. In *Que nostre desir s'accroit par la malaisance,* one of the most interesting among the shorter essays with its theme of the contradiction between desire and fulfilment, the final Bordeaux Copy addition completely transforms the structure by introducing a new argument (the best defence is no defence), which approaches the main theme from a different angle and above all in a different proportion. Of course there are cases, inevitably, where an interpolation produces a breach of continuity, but they are the minority. More often, it serves to bridge a gap, as we have seen in *Des coches.* Another example may show how this works in detail. In the first (1580) version of *De la solitude* Montaigne is developing the Stoic topos of the necessity of freeing oneself from the ties of family and friendship:

> Nostre mort ne nous faisoit pas assez de peur; chargeons nous encore de celle de nos fames, de nos enfans et de nos gens. Nos affaires ne nous donnoient pas assez de peine; prenons encore à nous tourmenter et rompre la teste de ceux de nos voisins et amis.
> [a quotation from Terence, on self-love, follows.]
> Or, c'est assez vescu pour autruy; vivons pour nous, au moins ce bout de vie.[1]

There is continuity here certainly, but it is strengthened by the Bordeaux Copy insertion, after the quotation:

> La solitute me semble avoir plus d'apparance et de raison à ceus qui ont doné au monde leur eage plus actif et fleurissant, suivant l'exemple de Thales.[2]

which looks forward to 'ce bout de vie'.

Interpolations like this are a special case of the links which attach themes to themes and digressive movements to the central axis (when there is one). Sometimes these links are of the clumsy and blatant type, recurrent expressions like 'pour revenir à mon propos' which draw attention to the digression. In spite of their

---

[1] I, xxxix: DB i, 202–3: TR 236(*a*).
[2] I, xxxix: EM i, 315; TR 236(*c*).

relative frequency, such phrases are scarcely noticeable and do little to break the continuous flow, which, as we have suggested, depends above all (at this verbal level) on keywords, the 'mot en un coin'. One further example may be added to those already given. The true subject of *Du jeune Caton* is, as we have seen, poetry (but illustrated by lines on Cato). The essay begins (indirect entry) with Montaigne's declaration that he does not judge other people by himself. In spite of his weakness he admires heroic souls and great virtue. In his own time virtue has become hypocrisy. Not only this, judgement is so corrupted that virtue is not even recognised. Then follows the argument against detractors which we have already discussed. At this point he introduces an apparently casual example of the attribution of false motives:

> ... ou, comme je pense plustost, pour n'avoir pas la veuë assez forte et assez nette pour concevoir la splendeur de la vertu en sa pureté naifve, ny dressée à cela: comme Plutarque dict que, de son temps, aucuns attribuoient la cause de la mort du jeune Caton à la crainte qu'il avoit eu de Cæsar . . .[1]

This is the first mention of Cato and it comes obliquely, as part of an illustration not of the main argument, with perfect naturalness, without the slightest jerk. Once this chord has been struck there is an easy progression to the virtue of Cato and the way the poets have treated it: the minor key becomes major, the 'mot en un coin' leads into the dominant theme of the essay.

We have seen that Montaigne himself frequently emphasises the disorder and formlessness of the *Essais*, and he has often been taken at his word. The notion of form seems to imply a completed whole, in which all the parts fit neatly, or at least observably, together. But the essay as he practises it is incomplete of its essence: it is always possible to add some more of these haphazard reflections, as the interpolations show (and this is another reason for considering them indispensable to any discussion of the form). In another of his most profound remarks on the character of the book, he puts the point incomparably well:

> Qui ne voit que j'ay pris une route par laquelle, sans cesse et sans travail, j'iray autant qu'il y aura d'ancre et de papier au monde?[2]

[1] I, xxxvii: EM i, 302; TR 227.
[2] III, ix: EM iii, 204; TR 922.

He is embarked on an enterprise which can go on for ever, or at least as long as his life. There was never a more absolute case of the *homo unius libri*: one book is capable of accommodating all that he might ever have to say. There is no theoretical limit to the number of essays he could write; none the less, after 1588 and to some extent before, he prefers to add to the essays already written. It thus appears that not only the book as a whole but each individual essay is infinitely expandable. Of course we can only take into account the work as we have it, but its potential expansion cannot be ignored either (or its real expansion if we compare the first with the later editions). This is an inherent and not accidental feature of the *Essais* and suffices to distinguish them from all works which are harmoniously complete and perfect, which conform to Aristotle's criterion of having a beginning, a middle and an end. We have also seen that they are distinguished from superficially similar genres by what constitutes the greatest among their many originalities, the depiction of spontaneous and moving thought as opposed to the symmetrical classifications of systematic writers. This spontaneous thought is bound to be formless, at least in an aesthetic sense.

But our argument suggests, that all this, though perfectly true, is only half the story. Again he brings the two sides together:

> Aus fins de ranger ma fantasie à resver mesmes par quelque ordre et projet, et la garder de se perdre et extravaguer au vent, il n'est que de doner corps et mettre en registre tant de menues pensées qui se presentent à elle. J'escoute à mes resveries par ce que j'ay à les enrooller [record them].[1]

This is another passage where every word counts, another of the capital statements about the nature of the work. The act of writing itself has the effect of modifying the process of thinking, and to some extent of fixing it ('de choisir et *arreter* tant de menus airs de ses agitations'). The *Essais* are the depiction of spontaneous thought, but this is not quite the same thing as spontaneous thought itself, an aesthetic dimension has been added. The essay is the ideal form for this purpose because, in fact though not, as we have seen, in potentiality, it sets a limit to endless fancies and reflections and establishes a centre round which they can move.

[1] II, xviii: EM ii, 454; TR 648(*c*).

There is a striking contrast between the circular form which we have found to be characteristic of the essay and the linear progression implied in 'de jour en jour, de minute en minute'. What is happening therefore is that thought progressing from moment to moment in a moving present is also being shaped into certain patterns which depend in the first instance on the breaking up of the undifferentiated flow of time into more manageable units. An interesting, if slightly old-fashioned, remark is made by Édouard Ruel:

> ... s'il y a des chapitres dans son livre, c'est à peine si c'est sa faute; ne distingue-t-on pas les heures dans le jour, et les jours dans l'année? Un chapitre, pour lui, c'est ... une heure ou une matinée de vie.[1]

This tells us a great deal about Montaigne but when it is formulated like this we see at once that it is not true. The essays are not temporal units (like entries in a diary) but thematic units in which the continuous flow of inner time can be successfully concentrated. To speak of a circular form is slightly misleading: the outline is too irregular. And, as we have seen, many essays do not fit exactly into this shape. There are the binary and ternary essays which have more than one centre; there are those like *De la vanité* where themes are interwoven, a highly complex pattern of varied strands emerges, and circular movements can be observed within the circle of the essay; or like *Des coches* (though it is probably unique) where one theme leads to another by association and the circular relation between them is revealed only at the end. In fact each essay has its own shape: what they have in common (apart from the early ones and the rare cases of strict logic) is the use of oblique movements, indirect links, concealed arabesques. This is certainly form but it is, as I have suggested, organic not mathematical: the form of a tree rather than that of a temple. Growth is indeed an essential property of it, the visible growth represented by the interpolations and the (almost) invisible growth of the movement from one thought to another. Form is thus an aspect of the content, developing naturally from it, and not a superimposed arrangement. We need hardly ask whether it is consciously achieved, a question which is not critically fruitful;

---

[1] *Du sentiment artistique dans la morale de Montaigne*, 1902, p. 48.

but it is not accidental, there is a sort of deliberateness about it, as we see from the way in which the interpolations tend to reinforce it. And it is clear from a number of our quotations that, whether or not he knew what he was doing, Montaigne was very well aware of what he had done; the critic, the observer of the observer, perceives and describes the process with uncanny accuracy.

K

12

Montaigne's Style

ONE way of looking at style is as form on a larger scale (I mean in the strict sense according to which a large-scale map is one that shows more detail); it is the form of the word and the sentence rather than the form of the chapter or the book. This view of style is not wholly adequate, especially with a writer like Montaigne whose large-scale and small-scale effects are so closely related, but it will do as a starting-point. We are naturally confronted with the same difficulty as before, that style is content, but as before we can ignore the theoretical problems unless they force themselves upon us.

Montaigne was deeply interested in language and style, and his numerous observations supply further evidence of his consciousness of his own procedures as a writer (which, as we have seen, is not the same as saying that the procedures themselves were conscious). His sensitivity, which we have already found reflected in his criticism, expresses itself in an appreciation of the corporal substance of words: 'J'avois trainé languissant apres des parolles Françoises, si exangues, si descharnées et si vuides de matiere et de sens . . .'.[1] but still more of their meaning, as in the passage where he describes his personal dictionary: 'J'ay un dictionaire tout à part moy: je passe le temps, quand il est mauvais et incommode; quand il est bon, je ne le veux pas passer, je le retaste, je m'y tiens.'[2] This subjection of familiar clichés to a penetrating scrutiny is one source of the originality of his language. In the same way grammatical and rhetorical categories are translated into the experience of ordinary life, as when he remarks that the

[1] I, xxvi: EM i, 190; TR 145.
[2] III, xiii: EM iii, 424; TR 1091.

280

technical terms of architecture (enumerated) are just the pieces of his kitchen door, or better still:

> Oyez dire metonomie, metaphore, allegorie, et autres tels noms de la grammaire, semble-il pas qu'on signifie quelque forme de langage rare et pellegrin? Ce sont titres qui touchent le babil de vostre chambriere.[1]

Fond as he is of words, he always looks to the reality behind them. Before Vaugelas he observes that grammar is powerless against usage,[2] and, before Malherbe, the usage he appeals to is that of simple people, the language of the Halles or the fishwives of the Petit Pont.[3] However, Malherbe is attracted by the simplicity of popular language, Montaigne rather by its vigour and picturesque elements. All this suggests that language is for him a social pheno-menon, and here he anticipates some trends in modern linguistics. Speech is an affair of two, not one: 'La parole est moitié à celuy qui parle, moitié à celuy qui l'escoute.'[4] What is said depends on the hearer, in the same way that a tennis-player's movements correspond to those of his opponent. Thus language is the funda-mental bond of society (hence his hatred of lying).[5] He is also aware of the philosophical defects of language and remarks that Pyrrhonism would require a new language to express its concep-tions adequately.[6] On the other hand, however unsatisfactory language may be from a philosophical point of view, he knows its literary power and the efficacity which great writers confer on it, an idea given wide currency by Pound and Eliot. His brilliant statement of this argument is worth considering as another ex-ample of his modernity, the direct look at things which remove him from a too narrow historical context:

> Le maniement et emploite des beaux espris donne pris à la langue, non pas l'innovant tant comme la remplissant de plus vigoreux et divers services, l'estirant et ployant. Ils n'y aportent point des mots, mais ils enrichissent les leurs, appesantissent et enfoncent leur signification et leur usage, luy aprenent des mouvements in-accoustumés. . . .[7]

This account applies very well to Montaigne himself.

---

[1] I, li: EM i, 394; TR 294(*b*).
[2] III, v: TR 853.
[3] I, xxvi: TR 169, 172.
[4] III, xiii: EM iii, 391; TR 1066.
[5] I, ix: TR 37–8; II, xviii: TR 650.
[6] II, xii: TR 508.
[7] III, v: EM iii, 112; TR 851.

Among his remarks on his own style the best known are those which emphasise its colloquial character, and in particular the famous (though not always quoted in full):

(*a*) Le parler que j'ayme, c'est un parler simple et naif, tel sur le papier qu'à la bouche: un parler succulent et nerveux, court et serré, (*c*) non tant delicat et peigné come vehement et brusque:
        Hæc demum sapiet dictio, quæ feriet,
(*a*) plustost difficile qu'ennuieux, esloingné d'affectation, desreglé, descousu et hardy; chaque lopin y face son corps; non pedantesque, non fratesque [monkish or friar-like], non pleideresque, mais plustost soldatesque, comme Suetone appelle celuy de Julius Cæsar; (*c*) et si ne sens pas bien pour quoi il l'en apele.[1]

This is another passage where every word counts and has an important bearing on the interpretation of the *Essais*. We are confronted with the same problem as with form: is it true that Montaigne's style is colloquial not literary, disjointed not composed? When, similarly, he says 'Mon stile et mon esprit vont vagabondant de mesmes',[2] is the impression of nonchalant disorder fully justified? At any rate by this time we are bound to view 'simple et naif' with considerable suspicion (it is fair to add that he does not directly assert the identity of this ideal of style with his own but it seems to be strongly implied). Apart from colloquialism the passage insists on compression ('court et serré'), and this again is taken up more fully elsewhere, in an almost equally interesting addition to *Consideration sur Ciceron*, where he maintains the primacy of sense over style in his writing:

Si suis je trompé, si guere d'autres donent plus à prendre en la matiere; et, comant que ce soit, mal ou bien, si nul escrivein l'a semée ny guere plus materielle ny au moins plus drue en son papier. Pour en ranger davantage, je n'en entasse que les testes. Que j'y atache leur suite, je multiplierai plusieurs fois ce volume.[3]

Here he brings confirmation of the limits to endless flow imposed by the essay form; what seems to be so spontaneous is in fact condensed by omission so that only the heads of the arguments are left (exaggerated but not therefore to be ignored). It will be seen that both vocabulary and syntax are involved in this pregnancy: words are chosen for their maximum concreteness and

---

[1] I, xxvi: EM i, 222; TR 171.
[2] III, ix: EM iii, 270; TR 973(*c*).
[3] I, xl: EM i, 326; TR 245(*c*).

particularity ('succulent et nerveux', 'plus drue'); sentences are pared so that only the minimum of necessary connection is made. Here again the point about syntax is expressed more fully and clearly in another essay (this pursuit of his idea of style from essay to essay in itself tells us a great deal about his form and method):

J'entends que la matiere se distingue soy-mesmes. Elle montre assez où elle se change, où elle conclud, où elle commence, où elle se reprend, sans l'entrelasser de paroles, de liaison et de cousture introduictes pour le service des oreilles foibles ou nonchallantes, et sans me gloser moymesme.[1]

This omission of logical links and substructure leads us to expect, translated into technical terms, a predominance of asyndeton and anacoluthon. More important is the end served, the allusive style which relies on the complicity of an intelligent reader (and this leads on to remarks we have already quoted about reading between the lines). But the most obvious consequence is a generally disjointed or chopped-up effect, suggested in more than one of the passages quoted. There are a number of references to this *style coupé*, contrasted with the smooth and flowing periods of artistic prose:

. . . il n'est rien si contrere à mon stile qu'une narration estendue: je me recoupe si souvant à faute de haleine, je n'ay ny composition, ny explication qui vaille. . . .[2]

J'ay naturellement un stile comique [familiar] et privé, mais c'est d'une forme mienne, inepte aux negociations publiques, comme en toutes façons est mon langage: trop serré, desordonné, couppé, particulier.[3]

It even comes into his instructions to the printer in the Bordeaux Copy, where he speaks of 'un langage coupé' and marks his preference for full stops rather than colons.[4] Similarly he expresses a liking for the minor cadence as opposed to the resounding Ciceronian close (we have already observed one or two examples in his own prose): 'Pour moy, j'ayme mieux une cadance qui tombe plus court, coupée en yambes [iambic feet].'[5] His models, though this is also his natural style, are Sallust and Seneca.[6] Here he

---

1 III, ix: EM iii, 271; TR 974.
2 I, xxi: EM i, 134; TR 105(c).
3 I, xl: EM i, 327–8; TR 246(b).
4 EM i, 428.
5 II, x: EM ii, 113; TR 395.
6 II, xvii: TR 621.

represents not only his own inclinations but a general reaction against the Ciceronianism of the early Renaissance and in favour of Seneca's terser language, a reaction which has been studied by Morris Croll, followed by others, and identified by him with the baroque style.[1] All this is extremely coherent. It does, however, seem to contradict what we have discovered about the continuity of his writing and his representation of time. Of course, so far we have been studying what he says about his style and though this is privileged it is not necessarily true or not necessarily the whole truth. One addition in the Bordeaux Copy does strike a rather different note:

> ... aumoins si je dois nommer stile un parler informe et sans regle, un jargon populere et un proceder sans definition, sans partition, sans conclusion, trouble, à la guise de celluy d'Amafanius et de Rabirius.[2]

The reference to Amafanius and Rabirius is from Cicero, who says much the same thing about their lack of definitions, divisions, and conclusions. Montaigne still stresses the disorder of his style and the absence of logical connections, but a rather different light is thrown on these features by the reference to the lack of formal divisions and conclusions, which suggests a continuity not altogether at one with terseness and disjointedness.

Before we try to resolve the difficulty it is perhaps necessary to say a word about the Gasconisms for which Montaigne excuses himself in the dedication of the Sabunde translation as well as in the *Essais* and for which he was attacked by some contemporaries, including Pasquier.

> Mon langage françois est alteré, et en la prononciation et ailleurs, par la barbarie de mon creu: je ne vis jamais homme des contrées de deçà qui ne sentit bien evidemment son ramage et qui ne blessast les oreilles pures françoises.[3]

The question has been studied by Robert Lafont, who distinguishes between the elements of different south-western dialects in Montaigne's writing.[4] He concludes that there are a number

---

[1] 'The baroque style in prose' (1929), reprinted in '*Attic*' and baroque prose style, 1969. On Montaigne's style in general see F. Gray, *Le style de Montaigne*, 1958; Zoe Samaras, *The comic element of Montaigne's style*, 1970.

[2] II, xvii: EM ii, 415–6; TR 620(c).

[3] II, xvii: EM ii, 418; TR 622.

[4] '*Que le gascon y aille si le français n'y peut aller:* réflexions sur la situation linguistique et stylistique de l'œuvre de Montaigne', *Le français moderne*, xxxvi (1968).

of Gascon, or more strictly Occitan, words like *bonnetade, harpade, stropiat, bihorre*; some syntactic features like the transitive use of intransitive verbs (one of Pasquier's criticisms); some variations from standard French genders like *couple* and *rencontre* treated as masculine. All this does not amount to very much and for the modern reader the Gasconisms are for the most part absorbed into the general idiosyncrasy or archaism of the language. As a broad principle, open to many objections, it may be said that effects of style spring from the impact (not necessarily conscious) on the reader and that those which require elaborate historical reconstruction do not really exist. The case of Latinisms is rather different because they are still very noticeable. The fact that Latin was more or less Montaigne's native language does raise the question how far his French style was influenced by it. In fact Latinisms of vocabulary and syntax are present in abundance and must be regarded as an outstanding characteristic of his style. However, he says that he no longer finds it easy to talk or write Latin,[1] and it is doubtful whether the degree of Latinisation exceeds that of other humanistically trained writers of the period. Mlle de Gournay replies to criticisms on this score, absurdly, that most French words come from Latin but also, sensibly, that extraordinary thoughts demand extraordinary means of expression.[2]

Among these means vocabulary is, if not the most important, certainly the most obvious. Gasconisms and Latinisms are part of an effort to enlarge vocabulary to the limits. There is no concordance (a vast undertaking in itself) and the Lexique of the Édition Municipale, though most useful, is sadly incomplete. But even without statistics it can be asserted that sheer size and variety are the first qualities to be taken into account. The range extends from the very learned, even obscure, to slang, and includes the technical, the popular and the dialectal (as we have just seen). Examples of learned words, and Latinisms, are *exagite, inculcation, titillation, confabulations*, or diminutives like *appendicules, adminicules*. Technical terms are occasionally legal (*hypotheques*), grammatical or rhetorical, more often military (*argolots, estacade, bicoque*), very often medical, where his own experience is clearly reflected (*ureteres, micraines, scarification, apostumes, opiate*). Among familiar or popular words are *caignart* (hovel), *embuffler* (to lead by the nose), *capirotade* (stew), *tintouiner* (to

1 II, xvii: TR 622.
2 *Les essais*, 1595, Preface, ã3ᵛ.

ring). Neologisms and coinages are quite numerous, though, as always, difficult to pinpoint with certainty. Definite examples seem to be *ombrelles* (parasols in Italy)[1] and *quartelets* ('tant nous avons de tiercelets et quartelets de Roys').[2]

These are scattered illustrations. But mere lists of words, even if complete, are bound to be arid and lifeless. To appreciate the richness of Montaigne's vocabulary it is necessary to look at words in juxtaposition, actively at work in the sentence, as in the description of a ragged beggar 'aussi scarrebillat [merry] que tel qui se tient emmitoné dans les martes'[3] or, more fully developed:

> Je vois avec despit en plusieurs mesnages monsieur revenir maussade et tout marmiteus du tracas des affaires, environ midy, que madame est encore après à se coiffer et atiffer en son cabinet.[4]

The effect depends on the accumulation of unusual and highly concrete words. The second example is marked by strong alliteration (*mesnages, monsieur, maussade, marmiteus, midy, madame,* not to speak of *coiffer* and *atiffer*). Alliteration is one of the most prominent features of Montaigne's prose: here it further emphasises just those words which stand out anyway and brings them into a rhythmical unison with each other and the rest of the sentence. Later corrections show with particular clarity the preference for the rarer or more vigorous word. Thus 'je vainqueray ce silence'[5] in the 1588 edition becomes in the Bordeaux Copy 'je vainqueray ta taciturnité';[6] 'apres avoir rendu de son ventre'[7] becomes 'apres avoir vomi de son ventre';[8] 'contenance magistrale'[9] becomes 'troigne magistrale'.[10]

The enrichment of vocabulary by all available means, especially technical, learned and dialectal terms, is in line with the programme of the Pléiade, and though Montaigne objects to affected novelty in language as in everything else it may be thought

---

[1] III, ix: TR 951. Cf. Bloch and Wartburg, *Dictionnaire étymologique de la langue française,* 1968, which gives this as the first appearance of the word.

[2] I, xliii: EM i, 347; TR 261(*b*). See also EM (Lexique), where neologisms are starred; the starring of course represents the state of knowledge in 1933.

[3] I, xxxvi: EM i, 295; TR 222.

[4] III, ix: TM iii, 243; TR 952.

[5] I, i: MJ i, 8.

[6] EM i, 7; TR 14.

[7] III, vi: MJ vi, 56.

[8] EM iii, 156; TR 884.

[9] III, xiii: MJ vii, 45.

[10] EM iii, 394; TR 1068.

that he is adopting their principles, which is partly true. Certainly both stand in sharp contrast with Malherbe's reforms and the restriction of vocabulary which characterised the seventeenth century and classical French generally (this in spite of Montaigne's anticipation of Malherbe in the appeal to popular speech). There is, however, an essential difference. For the Pléiade the enrichment of the French language was a high and deliberate purpose and its results were often grand but laboured and sometimes slightly ridiculous. For Montaigne the enrichment was an accomplished fact and no theoretical aim was required. He finds a language enriched and continues to enrich it. His immense vocabulary is no poetic ornament but one more instrument (the most important no doubt) in his total grasp of reality.

Discussions of vocabulary tend to concentrate on nouns as carrying the main weight of substantial meaning, and most of our examples have followed this tendency. Another characteristic of Montaigne's style is his mastery of all the parts of speech which are capable of contributing actively to the meaning of the sentence. This is especially true of verbs, often the deadest element in a writer's equipment but here astonishingly varied and lively. Verbs like *baguenauder*, *se gorgiaser* ('ils se gorgiasent en la nouvelleté'),[1] *mercurializer* or *tournebouler* ('qu'il se tourneboule et tracasse à sa fantasie')[2] display the qualities of vigour and rarity we have already observed. He shows great ingenuity in exploiting or perhaps inventing new verb forms by the use of affixes:

je naturaliserois l'art autant come ils artialisent la nature.[3]

O que n'ay je la faculté de ce songeur de Cicero qui, songeant embrasser une *garse*, trouva qu'il s'estoit deschargé de sa pierre emmi ses draps! Les mienes me *desgarsent* estrangement [approximately 'my gall-stones turn me away from any thoughts of girls']![4]

Almost more striking is the precision with which quite ordinary verbs are used, frequently in order to make psychological and moral discriminations, as on the death of Moneins:

sa faute ... ce fut d'avoir pris une voye de summission et de

---

[1] III, v: EM iii, 112; TR 851.
[2] II, xxxvii: EM ii, 579; TR 739. The Bordeaux Copy substitutes *tourneboule* for the more ordinary *tremousse*, but the alliteration is preserved.
[3] III, v: EM iii, 113; TR 852.
[4] II, xxxvii: EM ii, 580; TR 740(c). Italics mine.

mollesse, et d'avoir voulu endormir cette rage, plustost en suivant que en guidant, et en requerant plustost qu'en remontrant.[1]

Adjectives are also surprising and appropriate as in 'la santé mesme, si sucrée'[2] or (of sexual conquests) 'il y a des jouyssances ethiques et languissantes' (*ethiques* is modern French *étiques*, 'emaciated' or 'shrunken'). What he does constantly is to break the collocation of stock adjective and expected noun and substitute his own vision for the conventional one: 'je loüe une vie glissante, sombre et muette'.[3] Adverbs too are capable of conveying the principal meaning of a sentence. We have seen the importance of *naturellement* at the end of *De l'experience*. The whole meaning is contained in the adverbs in 'Ils disent assez veritablement et utilement, s'ils disent ingenieusement'.[4] More thoroughgoing, though perhaps less effective because of its excess, is:

(b) Je dis pompeusement et opulemment l'ignorance, et dys la science megrement et piteusement; (c) accessoirement cete cy et accidentalement, cele la expressement et principalement.[5]

Eight adverbs in a short sentence, half of them in the interpolation: it is easy to see that, as in other such cases, the predominance of adverbs puts all the emphasis on the mode of thinking and that this interests Montaigne as much as the thought itself. Exclusive preoccupation with imagery in studies of style has often diverted attention from linguistic features like this, which may be just as significant. There is not much to be said about pronouns, with one important exception. The first person *je* is naturally used a great deal. However, he is equally if not more fond of the plural *nous* and *nos*. Sometimes this means the French, more often Christians or Europeans, sometimes his contemporaries (often opposed to antiquity), sometimes the old, sometimes the male sex, sometimes humanity. From this variation between *je* and *nous* and between the different senses of *nous* we can discern in microcosm the continual movement between the self-portrait and the human condition in its multiple aspects.

We can now consider in rather more detail one quality of Montaigne's vocabulary which we have seen to be central, its

[1] I, xxiv: EM i, 167; TR 129–30(b).
[2] III, x: EM iii, 289; TR 988(c).
[3] III, x: EM iii, 303; TR 999. There are perceptive remarks on the use of adjectives in Gray, *Le style de Montaigne*, pp. 43–4.
[4] III, vi: EM iii, 145; TR 876.
[5] III, xii: EM iii, 350; TR 1034.

concreteness. This will lead inevitably to imagery. But we are confronted at once with a difficulty, perhaps only of terminology, perhaps not. In modern criticism and stylistics the word 'image' refers almost entirely to figures of comparison or substitution, chiefly simile, metaphor, metonymy and synecdoche. Such figures are usually though not always concrete. However, there are innumerable cases where concrete words are used quite literally, with no figure involved (unless it is hypotyposis or vivid description, but that is hardly figurative in an ordinary sense). Yet the effect is not notably different from that of imagery. In a writer like Montaigne the difficulty is even more acute because, as we have seen, his whole apparatus of thought and way of thinking are concrete (thought and image are one, to quote Sainte-Beuve again). From this point of view it might be argued that every concrete expression that occurs in the *Essais* is an image, is metaphor or parable or apologue, is a means of rendering abstract thought in terms of physical existence. But even this suggests a separation which is not always or usually present. In short it is often very hard to decide whether a given expression is an image in the technical sense or not and the answer may depend on whether we take it in conjunction with the immediate or a broader context. The best way to proceed will be to look at what actually goes on, as far as possible without preconceptions.

Beginning with examples of what at least appears to be concreteness for its own sake, we have noticed Montaigne's love of magnificence. Even in the grim story of the queen of Naples who strangles her husband he cannot resist the physical beauty of objects:

Jane, Roine de Naples, fit estrangler Andreosse, son premier mary, aus grilles de sa fenestre à tout un laz d'or et de soie tissue de sa main propre. . . .[1]

This is a straightforward case. A more ample one is the expedition of Dionysius to the Olympic Games:

. . . aveq des charriots surpassans tous autres en magnificence, il envoia aussi des poetes et des musiciens pour presanter ses vers, avec des tantes et pavillons dorez et tapissés Royalemant.[2]

The rich weight of the words corresponds to the theme. But this is from the essay on presumption and the contrast between this

1 III, v: EM iii, 129; TR 864(c).
2 II, xvii: EM ii, 413; TR 619(c).

splendour and the disastrous performance at the games themselves epitomises the argument of the essay: the description is
not gratuitous. This becomes still clearer in *Des coches*, where
the warlike magnificence of the Spaniards is contrasted with the
simplicity of the Indians, 'qui, pour le miracle de la lueur d'un
miroir ou d'un cousteau, alloyent eschangeant une grande richesse
en or et en perles . . .'.[1] We cannot exactly say that the mirror and
the knife, the gold and the pearls, are symbolic, but the whole
clash between two cultures is concentrated in a series of visual and
tactile impressions (of which this is only part). The liking for
magnificence appears also in the *Journal du voyage,* for example
in the description of the Pope's retinue (again an extract only):

> vint cinq chevaus . . . parés et houssés de drap d'or, fort richemant
> accommodés, et dix ou douze mulets, troussés de velours cramoisi
> . . . quatre homes à cheval portoint, au bout de certeins batons,
> couverts de velours rouge et dorés par le pouignet et par les bous,
> quatre chapeaus rouges.[2]

The repetition of gold and red is characteristic and produces a
brilliant picture. Such passages, however, in the *Essais* as in the
Journal, though numerous, are also exceptional and perhaps the
more striking for this reason. Concrete objects are more often
of the homely kind, as in the enumeration where Montaigne is
proclaiming his adaptability to different national habits: 'Soyent
des assietes d'estain, de bois, de terre, bouilly ou rosty, beurre ou
huyle de nois, ou d'olive, chaut ou froit . . .'.[3] Again, though there
is no symbolism, these words take on an almost emblematic
character (we might compare the use of foods, macaroni, frog or
rosbif, as national designations) and help to concretise the travel
theme of *De la vanité.* In this case visual and tactile elements are
present, and temperature also. We have already seen Montaigne's
personal sensitivity to smells and this naturally finds expression
in his descriptions, as in the wonderful cooks of the King of Tunis
(from *Des senteurs* of course):

> On farcissoit ses viandes de drogues odoriferantes . . . et quand
> on les despeçoit, remplissoint non sulement la sale, mais toutes les
> chambres de son palais, et jusques aus maisons du voisinage, d'une
> tressouefve vapur qui ne se perdoit pas si tost.[4]

[1] III, vi: EM iii, 160; TR 888.
[2] TR 1235.
[3] III, ix: EM iii, 258; TR 964.
[4] I, lv: EM i, 407; TR 302(c).

Concreteness must not in fact be confused with solidity: it includes all that is manifest to the senses, however intangible, like smells or the *lueur* just quoted, the gleam of the knife and the mirror rather than the objects themselves. All the same solidity and plenitude are essential characteristics of Montaigne's style and the world it creates, a world densely packed with concrete objects which have their own substantial existence quite apart from their functions as illustrations, examples, metaphors and so on. This plenitude does not, admittedly, derive only from the use of concrete words.

So far we have been looking at cases towards one end of the spectrum, where concrete words are used more or less for their own sake, though even then it often proved difficult to detach them completely from their context of abstract thought. As we move towards the other pole, that of figurative expression or imagery, the difficulty naturally increases. We can begin with an example which is very like those already discussed (the argument is that kings are no happier than anyone else): 'Ce ciel de lict, tout enflé d'or et de perles, n'a aucune vertu à rappaiser les tranchées d'une verte colique.'[1] This is not metaphor, it is not quite metonymy, though very close to it (the gilded bed standing like a throne as the concrete representation of royal splendour), since the bed is particularised by the demonstrative *ce* and we have to accept it as literally present in the imagined bedchamber of an emperor. The image is nearer still with the illustration of fear in *De la peur*:

Mais, parmy les soldats mesme ... combien de fois a elle changé un troupeau de brebis en esquadron de corselets? des roseaux et des cannes en gens-d'armes et lanciers? nos amis en nos ennemis? et la croix blanche à la rouge?[2]

The abstract emotion of fear is now embodied in a series of visual objects; also and more strikingly in a series of transformations which almost take the form of the simile. But these are hallucinations and as descriptions of hallucinations are to be interpreted quite literally. Yet the imaginative process is exactly, and the formal structure almost, that of simile or metaphor. The characteristic note of colour at the end hardly needs further comment. A last example, again on travel in *De la vanité*, looks simpler:

[1] I, xlii: EM i, 337; TR 253.
[2] I, xviii: EM i, 92; TR 75.

Absent, je ... sentirois moins lors la ruyne d'une tour que je ne faicts present la cheute d'une ardoise.[1]

Is this admirable rendering of the different proportions assumed by disaster when one is far away or close at hand an image? The element of comparison is fully present and the form now is exactly that of a certain type of simile. The answer is no, none the less, because of course the collapse of the tower and the fall of the slate are both regarded as equally real events. However, the effect on the reader is scarcely distinguishable from that of a true simile. This, and most of the other examples, can certainly be considered an image in the wider though not in the technical sense. What our argument goes to show is that Montaigne's well-known way of thinking in images must be extended beyond the use of tropes to his whole array of concrete depiction of the world.

Though concrete words predominate and give the style of the *Essais* its fundamental character, this is not to say that abstract words are rare, or could be in a book which deals to such an extent with philosophical problems. There is not much point in illustrating this at length and one main example will suffice, among many like it:

... nous avons pour nostre part l'inconstance, l'irresolution, l'incertitude, le deuil, la superstition, la solicitude des choses à venir, ... l'ambition, l'avarice, la jalousie, l'envie, les appetits desreglez, forcenez et indomptables, la guerre, la mensonge, la desloyauté, la detraction et la curiosité.[2]

These abstracts are not unmixed with semi-concrete expressions and in general the use of abstracts does not diminish the effect of solidity and plenitude. One more example will make this plain (on the deceits of female beauty):

Nous avons beau sçavoir que ces tresses sont empruntées d'un page ou d'un laquais; que cette rougeur est venue d'Espaigne, et cette blancheur et polisseure de la mer Oceane. ...[3]

The syntactical handling of the abstracts gives them life and flexibility and they follow a concrete term on the same syntactical level (*tresses*). More than this, they themselves refer to concrete objects (cosmetics) and behave like them (coming from Spain or the

---

[1] III, ix: EM iii, 216; TR 931.
[2] II, xii: EM ii, 204: TR 465.
[3] II, xii: EM ii, 356–7; TR 578.

ocean). Yet they have not lost their abstract character, redness and whiteness are what he is talking about, but there is a leap across an unexpressed middle term (such as rouge). The substitution of abstract for concrete is technically metonymy but the dramatically ambiguous effect here goes far beyond the conventional employment of the figure. Such leaps and concealed ellipses are typical of Montaigne but less frequent than the straightforward juxtaposition of an abstract and a concrete statement. Again one example will stand for a general procedure. Possessions are no use unless they can be enjoyed:

Les biens de la fortune, tous tels qu'ils sont, encores faut il avoir du sentimant pour les savourer. C'est le jouïr, non le posseder, qui nous rend heureux: [a quotation from Horace]. Il est un sot, son goust est mousse et hebeté; il n'en jouit non plus qu'un morfondu de la douceur du vin Grec, ou qu'un cheval de la richesse du harnois duquel on l'a paré.[1]

Obviously the abstract statement of an important theme, closely connected with the moral centre of the *Essais*, is immediately translated into concrete terms, and this typifies the constant interaction of abstract and concrete which we have seen to be the governing principle of Montaigne's thought. But we can appreciate also, in the first sentence, why the large number of abstracts does not detract from the densely concrete impression of the whole: the use of the verbal nouns *jouïr* and *posseder*, as well as the sense of *savourer*, explain this. The thought is already concrete enough even before translation; then, of course, the brilliant illustrations, the horse and its trappings particularly, give it still sharper definition and more vivid existence.

We can now approach imagery proper with rather less assurance that we know exactly what an image is or how abstract and concrete are distinguished in Montaigne. The subject has been quite fully dealt with elsewhere,[2] and we can be relatively brief. In particular Thibaudet's list of sources of imagery (vehicles) means that we need not spend much time on the details of classification. Montaigne, like other writers, draws his images for example from everyday life, from nature, from physiology and pathology (the last is especially characteristic of his time as a

---

1 I, xlii: EM i, 338; TR 254(*a*).
2 Thibaudet, *Montaigne*, pp. 505 ff.; Gray, *Le style de Montaigne*, pp. 151 ff.; and the articles of M. Baraz and Mrs C. E. Clark. Cf. also pp. 180–2 above.

comparison with Shakespeare or d'Aubigné will show). In the first group we find further evidence of the way in which intellectual and moral life is brought into close contact not only with the physical but with the most trivial and humdrum objects, like the description of the tyrannical frowns of old age as scarecrows in a hemp-field ('vrais espouvantails de cheneviere'),[1] or of the rhetorician's trade of making small things look big: 'C'est un cordonnier qui sçait faire de grands souliers à un petit pied.'[2] Nature images often perform the same function, as in the comparison of an active mind in an aged body to mistletoe on a dead tree[3] or, much more complex, original and poetic, the psychological distinction between external actions and inner being expressed in terms of springing water: 'Ce ne sount que filetz et pouintes d'eau fine rejalies d'un fond au demurant limoneus et poisant.'[4] But nature also serves to magnify, to introduce a wider dimension, as in the easy approach to virtue, 'd'une pente facile et polie, come est celle des voutes celestes',[5] or his state of mind oppressed by old age and illness: 'Je gauchis tout doucement, et desrobe ma veuë de ce ciel orageux et nubileux que j'ay devant moy.'[6] There is something again distinctly Romantic about this latter metaphor. Pathological images, like the comparison of war-torn France to a diseased body, are particularly abundant and in themselves highly conventional. *De la force de l'imagination* is notable for its fever images, which constitute an appropriate dominant of the essay. *Des mauvais moyens employez à bonne fin* offers a still more striking example. More deeply characteristic, though still conventional, are images of digestion and nutrition, applied to education, reading, learning, and finally to the *Essais* themselves.[7] When he writes 'Que nous sert-il d'avoir la panse pleine de viande, si elle ne se digere? si elle ne se trans-forme en nous? si elle ne nous augmente et fortifie?'[8] his rather ponderous identification of learning with digestion was as much a commonplace then as it is now. But when he says about the composition of an essay (*Des noms*) 'Quelque diversité d'herbes qu'il y ait, tout s'enveloppe sous le nom de

---

[1] II, viii: EM ii, 80; TR 373.
[2] I, li: EM i, 391; TR 292(*b*).
[3] III, v: TR 821.
[4] III, ii: EM iii, 28; TR 787(*c*).
[5] I, xxvi: EM i, 209; TR 161(*c*). Cf. p. 143 above.
[6] III, v: EM iii, 70; TR 818.
[7] On the conventional background of these pathological and nutritive images see Clark, 'Montaigne and the imagery of political discourse'.
[8] I, xxv: EM i, 177; TR 136(*a*).

salade',[1] the lightness of touch is accompanied by the renewal of a stock image. Above all he is not afraid to pursue the idea of digestion well beyond its conventional limits. We have already come upon the comparison of the *Essais* to excrement. The most vivid example of this recurrent image in the Third Book is perhaps 'Ce sont icy...des excremens d'un vieil esprit, dur tantost, tantost lache, et tousjours indigeste'.[2] His imagery, like the book in general, conveys the full range of human experience: nothing is too high or too low for him in affirming the relation between the life of the mind and the life of the body.

Some images, though still with a conventional basis, are given a more original bias or enter into a more organic relation with the central themes. One group among them is that drawn from art and especially architecture. The image of the state as a building is another commonplace, studied by Mrs Clark, and we have already come upon one example.[3] The same is true of the design of the universe and its great architect, particularly frequent in the *Apologie*. But individual images escape this conventional categorisation, like the description of the approach to love:

> Plus il y a de marches et degrez, plus il y a de hauteur et d'honneur au dernier siege. Nous nous devrions plaire d'y estre conduicts, comme il se faict aux palais magnifiques, par divers portiques et passages, longues et plaisantes galleries, et plusieurs destours

This produces a remarkable sensation of depth and movement, like 'les profondeurs opaques de ses replis internes' and the labyrinthine form of the *Essais* themselves. Imaginatively there is a kinship with Baudelaire's architectural imagery, though the immediate inspiration probably comes from the enchanted palace of the romances, Ariosto perhaps especially.[5] A full stylistic analysis even of this fairly brief sentence would take a long time, but it is worth noting how the sense is supported by the subtle pattern of alliteration, often in Montaigne a signal of heightened poetic intensity. Of other arts painting is the most often employed, and we have seen that it can be regarded in some ways as the central metaphor of the book (the writer as painter, 'c'est moy que je peins'). Here one example, not connected with the self-portrait,

1 I, xlvi: EM i, 354; TR 265(*a*).
2 III, ix: EM iii, 204; TR 923.
3 See p. 237 above.
4 III, v: EM iii, 122; TR 859.
5 *Orlando furioso*, canto XII.

may illustrate not only, again, his interest in the technique of painting but also the unexpectedness of his *rapprochements,* the wide angle of so many of his images. These are physicians who have not themselves had the disease they are treating and so cannot tell what it is really like:

> comme celuy qui peint les mers, les escueils et les ports, estant assis sur sa table et y faict promener le modele d'un navire en toute seureté.[1]

Music appears in the harmony of the spheres and is thus related to both the natural images of the heavens and the architectural images of the design of the universe. Here again we have a key image which does a great deal to illuminate the *Essais* as a whole, as in this rendering of a favourite idea, the primacy of judgement and wisdom in a man over merely specialised experiences:

> Come, en un concert d'instrumans, on n'oit pas un lut, un' espinete et la flutte, on oyt une harmonie en globe, l'assemblage et le fruict de tout cet amas.[2]

The thought is banal enough in itself but beautifully worked out. More than this, it suggests the harmony underlying the contradictions in Montaigne. With painting, the most frequent source of imagery drawn from the arts is most probably acting and the theatre. Again this is widespread at the time: Shakespeare offers obvious parallels, some of them quite close to Montaigne. In most cases what appeals to him is the contrast between the role and the man, the mask and the reality. The relationship is not, however, a simple one. He is not, like La Rochefoucauld, Molière and the classical moralists, tearing off the mask of other people's hypocrisy but showing how pretence works in everyone, including himself: sympathy rather than condemnation is uppermost. The main consideration is that we should not allow the inner reality to be overwhelmed by the part we are obliged to play:

> (*b*) La plus part de nos vacations [professions or occupations] sont farcesques. . . . Il faut jouer deuement nostre rolle, mais comme rolle d'un personnage emprunté. Du masque et de l'apparence il n'en faut pas faire une essence réelle, ny de l'estranger le propre. . . .
> (*c*) C'est asses de s'enfariner le visage, sans s'enfariner la poictrine.[3]

---

[1] III, xiii: EM iii, 380; TR 1057.
[2] III, viii: EM iii, 187; TR 909(*c*).
[3] III, x: EM iii, 290; TR 989.

It is hard to know what to admire most here: the constant inter-mingling of figurative and literal, so that we are never quite sure which is which (as we have suggested, an expression of Montaigne's deepest attitude); the psychological and moral pene-tration; or the insight into the workings of society, treated at once seriously and contemptuously, the instrument of analysis being one of the most commonplace of images. Superior strictly as an image, in the evocative treatment of the vehicle, and again typical in its complex reversal of the image itself and of the expected development of the tenor is:

Car, comme les joueurs de comedie, vous les voyez sur l'eschaffaut faire une mine de Duc et d'Empereur; mais, tantost après, les voyla devenuz valets et crocheteurs miserables, qui est leur nayfve et originelle condition: aussi l'Empereur, duquel la pompe vous esblouit en public . . . voyez le derriere le rideau, ce n'est rien qu'un homme commun, et, à l'adventure, plus vil que le moindre de ses subjects.[1]

This shows very well how imagery is a process of transmutation: the actors are turned into dukes and emperors and then turned back again (but this seems to be literal, though the whole essence of theatre may be regarded as metaphorical): then the emperor himself is exposed to the same process and turned into an actor (this is figurative perhaps but it is also real). In fact the distinction between figurative and literal has become totally blurred, and the distinction between appearance and reality. Imagery here is used at the highest poetic level. It also shows that style is an aspect of content. This is from *De l'inequalité qui est entre nous* and the basic equality of all men, the democratic feeling we have found in Montaigne, receives its most disturbing expression in the complexities of the simile.

The most important group, however, from the thematic point of view, is that composed of images of travel and movement, and with them we are still closer to the heart of the *Essais*. Again the basis is purely conventional: it seems natural to speak of thinking or writing in terms of a journey started or accomplished (moving from point to point, making a detour, arriving at a conclusion, looking back, and so on). Thus when Montaigne says 'Je marche plus seur et plus ferme à mont qu'à val',[2] there is nothing very remarkable about it, except that it reflects the general mobility

[1] I, xlii: EM i, 336; TR 253(*a*).
[2] I, xxvi: EM i, 195. TR 149.

of his thought and the differences of tempo.[1] But sometimes such images are sustained in long developments. *De la præsumption* is particularly interesting for the continuous use of comparisons (travel, road, ship, and so on) to denote mental phenomena, in this case his own character and conduct:

> Tout ainsi que des chemins, j'en evite volontiers les costez pandans et glissans, et me jette dans le battu le plus boueux et enfondrant, d'où je ne puisse aller plus bas, et y cherche seurté: aussi j'ayme les malheurs tous purs . . . qui, du premier saut, me poussent droictement en la souffrance.[2]

As often in his explicit comparisons the vehicle precedes the tenor, which gives greater prominence to the image than to the literal sense: it is a poetic rather than a prosaic order. In this case the vehicle is reintroduced into the tenor ('du premier saut') with the characteristic blurring effect between the two parts of the image. The hackneyed notion of life itself as a journey gives rise to some less developed but at least equally striking images:

> La goutte, la gravelle, l'indigestion sont simptomes des longues années, come des longs voiages la chalur, les pluies et les vens.[3]

The perfectly balanced chiasmus, with three items on each side of the fulcrum, is elaborately rhetorical, though the beauty of the image and the familiarity of its components may obscure the fact that it is anything but spontaneously colloquial. Even the simplicity of the comparison of youth and age: 'elle va vers le monde, vers le credit; nous en venons',[4] with its repetitions and antithesis is not quite as simple as it looks. It is certainly powerful and moving.

With movement, and in apparent opposition to it, may be associated another numerous group, that of barrier images, employed to represent the constraints imposed on human thought and conduct by custom and authority. As we should expect, the treatment of the image is ambiguous: sometimes it is favourable, sometimes unfavourable.

> Il faut contraindre l'homme et le renger dans les barrieres de cette police [of nature].[5]

[1] On which see Gray, *Le style de Montaigne*, pp. 70 ff.
[2] II, xvii: EM ii, 426; TR 627-8.
[3] III, xiii: EM iii, 393; TR 1067(*c*).
[4] III, v: EM iii, 72; TR 820.
[5] II, xii: EM ii, 168; TR 437(*a*).

On a raison de donner à l'esprit humain les barrieres les plus contraintes qu'on peut.[1]

But in the second case he goes on to explain the difficulty of erecting and maintaining such barriers against the fluidity of the human mind. In the last analysis the breaking down of barriers receives stronger emphasis:

Où que je vueille donner, il me faut forcer quelque barriere de la coustume, tant ell'a soigneusement bridé toutes nos avenues.[2]

In spite of the ideal desirability of restraint it is hardly possible, and Montaigne's dominant theme is liberation. It is easy to see that his moral and political position is to a large extent concentrated in his handling of this single metaphor.

In studying isolated images as we have necessarily done we miss something of the highest importance, their succession and interrelation. In Montaigne as in Shakespeare they tend to pour out in a spate without too much regard for consistency. One example, unfortunately too long to quote in full, though brilliant, is not exceptional. In *De l'inequalité qui est entre nous* he argues, as we have seen, that a man should be judged by his intrinsic worth, not by external trappings. To give concrete life to this idea he uses ten metaphorical expressions (image-counting is not an exact science of course): a horse and its harness; a greyhound and its collar; a bird (hawk) and its leash and bells; a cat ('un chat en poche'); a horse again (stripped for sale); a sword and its sheath; high pattens; a statue and its pedestal; stilts; and shirt-sleeves: 'qu'il mette à part ses richesses et honneurs, qu'il se presente en chemise.'[3] This is a case of serial or consecutive imagery. Interrelation is more complex and therefore harder to illustrate but we might take a relatively simple example:

c'est l'orgueil qui jette l'homme à quartier des voyes communes, qui luy fait embrasser les nouvelletez, et aimer mieux estre chef d'une trouppe errante et desvoyée au sentier de perdition, aymer mieux estre regent et precepteur d'erreur et de mensonge, que d'estre disciple en l'eschole de verité, se laissant mener et conduire par la main d'autruy, à la voye batuë et droicturiere.[4]

---

1 II, xii: EM ii, 306; TR 541(*a*).
2 I, xxxvi: EM i, 294: TR 221(*a*).
3 I, xlii: EM i, 335; TR 251.
4 II, xii: EM ii, 220; TR 478.

The two images, the rebel chieftain (combined with the travel motif) and the teacher of error, interlock and the second is enclosed in the first; the pictorial effect is considerable. Incidentally there are echoes here of the Sabunde translation, for example: 'celuy ... qui s'est jetté à quartier et hors de la carriere commune de toutes les creatures ...'.[1]

A vital and sometimes neglected aspect of imagery is its syntax, the way it is introduced, and attached to the sequence of the text. We can confine ourselves to one or two methods which seem characteristic of Montaigne, leaving aside the majority which are perfectly ordinary, like the use of *comme*. Some examples have already appeared in the discussion of types of image, like the placing of the vehicle before the tenor. A frequent alternative to *comme* or *ainsi que* in the introduction of similes is *c'est*, as in the description of life without La Boétie:

> si je la compare, dis-je, toute aux quatre années qu'il m'a esté donné de jouyr de la douce compagnie et societé de ce personnage, ce n'est que fumée, ce n'est qu'une nuit obscure et ennuyeuse.[2]

What happens here is that very heavy emphasis is laid on the machinery of comparison, a typically prosaic effect, and in this way the language of mysticism in the vehicle is kept in check. On the other hand, as always when *c'est* is used, the identification of the two terms is more complete than with an expression of comparison and syntactically the vehicle occupies the main, not a subordinate, clause. The principal result is therefore to enhance the prominence of the image and with it the poetic feeling. We have already looked at several examples of the sustained or epic simile, in which all the consequential details are drawn out in order to build a picture. This is less typical of Montaigne than the sudden illuminating metaphor but it does occur often: it is clearly rhetorical, literary, and at variance with the procedures of everyday speech. More interesting is the concealed comparison. *De l'institution des enfans* begins: 'Je ne vis jamais pere, pour teigneux ou bossé que fut son fils, qui laissast de l'avoüer.'[3] This appears to lead straight in to the subject of education, and in a way it does, but it is in fact an analogy, revealed at the begnning of the next sentence but one ('Aussi moy'), for Montaigne's own

---

[1] *Œuvres complètes*, ed. Armaingaud, ix, 128.
[2] I, xxviii: EM i, 252; TR 192.
[3] I, xxvi: EM i, 187; TR 144.

relation to his work. Again we see the absence of a normal subordinating link, like *comme,* and the substitution of a delayed coordinating link. The image thus acquires a much greater degree of self-sufficiency: in fact it is some time before we realise that it is an image at all. The ambiguity is typical but so is the harmony between image and general theme.

So far we have considered vocabulary and imagery, the latter slightly out of its conventional place because, though it cannot be limited to the single word, it contributes massively to the plenitude of Montaigne's style and his concrete grasp of the world. We can now proceed from single words to groups of words. The most immediately obvious feature of Montaigne's style, even to a casual reader, is the doubling of words, usually, not always, synonyms or near-synonyms. We find it in the opening sentence of the first essay: 'La plus commune façon d'amollir les cœurs de ceux qu'on a offensez . . . c'est de les esmouvoir par summission *à commiseration et à pitié*',[1] and from that point on such pairs verge on the innumerable.[2] The usage is not of course confined to Montaigne. It is characteristic of, and perhaps originated in, the language of law and administration ('last will and testament'). In sixteenth-century prose-writers, especially argumentative like Calvin and Amyot, it is nearly universal. Shakespeare's predilection for the figure is well known: Polonius's 'the origin and commencement of his grief'[3] is a straightforward example. How it can be made to produce supreme poetic effect appears in Antony's meeting with Cleopatra:

> . . . when such a mutual pair
> [*Embracing*
> And such a twain. . . .[4]

Meaning and rhetorical form echo and re-echo each other in a way both simple and highly complex. It may be doubted whether Montaigne quite equals this. Still, we see that his characteristic procedure is also characteristic of his time.

The most striking effect of the single pair taken in isolation is of weight and emphasis, the reinforcement of a notion by sheer repetition in a different form: 'd'une vifve et vehemente esper-

[1] I, i: EM i, 3; TR 11(*a*).
[2] But Miss Samaras has counted them and she makes the total 2045 (*The comic element,* p. 23).
[3] *Hamlet,* III, i.
[4] *Antony and Cleopatra,* I, i.

ance',[1] 'on faict fructifier et foisonner le monde'.[2] These examples are alliterative and this is true in a high proportion, perhaps even a majority of cases, a first distinguishing characteristic of Montaigne's use of the word-pair: clearly alliteration binds the pair more firmly in a single unit, and this unity is always present. But the contrary is also true: a single concept is diversified by the doubling of its expression. The pair, established literary device though it is, contributes to the conversational tone of Montaigne's writing: in conversation it is natural to try out different words for the same thing, to fumble and hesitate. More importantly, we have seen that his thinking proceeds by fine distinctions, and the word-pair is one of the instruments by which distinctions are made, as in one of the most beautiful, already quoted, describing the effects of poetry on judgement, 'elle le ravist et ravage',[3] not only ravishes or carries away but ravages, profoundly devastates and transforms. This example shows that phonetic repetition goes well beyond simple alliteration. Very common are identical prefixes, 'me transpercer et transporter';[4] less common the use of like endings, 'un peu plus grassement et gratieusement'.[5] A further stage is the rhyming pair, rarer but highly characteristic: 'de creinte et de contreinte',[6] 'les larmes ... ou feintes ou peintes'.[7] These assonances and echoes establish the unity of the pair even more securely; and they are, especially rhyme, essentially poetic devices.

They also reveal an interest, which we associate with Rabelais, Joyce or Queneau rather than with Montaigne, in language for its own sake, in playing tricks with the code (this in itself is bound to cast some doubt on his own description of his style as merely recorded talk). Certain kinds of word-play are so close to the word-pair as to be virtually inseparable from it. The most obvious of these is a type of paronomasia in which two words have different senses but very similar sounds (subtly but importantly different from the pun where the sounds are identical). Examples, as with the rhyming pair, come from the later phases of the text. The mechanism depends on the substitution (addition, subtraction) of

1 III, xiii: EM iii, 429; TR 1095.
2 III, xiii: EM iii, 363; TR 1043-4.
3 I, xxxvii: EM i, 303; TR 228(*c*).
4 ibid.
5 III, xiii: EM iii, 417; TR 1086.
6 I, xxvi: EM i, 209; TR 161(*c*).
7 II, xi: EM ii, 132; TR 409(*c*).

one or two phonemes: 'ny les choses qui nous oignent, au pris de celles qui nous poignent',[1] 'tout ce qui plait ne paist pas'[2] or best of all perhaps, speaking of Tacitus, 'qu'il nous peinct et qu'il nous pinse'.[3] All this bears a strong resemblance to the tricks of euphuism. A near-contemporary, the rhetorician Peacham, remarks on the element of affectation in paronomasia:

This figure ought to be sparingly used, and especially in grave and weightie causes, both in the respect of the light and illuding forme, and also forasmuch as it seemeth not to be found without meditation and affected labor.[4]

The same is true of similar word-plays which are not quite paronomasia, like 'Platon en sa plus verte vertu'[5] or the women of Sparta 'asses couvertes de leur vertu sans vertugade',[6] sufficiently covered by their virtue without farthingales, or petticoats. It is a short step to the extraordinary circular ingenuity of 'Nous veillons dormans, et veillans dormons'.[7] Of other figures in the same spectrum the most important are oxymoron ('si vilement victorieuses',[8] of the Spanish conquests) and syllepsis ('Ceus qui courent un benefice ou un lievre').[9] In both we find the cultivation of deep paradox and the union of contraries.

It will be seen that all these are variations on the basic form of the word-pair, that all contain a strong element of artifice and a professional writer's concern with language. Yet in Montaigne, and this is what distinguishes him from most of his euphuistic or mannerist contemporaries, such devices are never merely verbal tricks: always, I think, as in 'qu'il nous peinct et qu'il nous pinse', phonetic variation is a means of sharpening and intensifying a thought drawn from direct experience of reality. It is for this reason that it is important to grasp the difference between variation and identity, between Montaigne's devices and the true pun. Both are playful, both have something of Peacham's 'illuding forme', and certainly Montaigne plays with ideas and life as well as words. Yet this playfulness can be overstressed and should not

---

1 III, x: EM iii, 303–4; TR 999.
2 III, xii: EM iii, 326; TR 1016(c).
3 III, viii: EM iii, 201; TR 920.
4 *The garden of eloquence*, ed. Crane, Gainsville, 1954, p. 56.
5 II, xx: EM ii, 466; TR 656. The Bordeaux Copy substitutes *verte* for *nette*.
6 III, v: EM iii, 95; TR 838.
7 II, xii: EM ii, 360; TR 581(c).
8 III, vi: EM iii, 160; TR 888.
9 III, ix: EM iii, 247; TR 955(c).

blind us to the underlying seriousness. The pun achieves a union of disparates in identity, sudden surprise, laughter, even a poetic effect but usually at a superficial level: the symmetry is too perfect and too obvious. With paronomasia the slight differentiation of sound confirms a significant difference of idea, and the thought progresses instead of turning back on itself, another factor in the forward movement of the essay.

Like the image, the word-pair cannot be fully appreciated in isolation. The combination of pairs produces a variety of consequences, especially rhythmical, often the slowing down of the movement of thought, as in the argument that intellectual activity needs moderating rather than stimulating, supported by an elaborate comparison with the martial music of the Spartans (inessential matter is omitted):

Ainsi, comme la vaillance Lacedemonienne avoit besoing *de moderation et du son doux et gratieux* du jeu des flutes . . . depeur qu'elle ne se jettat *à la temerité et à la furie,* là où toutes autres nations . . . employent *des sons et des voix aigues et fortes* qui *esmouvent et qui eschauffent* . . . le courage des soldats, il me semble . . . qu'en l'usage de nostre esprit nous avons . . . plus besoing de plomb que d'ailes, *de froideur et de repos* que *d'ardeur et d'agitation.*[1]

One sentence contains eight pairs, nouns, verbs and adjectives. Though it would be an exaggeration to say that they express the theme, they certainly support it: the slowness of the movement corresponds to the soothing influence of the music. We may also perceive a connection between this slow unfolding and the aim of painting the changes of mood and mind not from age to age but from minute to minute. But other effects than slowness are possible. In a short sentence crammed with word-pairs almost to the point of parody: 'Pouvons nous pas mesler au tiltre de la *conference et communication* les devis *pointus et coupez* que *l'alegresse et la privauté* introduict entre les amis, *gossans et gaudissans plaisamment et vifvement* les uns les autres?'[2] the five pairs (two alliterative) create a dancing rhythm of cheerfulness, a two-way communication (emphasised by the final reciprocity of 'les uns les autres', as well as by the rising pitch of the question form).

The word-pair is, then, an essentially conventional feature and

---

1 III, iii: EM iii, 44–5; TR 799.
2 III, viii: EM iii, 197; TR 917.

its synonymous character prevents it as a rule from surprising, though we have seen that multiplication produces original effects. The group of three is very different. The replacement of an even by an odd number is enough in itself to break the perfect symmetry, and now a dynamic and liberating energy comes into play. This seems to remain true even when the three terms are near-synonyms, which is much less often the case. As with the pair all the main parts of speech are involved, though adjectives tend to predominate, as also in Proust, for example 'odeurs ... casanières, humaines et renfermées, gelée exquise, industrieuse et limpide ...',[1] or in Montaigne 'selon son estre insatiable, vagabont et versatile'.[2] Here the last two words are nearly synonymous. Where this is not so freedom is still greater, as in 'son goust est plus momentanée, fluide et caduque'[3] (of erotic pleasure) or, very similarly, 'nos necessiteuses commodités, fluides et ambigues'.[4] Fluidity and ambiguity are vital elements in Montaigne's thought as in his style, and the group of three with its broken symmetry and freer rhythm is ideally fitted to convey them. As these examples suggest, a large number of cases come from the Bordeaux Copy.

Yet although perfect symmetry is broken in the group of three it has not been eliminated, there is still a residual organisation. The next stage is enumeration proper, where symmetry has usually gone altogether though structure remains since all the items of an enumeration normally stand in the same syntactical relation to the rest of the sentence and belong to the same part of speech and the same semantic field. Within the limits imposed by this structure freedom is more or less absolute. To mark the extreme point we have the Rabelaisian series of sixty-eight verbs in the first person plural illustrating the language of gesture ('nous requerons, nous prometons, apelons ...').[5] Many other cases work on the same principle though they are on a smaller scale and often much more complex than an alignment of identical verb-forms. Enumeration is one of the most familiar stylistic devices, frequently studied, though not very much in Montaigne.[6]

[1] *A la recherche du temps perdu*, Pléiade ed., Paris, 1960, i, 49.
[2] III, xiii: EM iii, 417; TR 1086(c).
[3] I, xx: EM i, 101; TR 80(c).
[4] III, xiii: EM iii, 429; TR 1095(c).
[5] II, xii: EM ii, 161; TR 431(c).
[6] But see Recksiek, *Montaignes Verhältnis*, pp. 202 ff.; Butor, *Essais sur les Essais*, pp. 193 ff. Neither, however, analyses to any great extent.

Still, it will hardly be necessary to dwell on the simpler manifestations: our purpose must be to seek those forms and functions which are specially characteristic.

Montaigne's enumeration is neither the uninhibited flow of Rabelais nor the carefully organised sequence of Bossuet. Rather the impression given is one of completeness, everything is included that is necessary. An example is the caricature of medical practice:

> le nombre imper de leurs pillules, la destination de certains jours et festes de l'année, la distinction des heures à cueillir les herbes de leurs ingrediens, et cette grimace rebarbative et prudante de leur port et contenance. . . .[1]

Variation is clearly a much more important element of enumeration than of the word-pair. A slight change of register without change of form is enough to affect a transposition from the caricatural to the poetic:

> Un souffle de vent contraire, le croassement d'un vol de corbeaux, le faux pas d'un cheval, le passage fortuite d'un aigle, un songe, une voix, un signe, une brouée matiniere. . . .[2]

(These are the trifles which can overthrow man in his pride.) The progression is notable (four precise phrases, three rapid, vague and sinister nouns, the final delicate picture of a morning mist), but even more striking is again the variation, the inexplicable collocation of disparate phenomena. Or concrete enumeration can be used to bring a vast area of experience within a single conspectus, as in a passage quoted earlier:

> ce branle admirable de la voute celeste, la lumiere eternelle de ces flambeaux roulans si fierement sur sa teste, les mouvemens espouvantables de cette mer infinie. . . .[3]

This multiplication of subjects expresses, again in a Pascalian vision, the immensity of the universe which crushes man. And we have here what is no doubt the principal function of enumeration as of imagery: the direct grasp of the physical world, of tangible reality, so organised as to be manageable and to receive a structured form. The examples have been brief because they are

[1] II, xxxvii: EM ii, 591–2; TR 749.
[2] II, xii: EM ii, 189; TR 453–4.
[3] II, xii: EM ii, 156; TR 427.

quotable, but the same principles apply, though the element of variation and extraordinary collocation is even more pronounced, to such large-scale enumerations as the series of (if the count is correct) forty-three clauses beginning with *où* which constitute in *De la coustume* the main statement of the relativity of human behaviour and moral codes,[1] or thirty direct objects (approximately) of the verb *rencontra* in the description of American customs.[2] Though hardly an objectively verifiable stylistic feature, the immense enjoyment of passages like these is most powerfully communicated, a mind playing (but playing seriously) with the whole of nature and human existence.

As with the word-pair, double and multiple enumeration are common. Here is a relatively simple case of double enumeration of nouns and adjectives:

> La santé, la conscience, l'authorité, la science, la richesse, la beauté et leurs contreres se despouillent à l'entrée, et reçoivent de l'ame nouvelle vesture, et de la teinture qu'il luy plaist: brune, verte, clere, obscure, aigre, douce, profonde, superficielle. . . .[3]

The profundity of the thought (the transformation of experience by the mind) would require long elucidation, but stylistically the point seems to lie in the contrast between the comfortable abstracts (health, conscience, wealth) and the dismayingly unexpected adjectives (brown, green, sour) which qualify them in their transformed state. Especially characteristic of Montaigne is negative enumeration. The finest example, the 'C'est une nation' passage from *Des cannibales*, has already been quoted.[4] It will probably be agreed that its fourteen negations taken together offer a very positive picture of the life and character of the American Indians, but equally important is the condemnation of European society: they are not what we are. The negative enumeration thus permits a double view, comparison, ambiguity, and relativity once more. Most of the examples have exhibited asyndeton, the omission of conjunctions, which makes for a sense of pressure or urgency, as in this list of remedies inflicted by his doctors on their helpless patient: 'tant de puans breuvages, cauteres, incisions, suées, sedons, dietes . . .'.[5] All these ills come crowding in at once.

[1] I, xxiii: TR 110–3.
[2] II, xii: TR 557–8(*b*).
[3] I, 1: EM i, 388; TR 290(*c*).
[4] p. 192 above.
[5] III, xiii: EM iii, 399; TR 1072.

But a few lines before we have a very different picture of the restoration to health: 'avant qu'on vous aye rendu l'usage de l'air, *et* du vin, *et* de vostre femme, *et* des melons . . .'.[1] Polysyndeton, the multiplication of conjunctions, is one more delaying device, one way of savouring enjoyment and making it last, which we have seen to be a main theme of this essay (*De l'experience*). Polysyndeton with *ou,* also frequent, is obviously a vehicle for the expression of sceptical alternatives and doubts.

With asyndeton and polysyndeton we have reached syntax, though the borderline between semantics and syntax is not easy to draw. Sentence structure is of capital importance in Montaigne as in any prose-writer. We may begin with the external form and the brief sentence, which is the least characteristic perhaps but none the less very frequent. In fact extreme laconicism is one of the modes of Montaigne's style. It is necessary to repeat a warning already given, that we cannot always trust the punctuation of modern editions. One example of a series will be enough to illustrate (at the end Montaigne has, in the Bordeaux Copy, broken up a longer sentence):

> Aux evenemens je me porte virilement; en la conduicte, puerillement. L'horreur de la cheute me donne plus de fiebvre que le coup. Le jeu ne vaut pas la chandelle . . . La plus basse marche est la plus ferme. C'est le siege de la constance. Vous n'y avez besoin que de vous. Elle se fonde là, et appuye toute en soy.[2]

Such sentences often come in bursts like this and seem particularly suited to aphorisms and proverbial expressions, as here, or to situations marked by a sense of urgency. Perhaps they are found above all when he has dominated a question and can reduce it to the briefest form. Long sentences, on the other hand, are required for narration, argument and the exploration of the mind. In this particular case the tone is determined by the opening sentence: the laconic statements themselves convey the firmness he claims to show in the face of events. To brevity in the external form naturally corresponds ellipsis within the sentence. The omission of a verb is particularly frequent: 'Actes de son personage, non pas du nostre.'[3] More interesting are cases of actual syntactical disloca-

[1] ibid.
[2] II, xvii: EM ii, 426; TR 628(*b*).
[3] I, xxiii: EM i, 155; TR 121(*c*).

tion, anacoluthon, or imprecision, of which one more example
may be given, about Pyrrho:

> Et par ce qu'il maintenoit la foiblesse du jugement humain estre
> si extreme que de ne pouvoir prendre party ou inclination, et le
> vouloit suspendre perpetuellement balancé, regardant et accueillant
> toutes choses comme indifferentes. . . .[1]

It is impossible to be sure whether the subject of *pouvoir* is
jugement or Pyrrho: the ambiguous syntax exactly reflects the
hesitant thought. We have seen the part that such dislocations play
in the depiction of moving thought.[2]

The typical form, however, is the long sentence: it would not
be quite accurate to call it a period, which suggests a symmetrical
pattern. It is obviously impossible to illustrate without quotations
of inordinate length and one example will therefore have to stand
for all the rest, of exceptional complexity even for Montaigne but
not unique (it is not surprisingly from *Des coches* and part of it
has already been quoted):

> (*b*) Car, pour ceux qui les ont subjuguez, qu'ils ostent les ruses et
> batelages dequoy ils se sont servis à les piper, et le juste estonnement
> qu'aportoit à ces nations là de voir arriver si inopinéement des gens
> barbus, divers en langage, religion, en forme et en contenance, d'un
> endroict du monde si esloigné et où ils n'avoyent jamais imaginé
> qu'il y eust habitation quelconque, montez sur des grands monstres
> incogneuz, contre ceux qui n'avoyent non seulement jamais veu de
> cheval, mais beste quelconque duicte à porter et soustenir homme
> ny autre charge; garnis d'une peau luysante et dure et d'une arme
> trenchante et resplendissante, contre ceux qui, pour le miracle de
> la lueur d'un miroir ou d'un cousteau, alloyent eschangeant une
> grande richesse en or et en perles, et qui n'avoient ny science ny
> matiere par où tout à loisir ils sçeussent percer nostre acier; adjoustez
> y les foudres et tonnerres de nos pieces et harquebouses, capables
> de troubler Cæsar mesme, qui l'en eust surpris autant inexperimenté,
> et à cett'heure, contre des peuples nuds, si ce n'est où l'invention
> estoit arrivée de quelque tissu de cotton, sans autres armes pour le
> plus que d'arcs, pierres, bastons (*c*) et boucliers de bois; (*b*) des
> peuples surpris, soubs couleur d'amitié et de bonne foy, par la curiosité
> de veoir des choses estrangeres et incogneues: contez, dis-je, aux
> conquerans cette disparité, vous leur ostez toute l'occasion de tant
> de victoires.[3]

---

[1] II, xxix: EM ii, 505; TR 683–4.
[2] pp. 105–6 above.
[3] III, vi: EM iii, 159–60; TR 887–8.

This marvellous sentence practically defies grammatical analysis of the ordinary kind. Yet in spite of all the ramifications of its hypotaxis it is perfectly clear, as might be someone's vehement persuasion in verbal argument even though he was completely ignoring the rules of syntax. This is due to a firm underlying structure, whether we call it syntactical or rhetorical. The main statement is in fact the last ('vous leur ostez . . .'): all the rest is a series of three jussives or imperatives, used as conditionals ('if' understood). The matter is complicated by the switch from the third person ('qu'ils ostent') to the second ('adjoustez') which further adds to the impression of syntactical formlessness. Within this basic structure goes another directional element, the repetition of *contre* ('contre ceux . . . contre ceux . . . contre des peuples'), which works into the structure the clash and disparity between two civilisations which is the theme of the first or hypothetical part of the sentence. The second part, by a further contrast, cancels out the disparity and the Spanish victories which it produced. There is yet another disparity, of length, between the enormous protasis and the abrupt apodosis, recalling the similar disequilibrium in the total structure of the *Apologie*. This can only be a hurried outline of the shape of the sentence, neglecting all the details, which are of considerable interest. In one respect it is not entirely typical: its tone is that of eloquent pleading, not the representation of the processes of silent thought. Syntactically, however, the methods are not fundamentally different (though each sentence in Montaigne, like each essay, must to some extent be regarded as a special case). What we find then in sentences like this is extreme complexity, the appearance of conversational incoherence, a firm underlying structure, a correspondence between the syntax and the thought and, inevitably when one considers Montaigne's way of proceeding, between the form of a sentence and the form of an essay.

A full study of word order would again be excessive but one or two of the more significant features may be noted. Latin influence, as in vocabulary, is strongly marked:

Combien insolammant rebroüent Epicurus les Stoiciens sur ce qu'il tient l'estre veritablement bon et hureus [heureux] n'apartenir qu'à Dieu. . . .[1]

----

[1] II, xii: EM ii, 264; TR 509(*c*).

Here we find not only the inversion of subject and object but also an adaptation of the accusative and infinitive construction. The Latin or Latinate freedom of order is naturally congenial to Montaigne and permits one of his characteristic effects, postponement:

> Ce n'est pas au subject des substitutions seulement que nostre esprit montre sa beauté et sa force, et aux affaires des Roys.[1]

This sort of afterthought constitutes another element of dislocation; and it again combines the appearance of spontaneity with a rhetorical structure. It also, as here, furnishes examples of the cadences to which I have more than once referred. Particularly at the end of essays he cultivates understatement and a dying fall, which leaves a haunting echo in the mind:

> Car Dionysius, pour ne pouvoir esgaller Philoxenus en la poësie, et Platon en discours, en condemna l'un aus carrieres, et envoya vendre l'autre esclave en l'isle d'Ægine.[2]

Or, most beautiful of all no doubt, the close of *De la moderation* which, with the Indians bearing presents to Cortez, leads directly into the following essay (*Des cannibales*):

> Seigneur, voyla cinq esclaves; si tu és un Dieu fier, qui te paisses de chair et de sang, mange les, et nous t'en amerrons d'avantage; si tu és un Dieu debonnaire, voyla de l'encens et des plumes; si tu es homme, prens les oiseaux et les fruicts que voicy.[3]

This exquisite (but again rhetorical) simplicity, based on an Italian translation of Gomara, conveys his pastoral vision of America almost better than *Des cannibales* itself.

Sentences are not isolated, of course, and frequently a similar pattern (sometimes of successive questions) links contiguous sentences, adding to the impression of continuous movement. Again the subject would require illustration on a large scale and here a single, fairly subtle, example must suffice, six sentences from the description of virtue in *De l'institution des enfans*:

> En les rendant justes elle les tait.... Les moderant, elle les tient.... Retranchant ceus qu'elle refuse, elle nous aiguise.... Si la

---

[1] III, iii: EM iii, 48; TR 802.
[2] III, vii: EM iii, 173; TR 899. This is from Amyot, but Montaigne's subtle alteration makes all the difference: 'en envoya vendre l'autre comme esclave en l'isle d'Ægine' (Plutarch, *Œuvres morales*, 1572, f. 72ᵛ).
[3] I, xxx: EM i, 263; TR 199–200(*b*).

L

fortune commune luy faut, elle luy eschape ou elle s'en passe. . . . Elle sçait estre riche. . . . Elle aime la vie. . . .[1]

In the first four sentences we have postponement of the subject and what may be called disguised anaphora. In the last two (the climax) postponement and disguise are dropped and the most positive statements stand out with all the greater force.

We are now in a better position to answer the questions with which this chapter began. The conversational disorder of Montaigne's style is like the disorder or formlessness of the *Essais* as a whole. The impression of spontaneity is wonderfully created, but underneath it there is abundant evidence of rhetorical patterns and devices, of cunning echoes and modulated cadences which do not abolish spontaneity but endow it with the consistency and durability of art. In fact he comes very close to the ideal of 'Longinus':

> For art is then perfect when it seems to be nature, and nature, again, is most effective when pervaded by the unseen presence of art.[2]

On the other and more difficult question of broken against continuous style we have found brief sentences, ellipsis, asyndeton, anacoluthon; but long and convoluted sentences, repetition, redundancy (the word-pair) have turned out to be much more characteristic. Far more than the style of spontaneous conversation, Montaigne's is the style of spontaneous thought, and in general he uses the figures and syntactical forms best fitted to depicting it. In this perspective even the dislocations of syntax we have so often noticed do not produce an effect of abruptness: on the contrary, they contribute to ambiguity and multiplicity of meaning, to the impression of thought in the process of formulation. However, it would be wrong if redundancy and ambiguity suggested any slackness or looseness in writing. Every word tells and is packed with richness of meaning (in the corrections a more vigorous, precise or concrete expression is almost always substituted). But even this is inadequate to convey the range and poetic intensity of his writing: as the quotations show he is capable not only of colloquial raciness but, when it is required, of the loftiest eloquence.

[1] I, xxvi: EM i, 210; TR 161–2.
[2] *On the sublime*, tr. Havell, in *Theories of style*, ed. Cooper, New York, 1912, p. 130.

☙ 13 ☙

Renaissance, Mannerism and Baroque

IN the last two chapters we have been studying the form of
the *Essais* for the most part intrinsically, without more than
incidental reference to other works of the period. This was
both desirable and inevitable, since Montaigne reigns virtually
alone in the genre he has himself created (a comparison with Bacon
would be possible but it would reveal far more differences than
similarities). However, we can hardly avoid considering him in
relation to the great movements in the art and literature of his
time, and this involves some discussion of the confused question
of mannerism and baroque, a question which includes content as
well as form.[1] Anything like a firm definition of concepts which
have given rise to so much speculative interpretation and controversy is not possible in a brief space. Both mannerism and baroque
are best regarded as developments of Renaissance art, modifying
its forms and revealing in it new characteristics and potentialities.
If we accept a broad segment of critical opinion (but by no means
universally accepted) mannerism extends from 1520 to about 1600
and is characterised formally by artifice, distortion, disproportion,
disunity, and ideologically by various arguments which may be
thought to correspond to them. Baroque is essentially the art of
the seventeenth century: distortion of Renaissance forms
continues, but a new kind of unity is achieved, the harmony of
parts in the classical Renaissance style being fused in a single

---

[1] See Sayce, 'Baroque elements in Montaigne'; Buffum, *Studies in the
baroque from Montaigne to Rotrou*, 1957; Recksiek, *Montaignes Verhältnis
zu Klassik und Manierismus*. More general works on mannerism are Hauser,
Mannerism, 1965; Shearman, *Mannerism*, 1967. Those on baroque are very
numerous: Wölfflin's *Kunstgeschichtliche Grundbegriffe*, 1915 (tr. as *Principles
of art history*) remains the most illuminating.

dynamic whole, with movement everywhere dominant. Chronologically Montaigne belongs to the mannerist period, though it might be said that he stands on the threshold of the baroque. It is hardly necessary to point out the dangers of transferring categories from art history to literature in this way, especially the chronological limits, which may differ considerably. Suspicion will be reinforced in anyone who reads some of the more ambitious work on the subject, with its forced syntheses, contradictions, and sometimes nonsense. However, this work also has two great merits. It draws attention to phenomena which really exist: some important changes certainly occurred in the arts in the course of the sixteenth and seventeenth centuries. And it may lead to the discovery of resemblances and affinities between works of a widely separated nature and their relation to thought and life. What is essential is to avoid becoming the prisoner of words, to look for the realities behind them, and especially to treat terms like mannerism and baroque as hypotheses only, to see how the conceptions on which they are based work out when applied to an individual case. In dealing with Montaigne the best method seems to be to examine the ways in which he deviates from the principles of the Renaissance and then to see what sort of picture emerges (in all this the Renaissance is taken as a fixed point, which might itself be the subject of much argument).

First of all, however, we cannot overlook the fact that he has been traditionally considered as belonging to the Renaissance, indeed as one of its outstanding figures. To quote a random example, a statement by an anonymous writer of a generation ago: 'They [Montaigne and Shakespeare] are the imperishable monuments of the high Renaissance in Europe.'[1] This is entirely at variance with more recent views of historians, especially of art historians, for whom the high Renaissance ended about 1520. All the same, without quibbling on the meaning of 'high', we can say that in the deepest sense it is still true: the greatness of Montaigne and Shakespeare is only fully comprehensible in the light of their affiliation to the Renaissance. Montaigne belongs to it, as we have seen, by his passion for the ancients, his capacity for bringing antiquity to life, his constant appeal to its great men, Cato, Epaminondas, Socrates, as his mentors and models of virtue, the whole literary background of the *Essais* and the classical quota-

---

[1] *Times literary supplement*, 16 March 1933, p. 174.

314

tions, the philosophical systems with which his thought is impregnated. The style too may be Senecan rather than Ciceronian; it
is still in many important respects Latinate. The form of the essay,
wholly original though it is, could hardly have matured without
the example of Plato's *Dialogues,* Seneca's *Letters,* and above all
the *Moralia* of Plutarch. With the immense debt to antiquity goes
naturally the learning of the Renaissance scholar. Beside the
Scaligers, Turnebus or Lipsius, Montaigne's learning is nothing
much: to the modern reader it remains formidable, and the *Essais,*
apart from anything else, constitute almost an encyclopaedia of
antiquity. Like Erasmus or Rabelais he makes fun of the Middle
Ages, the monastic ideal, the philosophy and education of the
schoolmen, the glosses of the jurists, most of all perhaps the
formalist logic. He is a humanist in the broad as well as the
narrow sense: in his tolerance, his liberalism, his cosmopolitanism, his terrestrial morality, his belief in the development of the
whole man against the limits of specialisation, even his final confidence in human nature (though this is subject to reservations). We
have here not a separate compartment of his thought but a spirit
which animates all that he writes.

Yet, though it is all, it is not all. The confidence in man is
balanced by distrust, pessimism, even horror. The contradiction
is partly explicable by chronology: we have seen that the dark
picture of man in the *Apologie* gives way to the generous attitude
of *De l'experience.* But even in the Third Book there is plenty to
offset a too rosy view of human nature. The extravagant hopes of
the early humanists were bound, as we have seen, to be disap-
pointed. The disillusionment could scarcely be better expressed
than in the opening of the *Apologie,* where Montaigne contrasts
his own attitude to the Renaissance with that of his father's generation, very much as Rabelais had done in Gargantua's letter to
Pantagruel. For Gargantua 'par la bonté divine, la lumière et
dignité a esté de mon aage rendue ès lettres'. Printing has been
invented 'par inspiration divine', 'tout le monde est plain de gens
sçavans, de precepteurs tresdoctes'.[1] This paean is taken up by
Montaigne, almost in the same words:

car mon pere ... eschauffé de cette ardeur nouvelle dequoy le
Roy François premier embrassa les lettres et les mit en credit, recercha
avec grand soing et despence l'accointance des hommes doctes, les

[1] *Pantagruel,* ed. Saulnier, 1946, pp. 43–4.

recevant chez luy comme personnes sainctes et ayans quelque particuliere inspiration de sagesse divine, recueillant leurs sentences et leurs discours comme des oracles, et avec d'autant plus de reverence et de religion . . .

Montaigne's father shares Gargantua's enthusiasm. But the doubly ironic continuation completely overturns the splendid vision:

. . . et avec d'autant plus de reverence et de religion qu'il avoit moins de loy d'en juger, car il n'avoit aucune connoissance des lettres, non plus que ses predecesseurs. Moy, je les ayme bien, mais je ne les adore pas.[1]

The illiterate father worships letters and learning, the learned son looks at them with a coolly sceptical eye. There can be little doubt that Montaigne here speaks for his generation as well as himself; for reasons we have already considered the enthusiasm for antiquity shows a progressive decline in the course of the sixteenth and seventeenth centuries. Ancient models continue to influence, even to dictate, form in art, mythology continues to supply themes and illustrations but more and more as ornament, with less and less deep commitment. If we compare say Mantegna and Vasari the point becomes clear: earnest striving has turned into erotic play. In so far as this mood, part reaction against the Renaissance, part development from it, is mannerist, Montaigne can be said to share it.

There can be no doubt whatsoever about the genuineness of his passion for antiquity, but it comes under the scrutiny of an ironical observer, who distrusts passion and enthusiasm and all the exaggerated hopes of the earlier generation. Passion is thus (and not only in this respect) contained and divided; this constraint and the doubling of personality, the observer observed, correspond well enough to the definitions of mannerism usually given. Doubling is indeed an inadequate word, since we have found something like an infinite regress:[2] we might compare the technique of the mirror in painting, for example in Parmigianino's self-portrait (Vienna).

The overthrowing of values goes far beyond humanism, literature, learning and antiquity. It is not only the Renaissance that is questioned but everything: science, medicine, law, but above all

[1] II, xii: EM ii, 140; TR 415(a).
[2] On the infinite regress in the scepticism of Sextus Empiricus see Popkin, *The history of scepticism*, pp. 3, 52, 126.

perhaps the system of logical classification and definitions which enables us to believe that we can make some sense of the world. We are lost in a universe where all the familiar landmarks have started to shift. Instead of the 'sustantificque mouelle' of the dog's bone in Rabelais,[1] philosophy according to Montaigne gives us 'à ronger cet os creus et descharné'.[2] We have considered his scepticism mainly in itself and in relation to its ancient sources, but it is also part of a general movement.[3] Again most definitions of mannerism include scepticism, the overturning of values, and the loss of confidence in every kind of certainty. These ideas, it is true, can already be found not only in Cornelius Agrippa but also, especially the praise of ignorance and the attack on science and medicine, in Erasmus: chronological schemes of this kind have to be treated with caution. At least we see one more indication that what is called mannerism only develops tendencies already latent in the Renaissance itself. Finally, and principally, Montaigne's scepticism, like his Stoicism, is itself evidence of his debt to the Renaissance. Without Pyrrho and Sextus Empiricus there would have been no *Apologie* and no scepticism, at least of a seriously philosophical kind. Even when he is undermining the cult of antiquity he remains faithful to his ancient masters and borrows from them the arguments he uses so effectively.

With scepticism goes the mobility we have found to be so profoundly characteristic. In the visual arts the evolution from static to dynamic conceptions is most striking: a comparison between Raphael and Rubens would show it in a fairly extreme form. Instability and uncertainty appear in the reactions to the sudden expansion of the world, both of the earth after the great geographical discoveries and (perhaps most apparent in Bruno) of the cosmos after the Copernican revolution with its shattering of the limits constructed by traditional or Aristotelean cosmology. We have seen that Montaigne reveals a keen and, in the second case at least, precocious awareness of the consequences of both. However, it is inner or psychological movement which is most immediately relevant. If opinions, thoughts and attitudes are in a state of continual flux there are no general psychological laws and, as we have seen, it becomes impossible to know the mind, the motives

---

1 *Gargantua*, Prologue (ed. Plattard, 1946, p. 5).

2 II, xii: EM ii, 234; TR 488.

3 On which see Popkin, *The history of scepticism*, and Hauser, *Mannerism*; also Haydn, *The Counter-Renaissance*, 1950.

and the deeper character of anyone else. The resulting dissolution of the notion of a single unified personality goes a long way towards destroying the confidence in man which seems to be one of the characteristics of the Renaissance: towards destroying not perhaps confidence in men individually but in a symmetrical abstraction of noble attributes. Our whole feeling of solidity and solidarity is undermined:

> Mais quoi, nous somes par tout vent. Et le vent encore, plus sagement que nous, s'aime à bruire, à s'agiter, et se contante en ses propres offices, sans desirer la stabilité, la solidité, qualitez non sienes.[1]

Our life is nothing but appearance, shadow and dream: 'Ceux qui ont apparié nostre vie à un songe ont eu de la raison, à l'avanture plus qu'ils ne pensoyent', which leads to the haunting phrase already quoted: 'Nous veillons dormans, et veillans dormons'.[2] There is not only the dream but the dream within the dream (appropriately in parentheses):

> Il m'en advient comme de mes songes: en songeant, je les recommande à ma memoire (car je songe volontiers que je songe). . . .[3]

The history of the idea of life as a dream is a long one and goes back to antiquity (Sophocles in one of the sentences painted in Montaigne's library, for example), but it exercised a peculiar fascination on the minds of men of this period. Prospero's speech in Act IV of *The Tempest* and Calderón's *La vida es sueño* are only the best-known instances. The insubstantiality of things goes naturally with movement and instability. Of course there is here as usual contradiction and paradox. We have seen that few writers are more gifted than Montaigne, or we might add Shakespeare, for the rendering of concrete experience in all its variety. We can only admire the more the magician's skill which can make it all vanish in the doubts of scepticism or the flux of mobility. To the dream, and again the parallel with Shakespeare is very close, we must join the persistent use of theatrical imagery. As with the dream so with the stage, life is presented as evanescent and unreal. The things we take most seriously are even more an illusion than the rest: we have seen that, stripped of the finery of his stage

[1] III, xiii: EM iii, 417; TR 1087(c).
[2] II, xii: EM ii, 360; TR 580–1(b,c).
[3] III, v: EM iii, 116; TR 854.

costume, an emperor is as wretched a creature as the least of his subjects. This is true not only of individuals but of the whole of political activity:

> N'est-ce pas une noble farce de laquelle les Roys, les choses publiques et les Empereurs vont jouant leur personnage tant de siecles, et à laquelle tout ce grand univers sert de theatre ?[1]

Yet the illusion is not entirely unconnected with reality, the two tend to mingle:

> Mais quelque personnage que l'home entrepraigne, il joue tousjours le sien parmy.[2]

We cannot be sure which is which and the ambiguity and confused perspectives which result are typical. Similarly an actor's feigned emotions can become true (an idea Montaigne takes from Quintilian):[3] this is the subject of Rotrou's *Saint Goncst* (1647). In general the theme of theatrical illusion and the play within the play are widespread in the drama of the following period, not only in Shakespeare but in Corneille (the *Illusion comique*) and many minor French playwrights as well.

Montaigne's diversity is again characteristic of the art of his period.[4] Like contemporary princes, with their cabinets of curiosities, like Francesco de' Medici in particular, whose creations he admired in Florence:

> il prend plesir à besoingner lui-mesmes, à contrefaire des pierres orientales et à labourer le cristal: car il est prince souingneus un peu de l'archemie et des ars mechaniques, et surtout grand architecte.[5]

he made his own small collection of objects from America;[6] but the *Essais* themselves are his real cabinet of curiosities with their anecdotes and incidents, strange customs from all over the world, exotic animals, marvellous coaches, freaks and monsters (*D'un enfant monstrueux* for example), grotesques (the word he uses himself) of all kinds. In the *Journal du voyage*, where he gives this kind of curiosity free rein, he reveals a particular interest in machinery: the city gates of Augsburg which open of their own

[1] II, xxxvi: EM ii, 569; TR 732.
[2] I, xx: EM i, 101; TR 80(c).
[3] III, iv: TR 816.
[4] See for example Hauser, p. 25; Shearman, pp. 139 ff.
[5] *JV*: TR 1195.
[6] Cf. p. 92 above.

accord, automata, or in Florence an artificial rock spouting water to work mills and church bells, soldiers and hunting scenes. It is in general their ingenuity rather than their utility which impresses him. But the most wonderful machines of all are the fountains he describes whenever he finds them, at Augsburg, Pratolino, Caprarola, Bagnaia, and especially Tivoli, where at the Villa d'Este he notes 'Ce rejallissemant, d'un infinité de surjons d'eau bridés et eslancés par un sul ressort qu'on peut remuer de fort louin ...', water organs and artificial trumpets, and the perpetual rainbows produced by the mingling and collision of water from different fountains.[1] Most of the gardens he describes have machinery for drenching visitors with water. In this respect at any rate he exhibits a lively appreciation, at once childlike and technical, of one of the most characteristic expressions of mannerist art.[2]

The self-portrait too, in spite of its extreme originality, has some connections with the general spirit of the time: it can be regarded as the reflection or the focus of the universal movement and uncertainty we have been discussing. One example, very like many already quoted, gives the key:

> Car en ce que je dis, je ne pleuvie autre certitude, sinon que c'est ce que lors j'en avois en ma pensée, pensée tumultuaire et vacillante.[3]

As we have seen, the self-portrait itself forms part of the group of major themes centred on mobility. But more than this, the retreat into the self is a logical consequence of the view of the world as uncertain and unknowable. If everything is uncertain and a familiar world is collapsing (both politically and intellectually) it is natural to seek certainty and security in one's own consciousness. We have seen that this is the principal explanation of the contemporary vogue of Stoicism. Of course this logical consequence does not necessarily imply, in the case of Montaigne, an order of events in time: the chances are that the view of the world and the self-portrait developed together. At any rate the narcissism we have discovered in the *Essais*[4] is treated by Hauser, but without specific reference to Montaigne, which strengthens his case, as a prominent feature of mannerist art (Hamlet is the most convincing of his examples).[5] The word narcissism is liable to

---

[1] *JV*: TR 1237–8.
[2] Cf. Shearman, pp. 112–3.
[3] III, xi: EM iii, 318; TR 1010(*c*).
[4] p. 53 above.
[5] Hauser, pp. 115–30.

shock when applied to Montaigne: his preoccupation with himself is so robust and healthy, it is presented to the reader with such modesty and good humour, it is so remote from the posturings of a Rousseau or a Chateaubriand, that a description of it which may appear pejorative is hard to accept. But praise or blame is irrelevant in the historical perspective we are adopting for the moment: the passages quoted earlier prove beyond doubt that his self-preoccupation is also self-regarding and self-obsessed, fortunately, it may be added, since it is doubtful whether any great autobiographical work could be written without this quality. At all events, it is a quality which seems to link him with some of the general tendencies of the art of his period.

The same may be true of his treatment of the erotic. Certainly this is a most powerful element in the art and literature of the sixteenth century and one that is considerably attenuated or at least represented less disturbingly in the seventeenth. In literature we have not only Rabelais and Brantôme, already mentioned, but Aretino and Ronsard, among many others; in painting the examples are innumerable. Of course the erotic is an all but universal theme of art: what distinguishes mannerism is an elegant, cool and refined perversity, of which the Fontainebleau School or Vasari's Studiolo in the Palazzo Vecchio at Florence (painted about 1570) offer outstanding evidence. This does not seem to fit Montaigne at all : we have seen the eminent sense and sanity with which he treats the subject. Yet we have also seen the range of sexual experience he brings in, not all of it by any means of a perfectly straightforward kind. Elegance is also present, though it is obscured, as with other sixteenth-century writers, by the language which strikes us as in some way naïve because of what are to us its archaisms. We know that Montaigne has an astonishingly exact command of language but the archaisms seem to impart to it a slight clumsiness or even a comic quality which is often but not always there. When we have made allowances for this obstacle, which may affect different readers in different degrees, he is perhaps closer to contemporary painters than might at first appear. The description of Jupiter and Juno[1] is an excellent example of the kind of erotic encounter which had a special appeal for mannerist painters. A detail is the reference to Bradamante and Angelica (in Ariosto): 'l'une travestie en garçon, coiffée

---

[1] Cf. p. 131 above.

d'un morrion luysant, l'autre vestue en garce, coiffée d'un attiffet enperlé.'[1] Shakespeare again offers the most obvious instances of the fondness for girls in male disguise, but female warriors, helmeted like Bradamante here, are particularly frequent in the art and literature of this and the succeeding period (in Rubens for example). The phenomenon illustrates both the playing of variations on ordinary love and the growing strength of feminism which becomes highly important in the baroque period.

The forms through which these themes are expressed are at least equally relevant to any consideration of Montaigne's affinities with the art of his time. We have noticed more than once the dominance of the oblique approach, the indirect entry, the discrepancy between titles and subjects, the tangential linking of themes. It may not be too fanciful to see a resemblance to the oblique vistas of Tintoretto or Palladio's Teatro Olimpico at Vicenza. But perhaps the most relevant passage is the description of the magnificent palaces of love with their porticos and passages, long galleries and numerous detours.[2] Shearman makes the excellent point that buildings of the mannerist period are not designed to be taken in at a single view but are composed of successive impressions.[3] Montaigne's imagined palaces are clearly very similar. What emerges here, beyond the purely formal aspect, is a sense of mystery and tortuousness, something which we are bound to feel in him and which has to be set against his open love of life and luminous common sense. Sainte-Beuve's image of the labyrinth[4] may be misleading as an explanation of Montaigne's religion but it does succeed in conveying much of the essential atmosphere. In an extravagant but interesting work, one half of which is entitled *Die Welt als Labyrinth*, G. R. Hocke claims that the labyrinth is the central symbol of mannerism and indeed expresses its quintessence. However suspicious we may be of his arguments in general, it must be admitted that this applies with remarkable aptness to Montaigne, who himself uses the word metaphorically to designate his picture of man, 'trouvant une si extreme varieté de jugemens, un si profond labyrinthe de difficultez les unes sur les autres, tant de diversité et incertitude

---

1 I, xxvi: EM i, 209–10; TR 161(c).
2 Cf. p. 295 above.
3 *Mannerism*, pp. 116, 125, 145.
4 Cf. p. 202 above.

en l'eschole mesme de la sapience . . .'.[1] The labyrinthine form is thus explicitly connected with the theme of diversity. However, it is not just a matter of a single isolated metaphor: he sees his whole work in the same way. The human mind is itself a labyrinth, 'les profondeurs opaques de ses replis internes', and this is reflected in the whole of his psychology. It is also reflected, as we have seen, in the form which carries this vision of man. The mature essay follows a sinuous, a serpentine line (also a characteristic of mannerism),[2] along which 'l'indiligent lecteur' and even a diligent one easily gets lost. It is noteworthy that the labyrinthine character of the *Essais* was already apparent to Florio: 'So was he [Diodati] to me in this inextricable laberinth like *Ariadnaes* threed.'[3] In short, if the labyrinth is mannerist, then Montaigne is too. Incidentally, we have here a good illustration of Wölfflin's central principle: things may remain the same, but the way of looking at them changes (the human mind is not a labyrinth for La Rochefoucauld or Locke or Voltaire).

We have seen that Montaigne forms part of the Senecan movement, the reaction against the Ciceronian period, at the end of the sixteenth century. The Senecan movement has been called baroque (by Croll) and mannerist (by Dr Recksiek). We need not settle this question, in view of the confused definitions of the two terms, but it may be that in this connection the use of the term mannerism leads to a more precise historical discrimination. A feature which can be attached with much more assurance to mannerism is paronomasia with its associated types of word-play. We have noted the parallel with euphuism and even with Shakespeare, and one might add the names of Marino and Góngora,[4] but we have also seen that such devices in Montaigne are always functional, which is not the case with their strictly mannerist employment, where the device is its own justification.[5] Enumeration can be found at most periods, is indeed almost a stylistic universal, but in the *Essais* it serves, among other purposes, to express the diversity of things, including the oddities and mons-

---

[1] II, xvii: EM ii, 411; TR 617(*a*).

[2] On the serpentine line in Montaigne cf. Thibaudet, *Montaigne*, pp. 410, 477; in mannerism generally Shearman, p. 81.

[3] *Essayes*, dedication to the Countess of Bedford. On the labyrinth see also Butor, *Essais sur les Essais*, pp. 111–3 (but rather forced).

[4] On paronomasia in Guarini see Shearman, p. 95.

[5] Cf. Croll's introduction to his edition of Lyly, *Euphues*, 1916.

trosities of the world, as in the remedies of the physicians, already mentioned but worth quoting:

> ... le pied gauche d'une tortue, l'urine d'un lezart, la fiante d'un Elephant, le foye d'une taupe, du sang tiré soubs l'aile droite d'un pigeon blanc ... des crotes de rat pulverisées. ...[1]

This presents an evident parallel with the witches' concoction in *Macbeth*, and it is not surprising that Montaigne compares such remedies to the spells of magicians.[2] Enumeration is also admirably fitted to convey the richness and splendour which constitute a notable though neglected quality of Montaigne's style in general. One further example, the preparations made by Heliogabalus for his suicide, is perhaps even more striking than some quoted earlier:

> ... et ... avoit fait bastir expres une tour somptueuse, le bas et le devant de laquelle estoit planché d'ais enrichis d'or et de pierrerie pour se precipiter; et aussi fait faire des cordes d'or et de soye cramoisie pour s'estrangler; et battre une espée d'or pour s'enferrer; et gardoit du venin dans des vaisseaux d'emeraude et de topaze pour s'enpoisonner. ...[3]

Here the elegance combined with perversity which we have seen to be typical of mannerist art is very much present, and the fact that it is a free translation from the late Roman historian Lampridius does not detract in any way from the force of the parallel. Apart from the vocabulary, the polysyndeton produces an effect of slow and even affected stateliness most appropriate to the subject. It is true that immediately afterwards Montaigne deflates it all with the remark that if he had really tried it Heliogabalus's nose would have bled, but for the moment he is himself under the spell, his stylistic range as capable of conveying decadence as robust humour. The result, whatever label we attach to it, is extremely beautiful.

We have found several characteristics which, if they are not mannerist, at least correspond very closely to what is generally said about mannerism: reaction against the optimism of the early Renaissance, doubling of the personality, scepticism, narcissism, oblique and labyrinthine forms, paradox, word-play. Against these

[1] II, xxxvii: EM ii, 591; TR 749.
[2] Cf. pp. 183–4 above.
[3] II, xiii: EM ii, 374; TR 591.

features, some apparently superficial but all in fact touching the deepest layers of the work, have to be set Montaigne's good sense, his frankness and hatred of feigning. If there is a political domin-ant of the mannerist period, it is Machiavellianism, illustrated practically by the assassinations and dark stratagems of the Italian princes or the court of Henry III (mirrored and exaggerated in Elizabethan and Jacobean drama). We have seen how firmly, if also with what subtle discriminations, Montaigne expresses his opposition to political immoralism. Of course it can always be argued that in spite of his detestation these currents of thought and action are as powerfully reflected in the *Essais* as they are in say Webster. The same is true of the perverse refinements, the sinister side, of mannerist art. We have seen that they are present, more than might at first be suspected, even when they are condemned. Still, they are none the less reduced to a sub-ordinate place by the sane and humorous outlook which generally predominates. Symptomatic perhaps is the dislike he expresses more than once for the *fêtes de cour*, the court masques and ballets, which rank among the most typical expressions of manner-ism[1] (the *Journal du voyage* where the direct impact of mannerist art is most apparent shows greater sympathy). It is perhaps his literary judgements which do most to confirm these reservations. He objects strongly to poets who cultivate *concetti* or the 'fantastic elevations' of the Spaniards and the Petrarchists.[2] His admira-tion goes, as we have seen, to classical simplicity and greatness, above all to Virgil, Horace and Lucretius.[3]

So far I have not attempted to distinguish at all rigorously (perhaps not rigorously enough) between mannerism and baroque, because there is no accepted body of definitions to which easy reference can be made: the whole question would have to be argued out. It could be done but only at great length. Briefly, what seems to link Montaigne to baroque tendencies, in contra-distinction to mannerist, is first of all the open form of the *Essais*, their infinite expandability, the fact that he can go on 'autant qu'il y aura d'ancre et de papier au monde'.[4] Open form is one of the criteria advanced by Wölfflin to distinguish between baroque and

---

[1] e.g. III, vi: TR 880–1. On the *fêtes de cour* see for example Yates, *The Valois tapestries*, 1959.

[2] II, x: TR 391.

[3] Cf. p. 48 above.

[4] On his open form see also Friedrich, *Montaigne*, 1967, pp. 312 ff., 327 ff.

Renaissance art; it also seems valid for the distinction between baroque and mannerism. With it in Montaigne goes the breaking down of barriers, the unbroken flow of thought from minute to minute, mobility, and above all the unity ('mon livre est tousjours un') which makes so many disparate themes and ideas convergent rather than divergent. Whether this is Wölfflin's multiple unity or unified unity (*vielheitliche Einheit* or *einheitliche Einheit*) is perhaps a matter for argument. As a footnote, we cannot help being struck by the resemblance between Montaigne's picture of himself and one of the greatest manifestations of baroque art, Rembrandt's series of self-portraits, especially in the representation of the ravaging processes of illness and old age. Of course the difference between visual and verbal art means that what Rembrandt had to do in a succession of static works could in Montaigne be presented as continuous motion. Seen in the perspective of mannerism and baroque, Montaigne stands at a point of transition but the baroque elements are perhaps the more significant.

It would indeed be absurd to apply either label to him in an all-embracing way, to call him mannerist or baroque, since, like Shakespeare, he so totally transcends them. The warning I gave in the Introduction has been confirmed by much of the subsequent argument: his view of the world and himself is too fresh and original to be tied to any historical scheme, even a more watertight one than that of the art historians. At the same time these parallels, however desultory and incomplete, have two advantages. They show that, though so original, he is not isolated, that he shares not only the abstract ideas of his contemporaries, which is obvious, but also their way of looking at things, their deeper sense of form. And by projecting a light from apparently quite remote sources they may reveal hidden aspects of his work which are likely to escape attention in a straightforward reading. If mannerism and baroque are characterised by the distortion and renewal of classical forms, the *Essais* furnish a very good example, as we can see by comparing them with such ancient prototypes as Plutarch and Seneca.

The Unity of the Essays

A S I suggested in the first chapter the most difficult problem in dealing with Montaigne is probably that of reconciling two impressions: an impression of disorder, formlessness, contradiction, and eclecticism; and an equally or more powerful impression of overriding unity, both in thought and form. Much of our discussion has been directed to just this point and many indications of a solution have, I hope, emerged, though inevitably in a scattered way. Before we try to draw them together we ought to look a little more closely at the solution which comes near to suppressing the problem, the theory of the evolution of the *Essais* associated with the great work of Villey but adopted by many others. That it was put forward at a time when evolution, under the influence of Darwinism, had become a leading intellectual fashion (Brunetière's evolution of genres having set the tone in France) does not of course mean that it is wrong. We have in fact considered it in relation to various particular questions and found it sometimes confirmed, sometimes not. If it is completely accepted, then Montaigne simply moves from one position to another, the contradictions are explained as largely changes of mind, and it becomes unnecessary to look for principles of unity, though they may still exist.

The presence of an evolutionary element is undeniable: it is implied inescapably in the depiction of moving and changing thought which we have studied in some detail. On the broadest scale it can be observed (and this is fundamental to the evolutionist theory) in the very real differences between the essays published in 1580 and the Third Book of 1588. However, we have seen that these differences are for the most part not direct opposi-

M

tions but rather the full development, amplification and elaboration in the late stages of themes and attitudes already stated earlier. A good example is the 'tout entier et tout nud' of the 1580 preface. Montaigne already expresses the desire to paint himself with total frankness and goes quite a long way in this direction in the first two books, but it is in the Third Book that all reticence is finally dropped and the naked man appears. It is equally true of the self-portrait in general and we have observed how early he begins to paint himself (though some cases are no doubt pre-1580 interpolations): the Third Book simply carries the process further. It is even true of the human condition, often presented as the great discovery of the Third Book: we have seen that the depiction of humanity in a single individual occurs from a very early point, though the idea only receives fully explicit statement in the famous passage of *Du repentir*. There is certainly evolution in his view of death, from death as the principal concern of the living and the object of strenuous preparation to death as a mere incident of no great account; even here the preoccupation with death remains though the manner of confronting it has changed, and the evolution is well under way by 1580, especially as we have seen, in *De l'exercitation* and *De la ressemblance des enfans aux peres*. The early attitude to death is one aspect of his Stoicism and, unquestionably, rigid Stoicism is more and more attenuated as he goes on but is never entirely abandoned. Equally scepticism is visible from the beginning, well before Villey's sceptical crisis, and continues to exert its influence until the end. The notion of three separate stages (which is to simplify Villey's argument somewhat) does not stand up to serious examination. A stronger case can be made out for the naturalism or epicureanism or hedonism of the Third Book. In particular there is a marked contrast between the dark pessimism of much of the *Apologie* and the joyful acceptance of life in *Sur des vers de Virgile* and *De l'experience*. It is worthy of remark, incidentally, that the *Essais* progress from pessimism to serenity and happiness as the bodily condition of their author moves in the opposite direction. Again, however, this undoubted contrast must not be exaggerated. There is a dark side to the Third Book, especially the picture of the civil wars, and the general impression given by the first two, even without the later additions, is far from pessimistic: humour and humanity keep breaking in, and, more particularly, the view of pleasure as the highest good is by no means absent. No doubt the most radically subversive essays, like *Des boyteux,* are found in the Third Book and the most revolutionary remarks are asides added at many points in the Bordeaux Copy. Still, there is plenty to disturb a conventional mind in the first edition, in the *Apologie, De la coustume* or *Des cannibales* for example. From the point of view of form there is an immense difference (often obscured by later additions) between the anecdotes of the very early essays and the convolutions of the Third Book, but again the mature type can be seen in its essentials in 1580, as in *Des cannibales, De la præsumption* or *De l'exercitation.*

On the whole, then, we can conclude that, though evolution undoubtedly exists and forms part of the basic structure of the work, the continuity of the *Essais* is much more striking. This can be seen for instance in the praise of ignorance which runs all the way through, more profoundly in the personality of the writer, whose wry modesty and self-mockery never changes, however much he may progress in the candour of self-revelation, or in the steadfast refusal to be taken in by appearances, to accept what is accepted. Most of all perhaps it is manifested in the conception of truth as contradiction and paradox, equally discernible in the first and last essay, vast though the difference is in the level of treatment. Evolution is an element which cannot be ignored, which has to be set alongside other elements rather than above them, but it offers no universal key, it cannot be used to explain away the equally fundamental contradictions.

These contradictions have appeared at every stage of our survey and for some of them at least solutions have been suggested. Before we go further it will be well to recapitulate the most important. Montaigne (or more accurately the author of the *Essais*) is completely self-centred, inward-looking, concerned only to depict himself, but he also depicts humanity mirrored in himself and he shows a capacity for observation of human conduct without restriction of time or space, moving through history and over the face of the globe, and a grasp of the concrete totality of the world, which place him among the great realist writers as well as among the great introspectives. This grasp of reality is in its turn contradicted by the scepticism which presents the world as unknowable and on a more intimate level by the sense of the fleeting, the evanescent, the illusory, which dismisses the wonderfully rich and solid universe he evokes for us as no more than flux, inconstancy or 'des joncs que l'air manie casuellement selon soy'. Flux and mobility themselves are contradicted by the notion of an underlying form of the human condition and of the individual and the feeling of a permanence in himself beneath the continuous change:

> Or de la cognoissance de cette mienne volubilité j'ay par accident engendré en moy quelque constance d'opinions, et n'ay guiere alteré les miennes premieres et naturelles.[1]

Mobility and the relativism which inevitably accompanies it seem at first to stand in opposition to the expressions of extreme conservatism, as the powerful attachment to custom is contradicted by the exposure of custom as irrational prejudice, the enemy of reason and humanity; on the one hand a clinging to familiar landmarks, on the other an unlimited receptiveness to new and disturbing ideas. In the same way the genuinely devout Catholic is also a free-thinker, a classical pagan, a deist or a pantheist. This conservative is is in fact a liberal and even a revolutionary. The passionate lover of antiquity and classical literature demolishes faith in letters and learning. The humour and playfulness of the *Essais* are the vehicle of deeply serious thoughts, and it is not always easy to tell which is which. Then there is the difference between the analytical intelligence, the capacity for perceiving distinctions which Montaigne regards as his dominant intellectual quality, and the almost if not quite equal ability to bring out hidden identities and resemblances, to reveal links between the most unexpected facts or topics. We can see an apparent contradiction between content and form, between the boldness of the ideas and the elusiveness of the form, and in the form itself between disorder, conversational style, spontaneous thought on the one hand and on the other the brilliant use of a full range of rhetorical devices, the creation of organic forms which turn the inchoate outpourings of the mind into supreme works of art. It would be easy to go on with this catalogue of contradictions: with one exception they have already been dealt with in earlier chapters.

However, what emerges from this list is that trying to reduce Montaigne to a straight series of polarised oppositions, as we have just done, falsifies him almost as much as a simple view which leaves the contradictions out of account. Instead we see the formation of a criss-cross pattern of multiple oppositions and identities. Each feature has several opposite poles (if that is logically poss-

[1] II, xii: EM ii, 321; TR 553(*a*). Cf. p. 68 above.

ible): thus conservatism is in contradiction not only with liberalism but also with flux and relativism; relativism is in contradiction not only with conservatism but also with liberalism, since the
liberal-humanitarian views are among the firmest, the least
touched by moral relativism: 'il ne se trouva jamais aucune opinion
si desreglée qui excusat la trahison, la desloyauté, la tyrannie, la
cruauté, qui sont nos fautes ordinaires.'[1] On the other hand
relativism is itself the foundation of liberalism, because of its
dissolvent effect on local absolutisms, political, religious or moral.
This is about as simple an example as could be found of the endless circularity of contradictions. Thus even a statement of the
contradictions soon confirms what I said in the Introduction, that it
is impossible to touch on any aspect of Montaigne without risking
involvement in all the rest. Contradiction is itself a principle of
unity and perhaps the most important, not surprisingly when we
consider his views on the contradictory nature of truth.

In fact, in spite of superficial disorder and contradiction, everything hangs together, one thing leads on to another, everything
brings in, or can bring in, everything else, 'les matieres se tiennent
toutes enchesnées les unes aux autres'. This is eminently true,
as we have seen, of the form of the individual essays, which pass
from one theme to another, apparently unrelated, with no breach
of continuity. There is naturally a close connection between this
inner form and the intellectual ideas expressed through it: the
movement of the essays and the painting of *le passage,* for example, convey in themselves scepticism, relativism, and the unreliability of reason. It is also true of the relation between themes,
abstracted from their treatment in individual essays: they interact
on many planes. Thus, to give a few examples, we can discern a
close connection between themes we have considered separately
and which might seem quite remote: between Montaigne's delicate sensory organisation, his love of beauty, and his hedonism;
between his temperament as revealed in the self-portrait and his
philosophical positions: 'L'incertitude de mon jugement est si
egalement balancée en la pluspart des occurrences que je compro-
mettrois volontiers à la decision du sort et des dets'[2] (scepticism
as a reflection of a naturally balanced and hesitant judgement);
between logic and morality (logic as the morality of the intellect);
between law, the self-portrait, relativism, mobility, and form (the

[1] I, xxxi: EM i, 274; TR 208.
[2] II, xvii: EM ii, 439; TR 638.

incompatibility between general laws and particular cases, the infinite regress of glosses and commentaries); between the unity of the universe, the unity of the state, and the unity of the *Essais* (in each no piece can be affected without affecting everything else). Such echoes and resonances are omnipresent. The whole matter is well summed up by Conche:

Les idées de Montaigne s'organisent, sans qu'il l'ait cherché, en une vision cohérente de l'homme et du monde.[1]

It is, as we should expect, even better summed up by Montaigne, following Amyot but considerably improving on him:

Nostre vie est composée, comme l'armonie du monde, de choses contraires, aussi de divers tons, douz et aspres, aigus et plats, mols et graves.[2]

The musical analogy, which we have come upon before, seems exactly right: the contradictions are harmonised in a superior unity. Certainly we can recognise, with Villey,[3] the unity of personality which is to be found in the works of most great writers. But it should now be clear that there is far more than this, that the major themes, mobility, relativism, scepticism, diversity, exoticism, primitivism, cosmopolitanism and contradiction itself, converge in the most remarkable way.

There is, however, one contradiction, the exception mentioned earlier, which has not so far been discussed as a whole and which must have struck the reader. It is perhaps the most difficult of all and is bound to affect our final judgement of Montaigne not only as a literary creator (in this respect his greatness has, I hope, been fully established) but as a humanist in the broadest sense, the champion of enlightened values and the enemy of inhumanity and obscurantism. On the one hand we have found self-centredness, mobility, scepticism, detachment, contradiction, paradox, above all obliquity and ambiguity, in form especially but consequently also in the thought which the form carries, on the other hand toleration, political and religious liberalism, subversion, liberation. There is no necessary contradiction between the two groups, perhaps, but it may seem that bold and dangerous ideas like these should be boldly and unequivocally stated, that there is

---

[1] *Montaigne ou la conscience heureuse*, p. 67.
[2] III, xiii: EM iii, 393; TR 1068.
[3] *Sources et évolution*, ii, 294.

some incongruity in a champion who approaches the combat by such devious paths. To put it in another way, we have on the one hand an aesthete and a dilettante (a word often used of him), infinitely preoccupied with the details of his own sensibility, reducing, it often appears, morality itself to aesthetic values, on the other the indignant defender of enslaved peoples and oppressed minorities. The most obvious answer to the dilemma is prudence, which must not be confused with lack of courage or conviction. The Bastille, said Lanson, gave wit to the writers of the eighteenth century, and we can see that Fontenelle, Montesquieu or Voltaire, for all their clarity, make their devastating attacks mainly through the medium of oblique irony. What the threat of fire and torture gave the revolutionary writers of the sixteenth century, like des Périers or Bruno, was not wit so much as a cloudy and nearly impenetrable mysticism. The danger was greater and the disguise therefore more complete. We have seen the exaggeration of the Armaingaud theory of camouflaged atheism in Montaigne but also that it is not entirely without foundation: ambiguity, as in the 'Perigordins ou Alemans' passage, or concealment under a frivolous-sounding title, as in *Des coches* or *Des boyteux*, allow ideas to be expressed which would otherwise have been foolhardy. But it is not only a question of prudence: contemporary habits of thought made it difficult to say certain things except obscurely or ambiguously, because the weight of accepted prejudices could not be shaken off all at once. And Montaigne, though he is ambiguous, is not obscure: indeed when we reach the core of an essay like *Des boyteux* through its layers of apparent irrelevance it is astonishing to see with what vigour and decisiveness he speaks. In the end he is all of a piece, in this as in other respects. Like most great writers perhaps (though we should not forget those who concentrate their attention on a narrow band of experience) he is offering us a total vision of life. The denunciation of cruelty and inhumanity is an important part of it, and the undermining of the ferocious beliefs which were used as their justification had to be a slow process, not to be accomplished by a single writer, and had to work at first by indirect means. Moreover, though an important part, it is negative: the positive side is the liberation of the whole man from the shackles of custom and parochial laws, which involves the exploration of the rich content of ordinary life neglected by those who, disastrously for humanity no doubt, think that great political and public questions are all that matter. The oblique, ambiguous and organic forms he creates are perfectly adapted both to the undermining process and to this exploration of life with its diversity, uncertainties, and infinite contradictions. His pragmatic conservatism is in no way at variance with all this: as we have seen, it is his very sense of mobility and uncertainty that makes him so keenly aware of the dangers of sudden and violent change. Auden's sonnet, though wrong in almost every detail, succeeds with poetic insight in characterising Montaigne's position in European history as well as anyone:

> Outside his library window he could see
> A gentle landscape terrified of grammar,
> Cities where lisping was compulsory,
> And provinces where it was death to stammer.
>
> The hefty sprawled, too tired to care: it took
> This donnish undersexed conservative
> To start a revolution and to give
> The Flesh its weapons to defeat the Book.[1]

Thus unity and diversity, unity in diversity, are Montaigne's outstanding characteristics, and the fullest emphasis must be given to both. We have seen that the reconciliation of contraries in this way can be linked with contemporary movements in the arts, with mannerism and baroque, but we have also seen that he transcends such temporal classifications. His feeling for diversity and the concrete particularity of things places him among the great realists, but one principal quality he possesses, which is intelligence, sets him apart from most of them. It gives him his capacity for fine discriminations and unexpected analogies, and the psychological penetration which has made so many readers, as remote from each other as Flaubert and Mme du Deffand, recognise themselves in him. It is not so much that we are like him as that he reveals us to ourselves. His intelligence also explains the freshness of his immediate perception of reality with his considerable independence of the pressure of historical circumstance, and his remarkable anticipations of later thought and modes of feeling. We have seen in how many ways he is the precursor of seventeenth-century classicism, and the thought of the Enlightenment, how he occasionally catches the mood of the Romantics. It is reasonable to say that no writer of his time, perhaps not even Shakespeare, speaks to us so directly.

[1] 'Montaigne', *Collected shorter poems 1927–1957*, London, 1966, pp. 193–4.

Select Bibliography

Works published before 1942 (the date of Tannenbaum's bibliography) are included only if they are of considerable importance or are mentioned in the text or notes. After that date a rather fuller, though still limited, coverage has been attempted.

I Editions of Montaigne (for details of the original editions see chapter 2).

Œuvres complètes, ed. Armaingaud, 12 vols., Paris, 1924–41.

Œuvres complètes, ed. Thibaudet and Rat (Bibliothèque de la Pléiade), Paris, 1962 (reprinted 1965).

Les Essais de Michel de Montaigne, ed. Strowski, Gebelin and Villey (Édition Municipale), 5 vols., Bordeaux, 1906–33.

Essais de Michel de Montaigne: texte original de 1580 avec les variantes des éditions de 1582 et 1587, ed. Dezeimeris and Barckhausen, 2 vols., Bordeaux, 1870–3.

Essais: reproduction photographique de la deuxième édition (Bordeaux, 1582), ed. Françon, Cambridge, Mass., 1969.

Les Essais de Montaigne, ed. Motheau and Jouaust, 7 vols., Paris, 1886–9.

Les Essais de Montaigne, ed. Courbet and Royer, 5 vols., Paris, 1872–1900.

Reproduction en phototypie de l'exemplaire avec notes manuscrites marginales des Essais de Montaigne appartenant à la ville de Bordeaux, ed. Strowski, 3 vols., Paris, 1912.

Trois essais de Montaigne (I–39 – II–1 – III–2), ed. Gougenheim and Schuhl, Paris, 1951.

Le livre de raison de Montaigne sur l'Ephemeris historica de Beuther: reproduction en fac-similé, ed. Marchand, Paris, 1948.

Journal de voyage, ed. Lautrey, Paris, 1906.

The Essays of Montaigne, tr. and ed. Zeitlin, 3 vols., New York, 1934–6 (with important introduction and notes).

Saggi, tr. and ed. Garavini, Milan, 1966 (with useful appendixes).

II   *Contemporary Sources (Sixteenth and Seventeenth Centuries)*

AGRIPPA, HENRICUS CORNELIUS, *De incertitudine et vanitate scientiarum*, Paris, I. Petrus, 1531.

AMYOT, JACQUES, *see* PLUTARCH.

BENZONI, GIROLAMO, *La historia del mondo nuouo . . . laqual tratta dell'isole, & mari nuouamente ritrouati, & delle nuoue città da lui proprio vedute, per acqua & per terra in quattordici anni*, Venice, F. Rampazetto, 1565.

BENZONI, GIROLAMO, *Histoire nouuelle du nouueau monde, contenant en somme ce que les Hespagnols ont fait iusqu'à present aux Indes Occidentales, & le rude traitement qu'ils font à ces poures peuples-la*, tr. Chauveton, Geneva, E. Vignon, 1579.

BODIN, JEAN, *Les six liures de la republique*, Paris, I. du Puys, 1576.

BODIN, JEAN, *De la demonomanie des sorciers*, Paris, I. du Puys, 1580.

BODIN, JEAN, *La méthode de l'histoire*, tr. and ed. Mesnard, Algiers, 1941.

BODIN, JEAN, *Colloquium Heptaplomeres*, ed. Noack, Schwerin, 1857 (repr. Stuttgart, 1966).

BRUÈS, GUY DE, *The dialogues of Guy de Bruès: a critical edition with a study in Renaissance scepticism and relativism*, ed. Morphos, Baltimore, 1953.

CHAUVETON, URBAIN, *see* BENZONI.

DESCARTES, RENÉ, *Discours de la méthode*, ed. Gilson, Paris, 1947.

DU VAIR, GUILLAUME, *Traictez philosophiques*, Paris, A. l'Angelier, 1606.

ERASMUS, DESIDERIUS, *Moriae encomium*, Strasburg, M. Schurerius, 1511.

ESTIENNE, HENRI, *Apologie pour Hérodote*, ed. Ristelhuber and Liseux, 2 vols., Paris, 1879.

GOMARA, FRANCISCO LOPEZ DE, *Histoire generalle des Indes occidentales*, tr. Fumée, Paris, M. Sonnius, 1584.

GONZALEZ, *see* MENDOZA.

GOULART, SIMON, *see* OSORIUS.

GOURNAY, MARIE DE, *Le proumenoir de Monsieur de Montaigne*, Paris, A. l'Angelier, 1594.

GOURNAY, MARIE DE, *Les advis, ou les presens de la Demoiselle de Gournay*, Paris, I. du Bray, 1641.

[HENRY II (ROUEN ENTRY)] *Cest la deduction du sumptueux ordre plaisantz spectacles et magnifiques theatres dresses, et exhibes par les citoiens de Rouen*, Rouen, R. le Hoy, R. & I. dictz du Gord, 1551.

[HENRY II (ROUEN ENTRY)] *L'entrée de Henri II roi de France à Rouen au mois d'octobre 1550*, ed. Merval, Rouen, 1868.

[INDEX] *Librorum expurgandorum, suculenter ac vigilantissime recognitus nouissimus index*, Madrid, D. Diaz, 1640.

LA BOÉTIE, ESTIENNE DE, *Œuvres complètes*, ed. Bonnefon, Bordeaux and Paris, 1892 (reprinted Geneva, 1967).

LANCRE, PIERRE DE, *Tableau de l'inconstance des mauuais anges et demons*, Paris, I. Berjon, 1612.

LE ROY, LOYS, *De la vicissitude ou variete des choses en l'vniuers*, Paris, P. l'Huilier, 1576.

LÉRY, JEAN DE, *Histoire d'vn voyage fait en la terre du Bresil, autrement dite Amerique*, La Rochelle, A. Chuppin, 1578.

L'ESTOILE, PIERRE DE, *Mémoires-journaux: Journal de Henri III*, ed. Brunet *et al.*, 3 vols., Paris, 1888.

LOPEZ, *see* GOMARA.

MACHIAVELLI, NICCOLÒ, *Il principe*, ed. Lisio, Florence, 1942.

MENDOZA, JUAN GONZALEZ DE, *Histoire du grand royaume de la Chine, situé aux Indes orientales*, tr. Luc de la Porte, Paris, I. Perier, 1589.

MEXIA, PEDRO, *Les diverses lecons de Pierre Messie*, tr. Gruget and du Verdier, Lyons, B. Honorat, 1577.

OSORIUS, HIERONYMUS, *Histoire de Portugal*, tr. Goulart, Paris, G. de la Nouë, 1581.

PASCAL, BLAISE, *Œuvres*, ed. Brunschvicg, Boutroux and Gazier (Les Grands Écrivains de la France), 11 vols., Paris, 1908–14.

PASCAL, BLAISE, *Pensées sur la religion et sur quelques autres sujets*, ed. Lafuma, 3 vols., Paris, 1951.

PASQUIER, ESTIENNE, *Choix de lettres sur la littérature la langue et la traduction*, ed. Thickett, Geneva, 1956 (pp. 43–52).

PEACHAM, HENRY, *The garden of eloquence (1593)*, ed. Crane, Gainesville, Florida, 1954.

PLUTARCH, *Les vies des hommes illustres*, tr. Amyot, Paris, M. de Vascosan, 1565.

PLUTARCH, *Les œuures morales & meslees*, tr. Amyot, Paris, M. de Vascosan, 1572.

POSTEL, GUILLAUME, *De la republique des Turcs, & là ou l'occasion s'offrera, des meurs & loy de tous Muhamedistes*, Poitiers, E. de Marnef, 1560.

POSTEL, GUILLAUME, *Des histoires orientales*, Paris, H. de Marnef and G. Cauellat, 1575.

RABELAIS, FRANÇOIS, *Gargantua*, ed. Plattard (Les Textes français), Paris, 1938 (reprinted 1946).

RABELAIS, FRANÇOIS, *Pantagruel*, ed. Saulnier (Textes littéraires français), Paris, 1946.

RAEMOND, FLORIMOND DE, *Erreur populaire de la papesse Iane*, Bordeaux, S. Millanges, 1594.

RONSARD, PIERRE DE, *Œuvres complètes*, ed. Laumonier, Silver and Lebègue, 18 vols., Paris, 1914–67.

TAHUREAU, JACQUES, *Les dialogues*, ed. Conscience, Paris, 1870.

THEVET, ANDRÉ, *Les singularitez de la France antarctique, autrement nommée Amerique*, Paris, les heritiers de Maurice de la Porte, 1558.

WIERUS [WIER], JOANNES, *De praestigiis daemonum, et incantationibus ac ueneficijs, libri V*, Basle, I. Oporinus, 1564.

WIERUS [WIER], JOANNES, *Cinq liures de l'imposture et tromperie des diables des enchantements & sorcelleries*, tr. Grévin, Paris, I. du Puys, 1569.

III   Critical Works and General Studies

ALLEN, DON CAMERON, *Doubt's boundless sea: skepticism and faith in the Renaissance*, Baltimore, 1964.

ARMSTRONG, ELIZABETH, *Ronsard and the Age of Gold*, Cambridge, 1968.

ATKINSON, GEOFFROY, *Les nouveaux horizons de la Renaissance française*, Paris, 1935.

AUERBACH, ERICH, *Mimesis: the representation of reality in Western literature*, tr. Trask, New York, 1953.

AULOTTE, ROBERT, *Amyot et Plutarque: la tradition des Moralia au XVIᵉ siècle*, Geneva, 1965.

AYMONIER, CAMILLE, 'Les opinions politiques de Montaigne', *Actes de l'Académie nationale des sciences, belles-lettres & arts de Bordeaux*, 6ᵉ série, xi (1937–8), 213–37.

BARAZ, MICHAËL, *L'être et la connaissance selon Montaigne*, Paris, 1968.

BARAZ, MICHAËL, 'Le sentiment de l'unité cosmique chez Montaigne', *Cahiers de l'Association Internationale des Études Françaises*, xiv (1962), 211–24.

BARAZ, MICHAËL, 'Les images dans les *Essais* de Montaigne', *BHR*, xxvii (1965), 361–94.

BARRIÈRE, PIERRE, *La vie intellectuelle en Périgord 1550–1800*, Bordeaux, 1936.

BARRIÈRE, PIERRE, *Montaigne gentilhomme français*, 2nd ed., Bordeaux, 1948.

BATTISTA, ANNA MARIA, *Alle origini del pensiero politico libertino: Montaigne e Charron*, Milan, 1966.

BERNOULLI, RENÉ, 'La mise à l'index des *Essais* de Montaigne', *BSAM*, IV, 8 (1966), 4–10.

BLINKENBERG, ANDREAS, 'Quel sens Montaigne a-t-il voulu donner au mot *Essais* dans le titre de son œuvre?', *BSAM*, III, 29 (1964), 22–32.

BOAS, GEORGE, *The happy beast in French thought of the seventeenth century*, Baltimore, 1933.

BOASE, ALAN M., *The fortunes of Montaigne: a history of the Essays in France, 1580–1669*, London, 1935.

BOASE, ALAN M., 'Montaigne annoté par Florimond de Raemond', *Revue du seizième siècle*, xv (1928), 237–78.

BOASE, ALAN M., 'Montaigne et la sorcellerie,' *Humanisme et Renaissance*, ii (1935), 402–21.

BOASE, ALAN M., 'Un lecteur hollandais de Montaigne: Pieter van Veen' in *Mélanges offerts à M. Abel Lefranc*, Paris, 1936.

BOASE, ALAN M., 'The early history of the *essai* title in France and Britain' in *Studies in French literature presented to H. W. Lawton*, Manchester, 1968.

BONNEFON, PAUL, 'La bibliothèque de Montaigne', *RHLF*, ii (1895), 313–71.

BONNET, PIERRE, 'Une nouvelle série d'annotations de Florimond de Raemond aux *Essais* de Montaigne', *BSAM*, III, 10 (1959), 4–23.

BONNET, PIERRE, 'Le texte des *Essais* de Montaigne: évolution de sa structure des origines à nos jours', *BSAM*, IV, 7 (1966), 70–81.

BOON, JEAN-PIERRE, 'Émendations des emprunts dans le texte des essais dits "stoïciens" de Montaigne', *Studies in philology*, lxv (1968), 147–62.

BOWMAN, F. P., *Montaigne: Essays*, London, 1965.

BROWN, FRIEDA S., *Religious and political conservatism in the Essais of Montaigne*, Geneva, 1963.

BRUNSCHVICG, LÉON, *Descartes et Pascal lecteurs de Montaigne*, New York and Paris, 1944.

BUFFUM, IMBRIE, *L'influence du voyage de Montaigne sur les Essais*, Princeton, 1946.

BUFFUM, IMBRIE, *Studies in the baroque from Montaigne to Rotrou*, New Haven and Paris, 1957.

BURY, J. B., *The idea of progress: an inquiry into its origin and growth*, London, 1920.

BUSSON, HENRI, *Le rationalisme dans la littérature française de la Renaissance (1533–1601)*, revised ed., Paris, 1957.

BUSSON, HENRI, *Littérature et théologie: Montaigne, Bossuet, La Fontaine, Prévost*, Paris, 1962.

BUTOR, MICHEL, *Essais sur les Essais*, Paris, 1968.

CAMERON, KEITH C., *Montaigne et l'humour*, Paris, 1966.

CHARTROU, J.-M., 'Les entrées solennelles à Bordeaux au XVIe siècle', *Revue historique de Bordeaux*, xxiii (1930), 49–59, 97–104.

CHATEAU, JEAN, *Montaigne psychologue et pédagogue*, Paris, 1964.

CHÉREL, ALBERT, *La pensée de Machiavel en France*, Paris, 1935.

CHINARD, GILBERT, *L'exotisme américain dans la littérature française au XVIe siècle*, Paris, 1911.

CITOLEUX, MARC, *Le vrai Montaigne théologien et soldat*, Paris, 1937.

CLARK, CAROL E., 'Seneca's Letters to Lucilius as a source of some of Montaigne's imagery', *BHR*, xxx (1968), 249–66.

CLARK, CAROL E., 'Montaigne and the imagery of political discourse in sixteenth-century France', *French studies*, xxiv (1970), 337–55.

COLIE, ROSALIE L., *Paradoxia epidemica: the Renaissance tradition of paradox*, Princeton, 1966.

CONCHE, MARCEL, *Montaigne ou la conscience heureuse*, Paris, 1964.

COPPIN, JOSEPH, *Montaigne traducteur de Raymond Sebon*, Lille, 1925.

CROLL, MORRIS W., *"Attic" and baroque prose style: the anti-Ciceronian movement*, ed. Patrick, Evans and Wallace, Princeton, 1969.

DÉDÉYAN, CHARLES, *Essai sur le Journal de voyage de Montaigne*, Paris, n.d.

DELÈGUE, YVES, 'Du paradoxe chez Montaigne', *Cahiers de l'Association Internationale des Études Françaises*, xiv (1962), 241–53.

DESGRANGES, GUY, 'Montaigne et l'histoire', *French review*, xxiii (1950), 371–7.

DESSEIN, ANDRÉ, 'Sur quelques citations cachées des *Essais*', *BSAM*, IV, 14 (1968), 39–41.

DRÉANO, MATHURIN, *La religion de Montaigne*, revised ed., Paris, 1969.

DRESDEN, S., 'Le dilettantisme de Montaigne', *BHR*, xv (1953), 45–56.

ELLERBROEK, G. G., 'Montaigne et les applications de la technique', *Neophilologus*, xxviii (1943), 1–6.

FAIRCHILD, HOXIE NEALE, *The noble savage: a study in Romantic naturalism*, New York, 1928.

FAURE, ÉLIE, *Montaigne et ses trois premiers-nés*, Paris, 1926.

FRAISSE, SIMONE, *Une conquête du rationalisme: l'influence de Lucrèce en France au seizième siècle*, Paris, 1962.

FRAME, DONALD M., *Montaigne's discovery of man: the humanization of a humanist*, New York, 1955.

FRAME, DONALD M., *Montaigne: a biography*, London, 1965.

FRAME, DONALD M., *Montaigne's Essais: a study*, Englewood Cliffs, New Jersey, 1969.

FRAME, DONALD M., 'What next in Montaigne studies?', *French review*, xxxvi (1962–3), 577–87.

FRANÇON, MARCEL, 'La chronologie des *Essais* de 1580', *Symposium*, viii (1954), 242–8.

FRANÇON, MARCEL, 'A propos des éditions des *Essais* de Montaigne', *BHR*, xxviii (1966), 89–90.

FRANÇON, MARCEL, 'Montaigne, J.-A. de Thou et les "guerres de religion"', *BSAM*, IV, 18 (1969), 33–42.

FRIEDRICH, HUGO, *Montaigne*, 2nd ed., Berne and Munich, 1967.

FRIEDRICH, HUGO, *Montaigne*, tr. Rovini, Paris, 1968.

GARAPON, ROBERT, 'Quand Montaigne a-t-il écrit les «Essais» du livre III?' in *Mélanges de langue et de littérature du Moyen Age et de la Renaissance offerts à Jean Frappier*, Geneva, 1970, i, 321–7.

GIDE, ANDRÉ, 'Essai sur Montaigne', 'Suivant Montaigne', *Œuvres complètes*, ed. Martin-Chauffier, Paris, xv (1939), 3–68.

GILLOT, HUBERT, *La querelle des anciens et des modernes en France*, Paris, 1914.

GRACEY, PHYLLIS, *Montaigne et la poésie*, Paris, 1935.

GRAY, FLOYD, *Le style de Montaigne*, Paris, 1958.

GRAY, FLOYD, 'The unity of Montaigne in the "Essais"', *Modern language quarterly*, xxii (1961), 79–86.

GRAY, FLOYD, 'Montaigne's friends', *French studies*, xv (1961), 203–12.

HALL, KATHLEEN M., ' "Certain mutations": thoughts on the evolution of one of Montaigne's earliest *Essais*', *L'esprit créateur*, viii (1968), 208–15.

HALLIE, PHILIP P., *The scar of Montaigne: an essay in personal philosophy*, Middletown, Conn., 1966.

HATZFELD, HELMUT A., 'Per una definizione dello stile di Montaigne', *Convivium*, xxii (1954), 284–90.

HAUSER, ARNOLD, *Mannerism: the crisis of the Renaissance and the origin of modern art*, 2 vols., London, 1965.

HAYDN, HIRAM, *The Counter-Renaissance*, New York, 1950.

HENSEL, PAUL, 'Montaigne und die Antike', *Vorträge der Bibliothek Warburg 1925–1926*, Leipzig and Berlin, 1928.

HOCKE, GUSTAV RENÉ, *Die Welt als Labyrinth: Manier und Manie in der europäischen Kunst*, Hamburg, 1957.

HOLYOAKE, S. JOHN, 'The idea of "jugement" in Montaigne', *Modern language review*, lxiii (1968), 340–51.

HUGUET, EDMOND, *Dictionnaire de la langue française du seizième siècle*, 7 vols., Paris, 1925–67.

HUNT, R. N. CAREW, 'Montaigne and the state', *Edinburgh review*, ccxlvi (1927), 259–72.

ILSLEY, MARJORIE HENRY, *A daughter of the Renaissance: Marie le Jars de Gournay, her life and works*, The Hague, 1963.

IVES, GEORGE B., 'Bibliography of the Essays' in *Essays of Michael Lord of Montaigne*, 3 vols., Boston and New York, 1902–4 (iii, 415–92).

JANSSEN, HERMAN JOZEF JOANNES, *Montaigne fidéiste*, Nijmegen and Utrecht, 1930.

JASINSKI, RENÉ, 'La composition chez Montaigne' in *Mélanges d'histoire littéraire de la Renaissance offerts à Henri Chamard*, Paris, 1951.

JEANSON, FRANCIS, *Montaigne par lui-même*, Paris, 1951.

JONES, P. MANSELL, *French introspectives from Montaigne to André Gide*, Cambridge, 1937.

JULLIAN, CAMILLE, 'Bordeaux au temps de la mairie de Michel Montaigne', *Revue historique de Bordeaux*, xxvi (1933), 5–18.

KELLER, ABRAHAM C., 'Historical and geographical perspective in the *Essays* of Montaigne', *Modern philology*, liv (1956–7), 145–57.

KELLER, ABRAHAM C., 'Optimism in the Essays of Montaigne', *Studies in philology*, liv (1957), 408–28.

KELLERMANN, FREDERICK, 'Montaigne's Socrates', *Romanic review*, xlv (1954), 170–7.

KELLERMANN, FREDERICK, 'The *Essais* and Socrates', *Symposium*, x (1956), 204–16.

KIES, A., 'Montaigne et saint François de Sales sont-ils baroques?', *Les lettres romanes*, xii (1958), 235–50.

KNÖS, BÖRJE, 'Les citations grecques de Montaigne', *Eranos*, xliv (1946), 460–83.

LABLÉNIE, E., *Montaigne auteur de maximes*, Paris, 1968.

LA CHARITÉ, RAYMOND C., *The concept of judgment in Montaigne*, The Hague, 1968.

LAFONT, ROBERT, '*Que le gascon y aille si le français n'y peut aller*: réflexions sur la situation linguistique et stylistique de l'œuvre de Montaigne', *Le français moderne*, xxxvi (1968), 98–104.

LANSON, GUSTAVE, *Les Essais de Montaigne: étude et analyse*, Paris, 1930 (reprinted 1948).

LANSON, GUSTAVE, 'La vie morale selon les *Essais* de Montaigne', *Revue des deux mondes*, February 1924, 603–25, 836–58.

LAPP, JOHN C., 'Montaigne's "négligence" and some lines from Virgil', *Romanic review*, lxi (1970), 167–81.

LEBÈGUE, RAYMOND, 'La littérature française et les Guerres de Religion', *French review*, xxiii (1950), 205–13.

LEBÈGUE, RAYMOND, 'Montaigne et le paradoxe des cannibales' in *Studi di letteratura, storia e filosofia in onore di Bruno Revel*, Florence, 1965.

LEVI, ANTHONY, *French moralists: the theory of the passions 1585–1649*, Oxford, 1964.

LEVIN, HARRY, *The myth of the Golden Age in the Renaissance*, Bloomington and London, 1969.

LORIAN, ALEXANDRE, 'Montaigne – de l'impératif (étude de style)', *Zeitschrift für romanische Philologie*, lxxx (1964), 54–97.

MCFARLANE, I. D., 'Montaigne and the concept of the imagination' in *The French Renaissance and its heritage: essays presented to Alan M. Boase*, London, 1968.

MCGOWAN, MARGARET, 'Form and themes in Henri II's entry into Rouen', *Renaissance drama*, i (1968), 199–251.

MARCHAND, JEAN, *Hypothèse sur la quatrième édition des Essais de Montaigne (1587)*, Bordeaux, 1938.

MARCU, EVA, *Répertoire des idées de Montaigne*, Geneva, 1965.

MÉGRET, JACQUES, 'Remarques sur le "Montaigne de 1595"', *Le bouquiniste français*, January 1962, 7–9.

MERLEAU-PONTY, MAURICE, 'Lecture de Montaigne', *Les temps modernes*, iii (1947–8), 1044–60.

MESNARD, JEAN, 'De la «diversion» au «divertissement»', 1964 (see PALASSIE).

MESNARD, PIERRE, *L'essor de la philosophie politique au XVIᵉ siècle*, Paris, 1936.

METSCHIES, MICHAEL, *Zitat und Zitierkunst in Montaignes Essais*, Geneva and Paris, 1966.

MICHA, ALEXANDRE, *Le singulier Montaigne*, Paris, 1964.

MICHA, ALEXANDRE, 'Art et nature dans les «Essais»', *BSAM*, II, 19 (1956), 50–5.

MICHEL, PIERRE, *Montaigne*, Bordeaux, 1969.

MICHEL, PIERRE, 'Bibliographie montaigniste (1580–1950)', *BSAM*, III, 1 (1957), 62–80.

MICHELET, JULES, *Histoire de France*, 17 vols., Paris, 1852–67.

MOORE, W. G., 'Montaigne's notion of experience' in *The French mind: studies in honour of Gustave Rudler*, Oxford, 1952.

MOORE, W. G., 'L'«Apologie» et la science', 1964 (see PALASSIE).

MOORE, W. G., 'Lucretius and Montaigne', *Yale French studies*, xxxviii (1967), 109–14.

MOREAU, PIERRE, *Montaigne l'homme et l'œuvre*, Paris, 1939.

MOREAU, PIERRE, 'Analyse et dilettantisme chez Montaigne et Stendhal', *Saggi e ricerche di letteratura francese*, iii (1963), 7–36.

MÜLLER, ARMAND, *Montaigne* (Les Écrivains devant Dieu), [Paris and Bruges], 1965.

NORTON, GRACE, *Studies in Montaigne*, New York, 1904.

PALASSIE, GEORGES (ed.), *Mémorial du Iᵉʳ Congrès International des Études Montaignistes*, Bordeaux, 1964.

Select Bibliography

PAYEN, J.-F., *Notice bibliographique sur Montaigne*, Paris, 1837 (supplements 1837 and 1860).

PERTILE, LINO, 'Su alcune nuove fonti degli *Essais* di Montaigne', *BHR*, xxxi (1969), 481–94.

PERTILE, LINO, 'Il problema della religione nel «Journal de voyage» di Montaigne', *BHR*, xxxiii (1971), 79–100.

PIZZORUSSO, ARNALDO, 'Montaigne e la delimitazione dell'umano', *Belfagor*, xxv (1970), 277–87.

PLATTARD, JEAN, *Montaigne et son temps*, Paris, 1933.

PLATTARD, JEAN, *État présent des études sur Montaigne*, Paris, 1935.

PLATTARD, JEAN, 'Le système de Copernic dans la littérature française au XVIe siécle', *Revue du seizième siècle*, i (1913), 220–37.

PLATTARD, JEAN, 'L'Amérique dans l'œuvre de Montaigne', *Revue des cours et conférences*, 1933–4 (I), 12–21.

POPKIN, RICHARD H., *The history of scepticism from Erasmus to Descartes*, Assen, 1960.

PORTEAU, PAUL, *Montaigne et la vie pédagogique de son temps*, Paris, 1935.

POUILLOUX, JEAN-YVES, *Lire les "Essais" de Montaigne*, Paris, 1969.

POULET, GEORGES, *Études sur le temps humain*, Paris, 1950.

PRÉVOST, JEAN, *La vie de Montaigne*, Paris, 1926.

RAYMOND, MARCEL, *Génies de France*, Neuchâtel, 1942 (includes an essay on 'L'attitude religieuse de Montaigne').

RECKSIEK, MARGOT, *Montaignes Verhältnis zu Klassik und Manierismus*, Bonn thesis, 1966.

ROSELLINI, ALDO, 'Quelques remarques sur l'italien du "Journal de voyage" de Michel de Montaigne', *Zeitschrift für romanische Philologie*, lxxxiii (1967), 381–408.

RUEL, ÉDOUARD, *Du sentiment artistique dans la morale de Montaigne*, Paris, 1902.

SAINTE-BEUVE, C.-A., *Port-Royal*, ed. Doyon and Marchesné, 10 vols., Paris, 1926–32.

SAMARAS, ZOE, *The comic element of Montaigne's style*, Paris, 1970.

SAYCE, R. A., 'Baroque elements in Montaigne', *French studies*, viii (1954), 1–15.

SAYCE, R. A., 'L'ordre des *Essais* de Montaigne', *BHR*, xviii (1956), 7–22.

SAYCE, R. A., 'Montaigne et la peinture du passage', *Saggi e ricerche di letteratura francese*, iv (1963), 9–59.

SCHNABEL, WALTER, *Montaignes Stilkunst: eine Untersuchung vornehmlich auf Grund seiner Metaphern*, Breslau and Oppeln, 1930.

SCHON, PETER M., *Vorformen des Essays in Antike und Humanismus: ein Beitrag sur Entstehungsgeschichte der* Essais *von Montaigne*, Wiesbaden, 1954.

SCLAFERT, CLÉMENT, *L'âme religieuse de Montaigne*, Paris, 1951.

SHEARMAN, JOHN, *Mannerism*, Harmondsworth, 1967 (reprinted 1969).

STAROBINSKI, JEAN, 'Montaigne en mouvement', *Nouvelle revue française*, January-February 1960, 16–22, 254–66.

STEGMANN, ANDRÉ, *Montaigne critico del pensiero umanistico* (Studi e ricerche di storia della filosofia, 36), Turin, 1960.

STROWSKI, FORTUNAT, *Montaigne*, 2nd ed., Paris, 1931.

TANNENBAUM, SAMUEL A., *Michel Eyquem de Montaigne (a concise bibliography)*, New York, 1942.

TELLE, E. V., 'A propos du mot «essai» chez Montaigne', *BHR*, xxx (1968), 225–47.

THIBAUDET, ALBERT, *Montaigne*, ed. Gray, Paris, 1963.

THORPE, LEWIS, 'Pieter van Veen's copy of Montaigne', *Rivista di letterature moderne*, iii (1952), 168–79.

TRAEGER, WOLF EBERHARD, *Aufbau und Gedankenführung in Montaignes Essays*, Heidelberg, 1961.

TREVOR-ROPER, H. R., *The European witch-craze of the 16th and 17th centuries*, Harmondsworth, 1969.

TRINQUET, ROGER, 'Note sur «Saint Michel et son serpent»', *BSAM*, II, 18 (1956), 45.

TRINQUET, ROGER, 'Les deux sources de la morale et de la religion chez Montaigne', *BSAM*, IV, 13 (1968), 24–33.

VILLEY, PIERRE, *Les sources et l'évolution des Essais de Montaigne*, 2nd ed., 2 vols., Paris, 1933.

VILLEY, PIERRE, *Montaigne devant la postérité*, Paris, 1935.

WEBER, HENRI, 'Montaigne et l'idée de nature', *Saggi e ricerche di letteratura francese*, v (1954), 41–63.

WEINBERG, BERNARD, 'Montaigne's readings for *Des cannibales*' in *Renaissance and other studies in honor of William Leon Wiley*, Chapel Hill, 1968.

WILDEN, ANTHONY, 'Par divers moyens on arrive à pareille fin: a reading of Montaigne', *Modern language notes*, lxxxiii (1968), 577–97.

WILLIAMS, W. D., *Nietzsche and the French: a study of the influence of Nietzsche's French reading on his thought and writing*, Oxford, 1952.

WILLIAMSON, EDWARD, 'On the liberalizing of Montaigne: a remonstrance,' *French review*, xxiii (1949), 92–100.

WITTKOWER, ELLY, *Die Form der Essais von Montaigne*, Basle thesis, 1935.

WÖLFFLIN, HEINRICH, *Kunstgeschichtliche Grundbegriffe*, Munich, 1915.

YATES, FRANCES A., *John Florio: the life of an Italian in Shakespeare's England*, Cambridge, 1934.

YATES, FRANCES A., *The Valois tapestries*, London, 1959.

General Index

Index of Essays